Conducting Personal Network Research

# Methodology in the Social Sciences

David A. Kenny, Founding Editor

Todd D. Little, Series Editor

*www.guilford.com/MSS*

This series provides applied researchers and students with analysis and research design books that emphasize the use of methods to answer research questions. Rather than emphasizing statistical theory, each volume in the series illustrates when a technique should (and should not) be used and how the output from available software programs should (and should not) be interpreted. Common pitfalls as well as areas of further development are clearly articulated.

## RECENT VOLUMES

BAYESIAN STATISTICS FOR THE SOCIAL SCIENCES
*David Kaplan*

CONFIRMATORY FACTOR ANALYSIS FOR APPLIED RESEARCH, Second Edition
*Timothy A. Brown*

PRINCIPLES AND PRACTICE OF STRUCTURAL EQUATION MODELING, Fourth Edition
*Rex B. Kline*

HYPOTHESIS TESTING AND MODEL SELECTION IN THE SOCIAL SCIENCES
*David L. Weakliem*

REGRESSION ANALYSIS AND LINEAR MODELS: Concepts, Applications, and Implementation
*Richard B. Darlington and Andrew F. Hayes*

GROWTH MODELING: Structural Equation and Multilevel Modeling Approaches
*Kevin J. Grimm, Nilam Ram, and Ryne Estabrook*

PSYCHOMETRIC METHODS: Theory into Practice
*Larry R. Price*

INTRODUCTION TO MEDIATION, MODERATION, AND CONDITIONAL PROCESS ANALYSIS: A Regression-Based Approach, Second Edition
*Andrew F. Hayes*

MEASUREMENT THEORY AND APPLICATIONS FOR THE SOCIAL SCIENCES
*Deborah L. Bandalos*

CONDUCTING PERSONAL NETWORK RESEARCH: A Practical Guide
*Christopher McCarty, Miranda J. Lubbers, Raffaele Vacca, and José Luis Molina*

# Conducting Personal Network Research

## A Practical Guide

Christopher McCarty
Miranda J. Lubbers
Raffaele Vacca
José Luis Molina

*Series Editor's Note by Todd D. Little*

THE GUILFORD PRESS
New York London

A Division of Guilford Publications, Inc.
370 Seventh Avenue, Suite 1200, New York, NY 10001
www.guilford.com



Printed in the United States of America

This book is printed on acid-free paper.

Last digit is print number: 9 8 7 6 5 4 3 2 1

Library of Congress Cataloging-in-Publication Data is available from the publisher.

ISBN 978-1-4625-3838-6

# Series Editor's Note

We all have personal networks comprised of our friends, family, acquaintances, colleagues, coworkers, and the like. Ever wondered how such personal networks affect who we are, how we feel, how we behave, how we are received, how productive we are? Of course you have! We all have. But how do we move beyond wondering to actively studying and understanding such personal networks as a research endeavor? The author network in this book, of Christopher McCarty, Miranda J. Lubbers, Raffaele Vacca, and José Luis Molina, have beautifully crafted an indispensable resource, *Conducting Personal Network Research: A Practical Guide*. They introduce the world of personal network modeling to us with an engaging and accessible voice.

This network of accomplished authors opens each chapter with a succinct and elucidating overview. These overviews provide an all-important view from the top of the mountain so that you don't get lost when you start hiking the trails of learning. They easily guide you through the seeming morass of details by starting you at the trailhead and gently leading you to the top of this all-important mountain of personal network research.

You'll find guide posts in the form of boxes that showcase many of the major published studies of personal network research. These engaging examples highlight principles and practices of personal network research. In other boxes, the authors lay out the important steps needed to traverse intersections on the trail. This author network, however, doesn't "tell" you what to do; instead, they elucidate the guiding principles needed to make informed decisions as you develop your personal network research. Additionally, the invaluable Appendix describes various software options available for conducting personal network research.

From the authors' wealth of experience, they offer insight for making informed design, measurement, visualization, and analysis decisions. On the way to the top of this majestic mountain, you'll find nuggets of rich jewels in the form of captivating examples that shine light on the insights that can be gained only in the context of personal network research.

McCarty, Lubbers, Vacca, and Molina will become key nodes in your personal research network composition and structure. McCarty, for example, is the author of EgoNet, which is the first software program specifically created for analyzing personal networks. Moreover, their work is now a shining node, if you will, in the growing network of accessible and authoritative resources that is the Methodology in the Social Sciences series. I'm very pleased to bring this work into our collection. As always, enjoy!

TODD D. LITTLE
*International Balloon Fiesta*
*Albuquerque, New Mexico*

# Prologue

Mariama[1] stepped off the train and walked up the street toward the center of Vilassar de Mar, a small seaside town in Spain. She had finished her high school classes about an hour before, but the train ride had taken about 45 minutes of that time. The time passed quickly as she chatted with her cousin Ousmane, who also commuted daily to Barcelona. After leaving the train station, she walked up the street with a group of passengers toward the city center. The group consisted of about 50 people, roughly half of Spanish origin, and the other half people from countries in North and West Africa, but also from Latin America and eastern Europe. Over the preceding two decades, the number of migrants in that part of Spain had increased substantially, but the economic crisis that started in 2008 suddenly halted the process. Many migrants came to Spain as an entry point to other European Union countries. Others, like those Mariama walked with that day, had chosen to make Spain their home.

Mariama's parents were among the latter. They were originally from The Gambia and had moved to Spain in 1989, seeking a better life for themselves and their children. Mariama was born in Spain. Her family lived in an apartment in a building near the center of Vilassar de Mar, which rented mostly to migrants from Senegal and The Gambia. That neighborhood was where Mariama's family was living because Mariama's uncle had moved there a few years before. Most migrants moved to an area after friends and relatives before them had established a bridgehead.

Mariama walked quickly. Her supervisor at her grocery store job near the apartment needed her to fill in for another employee who had been sick all week. Mariama would have to be there earlier than usual. Yet her mother still expected her to stop by the elementary school and walk her two younger sisters and younger brother home before

[1] The names of persons and the town mentioned here are changed in order to preserve anonymity.

work. She would have to take them home, prepare their meal, and hope her teenage brother arrived home in time for her to get to work.

At age 19, Mariama had most of the responsibilities of a young mother, only in her case she was caring for her younger brothers and sisters. She rarely went out with her friends, as her parents needed help with her siblings. Also, her family was Muslim, and it was unacceptable for Mariama to put herself openly in social situations where she might interact inappropriately with young men. She limited her friendships to a selected set of neighbors and cousins and a few people from work. None of these friendships took her too far from home. Mariama's daily routine consisted mostly of going to school and then to work. Other than that, she socialized with her immediate family and those who lived nearby.

Plate P.1[2] depicts Mariama's personal network. The circles and triangles, called nodes, represent 45 of the people she knows. The lines indicate whether, according to Mariama, the two people interact with each other independently of her, that is, when she's not around. The nodes are arranged by a visualization algorithm to account for the fact that some of the people she knows know each other and others do not. The colors of the nodes represent whether the person is one of Mariama's family members (dark blue and red) or not (light blue). There is a label for each node indicating where the person was born; the circles indicate women, while the triangles depict men.

This visualization is a representation of the social context, or the personal community, surrounding Mariama. As social scientists, we are interested in the characteristics of the people Mariama knows, how they know each other, and how these things might affect her. In this case, we see that she has a densely connected personal network, compared to others, with only a small group of Spanish people. As a second-generation migrant, Mariama still tends to associate with the same group of people as her parents. She socializes and works with people from Senegal and The Gambia and people who were born in Spain but whose parents were born in Senegal or The Gambia. It is only through her classes at the high school that Mariama is exposed to nonmigrants in a way that would allow them to become her friends or closer acquaintances.

The only sibling in the family for whom Mariama does not provide care is Awa, her 22-year-old sister, indicated as the red node in her network. With a difference in their ages of less than 3 years, Mariama and Awa grew up under very similar circumstances. They are both second-generation migrants born in Spain. They are both from a Muslim household, and both grew up in the same family and the same neighborhood heavily populated with migrants from North and sub-Saharan Africa, particularly Senegal and The Gambia. But that is where the similarities end.

As a child, Awa played with a variety of children, some of whose parents were from

[2] See the color insert for the seven plates.

Senegal and The Gambia, some from Morocco and countries in West Africa, and others from Spain. When she entered secondary school, Awa's gregarious nature gained her friendships with an even wider set of people, some of whom were unhealthy influences. Despite her Muslim upbringing, Awa experimented with smoking and drinking.

Eventually, Awa began selecting friendships that accommodated her lifestyle. Her father discovered that she was smoking and ordered her to stop, threatening to expel her from the apartment. Once she graduated from secondary school, Awa rebelled. She decided not to attend university, instead choosing a job that would earn her money she could spend on the weekends. Through her friends, she met people in nearby suburbs with whom she could stay on weekends and with whom she could attend parties. She was careful not to introduce them to each other for fear that information about her behavior would get back to her father or one of his friends or relatives. The migrant network in Vilassar de Mar is small and highly interconnected, and she knew that. She chose to smoke and drink with isolated friends who were connected to other groups but not to each other. None were even remotely connected to her family. She had never seen her personal network, or even thought about it before, yet Awa successfully compartmentalized her social world to accommodate her way of life.

Plate P.2 depicts Awa's personal network. It is shaped, sized, colored, and labeled in the same way as Mariama's. Yet it looks very different. A higher percentage of people in Awa's network were born in Spain and in other countries. Most notable are the network isolates stacked in the upper left hand of the figure. These are the people Awa knows, but who do not know anybody else in her network, according to Awa. Awa's network has less cohesion, owing in part to the absence of her father and his friends from her social life and her choice to associate with people in different social settings. Still, like Mariama, she has a large group of first- and second-generation migrants from Senegal and The Gambia who know each other, and her sister Mariama (the red node) has a central position in this group of people, meaning that Mariama knows many of Awa's network. A pair of people from Spain in the upper left corner of the figure represent the shopkeeper at a local bakery and the shopkeeper's daughter. Awa is not particularly close to them, but she sees them often and considers them friends.

These two examples illustrate the main ideas behind personal networks. Here we have two sisters who grew up in virtually identical circumstances, but they have different personalities and they took very different social paths. Many characteristics of their networks are the result of choices each made early on about whom to associate with and how to behave. Once they took a few steps down their respective paths, the social environment presented different choices for them, further exaggerating the differences between the two. Thus, looking at personal networks, we can find simultaneously the traces of structural circumstances, the life course, and the choices made by individuals, bringing us an excellent opportunity to study social life in all its complexity.

In sum, this book is about investigating these personal networks, how people manage their lives interacting in multiple contexts, and how these contexts constrain and influence people in multiple ways. Although each personal network is indeed unique, by looking at it in a given moment or following it up during a certain period, we can gain insights into the main factors structuring people's lives while keeping in mind the sources of variation, the narratives that people produce that give meaning to their lives, and how they identify and position themselves among others. In this regard, all the techniques and methods presented in this book are just a means to help the reader gain a better understanding of the complexities of people and, hopefully, a better understanding of themselves.

# Acknowledgments

This book is the result of years of work, which developed around numerous research grants, journal articles, consultancies, institutional research networks, and international conferences such as the International Network for Social Netwok Analysis (INSNA) Sunbelt Conference and the European Conference on Social Networks (EUSN). Over time, many people have contributed to our thinking and work in one way or another, through long-term research collaborations, short conversations over coffee during a break, or conference workshops on personal networks. So many people, in fact, that it would be impossible to name them all.

Yet among the many, we would like to thank some of the collaborators that we've had the privilege to work with in recent years, including Russ Bernard, Claire Bidart, Steve Borgatti, Başak Bilecen, Ulrik Brandes, Markus Gamper, Alejandro García-Macías, Marian-Gabriel Hâncean, Andreas Herz, Jeff Johnson, Peter Killworth, Till Krenz, Jürgen Lerner, Isidro Maya Jariego, Victoria Reyes-García, Mario Small, Tom Snijders, Mark Tranmer, Hugo Valenzuela, and Ashton Verdery—they have always been a source of invaluable advice and insights for our research. We are equally grateful to Janine Dahinden, Anuska Ferligoj, Michel Grossetti, Bernie Hogan, Bettina Hollstein, Eugene Johnsen, David Kennedy, Carlos Lozares, Joel Martí, Valentina Mazzucato, Ted Mouw, Félix Requena, Louise Ryan, Christian Steglich, Elizabeth Tracy, Paola Tubaro, Marijtje Van Duijn, Joan Miquel Verd, Beate Volker, and Barry Wellman.

This book has also greatly benefited from the nine editions of the Summer Course on Personal Network Research at the Universitat Autònoma de Barcelona, and is published as we prepare for its 10th edition in July 2019. The Barcelona Summer Course has given us the opportunity to meet some of the most passionate and brilliant students in the field of personal network research, including researchers and graduate students from Spain, the United States, Mexico, the United Kingdom, the Netherlands, Hungary, Italy, Iceland, Iran, and Israel: We are grateful to all of them for sharing their curiosity, research ideas, and scientific work with us over the years. Similarly, we would like to thank participants in our software workshops at the Sunbelt and EUSN conferences, as well as our (current and former) undergraduate and graduate students in Spain and Florida. Their comments, questions, and stories about motives and challenges of their research have been an extraordinary source of inspiration for our work.

Finally, we'd like to thank the enthusiastic and highly professional team at The Guilford Press for helping us to create this book and bearing with us through the long editorial process. Many insightful suggestions, comments, and critiques that greatly improved the text were provided by the initially anonymous reviewers whom we now thank by name: Barry Wellman, Director, NetLab Network, Toronto, Canada; Bernie Hogan, Oxford Internet Institute, University of Oxford, United Kingdom; Claude S. Fischer, Department of Sociology, University of California, Berkeley; and the other thoughtful reviewer from the Midwest, who continues to remain anonymous.

Our research on personal network theories, methods, and applications has been funded by various agencies and institutions over the years, including the U.S. National Science Foundation (BCS-0417429); the U.S. National Institutes of Health (UL1TR001427); the European Science Foundation (05-ECRP-026 and 10-ECRP-044); the Spanish Ministries of Science and Technology, Science and Innovation, and Economy and Competitiveness (SEJ2007-30289-E, CSO2009-07057, CSO2012-32635, CSO2015-68687-P, RYC-06081); and the Spanish Recercaixa Program (2015ACUP 00145). We are also grateful to the Center for Sociological Research in Madrid for working with us in the study "Social Cohesion and Trust" (study no. 3036). Our work would not have been possible without the very important support of all these organizations.

Nor would any of this have been possible without the collaboration of the respondents, informants, and community organizations that have participated in our research projects. They deserve a very special thanks for sharing their experiences, thoughts, and lives with us.

Last, as it goes, almost without saying, we are tremendously grateful to our families for supporting us all along the way. They are the heart and foundation of our personal networks.

# Contents

# 1

# Introduction

### *What Is This Chapter About?*

This chapter introduces the basic concepts of personal network analysis describing what personal networks are, why it is important to study them, and when it is appropriate to use a personal network approach. It also introduces a few basic concepts, such as ego and alter, node and edge, network size, composition, and structure, sociocentric, egocentric, and personal network approaches. Finally, the chapter provides an overview of the book's contents and structure.

## 1.1 EVERYONE HAS A PERSONAL NETWORK

We all have our own personal network. Who is in that network and how those people are connected to each other say something about us and impact the way we think and behave. From the moment of our birth, a combination of external factors and personal choices determines who will be in our network. Although the popular saying, "You can pick your friends, but you can't pick your family," has some truth to it, we can often choose the level of interaction we have with both friends *and* family. We also choose whether or not to introduce our friends to our family. In other words, we have a lot to say about who is and is not in our personal network, how we interact with them, and how (or even *if*) those people are connected to each other.

We do not, however, have complete control. We do not decide what country, social class, or ethnic group we wish to be born into. These factors affect the environment in which we are initially socialized, as well as the norms that govern social interaction patterns. In addition, we are born into a biological family, which will always constitute the set of biological family relationships from which we can choose. Yet throughout our lives, our decisions about what we do and where we live influence the set of people from whom we choose our contacts, friends, and acquaintances. Those contacts will, in turn, affect what we do and where we live, constraining the set of people we may potentially meet. The process is complex, with influence in both directions.

The consequences of this lifelong process of interacting with people and with the nonsocial environment, and the interplay between the social and nonsocial world give people different attitudes, behaviors, and outcomes. Personal network analysis attempts to explore the social environment and isolate its effect on people, using the variation from one person to another to explain the variation in what we think the social environment predicts or affects. In other words, personal network analysis is a way of operationalizing social context. Let's consider some examples.

Pam is a secretary in a county Health Department in Valdosta, Georgia, USA. She is 32 years old, married with three children, and was born in a small rural town not far from where she lives now. She went through grade school and middle school in her rural hometown, where most of the students were, like her, black. Her immediate family (father, mother, two sisters, and three brothers) moved to Valdosta around the time Pam entered high school. Valdosta has a small college that draws students from southern Georgia and northern Florida, with its faculty suited to accommodate those students. Pam's high school graduating class was a mix of races, family-income levels, and career tracks for parents. Her coworkers are a similar mix, including a few with whom she went to high school. She works with doctors, nurses, social workers, clerks, and janitors. Pam lives in a neighborhood that is predominantly black and middle class. She attends a Baptist church every Sunday. Her church members and neighbors, including her two sisters and two brothers and their families, make up the core of Pam's friends. Other than her two friends from high school, she does not create situations where people from work associate with her family and friends. Pam likes to keep things separate.

Allen is a software engineer for a company in Rochester, New York. He is 46 years old, white, and recently divorced, with two children who live with their mother. He was born and raised in San Diego, California, but went to college at Cornell University, a family tradition. While in college he joined a fraternity. He met his now ex-wife, a former sorority member, through the fraternity. He has maintained contacts with several fraternity brothers since college. It was through one of his fraternity brothers that he found out about an opening at his company more than 20 years ago. When Allen was married, he and his wife socialized a lot with a few other couples. He didn't have much contact with his brother and sisters at the time. Allen also had a set of friends from his work. The divorce caused some disruption in that set of friends, leaving Allen with a severely attenuated support group. He has recently tried to reconnect with his brother and two sisters, but that has proven difficult as they live in various parts of the country and have not visited each other regularly for many years. His company has laid many people off over the past several years, particularly in Rochester, and Allen's job is on the line. Some of his friends have already lost their jobs, and a few of them have moved away to work in other places.

Helen is a physical therapist in Seattle. She is 28 years old and single. She is an only child. Her father was in the diplomatic service, moving every couple of years until Helen went to high school, at which point they moved to Portland, Oregon. She finished high school there and then went to college at the University of Oregon in Eugene. She has lived in Seattle for the past four years. Helen is involved in several social groups surrounding her interests. She learned to play the cello as a child and participates in a string quartet that practices at least one night a week and performs at weddings and other formal gatherings. Helen belongs to a biking club that does long rides on Saturday mornings. She also belongs to a gym and conducts a yoga class twice a week. Her job is at a city hospital doing physical therapy with trauma patients. She regularly takes trips back to Portland where she visits her parents. She also maintains contact with a few high school friends, whom she sees when visiting her parents.

These three people clearly have some things in common, but they also differ in many ways. Some of those differences are ascribed (i.e., they cannot be changed): Pam and Helen are women and Allen is a man; Helen is 28, Pam is 32, and Allen is 46; Pam is black, and Helen and Allen are white. Most social scientists recognize the effect that sex, age, and race/ethnicity have on many outcomes, such as physical health, mental well-being, and income. For example, men and women are susceptible to some types of cancers specific to the genetics of their sex, such as breast or prostate cancer. The elderly tend to experience loss of memory and depression at much higher rates than young people. In many parts of the world, women and black people still experience discrimination in many job sectors, which affects their income. These outcomes are related to the unchangeable (or in the case of gender, difficult-to-change) attributes of these people.

Yet other personal attributes *can* be changed. Pam lives in Valdosta, Allen in Rochester, and Helen in Seattle. Pam never moved from the town where her family lives, Allen moved far from his biological family for his job, and while Helen moved, she stayed close enough to visit frequently. How far one moves from his or her family is a life decision that has significant consequences in both the shorter and longer run. On the one hand, being mobile means having more job opportunities. On the other hand, being far away means one cannot rely as much on family for tangible or emotional support. Such support becomes important at different stages of life. For example, the decision to move far from one's parents may cause hardships as those parents age and need their children's help on a regular basis.

Apart from the differences between Pam, Allen, and Helen in their ascribed and achieved personal attributes, we also perceive differences in their social environments. While "social environment" and "social context" are broad expressions that social scientists use to refer to many different things (e.g., the kind of neighborhood in which we reside, the religious and political organizations we belong to, or the type of welfare state we live in), our personal network—the personal community made up of all the close and distant relationships that we maintain—is obviously a major component of what we call the social environment.

The differences in Pam's, Allen's, and Helen's personal networks are in part related to the differences in their personal attributes. On the one hand, our age, sex, race or ethnicity, education, personality, and place of residence determine who we will meet and with whom of those people we will build stronger or longer lasting relationships. On the other hand, our friends and family may also influence our changeable personal attributes. For example, we may choose to live closer to our parents, quit smoking because our romantic partner doesn't like it, or attend a certain college because our friends go there.

Like personal attributes, personal networks can have a direct or indirect effect on outcome variables such as those we have mentioned: physical and mental health, well-being, occupation, and income. As networks are different, this may play out differently for different persons. Although Allen appears to be in a difficult position, through his work and his college experience he may have established contacts that can lead to other jobs similar to the one he has now. Helen works in a hospital with many doctors and nurses who know other doctors and nurses at other hospitals with knowledge of job openings for physical therapists. What is more, she is involved in groups, such as the yoga class and the string quartet, which might put her in contact with people who are aware of job opportunities. In contrast, in terms of job opportunities, Pam may be more constrained. Like Helen, she knows many people at her work, but the rest of her personal network consists of people who are in a similar position to her own—they have lived in the same place for a long time, many of them know each other, and she has few connections outside her circle of family and friends. With this personal network, Pam is probably not the recipient of a lot of new job information.

At the same time, Pam may receive a lot of emotional and tangible support from her network, another outcome that is in turn related to physical and mental well-being. She can rely on her family and neighbors for child care, rides to the doctor, or shoulders to cry on when things are not going well. Helen may have created a similarly supportive situation in the form of her many social groups and her proximity to her parents, even though her relations have a shorter duration, while Allen's network offers him little support in the "well-being" area at this stage of life.

## 1.2 THE SIZE, COMPOSITION, AND STRUCTURE OF PERSONAL NETWORKS

So far, the effects of personal networks that we have discussed are primarily concerned with the types of people in the network—that is, what the network is *composed* of. When we talk about network *composition*, we refer to the characteristics or attributes of the network members, or network "actors." Pam, for example, has a network composed of family members, friends from high school, neighbors, church members, and colleagues. These are all different roles played by Pam's network members. Helen's network also has high *role diversity*, although it has fewer family members than Pam's. Most of Pam's contacts live in the same town as she does, many even in the same neighborhood, so her network can be said to be mostly *local*. Helen's contacts, in contrast, are geographically more dispersed than Pam's network members. We also saw that Pam's colleagues are quite mixed in terms of social class and race, whereas Pam's other relations are more similar to hers.

Apart from differences in network composition, personal networks can also differ in *size*—that is, the number of people in the network—and in the way those people have relationships among themselves—that is, the *structure* of the network. Two personal networks with roughly the same composition in terms of the characteristics of actors can have very different effects on the person when their structures differ. We have alluded to these effects with Pam. The fact that most of Pam's family, friends, and neighbors all know each other means that they may tend to recycle the same sort of information. They may also talk openly to each other about Pam and her life, something that helps her in some circumstances but hinders her in others. Because Pam's network members communicate about her, Pam's children may be safer walking around the neighborhood, or she might readily get help with physical health problems were they to arise. However, if Pam became depressed, a condition still associated with social stigma in U.S. society, she might be reluctant to tell anyone in her network, or she might ask a friend for suggestions on how to seek treatment, since her contacts all know each other and could share information about her. She might worry that her entire personal network could be talking negatively about her at some point. Given the structural characteristics of her personal network, Pam's fear of being looked down on by her family and friends might actually serve to isolate her from her social network. In other words, the fact that many members of Pam's network know each other may increase her possibility of mobilizing social support when needed, but it also increases social control and pressure compared to others (like Allen and Helen) whose networks are less connected.

Finally, compositional and structural characteristics can be combined to gain an entirely new insight into the effects of personal networks. For example, Helen belongs to several groups: the hospital where she works, the string quartet, her yoga class, the biking club, and her family at home in Portland. Helen has a best friend, Wendy, whom she has known since high school and who, like Helen, moved to Seattle. Wendy has attended several of Helen's performances, has met her friends from work, and takes her yoga classes. Helen also knows Wendy's family. Wendy is in a structurally important position in Helen's network because she knows many of Helen's contacts and bridges several of Helen's groups. Wendy also has the characteristic of being Helen's friend from high school and main *confidante*. Helen tells her everything. Wendy's *central* position in the network, combined with her role as a high school friend and her function as Helen's primary support, can benefit Helen, as she can easily talk with Wendy about her life and the people in it. However, a falling-out between the two friends could be devastating to Helen, not only because of her relationship with Wendy, but also because Wendy is part of many of her social circles.

These examples show us that the people we know and the way they are connected to each other can affect our attitudes, behaviors, and outcomes. However, we are not passive participants in the composition and structure of these relationships. We make choices about who will be in our networks, who we will connect to one another, and how closely we will connect them. In part depending on our personality, some of us are more passive observers of what goes on in our network, while others carefully strategize and shape the composition and structure of their personal network. So, we are active agents in the construction of our networks, and at the same time, we are constrained by them. This complexity makes it challenging to study personal networks.

## 1.3 EGOS, ALTERS, EGOCENTRIC NETWORKS, AND SOCIOCENTRIC NETWORKS

Personal network research falls under a larger field of study called *social network analysis*—and, more recently, *network science*. Broadly speaking, social network analysis is the study of the pattern of relationships between social actors. While the term "social network" instantly evokes Facebook, Twitter, and the like, in the social sciences a social network is simply any set of actors (or *nodes*) and the ties among them (or *edges*, i.e., the lines connecting the nodes). These exist not only online but also offline. The network actors are usually people, but they need not be. Social network studies have been done on the collaborative relationships between organizations (Van de Bunt & Groenewegen, 2007), the migration flows between countries (e.g., Danchev & Porter, 2018), and even the affiliation patterns between animals (e.g., Mann, Stanton, Patterson, Bienenstock, & Singh, 2012). Actually, any set of relationships between organisms or groups of organisms can be analyzed using social network analysis.

Historically, social network analysis has comprised two broad approaches. The first is *egocentric network analysis*, which studies the social networks surrounding selected people. These focal persons, whose networks we are interested in, are called *egos*, and their network members are called *alters*. In the preceding examples, Pam, Allen, and Helen are the egos, and their family, friends, and acquaintances are the alters. Thus, an egocentric network is a social network among the contacts (alters) linked to a focal person (ego).

Egocentric network analysis can either be constrained to the social relationships that people have in a particular context, such as their workplace or school; or it can be unconstrained, in which case it is also called *personal* network analysis. Personal networks are thus egocentric networks across multiple social contexts or settings. We may be interested in the specific *egocentric* network of Pam's coworkers, or we may be interested in Pam's total *personal* network, including her family, friends, coworkers, and any other contact with whom she interacts. With personal networks, our goal is to study the effects of the set of relationships that surround an individual, regardless of the context from which they are drawn. Therefore, we usually need to ask respondents to tell us which people are in their networks, as they may be anyone.

*Sociocentric* or *whole networks* are quite different. Instead of focusing on the people who surround a particular person or set of persons and the effects these people have on that person or persons, whole network analysis studies the pattern of relationships between actors in a defined, bounded group or a community or a context. A good example is the network of relationships between students in a school. In fact, some of the earliest known whole network analyses were conducted in elementary school classrooms to understand how the interactions among students affected their performance (Heidler, Gamper, Herz, & Esser, 2014; Moreno, 1934). The network of romantic relationships among students in a college is a sociocentric network; so are the network of friendship relationships among residents in a village and the network of email communications among coworkers in a company.

An important difference between egocentric and sociocentric network analysis has to do with how we collect the data used in our study. With egocentric networks, we only observe (e.g., interview) the egos. While the alters are part of the ego's network, they are not directly observed. By contrast, with sociocentric networks we observe (collect data from) all network actors. Also keep in mind that with egocentric network analysis we deal with many separate networks, as we typically observe a sample of egos. For each of them, the network includes the ego, the ego's alters, and the relationships among the ego's alters. Usually, though, we are not interested in the relationships between the different egos or between the alters linked to different egos. By contrast, in sociocentric analysis we may deal with a smaller number of networks, or even a single network, in which all the actors may be directly or indirectly connected to each other.

## 1.4 SHOULD I USE PERSONAL NETWORK OR WHOLE NETWORK ANALYSIS?

The decision of whether to study personal or whole networks depends on the research questions and hypotheses you have, as well as the type of data collection that is feasible in your case. Suppose you are interested in adolescent smoking behavior. You believe that whether an adolescent *A* will experiment with cigarette smoking depends on the social influence exerted on *A*, that is, on the attitudes, views, and behavior of the members of *A*'s social network. You would like to use social network data and methods to test this hypothesis.

In one approach, you hypothesize that adolescents' smoking behavior depends largely on the actor attributes and pattern of relationships in their high school network: in other words, whether *A* will start smoking depends on *A*'s position in her school's social network—a whole network—and on the attitudes and views of *A*'s school mates. If this were your hypothesis, you would focus on a specific high school, and collect and analyze data about the whole network that exists among adolescents within that high school. This would be a *whole network approach*: you identify a group (the high school), and you look at the whole, bounded social network that exists within that group. This approach also allows you to look at broader, group-level processes, such as what cliques, subgroups, or factions form in the school network and why; whether the school has a core of very central actors (actors who are related to many others) and a periphery of more marginal ones; what "classes" of actors have structurally similar positions in the school network and why; and how ideas and behaviors spread among individuals or groups to the larger school network.

In a different approach, you could determine that while you are sure that an adolescent's network influences her decision to start smoking, you don't really know whether only the adolescent's school mates, or also her neighborhood friends and family members, play a role in this process. In other words, you know that *A*'s social network matters, but you don't know where to set the boundaries of the social network that is relevant to your outcome of interest. In this case, you would focus on *A* herself and on other similar adolescents (the egos), and you would collect and analyze data about the unbounded personal networks surrounding these adolescents, separately from each other. This would be a *personal network approach*: you identify the focal individuals (the adolescents), and you look at the unbounded social network that exists around each of them. This strategy gives you a deeper lens on the social environment around each adolescent. However, this comes at the expense of the ability to capture broader processes within a larger group such as the whole high school. Plate 1.1 illustrates this important difference between a whole and a personal network approach.

To make the difference clearer, let's consider some simple network data and visualizations. Whole network data can be collected in many ways, but one approach is to ask each member of the bounded group to evaluate their relationship with every other member. Let's consider a classroom of students. Table 1.1 depicts an *adjacency matrix* collected on the first day of a graduate class in social network methods. Each of the 12 students was asked to rate on a scale of 0 to 5 how well they knew every other student. The answers of each person were then recorded in a row in the adjacency matrix. For example, the first row represents the answers of Irene on how well she knows each of the 12 students. The diagonal running from the upper left to the lower right has all 5's, since each person knows him- or herself as much as possible. Sometimes these cells are also left empty, since researchers are usually not interested in relations to self. Notice also that this matrix is *asymmetric*, meaning that the two people need not agree on the level of their relationship. For example, Irene said she knows Christie at level 2 (the second number in the first row is a 2), but Christie said she knows Irene at level 1 (the first number in the second row is 1).

**TABLE 1.1. Adjacency Matrix of a Graduate Social Network Class**

| | Irene | Christie | Ruby | Tom | Darlene | Sally | Flora | Erma | Melissa | Kent | Mable | Andre |
|---|---|---|---|---|---|---|---|---|---|---|---|---|
| Irene | 5 | 2 | 2 | 0 | 0 | 1 | 0 | 3 | 1 | 0 | 2 | 0 |
| Christie | 1 | 5 | 5 | 0 | 0 | 0 | 0 | 1 | 0 | 0 | 2 | 0 |
| Ruby | 2 | 5 | 5 | 0 | 0 | 1 | 0 | 2 | 0 | 0 | 4 | 0 |
| Tom | 0 | 1 | 1 | 5 | 0 | 0 | 0 | 0 | 0 | 0 | 0 | 0 |
| Darlene | 0 | 0 | 0 | 0 | 5 | 0 | 0 | 0 | 0 | 0 | 0 | 0 |
| Sally | 2 | 0 | 2 | 0 | 0 | 5 | 5 | 2 | 0 | 0 | 2 | 0 |
| Flora | 0 | 0 | 1 | 0 | 0 | 5 | 5 | 5 | 0 | 0 | 2 | 0 |
| Erma | 4 | 3 | 1 | 0 | 0 | 1 | 5 | 5 | 0 | 0 | 3 | 0 |
| Melissa | 1 | 0 | 0 | 1 | 0 | 0 | 0 | 0 | 5 | 0 | 1 | 0 |
| Kent | 0 | 0 | 0 | 0 | 0 | 0 | 0 | 0 | 0 | 5 | 0 | 3 |
| Mable | 2 | 3 | 3 | 0 | 0 | 1 | 2 | 2 | 1 | 0 | 5 | 0 |
| Andre | 0 | 0 | 0 | 0 | 0 | 0 | 0 | 0 | 0 | 3 | 0 | 5 |

One way social network researchers analyze these data is by visualizing them. That is, we can create a drawing that shows us the network resulting from these numbers. Figure 1.1 is a network visualization of the data in Table 1.1, where the 12 nodes represent the 12 students and the arrows from one node to another represent the existence of a relationship from one student to another (at a level of 1 or higher, in this case). The wider the arrow, the stronger the relationship. For the sake of visual clarity, in the case of two people who agree that they know each other, but don't agree on the strength of that relationship, as was the case of Irene and Christie, the width represents the strongest relationship of the two. Self-relations have been excluded from this graph.

The figure is quite informative. For example, it shows that, on the one hand, Tom indicated that he knows Christie and Ruby a little bit, but the women didn't indicate they knew Tom. On the other hand, both women indicated that they know each other very well. This information is not so easily extracted from the adjacency matrix.

We can see from this visualization that a large group of people are connected in the class. These were all students in the Anthropology Department. Andre and Kent at the top, were from the management department, and Darlene in the upper right, an *isolate*, was a political science student. This visualization gives us a quick understanding of how the people within this group relate to each other.

Whole networks represent social groups that most people would agree *are* a group. For example, researchers have performed whole network analyses of the people in an office and in a karate club (Zachary, 1977), and even an archival study of the whole network of the Italian aristocracy in Renaissance Florence (Padgett & Ansell, 1993). A crucial point in whole network analysis is that the group has well-defined boundaries, and we are only interested in relations or interactions that occur within those boundaries. We know who is in the group and who is not, and the group has some reason to interact, such

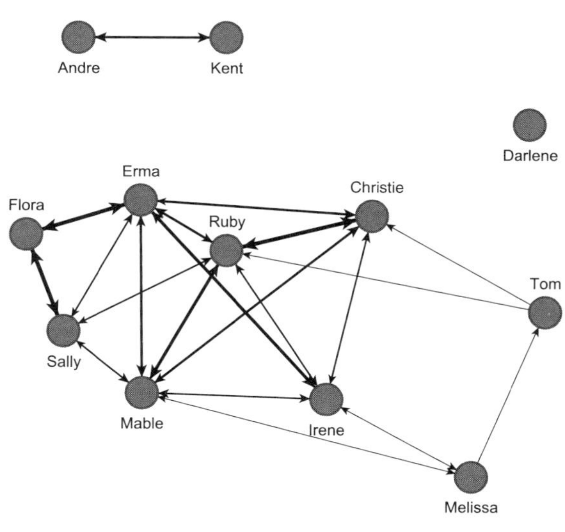


**FIGURE 1.1.** Network visualization of the adjacency matrix in Table 1.1.

as working together, playing together, or living near each other. We assume that only the relations or interactions that take place within the bounded group are relevant to the outcomes of interest, and we study the structural patterns that emerge from those relations.

In contrast, personal network analysis is about the *un*bounded networks surrounding individuals. This is an important conceptual distinction. In the preceding example, the whole network analysis of the graduate class informs us about what we can expect to happen when the students interact. For example, we would expect Andre and Kent to collaborate on a class project, and we might expect all the anthropologists to talk to each other about how to incorporate the methods into their dissertations. The conclusions we draw are limited to how these students interact within the context of their group, a graduate class in social networks.

While valuable for certain information, whole network analysis will not help us predict much about Andre or Kent as individuals outside of their class. For this we need personal network analysis because it accounts for influences from the many groups to which a person belongs. While both Andre and Kent belong to this graduate class, it is unlikely that this is the only group that influences them. Kent's family, his other professors, friends, and members of other social groups may all contribute to forming his attitudes and conditioning his behaviors. And while no two personal networks are exactly the same, similarities in personal networks affect people in similar ways.

Plate 1.2 shows Kent's personal network with 45 personal contacts (blue nodes are men and red nodes are women). The visualization is obtained from an egocentric adjacency matrix, a subset of which is in Table 1.2. This is very similar to the sociocen-

**TABLE 1.2. The First 12 Rows and Columns of a Personal Network's Adjacency Matrix**

| | Sheila | Kelly | Ivan | Amos | Rose | Alex | Bertha | Henry | Susie | Van | Jack | Erika |
|---|---|---|---|---|---|---|---|---|---|---|---|---|
| Sheila | 1 | 1 | 1 | 0 | 1 | 1 | 1 | 1 | 1 | 1 | 1 | 1 |
| Kelly | 1 | 1 | 0 | 0 | 1 | 1 | 1 | 1 | 1 | 1 | 1 | 1 |
| Ivan | 1 | 0 | 1 | 0 | 0 | 0 | 0 | 0 | 0 | 0 | 0 | 0 |
| Amos | 0 | 0 | 0 | 1 | 0 | 0 | 0 | 0 | 0 | 0 | 0 | 0 |
| Rose | 1 | 1 | 0 | 0 | 1 | 1 | 1 | 1 | 1 | 1 | 1 | 1 |
| Alex | 1 | 1 | 0 | 0 | 1 | 1 | 1 | 1 | 1 | 1 | 1 | 1 |
| Bertha | 1 | 1 | 0 | 0 | 1 | 1 | 1 | 1 | 1 | 1 | 1 | 1 |
| Henry | 1 | 1 | 0 | 0 | 1 | 1 | 1 | 1 | 1 | 1 | 1 | 1 |
| Susie | 1 | 1 | 0 | 0 | 1 | 1 | 1 | 1 | 1 | 1 | 1 | 1 |
| Van | 1 | 1 | 0 | 0 | 1 | 1 | 1 | 1 | 1 | 1 | 1 | 1 |
| Jack | 1 | 1 | 0 | 0 | 1 | 1 | 1 | 1 | 1 | 1 | 1 | 1 |
| Erika | 1 | 1 | 0 | 0 | 1 | 1 | 1 | 1 | 1 | 1 | 1 | 1 |

*Note.* The full adjacency matrix has 40 rows and columns and corresponds to the personal network in Plate 1.2.

tric adjacency matrix in Table 1.1, except that rows and columns are Kent's personal contacts, and each cell is 1 if Kent says that the two contacts in the cell's row and column know each other, 0 otherwise. Kent's personal network has a typical structure that consists of different cohesive subgroups, corresponding to the social circles that Kent interacts with. The dense group of nodes in the top left of Plate 1.2 is Kent's extended family. Kent has a large family in which, as we would expect, most relatives know each other; this results in a large, dense cohesive subgroup in Kent's personal network. The few blue nodes in the top right of the figure are Kent's old friends from high school. Some of them know Kent's family, while others don't. In the bottom left is the group of Kent's new friends in graduate school. They mostly don't know Kent's family, but some of them know Kent's old friends in the top right. In the middle is Kent, the ego, exposed to interactions with and influences from each of the social groups that form his personal network. Understanding these influences and their effects on people like Kent is the reason for studying personal networks.

One way of thinking about personal networks and whole networks is as different "slices" of, or windows on, social reality (Plate 1.3). Each of these windows has its pros and cons for understanding the social world—each of them shows something but hides something else. Personal networks offer an in-depth view on the social world of the individuals of interest (the egos), including contacts from any possible context, circle, and social setting. However, they are limited to the egos' direct contacts—what network analysts would call the *first-order neighborhood* of egos. Also, personal networks typically do not include information about connections among different egos or alters of different egos. In fact, if we sample individuals randomly from a larger population, we normally expect there to be no connection between different personal networks. By contrast, whole networks show us how the individuals of interest (the network actors) are embedded in a larger social structure, which includes the indirect contacts that are removed from an actor by several links or *degrees of separation*—in other words, the first-order and the higher-order neighborhoods of our individuals of interest. These individuals can be connected and share common contacts, unlike egos in personal network data. However, whole networks are limited to a single social setting, which in our example is the high school, and give us no information about the broader personal community of which each individual is part, beyond the selected setting.

In general, a whole network approach is more appropriate for your study if you can confidently assume that a single social setting, group, or organization (e.g., the high school) is what matters most for your outcome of interest (e.g., academic performance); or if you would like to capture the way in which individuals are embedded in the whole social structure of this group, including first-order and higher-order neighborhoods. You should also opt for whole networks if you are interested in group-level processes and outcomes: for example, looking at the whole networks of different high schools, how the cohesion of the school network is associated with the average performance of the school sport teams.

By contrast, you should choose a personal network approach if you are interested in a population of individuals, and the outcomes of these individuals (such as mental well-being, physical health, or occupational attainment) are likely affected by the broader

### *Combining Personal and Whole Networks*

Caterina Gouvis Roman and colleagues (2012) studied delinquency and gang membership among the youth in a small, disadvantaged, high-crime neighborhood in Maryland. They interviewed 147 young people between the ages of 14 and 21 in the neighborhood, for which they estimated the total number of youths to be 440. The researchers asked them to list 20 people they "hang out with or might see regularly in a typical day," about the characteristics of these alters (e.g., age, sex, place of residence, type of relation, perceived gang membership, and gang-related activities the ego knew about), and the relationships among the alters. After data collection, the researchers superimposed the personal networks of the respondents to create a whole, or sociocentric, network of the youth in the neighborhood and their relationships. Thus, they conducted both personal *and* sociocentric network analyses. Results showed that respondents with more numerous groups of relationships were less likely to be involved with delinquency. Also, those who were more central in the network of the neighborhood appeared to have a higher level of delinquency, but not of violence, than those less central.

social world or personal community in which they are embedded, including different circles and settings. Also, you should opt for personal networks if capturing each individual's entire personal community (but limited to direct contacts) is more important than knowing where each individual is located in the wider, first-order *and* higher-order social structure (but limited to a selected group).

Last, you can combine personal and sociocentric analysis if you are interested in the individuals in a bounded social group, such as a neighborhood, a school, or a prison, but you think that they are influenced by both the people in the group and the broader environment.

## 1.5 WHO IS THIS BOOK FOR?

This book focuses on research into personal networks. Personal network analysis is a way of operationalizing an important part of the social context: the immediate interpersonal environment. Anybody who is interested in describing that part of the social context of individuals, or who wants to predict an individual attitude, behavior, condition, or outcome they believe is in part due to differences in interpersonal environments may benefit from personal network analysis. In fact, personal networks are a particularly rich way of operationalizing the interpersonal context; they allow us to measure both the characteristics of the people who form an individual's social context (network composition) and the social structure that these actors create around the individual by interacting with each other (network structure). Personal network analysis helps us go beyond an individual analysis to incorporate contextual effects as explanatory variables for individual outcomes.

Figure 1.2 shows how personal network analysis can enhance a research design. On the left is the traditional model where respondent characteristics, such as age, sex, race/ethnicity, and income are used to predict some outcome of interest, such as physical or mental health, job attainment, or discriminatory experiences. On the right is the personal network model. The explanatory variables in this model include respondent characteristics but add to it characteristics of the personal network, such as the size, composition (e.g., the percent of alters the respondent can talk to about health issues), or structure (e.g., the cohesiveness of the network). These variables reflect characteristics of the respondents' social contexts, adding to the explanatory value of the model. Of course, prior knowledge of the field of study and theories can help us design different models. We may, for example, expect that personal network characteristics do not have a direct effect on the outcome, but rather that they alter or mediate the effect a respondent characteristic has on the outcome. For example, we may expect that introverted people (respondent characteristic) are more likely to get depressed (outcome) than extroverted people, but that a densely knit, supportive personal network (personal network characteristic) can form a buffer particularly for introverts, thus lowering the probability that introverts will become depressed. The precise mechanisms through which personal networks are thought to have an effect can differ from one model to another, but all personal network models have in common the use of personal network characteristics as explanatory social context measures in addition to respondent attributes.

Personal network analysis also allows us to understand the social organization of informal ties itself, at both a micro and macro level. Social cohesion in a population, for example, defined as the degree to which different subgroups in the population are connected by informal social relationships, can be studied by analyzing "*homophily*" (the tendency to associate with similar peers) in personal networks for a sample of individuals from the population (see Section 2.2).

As you will see, collecting personal network data can be time consuming and expensive. Therefore, the personal network approach should not be used when the variables you are trying to measure can be observed by asking more easily measured and

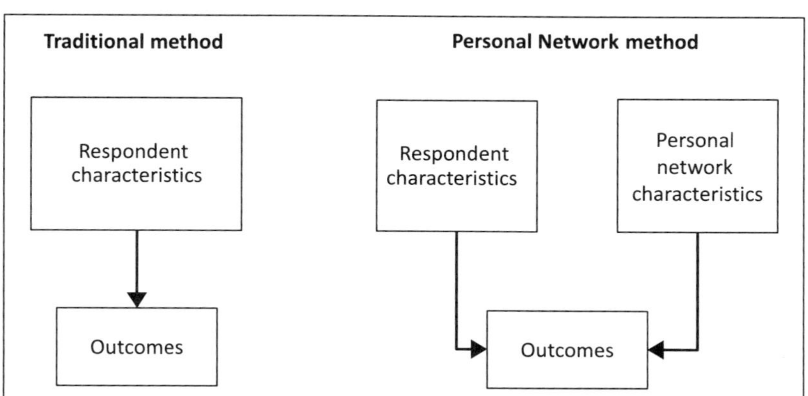


**FIGURE 1.2.** Models of social science research designs.

less intrusive proxy questions. In other words, if you can develop a model to predict smoking by simply asking respondents if their friends smoke, rather than collecting a lot of details about which friends smoke and how these friends interact with each other, you should not use the techniques described in this book. However, if you intend to study the interpersonal environment of the respondents, or a phenomenon dependent on that part of social context, and you think that a higher level of detail can provide important insight, personal network analysis offers a unique perspective that is often ideal for such studies.

This book is primarily aimed at readers who have no previous knowledge of personal networks or social network analysis. Most of the book should be easily understandable to students who are approaching social networks for the first time. It can be used on its own or as a companion to a book on the broader field of social network analysis, which would be typically more focused on sociocentric networks. Two such books are *Doing Social Network Research: Network Based Research Design for Social Scientists* by Garry Robins (2016) and *Analyzing Social Networks* by Stephen Borgatti, Martin Everett, and Jeffrey Johnson (2013). This book focuses primarily on personal network data collected through interviews and surveys, and we devote less attention to data extracted from online networking websites and applications, because we believe that in most cases online data are not a good substitute for data on offline social interactions. However, online data are valuable for understanding computer-mediated communication and can be used in tandem with personal network data (see Sections 3.4 and 6.7). Readers with an interest in mining online social networks are referred to *The Sage Handbook of Social Media Research Methods*, edited by Luke Sloan and Anabel Quan-Haase (2017). Matthew Salganik's *Bit by Bit: Social Research in the Digital Age* (2017) provides an excellent overview of the potential benefits and pitfalls of such data for the social sciences.

## 1.6 BOOK OVERVIEW

This book will guide the readers through the various stages of personal network research, extending from design and data collection to visualization and analysis. Chapter 2 gives a brief historical overview and presents the theoretical frameworks that have driven personal network research. Knowledge of these frameworks is important for developing a research question for a personal network project, which we discuss in Chapter 3. The research question will largely determine how you design your study.

Chapters 4 to 10 describe the design of personal network research. We focus primarily on a quantitative approach because the delineation of networks and even their structured visualization imply quantitative measurement. Nevertheless, we have often successfully used these methods in mixed-methods research, and we will often refer to it. Chapter 4 gets you started on the basics of surveys, particularly as applied to personal network research, and Chapter 5 presents questions you could ask about the respondents. As we explain in Chapter 4, personal network research is in part similar to any other survey or interview-based research, and therefore we review their basics in these two chapters. If you have experience in survey research, you may skip Chapters 4 and 5. Chapters 6–8 describe how to measure personal networks following the three steps most personal network researchers take: (1) To delineate the network using name generators or alternative approaches, (2) to ask questions about each network contact in order to measure network composition, and (3) to ask questions about the relationships between network contacts in order to measure network structure. The collection of these data allows researchers to visualize the networks, visualizations which they sometimes use during the interviews to collect more information. This is why we discuss visualization in Chapter 9. Chapter 10 reviews quantitative methods used to collect data about the characteristics of personal networks that do not involve the generation of a set of names. Usually, these methods focus on the larger personal networks (see Section 2.2).

After the discussion of the design of personal network research, we focus on analysis in Chapters 11 to 13. Chapter 11 discusses how you can summarize the relation-level data in aggregate or summary variables that describe network composition and network structure. Chapters 12 and 13 present more advanced topics in network measurement and statistical modeling, which require some previous familiarity with quantitative methods for the social sciences, mostly regression analysis. If you don't want to get into much detail, you may omit these two chapters and read Chapter 11 only.

The final chapter discusses research ethics. Of course, researchers need to take ethics into account during the whole research cycle, but we first want to give the reader a proper introduction to personal network analysis before delving into the sometimes tricky world of ethics. We encourage all readers to consult this chapter at the initial stages of research design and to keep its points in mind in later stages.

At the end of each chapter are suggestions for further reading that cover background concepts or more advanced treatment of the chapter's topics. The appendix, at the end of the book, lists software that has been specifically designed for personal network research. This list also includes software that is not specifically designed for it but is useful nonetheless.

## CHAPTER SUMMARY

This chapter presented the personal network as the network of social relationships surrounding an individual, where relationships can stem from different social settings. It further introduced some basic concepts and terminology: for example, "egos" and "alters"; the difference between personal, egocentric, and sociocentric network approaches; and the appropriate time to use them. Three cases (Pam, Allen, and Helen) illustrated some of the factors that affect the size, composition, and structure of personal networks, as well as the role of individual agency, social constraints, and the course of life within them. Although collecting data from personal networks can be a difficult task, it provides privileged insight into the immediate social environment of individuals and has proven useful in explaining many research problems. We will discuss this use in the next chapter.

# 2

# How Personal Networks Have Been Used So Far

*What Is This Chapter About?*

This chapter starts with a brief history of personal network analysis (Section 2.1) in order to provide an understanding of the theoretical precedents that shaped the field, whether from anthropology, sociology, social psychology, or other disciplines. We then summarize current knowledge of the size, composition, and structure of personal networks (Section 2.2) and discuss the main theoretical frameworks regarding the influence of personal networks on individual outcomes (Section 2.3). The final section discusses the latest developments. Throughout the chapter, we will introduce basic network concepts such as degree, dyad, triad, small worlds, tie strength, homophily, social foci, structural holes, social capital, social selection, and social influence.

## 2.1 A BRIEF HISTORY OF PERSONAL NETWORK ANALYSIS

### The Manchester School of Anthropology

The practice of looking at a person's social relationships to understand his or her attitudes and behaviors is not new. It goes back at least to Sigmund Freud and his creation of psychoanalysis. Freud and his followers developed methods to elicit discussions about relationships from a patient's social context and used them to help patients with psychological problems. They made generalizations about different conditions observed across individuals and how those conditions could be resolved. However, the focus of the method was on curing the individual rather than using these data to explain social phenomena or to inform a social theory.

Unlike psychoanalysis, personal network analysis involves the systematic collection of data on the social relations surrounding each set of individuals, together with analysis of the composition and structure of those social relations to understand social phenomena. Interestingly, the use of personal network methods has come full circle and today extends to applications in mental health counseling.

Personal network analysis was first applied by a group of British anthropologists working mostly in the British colony of Rhodesia (now part of Zambia and Zimbabwe) in the 1940s. Their studies were designed to complement the previous literature about social structure based mainly on normative groups by incorporating the analysis of actual relations among people across categories. Their leader was Max Gluckman, a South African who attended the University of Oxford as a Rhodes Scholar in the 1930s. There he learned about the structural functionalist theories of anthropologist Alfred Reginald Radcliffe-Brown, who regarded society as a complex system of norms, traditions, and institutions. Gluckman was also influenced both politically and academically by Marxist theory and combined it with the structural functionalist paradigm in his studies of conflict and power. Following his graduation from Oxford in 1936, he spent the next 10 years doing field research in central and southeast Africa.

Gluckman combined Radcliffe-Brown's notion of society as a system of relations among institutions, norms, and traditions with early concepts of acculturation to try to understand how traditional African tribal societies adapted to British colonial rule. He encouraged his students to collect data about conflicts arising from the interaction between traditional tribal society and British colonial society, and about the way individuals resolved those conflicts. Gluckman (1940, 1958) stressed that analyzing such situations should go beyond the system of institutions within the traditional culture and should take into account the ties between the colonized population and the British colonial rulers and administrators. His notion of ties that *bridge* cleavages in a social system was key to explaining how Africans successfully resolved conflicts within the evolving British colonial and African society. It also represents the first attempt to explain culture by using the concept of informal ties cutting across different types of groups—a personal network concept. From Gluckman's perspective, one could not understand the social structure of 1940s Rhodesia by observing what was happening within a single social group, British or African, because a new social system had evolved that cut across those boundaries. By focusing on individuals and their various daily interactions—their personal networks—Gluckman could examine what this system looked like and how it affected individuals.

In 1949, Gluckman was appointed the chair of social anthropology at the University of Manchester. Manchester, a British industrial town, lent itself well to Gluckman's theories on conflict and power in society. Recognizing that Manchester was not among Britain's flagship universities, Gluckman set up a seminar series to bring renowned anthropologists together from all over England, and as far away as the United States. The Manchester School seminars were largely responsible for disseminating the social network approach among other anthropologists.

Among those associated with the Manchester School were the anthropologists John Barnes, Elizabeth Bott, and Clyde Mitchell. These scholars are now widely acknowledged to be the first social scientists who systematically collected the type of data we would today consider to be personal network data. Each set out a program of research that focused on the network of relations surrounding a focal individual, or ego. While these egocentric networks were viewed as being part of a complete network of relations among all members of society (i.e., the whole network of society), the Manchester School researchers considered egocentric networks to be the primary research interest for anthropologists.

John Barnes, who did his fieldwork in a small fishing village in Norway in the 1960s, was the first to employ the term "network" to describe the set of informal social relations he observed in the village. Barnes was influenced by Jacob Moreno (1934), who first represented social relationships graphically with the so-called "sociogram." Like Gluckman, Barnes (1954) recognized that the Norwegian village he studied was made up of formal groupings or organizations, but he observed that the personal connections bridging these organizations often explained how things got done. This notion was similar to Gluckman's idea of the bridging ties between the traditional cultures of Britain's African colonies and the British colonial culture.

Barnes returned to Manchester from Norway and moved from Manchester to the London School of Economics and met Elizabeth Bott, a Canadian psychologist and anthropologist who had been working on a study of kinship relations among families in London. Bott used a similar approach to Barnes's, focusing on the set of relationships that surround particular married couples, and used the variability of those relationships to explain the level of segregation in conjugal roles. Unlike Barnes and Gluckman though, Bott did not seek to understand from her micro level data how a whole society functioned, which would be the so-called *extended case study*. Instead, she wanted to look at the workings of kinship, a traditional hallmark institution of anthropological study, and she used personal networks for this aim. Bott (1957) was the first researcher to recognize that there are different personal network types and that variability in these types affects people in different ways.

### *The Bott Hypothesis about Conjugal Roles and Social Networks*

Elizabeth Bott contributed to the Manchester School's studies on social networks with her classic work, *Family and Social Networks* (1957). In a study of 20 young married couples in Greater London, Bott posited a relationship between the degree of overlap among the couple's personal networks and the level of segregation of their conjugal roles. Her argument was as follows: when the new couple was embedded in a shared and dense network of relationships, the conjugal roles were likely to be more differentiated (what one spouse does at home the other does not) because of both pressure from outside the couple and help available. Conversely, when the couple's (personal) networks were more independent, the conjugal roles exerted in practice were less differentiated. The Bott hypothesis (see also Section 3.4) has been tested in a variety of situations and has proven influential in many fields, especially in family studies.

Clyde Mitchell continued the Manchester School tradition of research in British colonial Africa. Mitchell is often credited with formalizing social network theory in a way that also suggested *how* it should be studied. Mitchell (1969) introduced the term "ego-centered networks" to describe the data on the myriad social relationships surrounding a focal individual. He indicated that the ego-centered networks of the members of a community combine to form the *complete network* of that community. As an anthropologist, Mitchell realized that social relationships could be analyzed from the micro level (ego-centered networks) to the macro level (whole networks); he saw these approaches as complementary.

The Manchester tradition continued for another two decades in the work of Gluckman's and Mitchell's students, especially Bruce Kapferer. However, with few exceptions, such as Larissa Adler Lomnitz's masterly work on the support networks of people in a poor neighborhood in Mexico (Adler Lomnitz, 1977), personal network analysis never truly flourished among anthropologists. One reason was the lack of appropriate methods and computational power needed for dealing with the large amount of network data that would be collected during fieldwork. Nevertheless, it has continued to inspire qualitative research into social networks in different disciplines, which has become increasingly popular over the last decades.

While the Manchester School of anthropology was still active, sociologists in the United States, particularly at the University of Chicago and Harvard University, began to develop the methods of whole network analysis, based on the work of Jacob Moreno. Moreno is generally recognized as the founding father of *sociometry* (the quantitative measurement of social relationships) and the *sociogram* (the graphic representation of a network of relationships; Moreno, 1934). From the 1960s on, several lines of sociological

### *Clyde Mitchell and the Manchester School*

Clyde Mitchell (1969) edited one of the most influential books in the field of social network studies: *Social Networks in Urban Situations: Analyses of Personal Relationships in Central African Towns*. This book collected the contributions of a variety of anthropologists in different areas and with different foci of application in order to overcome the limitations of the structural functionalist framework. For example, Bruce Kapferer studied a strike in a Zambian factory, John Barnes suggested ways to apply social network methods to the study of political networks, and Arnold Leonard Epstein focused on the spread of gossip in a Copperbelt town, Ndola.

In the introductory chapter, Clyde Mitchell proposed a series of formulas and conventions for drawing social networks (some of which are still valid today). These included representation of the frequency of interaction with line width; relationship content with colors; direction with arrows; and intensity with the relative distance among nodes.

In 2010, the Mitchell Centre for Social Network Analysis was founded in Manchester by Martin Everett, one of Mitchell's students, and by Nick Crossley, in recognition of Mitchell's contribution to the social network field.

research into *personal* network analysis developed, moving personal network analysis toward structured measurement and larger samples.

## U.S. Sociology Takes the Baton

In the 1960s, Edward Laumann, then at the University of Michigan, was involved in administering a survey as part of the Detroit Area Study, 1965–1966 (Laumann, 1969b). The survey stemmed from an interest in *social distance,* that is, the separation between different social classes and religions in society. Under the direction of Howard Schuman, Laumann collected data about personal networks and studied their composition in terms of class and religion. The study was the first to collect personal network data about a small number of alters from a large and representative sample of egos (survey respondents), a method that would come to dominate personal network analysis for decades. As we will see in the next few chapters, personal network analysis often implies a trade-off between a more representative sample of respondents and more representative personal networks: the researcher has to decide whether to interview more respondents from a certain population and yet collect a smaller personal network from each; or collect larger, more representative personal networks from fewer respondents. Laumann's research focus was on understanding whether people in different social situations have different personal networks. This objective required sampling many respondents in order to capture the variability across these social situations.

A few years later, Mark Granovetter at Harvard University posited that acquaintance relationships, or "weak ties," had their own strengths: he saw them as indispensable for the social integration of communities (Granovetter, 1974/1995). He based his proposition on his work on *triads*—which are subsets of three actors and the ties they have among each other, just as *dyads* are subsets of two actors and the tie(s) between them. He suggested that the triad that is most unlikely to occur in social life is that in which actors A and B, and actors B and C as well, are strongly connected, but the tie between A and C is absent. He dubbed this the "forbidden triad." From this proposition, it followed that strong ties would never be bridging ties. Granovetter conducted personal network interviews with a sample of respondents regarding how they went about looking for a job (Granovetter, 1974/1995). His results indicated that people often found out about job opportunities through people they knew. Indeed, these opportunities typically came through acquaintances rather than through people the respondents knew well. This happened because acquaintances connected the ego to new, distant social circles, which had access to diverse information that the set of alters in ego's closest social circle didn't have. The notion of *the strength of weak ties* would become extremely important in later research and is still a crucial reference for contemporary social network studies.

Another researcher from Harvard, Nancy Lee (1969), used a similar method as Granovetter's to study how women found an abortionist in the late 1960s. Until 1973, abortion was illegal in the United States, so women had to use word of mouth to find doctors who were safe and who would perform the procedure illegally. By interviewing women who had an abortion, Lee was able to describe how women mobilized their personal network ties (the acquaintance network) to find a doctor. Later research would demonstrate how many consumer decisions, including finding a doctor or dentist, are typically taken based on social networks and word of mouth. The approach that both Granovetter and Lee applied focused on the chain of ties that were activated in the process of accessing resources. This approach is similar to that of Stanley Milgram's famous Small World Experiment, which falls somewhere between personal and sociocentric networks. Nevertheless, their results are of great importance for personal network analysis.

Around the same time as Granovetter's and Lee's research, Donald Coates and Barry Wellman conducted a large personal network study in Canada, in a suburb of Toronto, using methods similar to Laumann's. This project would become known as the first East York Study. Wellman and colleagues interviewed 845 respondents, asking them to list six people whom they felt closest to. Wellman (1979) was interested in "the Community Question": he wanted to understand how people formed communities in contemporary cities and how modern industrialization and bureaucratization had changed the local, densely knit communities of the past. He discovered that despite the common wisdom that people in urban situations had lost their sense of community, communities still existed through sometimes distant network linkages ("glocalization"). Wellman later

### *The Small World Experiment*

In the 1960s, the psychologist Stanley Milgram (1967) conducted one of the most popular social science studies ever undertaken: the Small World Experiment. The project aimed to identify the distribution of chains of acquaintances in the "world" (the United States, actually) through an innovative approach: a group of participants in Nebraska and Kansas was asked to send a letter to a "target" (a person located in Boston from whom just a few details were provided) using their personal contacts. The contacts in the chain had to forward the letter to the person they thought was more likely to know the target. A total of 64 of the 296 starting letters reached their destination, traveling through chains of 5.2 contacts on average. Based on this finding, the researcher claimed that there are only six degrees of separation among two randomly chosen individuals in the world.

The experiment has been replicated several times and in different versions, including for email communications (Dodds, Muhamad, & Watts, 2003) and Facebook connections (Ugander, Karrer, Backstrom, & Marlow, 2011). Few experiments have proven to be so influential in so many areas of science, as well as in the development of current social media. (The first social networking website, launched in 1997, was *www.sixdegrees.com*.) This and other research about so-called relational chains (Grossetti, Barthe, & Chauvac, 2011) fall between sociocentric network research, as its interest lies in the network structure of a (large) population, and personal network research, as it starts with a sample of unrelated individuals and explores their relationships to others. Schnettler (2013) gives a thorough overview of Small World research.

**The East York Studies**

The East York studies, a large initial survey taken in 1968, a smaller follow-up in 1979, and a new large survey in 2004 and 2005 (the "Connected Lives" study) were conducted in Toronto over almost four decades, first by Donald B. Coates and Barry Wellman (e.g., Wellman, 1979) and later by Wellman and collaborators (Wellman, Carrington, & Hall, 1988). These studies have empirically assessed the structure, composition, and evolution of personal networks over time and represent a turning point in community and urban sociological studies. Among other findings, the researchers demonstrated the geographically dispersed nature of networks of support, the specialization of support roles depending on the type of relationship, and the influence of distance both before and after the diffusion of the Internet and contemporary telecommunication technologies.

adapted this concept to studies of community that used the Internet as a medium ("networked individualism") and became a leading scholar in the study of online communities (e.g., Rainie & Wellman, 2012; Wellman, 2002). He also founded the International Network for Social Network Analysis (INSNA) in 1977, the primary professional organization for social network analysis (*www.insna.org*).

One of the most well-known works on personal networks is *To Dwell among Friends: Personal Networks in Town and City* (1982a) by Claude Fischer, who conducted the Northern California Community Study in 1977. Using a large representative survey, Fischer took the community studies of Wellman and Laumann one step further. He analyzed in detail how personal networks were composed and structured and how urbanization influenced them. Multiple questions were used to elicit the personal networks, leading to larger networks of 18.5 contacts on average (see Section 6.4). Apart from his results about the differences in networks between cities and small towns, Fischer also showed how networks were shaped by socioeconomic variables such as age, education, and income. Replications of his study were carried out by Claude Fischer and Yossi Shavit (1995) in Israel and by Michel Grossetti (2007) in France. Beate Volker and Henk Flap (2001) and Marina Hennig (2007) also used adapted versions of Fischer's multiple name generator approach for addressing the "Community Question" posed by Wellman (1979) in Germany.

In the 1990s, Ronald Burt (1984) was instrumental in adding questions about the personal networks of respondents to the General Social Survey in 1985, a recurring nationally representative survey of Americans about their social characteristics, behaviors, and attitudes. The network module was again added in 2004. These data have led to a wealth of scholarly works on personal networks (e.g., Beggs, Haines, & Hurlbert, 2010; Marsden, 1987; McPherson, Smith-Lovin, & Brashears, 2006; Moore, 1990).

Along with Nan Lin (Lin, 2001; Lin & Dumin, 1986), Burt also developed measures of social capital based on the presence or absence of certain types of social ties (see Section 2.3). His most notable work studied the egocentric networks of managers in business settings. As part of this research, Burt (2000) developed the concept of *structural holes*: whenever groups of people in an organization do not interact with each other, a hole in the network structure exists. Brokers whose egocentric networks are rich in structural holes, creating indirect bridges among otherwise unconnected groups, can reap specific advantages in terms of information and power. Despite the original focus of Burt's research, his ideas about how networks stimulate individual creativity may be applicable outside of organizational settings.

## Personal Relationships across the Life Course

A history of personal network analysis would not be complete without recognizing the pivotal role social psychologists have played in this area. Social psychologists have long studied the nature and dynamics of personal relationships, as well as the supportive role that personal networks play in mental and physical health (e.g., Cantor, 1975; Cobb, 1976; Cohen & Wills, 1985; Taylor, 2011; Wills, 1985). Sheldon Cohen and collaborators (1997), for example, showed that variability in personal network characteristics is associated with stress levels, affecting even people's susceptibility to the common cold. This literature has proven fundamental in understanding the supportive nature of relationships, and it now forms the basis of the rich literature on social support (see Section 2.3).

An essential contribution to personal network analysis (a subject that is also discussed in Chapter 6) was the *social convoy model* of Robert Kahn and Toni Antonucci (1980), a model that emphasized the life-course nature of social relationships. The concept of a convoy evoked the idea that coetaneous people adopt different supportive roles over time, depending on the changing needs of the people related to them. In their seminal work, the authors described the protective role of personal networks by envisioning them as concentric circles with a stable center of a few close, supportive ties—with the spouse, close family, and friends—that change slowly, and two outer rings characterized by increasingly more contacts, a higher role relatedness, lower emotional closeness, and faster turnover in time. The *concentric circle model* they used, also called the target diagram or the hierarchical map, introduced earlier by Mary Northway (1940), has been widely adopted in personal network research.

The idea that personal networks are dynamic and change over the life course has led researchers from a variety of disciplines and in many different countries to investigate how personal networks change across life events, such as parenthood (Bost, Cox, Burchinal, & Payne, 2002; Gameiro, Boivin, Canavarro, Moura-Ramos, & Soares, 2010), divorce (Morgan, 1989; Terhell, Broese van Groenou, & van Tilburg, 2007), widowhood (Guiaux, van Tilburg, & Broese van Groenou, 2007; Morgan, Neal, & Carder, 1997), migration (e.g., Lubbers et al., 2010), unemployment (Jackson, 1988), the transition from school to work (Hollstein & Wagemann, 2014), and imprisonment (Volker et al., 2016). Simultaneously, personal networks can buffer these life events. In France, Claire Bidart, Alain Degenne, and colleagues have contributed to the study of the life course through analysis of a panel of young people entering into adult life over a period of nine years

(Bidart & Lavenu, 2005; Bidart, 2017; Degenne & Lebeaux, 2005). This unique research shows how personal networks undergo deep transformations over the life course, with changes in work and family life playing a predominant role.

## 2.2 WHAT WE CURRENTLY KNOW ABOUT PERSONAL NETWORKS

Now that we have briefly—and necessarily incompletely—described the history of personal network research, we will summarize what we currently know about network size, composition, and structure. These features of personal networks are of great interest because they show how humans organize their sociability and, at a higher level, how well communities and societies are integrated.

With regard to personal network size (also called *degree*, i.e., the number of alters), evolutionary anthropologist Robin Dunbar has done unique research. He suggests that the ability of people to know other people is constrained by the cognitive organization of family, friends, and acquaintances in memory, as well as time and cognitive resources. This limits networks to an average of 150 people (Dunbar, 1993). He points to the tendency for various human social groups to stabilize at around the same size. As we will discuss in more detail in Chapter 10, other researchers, applying a diversity of definitions and methods, have generally estimated network size to be higher, with medians varying between approximately 300 and a few thousand.

Earlier research (e.g., Kahn & Antonucci, 1980) showed that personal networks typically involve a few *core ties*, with a high contact frequency and emotional closeness, and many *peripheral ties*, with progressively lower contact frequency and emotional closeness. Dunbar also studied this layered structure. Interestingly, he suggested that there is a scaling ratio of about 3:1 that consistently emerges between the number of alters in the various layers in the network, with approximately 5, 15, 50, and 150 alters included within the first (support clique), second (sympathy group), third (active or close network), and fourth layer (personal network), respectively. His ideas have been tested beyond face-to-face environments, showing that this basic structure prevails for reciprocal relationships even in the social media and phone networks (i.e., who exchanges tweets, messages, phone calls with whom intentionally; cf. Dunbar, Arnaboldi, Conti, & Passarella, 2015; Dunbar & Sosis, 2017).

Both the early literature and more recent literature have focused mostly on the most intimate layers of personal networks. This research (e.g., Fischer, 1982a; Mollenhorst, Volker, & Flap, 2014; Wellman, 1979) shows that the relatively few core ties that people have are typically kin-centered, relatively stable over time, densely connected among each other, and give multistranded social support to ego. In comparison, the more numerous peripheral ties (e.g., Fu, 2007; McCarty, 2002) are less kin-centered, less stable over time, provide fewer types of social support (or no support), and are less connected among each other, although densely connected regions may be observed. Nevertheless, Barry Wellman (2012) warned against oversimplified ideas of personal networks, arguing that "personal networks are not tiered layer cakes. . . . The reality is not as simple as the closest layer providing support while the next closest layer only provides sympathy" (p. 175). Indeed, you will probably not have to search far in your own network to find examples of people whose romantic partner and parents can't stand each other, who have felt betrayed by a good friend, or who have obtained support from unexpected people. In reality, personal networks are complex and messy.

One important principle that structures personal networks and that does not fall neatly within these layers is that of *social foci*. Scott Feld used this term to refer to organizations and other entities or social contexts in which joint activities take place, such as the workplace, schools, voluntary organizations, bars, and churches (Feld, 1981). These foci thus create meeting opportunities (cf. Blau, 1977); social relationships are organized around them, explaining nonrandom interaction patterns between people. Mario Small (2009b) showed how the institutional conditions of such social foci, such as timetables, norms, and the allocation of space, have important consequences for the creation of ties and for what people can gain from them. In personal networks, cohesive subgroups (a set of alters with many ties among them) are often associated with a particular context. Contexts can overlap, and some people can cut across different contexts, which happens, for example, if you work in the same university department as your brother.

Partly because of the focused organization of ties, another principle that structures personal networks is *homophily*—that is, the tendency to have social relationships with people who are like oneself. The review article "Birds of a Feather: Homophily in Social Networks" (McPherson, Smith-Lovin, & Cook, 2001) shows that all sorts of ties are structured by homophily involving gender, age, education, religion, and political affiliations, among others. It is often believed that weaker ties are more heterogeneous in nature because we have more of them and they are less connected among themselves. However, even those ties exhibit certain levels of homophily (e.g., DiPrete, Gelman, McCormick, Teitler, & Zheng, 2011). This has pervasive consequences for the flow of resources and information.

Despite these general tendencies, networks can vary greatly in size, composition, and structure. Like snowflakes, no personal network is exactly the same when studied in sufficient detail. Researchers agree that the interindividual variance in personal network size is considerable. It has a log-normal distribution (e.g., McCormick, Salganik, & Zheng, 2010), with a few people having thousands of connections. These highly connected persons may form *hubs* in the whole network of society. The size, composition, and structure of personal networks are influenced by the ego's characteristics such as gender (e.g., Moore, 1990), age (e.g., Smith et al., 2015), residential mobility (e.g., Viry, 2012), and life events (see Section 2.1), as was illustrated with the cases of Pam, Allen, and Helen in Chapter 1. Personal networks reflect current socialization patterns, but they are also, at least partly, a product of the past.

The variation in personal network characteristics can have important consequences for individual outcomes, such as health, well-being, coping with adversity, behaviors, and occupational prestige. The following section briefly discusses the main theoretical frameworks that scholars have adopted to address the effects of personal networks on individual outcomes.

## 2.3 THEORETICAL FRAMEWORKS FOR EFFECTS OF PERSONAL NETWORKS ON INDIVIDUAL OUTCOMES

In Chapter 1, we discussed the idea that personal networks, conceptualizing the immediate social environment of individuals, affect individual outcomes. To investigate such effects, scholars often offer theoretical assumptions about the underlying mechanisms that connect networks and outcomes. Usually, they suspect that relationships transmit something, whether that is affection, material resources, money, information, ideas, advice, sanctions, conflict, germs even, and so on. Three main frameworks have been proposed for how transmission takes place: social capital, social support, and social influence.

### Social Capital

The theory of social capital, developed among others by Pierre Bourdieu, James Coleman, Nan Lin, and Robert Putnam, proposes that social networks constitute a form of capital that people can use for both collective and individual benefits. At the collective level, the theory assumes that communities that are knit together by dense webs of reciprocal relationships and repeated interactions develop social solidarity and trust, which enhance democracy and intergroup tolerance (Putnam, 1993, 2000). Such dense webs of relationships are the result of social participation (participation in cultural, religious, or political associations, volunteering) and informal networks.

At the individual level, social scientists have long studied how individuals access and mobilize resources embedded in their personal networks, for both expressive and instrumental purposes. These resources can help them in different situations. Various aspects of personal networks have been studied in their capacity to provide benefits to individuals. For example, Nan Lin (2001) proposed measuring the diversity of occupations among a person's network members, and in particular the extent to which a person has access to higher occupational positions through her network (e.g., whether she knows a surgeon, judge). James Coleman (1988) made the useful distinction among bonding ties and bridging ties. Bonding ties refer to the relationships among individuals who belong to the same social circle or group—that is, to a group of people who exhibit *network closure*. These relationships are thought to provide social support in all its dimensions. In contrast, bridging ties are relationships among people who belong to different social groups or who possess different categorical characteristics, which provide access to new resources or social positions.

This distinction is related to Mark Granovetter's notion of strong and weak ties (see Section 2.1) and to Ronald Burt's idea of *structural holes*. Alejandro Portes (1998) reviewed a large number of studies and theoretical arguments on social capital, mostly in sociological research. The social capital framework helps personal network researchers to identify both potentially and actually accessed resources that exist in individuals' personal networks in a variety of situations, such as when looking for a job, starting a business, migrating and adapting to a new country, or fighting a chronic illness. As we indicated earlier, networks beneficial in one situation may not be so beneficial in another, so expectations about the benefits depend on the outcome studied.

## Social Support

The concept of social support refers to the aid available to individuals from their informal social relationships that can help them cope with major life stressors (e.g., illness, loss of a job, divorce, widowhood) as well as with the challenges of daily life. This concept overlaps partly with that of social capital at the individual level, but its focus is different: Studies that use a social support framework mostly describe the role of personal networks for individual health. Social epidemiologist Lisa Berkman and her colleagues (2000), for example, proposed a comprehensive model showing how perceived social support mediates the effects of certain psychological and physical conditions.

Taxonomies have been developed that distinguish between different dimensions of social support, such as emotional support, tangible support (material and financial), intangible support (e.g., help with chores), information, and social companionship (e.g., Barrera, 1980). Furthermore, scholars have distinguished between available support (even when not needed), actually exchanged support in a given time period, and perceived support, all of which may affect outcomes.

It is now a well-known fact that personal networks matter to mental and physical health (House, Landis, & Umberson, 1988). The effect of networks is generally positive: the more social relationships an individual has, the better his or her chances for good health or fast recovery; conversely, more social isolation is associated with worse health indicators (Song, Son, & Lin, 2011). Why do these effects occur? Several mechanisms have been proposed (e.g., Berkman & Glass, 2000; Ertel, Glymour, & Berkman, 2009). First, the availability of social support through one's social network may have a positive *direct effect* on health as close ties promote healthy habits and behaviors. Second, social relations can create a *buffer effect* on the stress provoked by illness or other personal problems (Cohen, Underwood, & Gottlieb, 2000). By giving emotional or tangible support, people are better able to cope with health problems when they occur. In that case, social relations do not directly affect health but, rather, attenuate the effect of stressors on health. Some researchers have also suggested a *long-term effect* of social support: those who consistently enjoy social support over a long period of time develop better coping strategies to handle stress in the future.

Bernice Pescosolido (1991, 1992) proposed a more integrated model, the so-called network episode model. An "episode" is a disruptive life event, in this case, the onset of mental illness. Pescosolido argued that the usual individual cost-benefit analyses failed to explain health care utilization and adherence. Therefore, she proposed an alternative theoretical model that allows researchers to model individual agency in the utilization of health care and recovery, as embedded within dynamic structures of formal and informal support. She further formulated the functional specificity hypothesis, which states that the individual's specific needs determine which ties are activated and mobilized for help.

Since the 1970s, social support has been one of the dominant themes in personal network research, and personal network methods have become the primary approach of social support studies. Social support research based on personal network data and analysis is vast and diverse, spanning different decades and disciplines, such as anthropology, sociology, and epidemiology. Part of this research intersects with social scientists' work on the Community Question (in particular, the work of Claude Fischer, 1982a). More recently, social and health scientists have been using increasingly sophisticated statistical models for personal network data (see Chapters 12 and 13) to investigate patterns of social support and health outcomes in different populations. We will cite and discuss several further examples of social support research in the rest of this book.

## Social Influence through Diffusion

The third theoretical framework concerning network effects is that of social influence through diffusion, or contagion. In this framework, the concept of diffusion refers to ideas, knowledge, rumors, protest, behaviors, innovations, infectious diseases, and so on spreading through social networks.

Everett Rogers's (2003) theory of the diffusion of innovations models diffusion through social structure in three stages: knowledge, use, and adoption. The process follows a logistic curve: slow development at the beginning, a tipping point after which the growth is exponential, and finally a long phase of saturation. Thomas Valente (2010) has further developed this theory, modeling the conditions that account for adopting a new behavior based on the concept of the personal network *threshold*, that is, the number of adopters among a person's contacts. Typically, this threshold is different for different people, which explains that some people are early and others are middle or late adopters. The speed and scope of diffusion through a network depend on the structure of the network.

Longitudinal models are ideal for the study of diffusion because the simple fact that an individual adopts similar behaviors or traits to those of her network members at a single point in time does not sufficiently explain how contagion or influence has occurred. Denise Kandel (1996), among others, argued that similarity among contacts may be a consequence of social influence, but it may also result from social selection. In the case of social influence, a person is impacted by her existing contacts and therefore becomes similar to them *after* ties have been established. In the case of social selection, however, a person selects contacts who are already similar to her; therefore, similarity between individuals exists *before* the ties are created. Both influence and selection processes lead to *homophily*. To disentangle influence and selection effects in longitudinal data, Tom Snijders and collaborators (Snijders, van de Bunt, & Steglich, 2010) developed a class of statistical models for the coevolution of sociocentric networks and individual behaviors in longitudinal data, called Siena or stochastic actor-oriented models (SAOMs; see Chapter 13). These models are particularly designed for sociocentric data.

While sociocentric network data are better suited to study of the spreading process itself, personal network research has helped us to understand both social influence through diffusion and contagion at an individual level and infectious diseases in various ways. First, to study diffusion processes, personal network data collected from individuals in geographically bounded settings have sometimes been used to create a sociocentric network of that setting by interconnecting the networks (e.g., Christakis & Fowler, 2007; Fowler & Christakis, 2008; Klovdahl et al., 1994). Second, personal network studies are applied to investigate not the spreading process of the innovation or disease itself but rather the conditions that enable its transmission. For example, Thomas Valente (1996) studied how adoption of an innovation by network members affected the probability that an individual adopted the innovation; he presented precise, external information about the time of adoption of both egos and alters. Carl Latkin et al. (1995), investigating how personal network characteristics affect needle-sharing among intravenous drug users, identified needle-sharing as the primary mode of HIV transmission. Mossong et al. (2008) studied the contact patterns of individuals in a large population to investigate the mixing patterns relevant for the spread of diseases. Both personal network data and sociocentric network data are better sources for calibrating mathematical and agent-based models of social influence (e.g., Eames, Bansal, Frost, & Riley, 2014; Mossong et al., 2008).

## 2.4 FINAL REMARKS

Despite the many contributions researchers have made in the area of personal networks, much remains to be learned. Personal networks are complex, dynamic entities, and collecting data about them, as we will see, is not easily done. For instance, we still have relatively little knowledge about how and why personal networks change over time, as relationships form, strengthen, change in content, dissolve, water down, or are dormant, being partly coordinated with other ties and partly in isolation. Also, relatively little is known about the larger acquaintanceship networks, with its many weak ties.

In the last few years, the pervasive growth of new communication and Internet technologies, ranging from smartphones to social media to instant messaging apps, has given new meaning and significance to the notion of the personal network. The development of applications and platforms such as Facebook, Twitter, Google Plus, LinkedIn, YouTube, WhatsApp, and Skype has been largely based on social and personal networks, and on new discourses and rhetoric about them. These technologies have transformed the way we communicate, start and end friendships, get news, and participate in politics, among other things. In the process, they have encouraged us to think about our personal network—to examine it, expand it, manipulate it, and divide it into "circles" or "lists." These tools have become increasingly useful in tracking social interactions and predicting individual attitudes and behaviors. New fields of scientific inquiry, such as computational social science (Lazer et al., 2009) and the study of Big Data (Lazer & Radford, 2017), have developed in part from the expansion of these technologies. Personal network analysis has reflected these developments, with a growing number of personal network studies using trace data from the Internet and social media, either alone or in combination with survey data. Some of these studies are discussed in Chapters 3 and 6. Big Data also gives us new impulses in our thinking about what relationships mean in a globalizing, increasingly connected world; how social networks are connected with other contextual factors; and what our unique perspective, as social scientists, is on Big Data.

## CHAPTER SUMMARY

In this chapter, we have briefly reviewed the intellectual origins of the personal network approach. We have seen that the thinking about the interplay among cultures, institutions, and informal relationships led the Manchester School researchers to develop a set of methods for capturing this intermediate or meso level of social reality. This line of research was further developed by mostly American sociologists who collected data from large representative samples of the population and conducted longitudinal studies, motivated by the Community Question, and by social psychologists, who studied personal networks as sources of social support. We have discussed what we know about the size, composition, and structure of personal networks, and we have laid out the different theoretical mechanisms through which personal networks influence individual effects: social support, social capital, and social influence.

### FURTHER READING

Chua, V., Madej, J., & Wellman, B. (2011). Personal communities: The world according to me. In J. Scott & P. Carrington (Eds.), *The SAGE handbook of social network analysis.* London: SAGE.

Fischer, C. S. (1982). *To dwell among friends: Personal networks in town and city.* Chicago: University of Chicago Press.

Freeman, L. (2004). *The development of social network analysis: A study in the sociology of science.* Vancouver, BC, Canada: Empirical Press.

Wellman, B. (1979). The community question: The intimate networks of East Yorkers. *American Journal of Sociology, 84*(5), 1201–1231.

3

# Developing a Research Question

### *What Is This Chapter About?*

The next few chapters will describe the steps needed to design and implement a personal network study. Before we do so, we will help you think through some of the research aims and questions you could address using personal network methods (Section 3.1). Our main recommendation is to use this method when the research suggests that social context plays a vital role in explaining the outcome variables (Section 3.2). After addressing the issue of what type of information we are dealing with (Section 3.3), we review some examples of research that uses this approach (Section 3.4) in the fields of family roles, social support and health, risky behaviors, mobility and migration, the life course, and online communication on social media.

## 3.1 RESEARCH QUESTIONS, HYPOTHESES, AND OBJECTIVES

In social science articles and research proposals, we often read about research questions and hypotheses, as well as research objectives, goals, or aims. To see how these concepts apply to personal network research, we should first clarify what these terms mean. Let's start by considering the following example:

- *Research objective:* Explore personal network structure as it relates to individual well-being.
- *Research question:* What characteristics of personal network structure are associated with higher individual well-being?
- *Hypothesis:* Cohesion in personal networks is positively associated with individual well-being.

Formulating a specific, fully developed research question is the first step in any successful research project. Some questions may be more open and exploratory, with the aim of describing and exploring network mechanisms, context, temporality, or content and meaning (among others), whereas others are more closed, with the aim of describing the prevalence of characteristics or of testing hypotheses about relationships between variables or comparisons among groups of people. These two types of research questions are equally valid. On one hand, personal networks are complex because they involve multiple relationships that are to some extent interconnected and dynamic. Although knowledge about personal networks is steadily increasing, many areas are still not well understood. Open-ended questions are tailored to such situations, and they usually involve more qualitative research methods. On the other hand, the different theoretical models and prior research findings also make it possible to specify detailed expectations that can then be tested in empirical research. This may lead to more closed-ended questions that are often answered using quantitative or mixed-methods research designs. In either case, we encourage you to formulate your questions as clearly and as specifically as possible, for this will help you to define the type of evidence you need to collect.

An issue that often comes up in designing a research project, especially with closed research questions, is whether you need a hypothesis. Broadly speaking, a hypothesis is an explanation of something that is observed. In many cases, a hypothesis is a possible answer to the research question. You typically have some confidence that this answer is true and that, therefore, it will be supported by the data you collect. In the preceding example, the hypothesis offers an explanation for the observation that certain individuals have higher well-being, while others have lower well-being; different levels of personal network cohesion account for this variation. This hypothesis is also an answer to the research question of which characteristics of personal networks are associated with higher well-being. Hypotheses are often derived from a theory—that is, a coherent set of statements and arguments about the social world that explain why and how a certain phenomenon happens or a certain outcome (e.g., well-being) is produced. Thus, analyzing empirical data to test one or more hypotheses derived from a theory is often a way to assess the validity of the broader theory.

Two crucial characteristics of a scientific hypothesis are testability and falsifiability: a hypothesis should be formulated with enough precision that we can test it and potentially falsify (i.e., reject) it based on how compatible it is with the evidence (data) we collected. While a research objective is less precise and only indicates a broad area of interest, hypotheses define a research project through their precise wording. Statements such as "personal network cohesion is associated with individual well-being," "students who are more central in school networks tend to use more recreational drugs," or "friends who share similar political views tend to provide more support to each other" are precise, testable, and falsifiable: that is, they are scientific hypotheses. Statements such as "good people have many friends," "immigrants are a negative influence on society," or "without guns we wouldn't be a free society" are not scientific hypotheses because they are too generic, not testable, and not falsifiable.

When you develop research questions and hypotheses about causal relationships involving personal networks, it is important that they have as much detail as possible. Say that you want to test whether personal networks influence the extent to which individuals adopt sustainable or "green" consumption behaviors. That is, the food or goods the individuals purchase are produced with minimal use of natural resources and toxic materials and minimal emission of waste and pollutants (e.g., Seyfang, 2006). Your starting hypothesis is thus: "personal networks influence individuals' sustainable consumption." But this hypothesis is still very generic.

First, to make it more specific, you may ask yourself what underlying causal mechanisms produce this effect. Is it because individuals learn new behaviors when they observe others displaying them, because of social pressure to conform to the prevalent norm, or because individuals exchange information that will help them make more environmentally informed choices? In other words, to be involved in these choices, should they *see* the behavior, *talk* about it, or *perceive* others to be involved in it? At an aggregate level, would it simply be the total number of people in one's social context that display or talk about the behavior, or the proportion, or a certain *network threshold* (see Section 2.3), or being embedded in a densely connected personal network where sustainability is the norm?

Second, and related to the first question, what kind of social relationship do you think might transmit such an effect? Which people are involved? As we will see in Chapter 6, typically we are not interested in the "whole" personal network of hundreds of people. Rather, we prefer an intentional subsample—significant others, family members, coresidents, or those with whom respondents go shopping or discuss purchases, or people in the network—whatever the precise relation—who are clearly "ecological citizens" (Seyfang, 2006).

Third, you can ask yourself under what conditions you expect social influence to occur? Does it happen always or only under certain conditions, such as a certain type of personality, an initial interest in the matter, or an urban versus rural environment? Answering these questions may help you think about possible relations, specify your hypotheses, and translate them into a research design. For example, a more specific hypothesis might be "the number of people in the network whom the ego perceives to shop sustainably influences the ego's own sustainable consumption" or "the shopping behavior of close alters will have a larger effect on the ego's consumption behavior than that of mere acquaintances."

It is equally important to think of alternative explanations that can be given for the same phenomenon. A compelling test of a theory is that it not only confirms the phenomenon but also eliminates alternative explanations. In the preceding example, one rival explanation for an observed relation between the network composition and sustainable consumption is a selection rather than an influence effect, as discussed in Chapter 2. People who are conscientious about the environment may be attracted to people who share this attitude. Furthermore, the individual's level of education may have an effect, as it may influence both one's own shopping behavior and the number of people one could meet. In that case, you would like to control for that to avoid so-called spurious effects. Also, it will be easier to buy plastic-free, organic products in some environments than in others. If that strongly determines your outcome, you will want to control for such a confounding effect, and perhaps incorporate it in the set of hypotheses.

## 3.2 OUTCOMES AND SOCIAL DETERMINANTS

A close examination of the research question and hypothesis in the preceding examples reveals that each has two parts: an outcome or a dependent variable (individual well-being in the example research question presented at the beginning of Section 3.1); and an explanatory or independent variable, sometimes called the determinant or factor, which affects the outcome (personal network cohesion in the first example). We will talk more about dependent and explanatory variables in Section 4.6 and Chapter 5, but certain ideas are worth establishing in this chapter.

Most research questions and hypotheses in the social sciences imply one or more outcomes and one or more explanatory variables. An outcome is a phenomenon that varies across people, and it's this variation that we want to explain. Why is it that certain people enjoy higher levels of well-being, while others have lower well-being? Why do certain people cope with poverty hardships better than others? Why are certain immigrants better integrated in society than others are? Variation is key: we can have no outcome, no research question, and no hypothesis if there is no variation in a phenomenon across people. We are typically interested in studying this variation and the determinants that influence it within a circumscribed population: for example, well-being among residents of Brazilian urban areas; livelihood strategies among evicted people in America; and socioeconomic integration among Asian immigrants in European countries.

An explanatory variable is a characteristic or condition that also varies in the population and that we think contributes to determining the outcome. In other words, the variation we observe in the outcome is, at least in part, explained by variation in the explanatory variable. In personal network studies, we are interested in outcomes that have a social component: that is, they can be explained, at least to some degree, by explanatory variables that describe characteristics of the social world. Thus, we will restrict our research question to those phenomena that we think are at least partly influenced by social context. In this book, this means the people and social groups around us and the way they interact with each other. This involves a wide range of outcome variables covering such diverse topical areas as health, economics, politics, and culture.

As it turns out, it is quite difficult to imagine an individual outcome that is not potentially impacted by the social context surrounding a person. Even variables that we popularly think of as biologically or genetically determined—such as weight and blood pressure—have been shown to be in part socially determined. Certain types of disease have well-known social components: for example, lung cancer is related to smoking, which is influenced by social context; colon cancer increases with the intake of certain kinds of foods, which is often related to who we know, talk to, and are influenced by in our food habits; and cardiovascular diseases are linked to our levels of stress, which are in part affected by our conflictive and supportive relationships.

Although most individual outcomes could in part be driven by social context, to justify a personal network study you should be specifically interested in the effect of social context or expect that social context will explain a *significant portion* of the variation of outcomes among people. In addition, you should expect this portion of variation to be explained by the specific characteristics of social context *composition* and *structure*, which personal network data can capture. Consider again the example of colon cancer, which is the second leading cause of death by cancer in the United States. A major contributing factor to colon cancer is genetic, and that has little to do with social context (although more recent research is showing that environmental exposures and social context might affect gene expression; see Landecker & Panofsky, 2013, for an interesting review). However, besides genetic endowment and gene expression, social context can interact in many ways with biology to result in cancer. Those around you may encourage, constrain, or otherwise influence you to eat foods that contribute to colon cancer. Or you might live around people who don't value cancer screenings or medical intervention generally, increasing your risk of mortality by colon cancer. Thus, the questions for us as social scientists (and for policymakers) become whether the social component plays an important role in explaining the outcome (here, colon cancer morbidity and mortality), whether it substantially increases our ability to predict who is going to have a certain outcome, and whether it contributes enough to the outcome that designing an intervention based on the results of our research is actually going to affect that outcome. For example, it is going to decrease colon cancer morbidity and mortality in a population.

Once we have assumed that social context in general and personal ties in particular play a role in our research questions and/or hypotheses, we should ask ourselves, "What is the nature of the personal network data we are collecting?" This question is addressed in the next section.

## 3.3 REAL OR PERCEIVED?

In the field of social network analysis, there is an ongoing debate regarding whether personal networks as measured by researchers are "real." That is, do they represent the actual composition and structure of the social networks surrounding respondents rather than the perception of the respondents about the networks, which may or may not be connected to reality? This question arises considering the way we typically collect personal network data, namely, asking respondents to report on them (see Chapters 6–8). Particularly controversial is the accuracy of respondent reports of ties between alters in their network. Can a person (ego) accurately describe the relationship between any pair of contacts (alters) she mentions?

While not everybody would agree that personal network data capture "real" networks, most researchers concede that even merely *perceived* personal networks still affect important outcomes. For example, respondents' perception that their friends behave in an environmental friendly way may affect their own behavior more than their actual behaviors, part of which may be more hidden to the respondent. Also, the social support you perceive you have may influence your well-being more than the actual support (Cohen & Janicki-Deverts, 2009). One could argue that *perceiving* a cohesive network is the main factor contributing to well-being, even if the structure of the actual network is fragmented. In this case, whether respondents' reports are accurate and "real" is not that relevant.

Although outcomes such as personal well-being have subjective and psychological components that make perceptions important, personal network variables have also been used to predict many other outcomes for which the mere *perception* of social context would not be sufficient to explain variation. For example, personal networks have been analyzed to explain outcomes such as transmission of infection due to the exchange of needles, the interactions leading to spread of the flu, the efficiency with which personal networks can accommodate needs such as transportation or child care, or people's ability to align those they know into groups around cultural or political activity. In all of these cases, the critical factor is the *actual* composition and structure of the personal network, not just the perception of it. As you read about personal network studies in the rest of this book, you should ask yourself whether the demonstrated association between personal networks and the outcomes of interest can be simply explained by the importance of perceptions; or whether it can only be justified if the personal networks reported by respondents are "real." We will discuss the challenges of personal network data collection in Chapters 6–8, but these are considerations to keep in mind when you are designing a research project or a network-based intervention.

## 3.4 SOME EXAMPLES OF QUESTIONS AND HYPOTHESES IN PERSONAL NETWORK RESEARCH

We conclude this chapter by presenting a few examples of research questions and hypotheses from personal network studies, some of which are cited in this book. By dissecting these studies, we can see how research questions result in hypotheses and how those hypotheses inform the research design of the study.

### Personal Networks and Family Roles

- **Research question:** How can the variation found in the way that husbands and wives perform their conjugal roles be interpreted?
- **Hypothesis (induced from the research):** If one or both spouses has a closely knit network of people with whom they spend most of their leisure time, then more fixed and stricter conjugal roles emerge.

We start with one of the early studies cited in Chapter 2, one that has become very famous among personal network students: Elizabeth Bott's *Family and Social Network*. Bott, a member of a group with a broad interest in understanding the social and psychological organization of urban families, designed an in-depth, exploratory study of 20 married couples in London. Bott and her colleagues observed that the couples differed in how they divided up household chores (who mows the lawn, who cooks, etc.) and how they chose to spend their leisure time. Some couples had rigidly set roles and spent their leisure time with their own friends, while others shared their chore activities more freely and spent most of their time with each other. Bott also observed that some couples received support from their friends and family, who often held strong beliefs about the respective duties of husband and wife. Early on, she realized that these differences were "related somehow to forces in the social environment of the families" (Bott, 1956, p. 346). These observations led to a more specific research question: "What relationship existed between the couple's personal network structure and the way they divided their household work?" Bott observed that if one or both spouses belonged to a closely knit network (a characteristic operationalized as *network density*; see Chapter 11), and if they chose to spend their free time with that group rather than with their spouse, then stricter conjugal roles seemed to emerge to dictate the assignment of household duties. By contrast, if the spouses' networks were less closely knit and if they overlapped with each other, then the spouses tended to communicate more freely regarding what needed to be done and were more flexible regarding the distribution of duties. It was on the basis of these observations that Bott formulated her hypothesis, now known as the Bott hypothesis. Later researchers tested the Bott hypothesis on a larger scale, with mixed results (e.g., Aldous & Straus, 1966; Gordon & Downing, 1978; Maryanski & Ishii-Kuntz, 1991).

## Social Support and Health

- **Research questions:** What is the relationship between discussion networks and health outcomes among people experiencing mental illness? Do generic discussion networks or health-specific discussion networks matter more for health outcomes?
- **Hypotheses:** (1) Generic discussion networks have little overlap with health-specific discussion networks. (2) Generic discussion networks have different characteristics from those of health-specific discussion networks (a larger proportion of women, more family and fewer friends, more health professionals, more people with similar health conditions, and more close and broadly supportive ties). (3) Characteristics of health discussion networks, such as size and closeness, are better predictors of the individual's health outcomes than characteristics of generic discussion networks.

Brea Perry and Bernice Pescosolido (2010) argued that the mechanisms through which networks affect individual outcomes such as health are still largely unknown. Based on the functional specificity hypothesis (see Section 2.3), they expected that people mobilize their network ties selectively and purposefully. Therefore, they believed that the people with whom individuals discuss generic important matters (a popular question for generating personal networks in large-scale surveys, see Section 6.4) will not be as good a predictor of health as the more specific network of people with whom an individual discusses health matters.

After formulating their research question and specifying hypotheses based on the literature, Perry and Pescosolido analyzed data from a personal network survey among people who made their first contact with mental health services in Indianapolis between 1990 and 1997. They compared the personal networks of contacts with whom respondents discussed "important matters" (the generic discussion network) and the personal networks of people with whom respondents discussed health matters specifically (the health discussion network). Their analysis found support for the three hypotheses listed earlier: unlike the characteristics of the generic discussion network, the size and average closeness of the health discussion network predicted patient outcomes such as confidence in doctors, satisfaction with mental health services, and improvement in mental health.

Many other researchers over the past several decades have used personal networks as a way to operationalize social support. Research questions in these applications are typically concerned with the support that people can obtain from their personal contacts, and in many cases with the relationship between such support and individual health outcomes, similar to Perry and Pescosolido's research. Studies of this type have been conducted in such diverse populations as migrant women (e.g., Hendrikson, 2010), people with problems of depression or alcoholism (e.g., Gariépy, Honkaniemi, & Quesnel-Vallée, 2016), and parents of autistic children (e.g., Smith, Greenberg, & Maylick Seltzer, 2012).

## Risky Behaviors and Infectious Diseases

- **Research question:** How do norms influence sexual risk behaviors, and which ties promote condom use norms among drug users in disadvantaged urban neighborhoods?
- **Hypothesis:** People with larger support networks tend to perceive more positive condom norms among friends.

Personal network methods have been used extensively in studies of infectious diseases and related risky behaviors. For instance, Carl Latkin and colleagues (Latkin, Forman, Knowlton, & Sherman, 2003) conducted a study based on the above research question and hypothesis. They collected data on personal support networks and condom norms and behaviors among impoverished inner-city residents in Baltimore City. The 1,071 respondents in their survey were drug users (or people in weekly contact with drug users) and at risk of HIV infection (or already HIV seropositive). In addition to specific personal network questions, the researchers asked about respondents' perceptions of condom norms among their friends: specifically, whether most of their friends talked about condoms, encouraged the use of condoms, and actually used condoms. The study found that people who had larger support networks (more network members who provided advice on health matters or could provide material support) were more likely to perceive that their friends talked about condoms, encouraged the use of condoms, and used condoms. In other words, larger support networks were associated with more positive condom norms among peers, which, in turn, were associated with a higher likelihood that respondents used condoms themselves.

Many early studies on personal networks and risky behaviors relevant to infectious diseases were conducted in the mid-1990s. Alan Neaigus et al. (1994) demonstrated the influence of the personal networks of IV drug users on their risk of HIV infection. Drug users who shared needles and had at least one high-risk personal network member were much more likely to contract HIV. Latkin et al. (1995) used personal network measures to explain needle-sharing behavior among IV drug users, as well as HIV transmission. In this study, drug users with larger and denser networks were more likely to share needles than those with smaller, less dense networks. Thomas Valente et al. (Valente, Watkins, Jato, van Der Straten, & Tsitsol, 1997) drew on ideas from the literature on diffusion of innovations to examine the association between women's personal networks and contraceptive use in Cameroon.

## Mobility, Migration, and Transnationalism

- **Research questions:** What is the role of social capital in the transnational entrepreneurial activities of immigrants in Germany? Can different types of transnational entrepreneurship be distinguished on the basis of the geographical location and other aspects of the support networks?
- **Expectations:** Transnational entrepreneurial activities among immigrants may be central to businesses they run. Alternatively, such activities are occasional and complementary to their main employment. Both transnational personal networks in the home country and local personal networks in the destination country can be crucial to sustaining such arrangements.

Elena Sommer and Markus Gamper (2018) explored whether the transnational entrepreneurial activities of immigrant entrepreneurs are supported by social capital embedded in local and transnational networks. To do so, they conducted a qualitative personal network study based on interviews with 62 immigrants from the former Soviet Union living in Germany, who were self-employed or had been self-employed prior to the interview. Over half of the interviewees (37 immigrants) were involved in transnational entrepreneurial activities, that is, business activities requiring regular or occasional interactions with people and companies in countries other than Germany. The semistructured interviews focused on the personal contacts whom respondents considered "important for their business" and were supported by visualizations of the respondent's business-related personal network. Using a grounded theory approach, the authors identified four types of transnational entrepreneurial activities and analyzed transnational networking strategies for each type. They found that most respondents engage in occasional transnational entrepreneurial activities, which are secondary and complementary to the entrepreneur's primary business. These transnational activities are sustained by premigration weak ties in the country of origin, as well as an important local network in the destination country.

A growing body of research has adopted a personal network approach to the study of mobility, migration, immigrant integration, and transnationalism (e.g., Bashi Treitler, 2007; Dahinden, 2005, 2009; Mazzucato, 2008, 2011; Menjívar, 2000). These studies investigate how migrant ties are maintained across borders, how they correspond to different modes of immigrant incorporation in destination societies, and their association with the well-being, identities, and livelihood strategies of immigrants. An interesting contribution to the research on personal networks and mobility comes from Kay Axhausen (2009), who proposed the concept of personal network geography: the network of places visited by an individual during the course of her activities during a given period of time. This concept can be used to classify different lifestyles and their relationship with other domains of social activity, such as everyday displacements and tourism. Juan-Antonio Carrasco and colleagues have conducted extensive research on the spatial patterning of personal networks, and the relationship between personal networks and individuals' mobility in different countries (e.g., Carrasco & Cid-Aguayo, 2012; Kowald et al., 2013). With regard to migration and transnationalism, recent research has explored the relationship between personal networks and ethnic identification (Lubbers, Molina, & McCarty, 2007), social support (De Miguel Luken & Tranmer, 2010), and cultural and economic assimilation (Vacca, Solano, Lubbers, Molina, & McCarty, 2018) among international immigrants. (We will discuss some of this research in more detail at different points in the rest of this book.) A recent special issue of the journal *Social Networks* focuses entirely on the application of social network analysis to migration studies and features further examples of personal network studies on mobility, migration, and transnationalism (Bilecen, Gamper, & Lubbers, 2018).

Sommer and Gamper's (2018) study also demonstrates the importance of qualitative and mixed methods in personal network research. Personal network data, measures, and visualizations are increasingly being used to support semistructured interviews in otherwise qualitative research. When interviewees are presented with the visualization of their own personal networks, new, unique, and insightful narratives emerge in the interviews. Their stories help researchers to give meaning to the quantitative measures of social environment returned by personal network methods and to more fully explore the role played by both structural determinants and personal decisions in social phenomena (Molina, Maya-Jariego, & McCarty, 2014). We will return to the topics of personal network visualizations and qualitative interviews in Chapter 9.

## Online Interactions and Social Media

- **Research question:** Do online personal networks mirror offline personal networks in their layered structure?

The explosive growth of Internet communication technologies, social media, and social networking websites in the past 20 years has opened up a whole new set of questions for social scientists—and for social network researchers in particular. How are social media changing the way we interact with people and make friends? Do social networking websites reduce, replicate, or expand offline social networks? Do our new online social networks work similarly to the old offline, face-to-face networks? Is the Internet really making us more connected, or is it making us more isolated?

British anthropologist and psychologist Robin Dunbar and his colleagues (2015) addressed some of these questions in a study of personal networks on Facebook and Twitter. They sought to determine if the Facebook and Twitter personal networks had a layered structure similar to the one they found in offline personal networks. In offline personal networks, owing to cognitive and time constraints, people seem to consistently organize their contacts into four groups or layers, with increasing size and decreasing frequency of contact and emotional closeness (see Section 2.2). However, given that online communication can overcome some of these time constraints that limit offline networks, they asked whether online networks may have different qualities.

The authors found that Facebook and Twitter networks worked in a similar way, at least in the earlier stages of their development (the study used Facebook data, collected between 2004 and 2009, and Twitter data, collected in 2012). Facebook and Twitter personal networks had a similar layered structure to offline networks, with three to four distinct clusters of alters based on online contact frequency, a scaling ratio of about 3:1 among layer sizes, and average rates of contact with each layer that were very close to those observed offline.

Egocentric data on online interactions have been used in many other studies to answer disparate research questions (see also Section 6.7). Many of these questions revolve around the broad and pressing issue of whether the Internet is changing our sense of community, feelings of isolation, and social cohesion. In the e-Neighbors project, sociologist Keith Hampton (2007) implemented an intervention in which three Boston neighborhoods were provided with a neighborhood email discussion list and website. Simultaneously, he conducted three yearly surveys among neighborhood residents about mobility, sense of community, and engagement with social networks. His research asked whether the Internet is part of everyday neighborhood life, what types of neighborhood are more inclined to online interactions, and how these interactions can promote the development of local, offline, and online social networks. Diana Mok and her collaborators (Mok, Carrasco, & Wellman, 2009) examined the effect of spatial distance on frequency of email exchanges (as well as phone and face-to-face contact) in personal networks. Yuri Takhteyev, Anatoliy Gruzd, and Barry Wellman (2012) studied the formation of ties on Twitter and how Twitter interactions are influenced by such factors as spatial distance, national boundaries, and language. The Dutch American research team of Bas Hofstra and collaborators (Hofstra, Corten, van Tubergen, & Ellison, 2017) used personal network data from Facebook to analyze ethnic and gender segregation in broad personal communities, including strong and weak ties. Drawing on personal network literature and concepts, Paolo Parigi and Warner Henson II (2014) reviewed different lines of research on social cohesion and isolation, focusing on the emerging issue of whether new social media and networking websites are increasing the sense of isolation and loneliness in contemporary societies.

### Difficult People, Difficult Ties

- **Research question:** Why do people maintain ties with individuals whom they find difficult?
- **Hypotheses:** (1) Ties to kin are more likely to be perceived as difficult than ties to nonkin. (2) Ties to nonkin in more constraining contexts are more likely to be perceived as difficult than ties to nonkin in less constraining contexts. (3) Ties to alters who provide critical types of support are more likely to be perceived as difficult than ties to alters who provide less critical types of support. (4) Nonreciprocal exchange ties providing unilateral benefits to ego are more likely to be perceived as difficult than reciprocal exchange ties.

Shira Offer and Claude S. Fischer (2018) posed an important question that the literature on personal networks has so far mostly neglected: Why do people maintain ties with individuals whom they find difficult? Offer and Fischer answered this question by analyzing the University of California Social Networks Study (UCNets) panel, including respondents from two age groups in San Francisco: 50- to 70-year-olds ($N$ = 666) and 21- to 30-year-olds ($N$ = 480). In total, the 1,100 respondents reported over 12,000 relationships using a multiple name generator approach (including role-based and exchange-based questions, and one question about people they "sometimes find demanding or difficult"; see Chapter 6).

Offer and Fischer identified two models in the existing personal networks literature that might explain why people hold on to difficult ties: the structure of opportunity model, which posits that egos feel pressure to retain a tie in certain normative contexts, such as with kin (hypotheses 1 and 2), and the agentic model, which posits that a tie is retained if it has a certain utility (hypotheses 3 and 4).

Results of the study showed that, although the proportion of difficult alters in a network was relatively small (and even smaller for those alters involved in supportive exchanges with the ego), people kept difficult relationships in their networks. The first two hypotheses were largely supported by the data, suggesting that normative constraints influence the existence of difficult ties (especially kin-based relationships and affiliation to hierarchical organizations). Hypotheses 3 and 4 were not supported: Alters perceived as difficult who provided more types of support were not more likely to be retained in the network than difficult alters who did not provide support. Finally, close kin, especially female relatives and aging parents, were particularly likely to be named as difficult alters.

## CHAPTER SUMMARY

This chapter discussed what type of research questions and/or hypotheses are best suited for personal network analysis and what kind of contributions we can expect from this approach. We concluded that personal network analysis is appropriate for research questions and/or hypotheses that assume a key importance of social context. This approach has been successfully applied in a wide range of areas, including health, mobility and migration, social media, and longitudinal studies of the life course. Personal networks provide unique insight into the social world, through an intermediate level of analysis that combines quality and quantity, agency and structure.

## FURTHER READING

Alvesson, M., & Sandberg, J. (2013). *Constructing research questions: Doing interesting research.* London: SAGE.

Bidart, C., Degenne, A., & Grossetti, M. (2011). *La vie en réseau: Dynamique des relations sociales.* Paris: Presses Universitaires de France.

# 4

# Getting Started

## *Selecting a Population, Survey Mode, and Sampling Frames*

---

*What Is This Chapter About?*

This chapter will discuss how to get started with a personal network study. We first consider whether personal network is the right approach, as opposed to whole network, or, possibly, a combination of both (see Section 4.1). Once you have determined that you indeed want a personal network study, the next step is collecting the personal network data. This is most commonly done with a survey. To design and implement a personal network survey, you need to establish your *population of interest* (Section 4.2); decide how you will interview people, referred to as the *survey mode* (Section 4.3); and decide how you will recruit respondents, referred to as the *sample frame* (Section 4.4). In order to best design the survey, you also need to be clear about the purpose of your study and to differentiate the dependent and independent variables in your research (Section 4.5). Most of the topics in this chapter are not specific to personal network research. While this book can only briefly discuss them in connection with personal network research, the Further Reading section at the end of this chapter lists survey methods textbooks that you may find useful for a more thorough study of these topics.

---

### 4.1 DECIDING WHETHER PERSONAL NETWORK ANALYSIS IS APPROPRIATE

You need to consider several things before you start collecting data (see Figure 4.1). Assuming you have decided that a network approach is appropriate for your research, you still need to decide whether you want to do a whole or personal network analysis—or both. It is worth reviewing the differences between the two methods (Section 1.3). Let's consider a few examples.

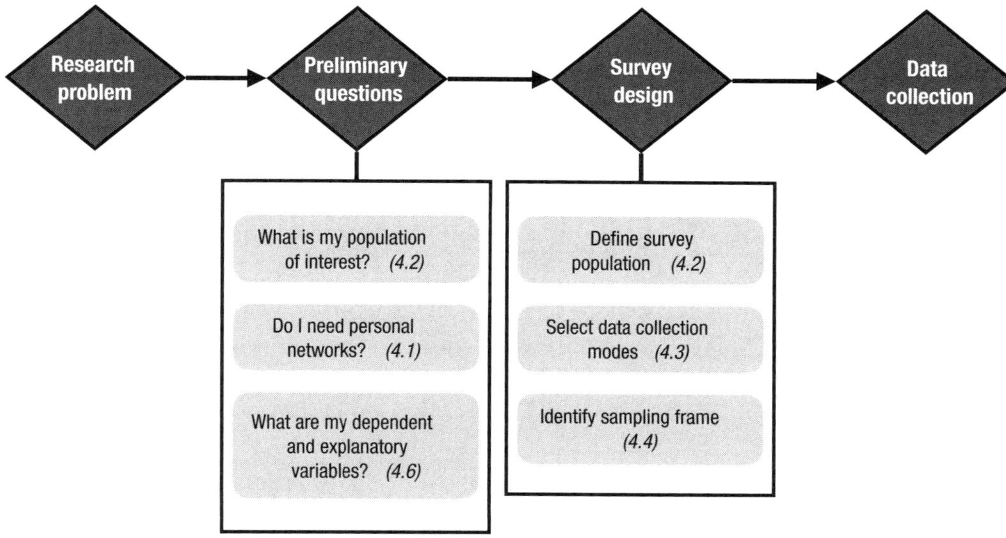


**FIGURE 4.1.** Designing a personal network survey and preparing for data collection. Numbers in parentheses indicate the section of this chapter that is relevant for each item.

First, we will look at a topic that is best researched using whole networks. Alice is a management consultant tasked with evaluating the efficiency of a corporate office. Her client has an organizational chart that indicates who reports to whom, but during the past year cases have emerged in which this practice was clearly not followed. As a consequence, several contracts have been lost because key personnel were not communicating as they should. The client wants Alice to make some recommendations about how to modify office communications. Alice determines that this is a great opportunity to use the whole network approach. She also realizes she might not get the best data by talking directly to the employees. She asks the client if she can have access to email transactions between the employees during the past year (see Chapter 14 on ethics and Borgatti & Molina, 2005a). She doesn't need to read the transactions, but only to record who sent an email to whom. She creates an adjacency matrix with all the office staff listed across the first row and down the first column. The cell intersecting two people contains the number of emails they sent to each other. With this matrix, Alice does her analysis and discovers that an office manager who has been with the company for more than 10 years is in a structurally important position. She concludes that employees may rely more on the office manager to get things done than on the organizational chart designed to maximize communication.

This case calls for a whole network approach. We are concerned with the interaction that takes place within a bounded group: the office within a company. While each person in the office knows people outside of it, we are not interested in the effect those outsiders have on the office. We are only interested in how the pattern of interaction in the office affects the way people behave.

Now let's consider a research topic involving people cutting across many groups. Joe is doing a study of depression among the elderly. He wants to understand why some seniors seek help for depression and others do not. He selects a sample of seniors consisting of different race, sex, and income levels—variables that are often significantly associated with depression. He also collects information on the personal networks of each elderly respondent. Among the questions he asks about each network member is whether or not he or she is someone with whom the respondent would talk to about depression. Joe finds that seniors who have many network members they can talk to about depression are far more likely to seek help than those who cannot talk to their network members about it, even after controlling for sex, race, and income differences. He also finds that less cohesive personal networks (those lacking much interaction between network members) tend to be associated with a lower likelihood of seeking help for depression.

This case is a good example of personal network analysis. We want to use characteristics of the personal network as attributes of the respondent, the *ego*, to predict some outcome of interest concerning the respondent himself. In this case, we are interested in predicting whether the respondent, an elderly person, will seek help with depression, and we may want to design an intervention based on our findings. To do this, we cannot limit the analysis to one specific bounded group the ego belongs to, such as a company, a school, or a neighborhood. We need to capture all the relationships around the ego, cutting across all groups and social circles the ego participates in. In other words, personal networks allow us to describe the entire social context surrounding the ego, measuring its composition and its structure.

Finally, let's consider a case that might benefit from both whole and personal network approaches. Henry is conducting a study of an isolated agricultural community in rural Mexico. Within the small village of about 300 households, half belong to an agricultural cooperative and the others do not; Henry wants to understand what explains that choice. He decides to use a mixed approach for his study, which means collecting data from the heads of each household about the household's reliance on every other household. He uses the data to construct an adjacency matrix representing the network structure of the entire village (whole network). He finds that only very central families in the network are in the cooperative. A clear difference like this suggests that there is a social mechanism behind the membership rather than randomness; this could be (at least partly) *structural* (see Section 1.2). He also selects a sample of households and elicits a personal network from each head of household. He finds that those outside the cooperative have a larger proportion of personal network ties *outside* the community, which seems to indicate that, while they are less central in the village, they may also be less reliant on the cooperative to market their produce.

In this case, both the whole and personal network approaches are appropriate. We can see that one approach is not necessarily better than the other. Some research questions call for whole network analysis, whereas others call for personal network analysis. For still other research questions, like Henry's question about what determines membership in the agricultural cooperative, whole and personal networks are complementary approaches that yield complementary, equally relevant findings.

Keep in mind, however, that not all studies need the kind of accurate data that personal networks provide. Personal networks require data that are typically more time-consuming and expensive to collect than traditional survey data. For some research questions, approximate variables about the respondents' social context suffice, which do not need a personal network survey but can be collected with less expensive survey questions such as "How many people are there in your family?", "How old are the people you typically hang out with?", and "How many African Americans do you know?"; or more sophisticated measures such as the ones explained in Chapter 10 of this book. At the same time, only by collecting actual personal network data will you be able to precisely measure, for example, the proportion of family, the average age of the personal contacts, or the proportion of African Americans in the social context surrounding the respondent. Moreover, the network *structural* characteristics of a respondent's social context can only be studied using personal network data. Thus, for example, you will need personal networks if you are interested in distinguishing the multiple cliques and subgroups or in identifying the most central personal contacts in the individual's social network. In other words, personal networks are the most accurate way to operationalize and measure the composition and structure of an individual's social context. At this point, you should have a good idea about whether your research interests would benefit from personal network analysis.

## 4.2 SELECTING A POPULATION

The first step in collecting personal network data is to select a population. This is the population that you plan to study. In the preceding examples, for Alice the population consisted of all the employees of a corporate office: for Joe the elderly; and for Henry the inhabitants of an agricultural village in rural Mexico. This is also the population in which you will recruit the survey respondents, that is, the egos of your personal networks. You will study the personal networks of individuals in this population and, typically, the way these personal networks are associated with other characteristics or outcomes of those individuals.

It is important to choose your population wisely and to define it properly. The process of population definition, though not unique to personal network analysis, is still vitally important for it. In the data collection stage, the way you define the population will determine the *modes* of data collection and the *sampling frame* available to you. In the data analysis stage, it will determine your ability to answer your research questions appropriately.

One way the population definition affects the mode of data collection is that certain characteristics tend to cluster spatially or to have lists available, whereas others do not. Spatial clustering is important for face-to-face surveys and less so for the other modes.

**Neighborhood Networks and Status**

Karen Campbell and Barrett Lee (1992) conducted a network study of 690 adults in 81 neighborhoods in Nashville, Tennessee, to study the association between various statuses (gender, age, family-cycle stage, and socioeconomic status) and neighborhood networks. The population comprised residents of Nashville who lived in the 81 neighborhoods. The two sociologists found that people who were socially more integrated (female, middle-aged, married, of high SES) had larger networks within their neighborhood. Conversely, lower SES residents maintained smaller networks, but their contacts in those networks were often more intense and more frequent than those of the more integrated group, possibly indicating they were mobilizing to help one another.

Geography obviously clusters well spatially, and for some projects it is enough to define your population using geographic boundaries—for example, a population consisting of the residents of a specific town, village, or neighborhood. In the example involving rural Mexico, Henry was interested in explaining why the members of a village did or did not join a cooperative. His population consisted of the members of the village. While this definition seemed to be straightforward, before beginning, Henry still had to settle specific questions about this population. Was it all members of the village? How would the boundaries of the village be defined? We can gain insight into the definition of population by contrasting his choice with another. For example, what would happen if Henry looked at a neighborhood in an urban setting rather than a village? Care must be taken to define the boundaries of the geography precisely.

Most of the time, however, we are *not* interested in studying the personal networks of those within a defined geographic space. Typically, we want to study people who have a particular characteristic in common, such as age or socioeconomic status. Sometimes those characteristics cluster spatially, which is again important for face-to-face data collection. Let's consider some examples.

Age is a characteristic that sometimes clusters in space. Children of school age can often be interviewed at school. Elderly respondents can be found at retirement homes or retirement villages. Recruiting elderly respondents in these settings, however, leads to potential bias, as seniors who live in retirement homes or retirement villages may be different from those who do not. If your research problem is to study the personal networks of all seniors (defined as those over age 65), then a spatial approach to sampling and data collection may bias your findings. Studies of the personal networks of 18- to 20-year-olds face a different problem, which is also related to space. In the United States and many other countries, this is an age at which many people are mobile and others are not. Some are leaving for college, others are staying home, while others are leaving the household for jobs elsewhere. A spatial approach to studies of this age group may also lead to bias a study toward a specific subpopulation of 18- to 20-year-olds. For example, if you interview 18- to 20-year-olds in a college campus of a renowned college town, you

**Emotional Support and Cognitive Functioning among the Elderly**

Teresa Seeman and colleagues (Seeman, Lusignolo, Albert, & Berkman, 2001) examined the relationship between social support and cognitive decline among the elderly in a longitudinal study (with an average time interval of 7.4 years). The researchers used data from three community-based cohorts of individuals aged 65 and older in Durham, North Carolina, East Boston, Massachusetts, and New Haven, Connecticut. The respondents selected were between 70 and 79 years of age and had high physical and cognitive functioning at the baseline assessment. For purposes of this assessment, the research team used a series of physical and mental tests to identify the participants in the top third of the age group. Their research shows that the level of emotional support received was positively related to the maintenance of cognitive functioning, regardless of other individual characteristics known to be related to cognitive aging.

should be aware that your study is only including those 18- to 20-year-old individuals who decided to go to college and who likely left their hometown to do so.

Another characteristic that tends to cluster geographically is income level, more specifically, poverty. Low-income families and individuals often concentrate in specific neighborhoods of cities—a pattern known as urban segregation. Social researchers are often interested in studying the impact of various phenomena on low-income populations. In the United States, poverty is specifically defined using a formula that considers income level and household size. It is not unusual for researchers to expand the population they are interested in by considering respondents who are at 200 percent of the poverty level.

Given the social and economic barriers present in the United States and other countries, race or phenotype also tends to cluster spatially as it is related to income. However, African Americans have achieved some upward mobility; thus, by focusing on the most segregated African American neighborhoods, researchers may tend to leave out middle- and upper-income African American households who live in other urban areas. Ethnicity is another characteristic that clusters, which is due largely to migratory patterns. Early immigrants establish *bridgeheads*, offering safe haven for later migrants. This pattern of chain migration may result in the formation of ethnic enclaves, neighborhoods with a high concentration of residences and businesses of immigrants in the same ethnicity. Unlike age and income, race and ethnicity are difficult to define and determine, and most survey methods rely on respondents' self-reports to identify them. For example, the 2010 U.S. Census asked respondents to self-identify their race as "White," "Black or African American," "American Indian or Alaska Native," "Asian," or "Native Hawaiian or Other Pacific Islander," and gave respondents the ability to select more than one race.

**_Social Support and Smoking in African American Adults_**

Patrick Romano, Joan Bloom, and Leonard Syme (1991) sought to explain higher levels of smoking among African Americans than among other populations in the United States. One of their hypotheses was that social factors mitigated the tendency to smoke. They sampled 1,137 African American adults in San Francisco and Oakland, California. From 1980 Census data they identified the neighborhoods of those cities that had at least 25% African American households. They then randomly selected households in those blocks and returned at least twice to identify those with at least one African American living in the household. The questionnaire included a set of questions about social support. They found that, for women, stronger social networks were related to less smoking. This effect was not present for men.

In a separate question, the 2010 U.S. Census asked respondents to self-identify their ethnicity as "Hispanic, Latino, or Spanish origin" or not.

## 4.3 THE SURVEY MODE

In general, four survey modes are used to collect survey data—face-to-face, telephone, postal mail, and the Web. Today online social networks such as Facebook and Twitter, as well as a variety of other online electronic footprints, provide some form of personal network data without the need to interview people. All the same, surveys remain the most appropriate means to collect accurate and comprehensive personal network data for most populations. Each of these modes varies to the extent that paper or computer-based instruments are incorporated. For example, you can do a face-to-face survey on paper or on a computer, using questionnaire-authoring software. And of course you can design a study that mixes modes, combining two or more of the four modes. Many surveys first use a mail survey, followed up with a telephone survey for those who do not complete the mailed version. In the past, most personal network data collection has been done face to face because of the high respondent burden. However, recently some interest has been shown in developing Web-based and telephone-based methods of personal network data collection.

The four survey/interview modes range from the method having the most contact with the respondent to the least, in the following order—face-to-face, telephone, mail, and Web. With regard to cost, this same order prevails. A little recognized fact about survey research is that the majority of the cost is not incurred in actually interviewing the respondent. The highest cost, rather, derives from the time needed up front to get a willing respondent to do the interview. So sending an interviewer to do face-to-face interviews in randomly selected homes over a large geographic area is extremely expensive. It is less expensive as the area gets smaller and even less so if you do face-to-face interviews in a single location, such as a mall or health clinic.

Depending on the extent of the personal network interview, you may have to interview respondents face to face. While this mode is the most expensive one, increasingly more advanced tools are being developed which reduce the respondent and interviewer burden in traditional face-to-face interviews. These tools include software programs that allow interviewers and respondents to draw personal networks using the mouse on a laptop computer, and even smartphone apps that researchers can use for conducting personal network interviews on a touch screen in the field (see the Appendix for these kinds of software).

Telephone and mail surveys are less expensive than face-to-face surveys. Many social-support studies are done by mail or telephone because they tend to focus on smaller sets of alters and result in a shorter interview. Although it may be possible (with the right incentive) to retain a respondent on the telephone for a long interview, such situations are rare. Also keep in mind that, depending on the population you are studying, there may be no convenient or practical *sample frame* for telephone or mail, that is, a list of telephone numbers or residential addresses for a sample of individuals in your population. For example, you will almost certainly have difficulty finding telephone numbers or residential addresses for migrants.

Researchers are intrigued by the prospect of doing personal network surveys over the Web. This is because Web surveys are by far the least expensive: All of the costs lie in programming the survey and managing the sample. The researcher does not have to pay for anyone to actually do the interviewing or type in the data—the respondent does all the work. In addition, the researcher can use the computer interface to present audio and visual cues to respondents and to do complex question authoring. Finally, an important advantage of Web surveys is that they negate the need for electronic data entry after data collection; the data are entered in an electronic format as they are collected.

Web surveys have some drawbacks, however. First, many people, particularly those who pique the interest of social scientists, do not have access to the Web and do not leave an electronic footprint. Lists of email addresses for specific populations are much harder to come by than are telephone numbers or mailing addresses. For example, you can obtain a list of addresses of households with at least one person over the age of 65, but because many seniors today do not use email, you cannot obtain a representative email list of seniors. While it is possible to generate random telephone numbers (random digit dialing), it is, and always will be, impossible to generate a random list of email addresses, as they vary extensively by provider and username. Although Web surveys are ideal for certain populations, it will be a long time before they are optimal for most populations.

Second, as we have already mentioned, Web-based surveys place all the work on the respondent. The respondent is supposed to complete the survey by himself, remain alone but focused throughout the process, and possess the necessary computer skills to do so. While this type of survey eliminates the need for interviewers, it also means that respondents will not take the survey without an adequate incentive. Because personal network surveys can be long and cognitively demanding, a high incentive, for example, in the form of electronic gift cards, might be necessary to convince respondents to click on the survey link and complete the questionnaire. Sitting in front of a computer for one or two hours by yourself, typing names of people you know, and indicating who knows whom among them make for a demanding job that you typically would not want to do for free. Furthermore, aside from the incentive, it might be difficult to complete a personal network questionnaire without any assistance. Respondents may have a hard time understanding questions or navigating the Web survey. This is particularly true among respondents with less advanced computer skills. If computer skills tend to be low in your population, for example, because you are studying farmers in a rural area of Sri Lanka or 70- to 80-year-old seniors in a nursing home, a Web-based survey might not be feasible irrespective of respondent incentives and compensations.

## 4.4 THE SAMPLING FRAME

Once you have defined your population precisely and have decided on the survey mode, you must choose a sampling frame to select your respondents. A sampling frame is nothing more than a list that represents, as closely as possible, all of the people in the population you wish to study. As is true in any social survey, if you plan to use your personal network data to make statistical inferences generalizable to the whole population of interest, you will want a sampling frame that is representative of the whole population you are studying.

To be representative of the whole population, the sampling frame must not overrepresent specific groups or characteristics. For example, if you are interested in studying the general population of seniors in the United States, and you know that 5% of American seniors live in retirement homes and 95% live in other residences, then your sampling frame should not include 95% seniors in retirement homes and 5% seniors in other residences. Rather, variability in your sample should reflect variability in the population of interest. Ideally, the proportions of those two groups of seniors in your sampling frame should be the same as they are in the general population. Although that might be difficult to obtain in practice, and you might need to subsequently *weight* your survey data to adjust for seniors in other residences being underrepresented, your sampling frame should at least include a positive percentage of seniors from both groups.

The problem of variability in the sampling frame is particularly critical if you are studying the relationship between personal networks and other characteristics, with personal networks being the independent or dependent variable in your model. As we will discuss further in Section 4.6, your sampling frame should exhibit sufficient variability in the dependent and independent variables of your model, or in characteristics that you are assuming will affect the independent variables. For example, if you are studying the relationship between personal networks (independent variable) and depression (dependent variable) among seniors, and you are assuming that living in a retirement home affects a senior's personal network, then your sampling frame should display variability in the characteristic "living in a retirement home." In other words, it should include both seniors who live in a retirement home and seniors who do not.

The combination of population definition and survey mode will suggest the sampling frames available. With face-to-face surveys you have several choices. You could use standardized spatial units, such as U.S. census tracts, to pick a sample within specific geographic areas. You could also use lists of addresses, such as membership directories, to select households to interview. Sometimes survey researchers are less concerned with geographic representation and instead use intercept surveys at a location. For example, respondents for a study about health issues might be recruited from a public health clinic. Finally, with extensive personal network studies, respondents may be asked to come to a specific location, such as a research lab, to be interviewed. In this case, the sampling frame may consist of the set of people who respond to an advertisement.

Qualitative and mixed-methods studies do not normally aim to obtain a statistically representative sample, but they follow other strategies in order to obtain rich information (Small, 2009a). These nonprobability strategies, which are not based on sampling frames, include purposeful sampling, quota sampling, and snowball sampling. Such sampling strategies are also followed if random sampling is not possible. Qualitative researchers may further adopt other strategies to maximize variation in the sample, find deviant cases, or continue sampling until saturation is reached and no new information is obtained from further cases.

In the case of personal network research, we would generally advise against snowball sampling with people who know each other really well, especially in small samples, given that their networks are likely to overlap at least partially. Thus, although they are different cases, their information may be to some extent redundant—though in some cases the information can be precisely of interest, as our case in the Prologue or as Elizabeth Bott's case with married couples. Having said that, when researchers wish to study both an individual and a community perspective by collecting personal network data and interconnecting them to form a whole network, sampling designs that use snowball principles, such as respondent-driven sampling (Heckathorn, 1997, 2002) or other link-tracing designs (Mouw, Chavez, Edelblute, & Verdery, 2014), are necessary.

## 4.5 INTEGRATION WITH LARGER SURVEYS

This book is structured to help you design a personal network study from beginning to end. However, some of the most impactful personal network studies have been the result of a small set of questions added to a larger study. Examples include the General Social Survey (Burt, 1984), Add Health (Harris, 2013), and the Framingham Heart Study (Fowler & Christakis, 2008). All three of these surveys have been fielded for many years and have consistently included questions regarding the personal networks of respondents during at least some of those years. The advantages of adding questions to an existing survey are many. The sample sizes of well-established surveys are typically large (> 1,000), many other questions are asked that can be included in your analysis as covariates, and these data collection efforts are among the highest quality in all of social science. In addition, data collection is often cost-prohibitive for a personal network component alone, but it can be justified when the personal network component is added to a larger battery of questions. While you may have to modify your survey questions to fit a larger existing study, this option is worth considering should the opportunity present itself. In fact, the ability to integrate egocentric data collection within existing, large-scale surveys is arguably one of the main reasons why personal network research has been gaining increasing popularity.

## 4.6 IDENTIFYING DEPENDENT AND EXPLANATORY VARIABLES

It is important to understand the purpose of your research. Personal network research typically has one of three goals—exploring network mechanisms in depth; estimating the distribution of a personal network characteristic in a population; or analyzing the relationship between personal network characteristics and an outcome that researchers want to predict. In the first two goals, personal networks are treated as a *dependent* variable, and in the third they are used as an *independent* or *explanatory* variable.

We first mentioned the difference between dependent and explanatory variables in Chapter 3. As a reminder, dependent variables are the final outcome you want to understand, explain, or predict. You typically posit the hypothesis that this outcome is affected by, or associated with, specific characteristics, factors, or conditions. These are called independent or (more appropriately) explanatory variables. Therefore, you are interested in studying whether the variability in the explanatory variables affects, explains, or predicts the variability in the dependent variable. We call a "model" a set of hypotheses about this relationship or association between the explanatory and dependent variables (see Figure 4.2 for an example).

Most personal network research uses personal networks as an explanatory variable. More precisely, specific characteristics of personal networks are treated as explana-

### *Loneliness and Dementia*

Laura Fratiglioni and colleagues (Fratiglioni, Wang, Ericsson, Maytan, & Winblad, 2000) hypothesized that living alone and/or with too few social connections affected the development of dementia. They selected a cohort sample of 1,203 nondemented people 75 years of age or older living independently in the Kungsholmen district in Stockholm, Sweden, and interviewed them intermittently over a three-year period. After three years, 176 had developed dementia. They found that the respondents who lived alone and without close social ties had 1.5 times the risk of developing dementia. Those living alone and single people developed dementia at almost twice the level of married people. The authors concluded that smaller personal networks increased the chance of developing dementia by 60%. In this study, personal network characteristics were used as explanatory variables to explain dementia, the dependent variable.

tory variables to predict an outcome of interest. For example, you might want to study whether seniors with a larger and more tightly knit personal network are more protected against depression than those without such a network. In this case, the outcome of interest is depression, which you want to explain or predict as a function of characteristics of the personal network, the explanatory variables. The proportion of family in the personal network, the average age of personal contacts, the proportion of co-ethnic contacts, the density of the network, or the number of network subgroups are all examples of personal network explanatory variables that might be incorporated in a model to predict such dependent variables as depression, immigrant acculturation, smoking behavior, or poverty. Figure 4.2, along with the textboxes in this section, show some examples of explanatory and dependent variables in social science models.

Fewer studies treat personal networks as the dependent variable and try to estimate the distribution of certain personal network characteristics in a population. For example, you might want to estimate the proportion of the personal network that is family in the U.S. population, separately for American men and women. In this case, the personal network and specifically the proportion of family in it, is the final outcome you wish to achieve—the dependent variable. You are trying to study the variability of this outcome across the variability of an explanatory variable—gender in this case. Other studies

### *Personal Networks and Ethnic Identity*

In their study of personal networks and immigrant acculturation, Miranda Lubbers and colleagues (Lubbers et al., 2007) found a significant association between personal networks and ethnic self-identification among migrants. The data were collected during 2004–2006 in Barcelona and Girona, Spain, through a questionnaire and a structured interview administered to Senegalese, Gambian, Moroccan, Argentinean, and Dominican migrants ($N = 294$). The personal networks were classified into five profiles on the basis of network structure (e.g., density, betweenness, centralization, and number of cohesive subgroups) and composition (e.g., alters' countries of origin and percentage of family members in the network). The network profiles were related to the different ways in which migrants described their ethnicity, including an "exclusive," a "plural or transnational," and a "generic" type of ethnic self-identification. On one hand, personal networks in which network members were mostly family and people from the same country of origin as the ego and tended to form one dense cluster were associated with exclusive ethnic self-identifications, even when controlling for individual characteristics such as country of origin, years of residence in Spain, gender, education, employment, and experiences of racial discrimination. On the other hand, more diverse and heterogeneous personal networks were associated with plural ethnic self-identifications. Their results show that both individual and network characteristics contribute to an understanding of ethnic self-identification. Figure 4.2 represents the model adopted in this study.

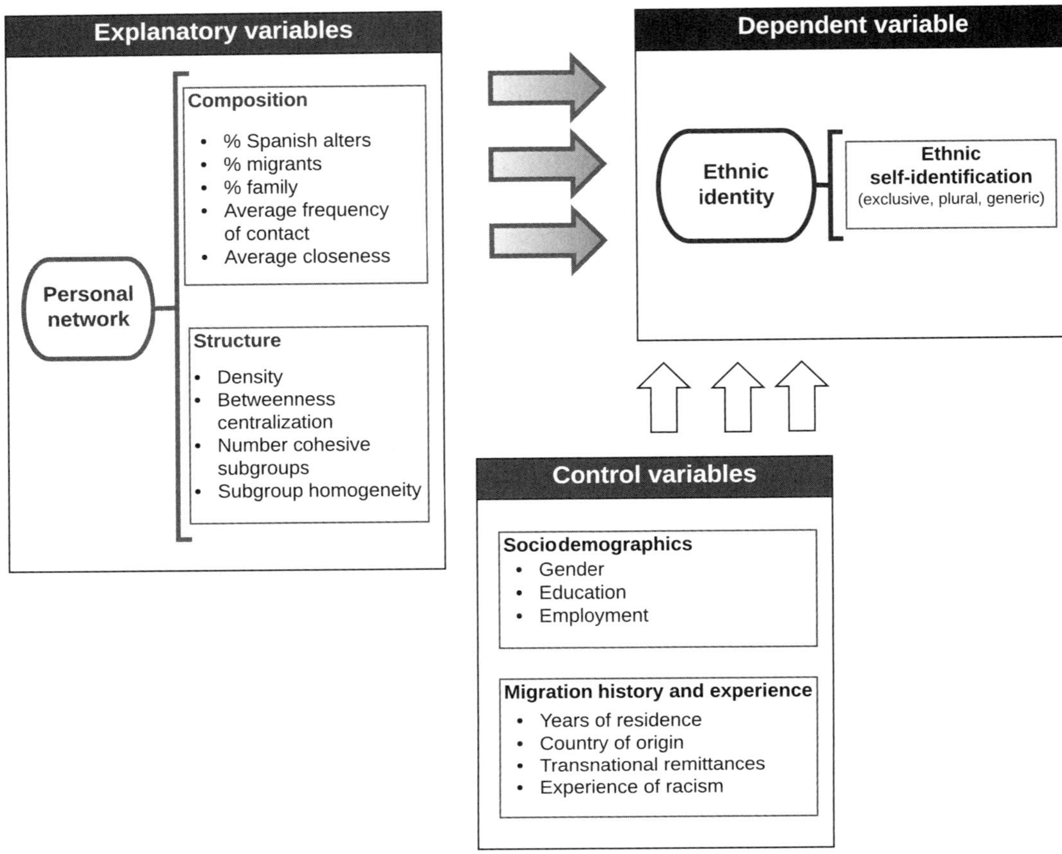


**FIGURE 4.2.** The model adopted by Lubbers et al. (2010). Personal network characteristics are treated as independent variables to explain ethnic identity among migrants while controlling for sociodemographic variables and migration history and experience.

have examined how the size of people's personal network is affected by life-cycle stages such as marriage or retirement.

Another expression you may encounter is "control variable," which is simply an explanatory variable that needs to be incorporated in the model. We seek to incorporate it not because we are specifically interested in it, but because its variability may confound the association between the outcome and other explanatory variables that interest us. For example, we might want to study how the proportion of family in the personal network (the main explanatory variable) affects mental health (the dependent variable) among Dominican immigrants in the United States. At the same time, it might be the case that Dominican immigrants who are married tend to be happier and to have more family in their personal networks, compared to those who are not married. In this case, marital status needs to be added as a control variable to our model. If we did not account for marital status, its variability could affect and confound the association that we are measuring between personal networks and mental health. We might conclude that Dominicans with more family in their personal network have better mental health, when in fact it is *married* Dominicans who have better mental health, and they also happen to have more family in their personal network. Only if we observe that personal networks with more family are associated with better mental health among Dominicans with the same marital status will we correctly establish that the proportion of family in the personal network has a positive effect on mental health. In other words, we need to examine the association between personal networks and mental health *while controlling* for marital status, or with the variable "marital status" being held equal.

The choice of dependent and explanatory variables has implications for your sampling frame. Again, keep in mind that you are trying to explain the variability in the dependent variable using the variability in the explanatory variable. If the dependent variable does not vary across respondents, you have nothing to explain. If the explanatory variables do not vary, you have no way to explain the dependent variable. This means that you want to design your sample to collect a wide range of data values for both the dependent and explanatory variables. For small sample studies, take care to ensure that this variability is captured. In many cases, researchers collect large sample sizes on the assumption that these will result in wide ranges of variability across both the dependent and explanatory variables.

Furthermore, if you have reasons to believe that a certain characteristic affects the explanatory variable in your population, your sampling frame should display variability in that characteristic too. Characteristics of this kind are typically included in a model as control variables, which we defined earlier. For example, you might want to study the relationship between personal networks (explanatory variable) and depression (dependent variable) in the general elderly population, including both seniors who live in retirement homes and seniors who do not. However, you might think that seniors who live in retirement homes tend to have a different personal network than those who live in other residences. In this case, living in a retirement home should be incorporated in your model as a control variable, and your sample should show variability in this characteristic, including seniors both inside and outside retirement homes. If your sample only included individuals in retirement homes, you would not be able to know what the personal network of a senior *outside* a retirement home looks like and how it affects depression. Therefore, you would not be able to study the relationship between personal networks and depression in the elderly population at large.

Similarly, when estimating the prevalence of a personal network characteristic within a population, the sample must be representative of the entire population. For example, if you want to estimate the proportion of the personal network that is family in the general U.S. population, and for men and women separately, your sample must be designed to ensure you get enough respondents who are men and women so that your estimates will have an acceptable *margin of error*. The margin of error is a way of measuring how far off your estimate is from the true value in the population. If the proportions of men and women in your sample are different from those in the general U.S. population, you will need to *weight* the results if you are trying to draw conclusions about the general population.

## CHAPTER SUMMARY

In this chapter, you learned when a personal network study is appropriate and how it can be combined with whole network analysis or even with large surveys. Personal network data can be collected from different sources, including the social media, but so far surveys (administered either through face-to-face interviews, telephone, Web survey, or email) are the most accurate and comprehensive way to address this type of research. In this regard, personal network surveys are to some extent no different from any social survey. In particular, this means that if you plan to use quantitative personal network data to make statistical inferences about that population in general, your sample frame has to be representative of your population of interest. Also, personal network variables can be used either as explanatory or dependent variables, depending on your research problem.

### FURTHER READING

Burt, R. S. (1984). Network items and the General Social Survey. *Social Networks, 6*(4), 293–339.

Dillman, D. A., Smyth, J. D., & Christian, L. M. (2014). *Internet, phone, mail, and mixed-mode surveys: The tailored design method.* Hoboken, NJ: Wiley.

Fowler, F. J., Jr. (2013). *Survey research methods.* Los Angeles: SAGE.

# 5

# Questions about the Ego

---

*What Is This Chapter About?*

This chapter deals with the part of a personal network study that is concerned with the individual characteristics of the respondents (the egos). This part is not specific to personal network research and is similar to any social survey. We first discuss how to determine what questions to ask about respondents on the basis of your research aims (Section 5.1). Responses to these questions generate different variables, which can have different levels of measurement. When you are wording questions, you must be mindful of the levels of measurement they generate and the kind of analyses you'll be able to run on the resulting variables (Section 5.2). There are different ways to word questions, including standardized survey instruments and open-ended questions. You should be aware of some common mistakes to avoid when writing these questions (Section 5.3). This is an introductory chapter that reviews basic concepts in statistics and survey research, including levels of measurement (Section 5.2) and question validity (Section 5.3). You might want to skip these sections if you are already familiar with survey research and data.

---

## 5.1 VARIABLES AND RESEARCH AIMS: WHAT QUESTIONS TO ASK

As we have seen, personal network analysis can be used as an approach to researching a variety of topics. As with most social science research, the problem that interests you will typically determine the population you want to study and how you go about studying it.

Once you have defined the population and selected a survey mode and sampling frame, you are ready to write your *survey instrument*—that is, the set of questions you will ask your respondents. In our discussion of instruments in personal network studies, here and in the next few chapters, we will distinguish four *modules* of a typical personal network study:

- Module 1: Questions about the ego.
- Module 2: Questions to elicit a list of alters (the *name generators*).
- Module 3: Questions about each alter (the *name interpreters*).
- Module 4: Questions about ties, or relationships, between alters (the *edge interpreters*).

Every personal network survey includes some elements of all four of these modules. The modules are typically, but not necessarily, separate and consecutive in a personal network survey. Module 1 consists of questions about the ego, the respondent, and is the subject of this chapter. It is normally the first part of the survey and is generally quicker and less cognitively demanding for the respondent. In face-to-face interviews, beginning the study with Module 1 often allows the interviewer and the respondent to become acquainted and familiar with each other before starting the more challenging Modules 2, 3, and 4. Later in the book, we will see that not all personal network studies use name generators and interpreters; alternative methods will be discussed in both Chapters 6 and 10.

In Module 1, you ask the egos to answer questions about themselves, and these typically include questions about your dependent variables, the outcomes that you believe personal networks help to predict or explain (see Chapter 3). These outcomes are normally ego-level variables, that is, variables that you observe of each ego. Outcomes could be a number of behaviors, attitudes, characteristics, or conditions we observe of the ego, including abstract characteristics, such as the ego's emotional well-being or ethnic identity; and more tangible characteristics, such as the ego's occupational prestige or smoking behavior.

The questions you ask respondents about themselves do not only generate the variables you want to predict or explain but also other variables you may want to use as explanatory or control variables (recall Figures 1.2 and 4.2). Personal network analysis seeks to increase the set of characteristics available to explain something about people in a population. With personal networks, we want to expand on, *not* replace or ignore, the variables that we normally measure about respondents. Characteristics like the respondent's sex, age, income, marital status, and education still help explain variability in a wide range of attitudes, behaviors, and other outcomes. By collecting personal network data, we are assuming that, *in addition* to these traditional variables, detailed information about the respondent's social context will allow us to do a better job of predicting attitudes, behaviors, and other outcomes.

This last point is important. Personal network variables must allow us to *better* predict or explain outcomes. Sometimes researchers go to great lengths to collect personal network data when other respondent-level variables already do an adequate job of predicting the dependent variable and are easier to collect. Also, keep in mind that you can sometimes ask very simple questions of the respondent that will be *proxies* for detailed personal network data. In other words, you may be able to get the same predictive power using a simple question about the family, friends, and acquaintances of a person, rather than collecting detailed information about their network. Let's consider an example.

Imagine we want to predict whether or not adolescents will try a cigarette. We know from the literature that peer influence is an important factor in determining whether adolescents will try cigarettes. Some researchers have attempted to capture these social influences by asking general (proxy) questions about the respondent's network. For example, you could ask adolescent respondents if their parents smoke, if most of their friends smoke, or if a friend ever offered them a cigarette. These are easy questions to ask the respondent and do not require any network analysis. Still, to some degree they measure the social influence of the respondents' personal network regarding smoking, although with less detail than a full personal network instrument.

With personal network research, you are assuming that the data you get from such simple proxy questions do not capture the detail you need to adequately explain the dependent variable. Continuing with the smoking example, we see that the critical factor that explains experimentation with tobacco might not be whether just any friend ever offered a cigarette, but *the proportion* of friends who did so, or whether a friend *who was very central* (e.g., with high degree score) in the adolescent's social network offered the cigarette. You can only test this with personal network analysis. In other words, with personal network analysis you hypothesize that the detail about the personal network composition and structure will be more predictive than simple questions you can ask respondents about themselves and about generic perceptions of their social environment.

When determining what questions to ask respondents about themselves, first remember that your research should suggest the question. This observation seems very obvious, but all too often researchers construct questionnaires with little regard for why they are asking a question. In many cases, researchers err on the side of asking unrelated and meaningless questions because they are unsure what is really important. Questions are added "just in case" they might prove useful in the analysis. This strategy is not a wise one when designing a personal network survey. In the next few chapters, we will describe Modules 2, 3, and 4, the parts of a personal network survey that make it a unique research instrument. These tend to be very time consuming and cognitively demanding for the respondent, resulting in a higher respondent burden than with traditional social surveys. For this reason, you should be careful not to add unnecessary questions to Module 1. As we have mentioned, Module 1 is typically the quick, easy part of a personal network survey, and you should try to keep it that way. At the same time, be sure to ask about all aspects of the respondent that you want to predict or use as explanatory variables later.

At this point, you should know the things you want to know about the respondent, but how do you form those into questions? Although it may seem premature, the first thing to ask yourself is what you will do with the answers to each question when you have collected all your data. You should not only know that you will use the data but also how you will actually analyze it. First, it is often helpful to match each question in your survey with the specific hypothesis you want to test, which involves a variable generated by that question. If a question cannot be matched to any hypothesis you have in mind, then you may consider removing that question from the survey. Second, for each question, it may be helpful to draw up an analysis plan for the variable generated by that question, indicating the specific type of analysis that will involve that variable.

This does not mean that you cannot ultimately explore other analytical options, but you should have some plan for each variable at the outset. If you can't come up with any meaningful type of analysis that involves the variable generated by a question, that is an indication that you might want to eliminate that question from the survey.

One way to determine whether a variable will ultimately be helpful is to create a set of *mock* or *dummy tables*. These tables may appear in your report or article, in which you put in some plausible values. The process of drafting mock tables helps you clarify your research questions and hypotheses because you will only be able to create a mock table if you are clear about what you are looking for in your variables. Mock tables also clarify whether you need each variable for your study. A common practice is to include plausible but extreme values in mock tables. This allows you to see if you would really use the data if they came out in a way you did not predict. If you don't see a variable in your mock tables or if you see a variable in a mock table that you do not find useful, you should consider removing the variable from your survey instrument.

The type of analysis you expect to apply will largely determine the way you will ask the questions. The data you need to construct a table is not necessarily the same as the data you need to test for differences between means or to build statistical regression models. Decide what you want to accomplish before you begin crafting questions.

### *Personal Networks and Social Support: Comparing Two Ethnic Groups in Southern California*

Thomas Schweizer, Michael Schnegg, and Susanne Berzborn (1998) collected personal network data from 91 respondents in Costa Mesa, an ethnically diverse town in Southern California. They asked a set of questions about egos that covered basic information such as the respondent's ethnicity, gender, age, marital status, occupation, and length of residence in Costa Mesa. This information was used to compare the characteristics of core personal networks and social support across different sociodemographic groups and different ethnicities. The authors focused on two ethnic groups of respondents, Anglos and Hispanics, and used the question about occupation to calculate the score of each ego on an occupational prestige scale. They found that personal networks and social support varied between egos of different ethnicity, gender, marital status, and occupational prestige class. Personal networks were much more local (concentrated within Costa Mesa) for Hispanics than for Anglos. Marital status and occupational prestige were important too, with married egos and egos in low-prestige jobs showing more social ties within the same town. Ethnic composition and gender composition of the personal networks changed across ethnicities and genders of respondents, respectively. Both Anglos and Hispanics had most social ties within their own ethnic group, and respondents mentioned more alters in their own gender. The authors concluded that, when considering strong ties of social support, Anglos and Hispanics live in ethnically segregated social worlds. Hispanic personal networks are based on kin, including extended family, while Anglos obtain social support from a mixed circle of associates, including relatives, friends, and neighbors.

## 5.2 LEVELS OF MEASUREMENT

The kind of analysis you can do with your variables is first affected by their *level of measurement*. Put simply, measurement is the description of a characteristic of observed units (e.g., of people) through numbers, and it always implies an act of differentiating and classifying units. The level or scale of measurement of a variable is the type of classification of observed units determined by that variable. There are four levels of measurement—nominal, ordinal, interval, and ratio. As will become clear, each level of measurement implies a different way in which observed units are distinguished and classified. As a consequence, levels of measurement determine the kind of mathematical operations a variable is amenable to, and therefore they have different limitations and advantages for your analysis.

*Nominal measures* (also called qualitative measures) are derived from questions whose possible responses form a set of mutually exclusive and exhaustive *categories* that have no inherent ranking. A typical example is the marital status question:

What is your marital status?

1 – Married

2 – Widowed

3 – Divorced/separated

4 – Never married

A nominal variable is generated by a multiple-choice question in which each choice must exclude all other choices (mutually exclusive) and all possible choices must be represented (exhaustive). You will normally use numbers in your dataset to represent each category or choice, with a label indicating the meaning of the number (e.g., 1=Married, 2=Widowed, 3=Divorced/separated, 4=Never married). With nominal data, however, the numbers are merely placeholders that represent a response category. They do not have any inherent meaning because there is no meaningful rank order of the categories; for example, you can't say that the category Married is "greater than" or "less than" Widowed. Therefore, you can represent the labels with any set of numbers, and that will not affect the results of the analysis. You can set 1=Married and 2=Widowed or 2=Married and 1=Widowed, with no consequences for the analysis.

Nominal data are typically analyzed using *frequencies*, the number and proportion of the respondents that chose each response category. The relationship between nominal variables is usually analyzed using cross-tabulations with a *significance test*, such as a *chi-square* test, which indicates how likely it is that the cross-tabulation frequencies in the table and the relationship they indicate between the variables are merely due to chance.

*Ordinal measures* (also called rank) have the same qualities as nominal measures, with the added attribute that the numbers representing the data do have rank order. Ordinal and nominal variables are also often called "categorical." Ordinal questions ask the respondent to rank something about them. A typical ordinal question, included in the 2014 American General Social Survey, is the following:

Do you agree that homosexual couples have the right to marry one another?

1 – I strongly agree

2 – I agree

3 – I neither agree nor disagree

4 – I disagree

5 – I strongly disagree

In social science, ordinal questions are often items of a *scale*, that is, a series of related questions used to measure a single concept. For example, a researcher may want to measure depression in respondents. Depression is a complex mental condition that cannot be captured with a single question, but it is more effectively measured with a scale. Several depression scales have been proposed, such as the Beck Depression Inventory (BDI), which consists of a set of items with answer choices ranging from 0 to 3, such as the following:

Please pick the statement that best describes the way you have been feeling during the past two weeks.

0 – I do not feel sad.

1 – I feel sad.

2 – I am sad all the time and I can't snap out of it.

3 – I am so sad and unhappy that I can't stand it.

You can see that a value of 1 means the respondent is more sad than if he or she picks 0, a value of 2 represents more sadness than 1, and so on. However, a value of 2 does not necessarily mean being twice as sad as 1, and the difference between the levels of sadness 1 and 0 is not necessarily the same as the difference between the levels 3 and 2. One person's evaluation of a level 2 of sadness may not be the same as another's, so distances between numbers are not meaningful and we cannot subtract values from each other. In other words, while we can say that the difference between 3 meters and 1 meter is 2 meters, it does not make sense to say that, in the ordinal variable above, the difference between a degree 3 and a degree 1 of sadness is 2 degrees of sadness. The data are mutually exclusive and exhaustive, and they have rank, but the numbers do not have an equal and meaningful distance between them.

Typically, researchers analyze ordinal data using frequencies and cross-tabulations as well. Because ordinal data share the same qualities as nominal data, this kind of analysis is fine. There is also a set of statistical analyses designed specifically for ordinal data in a cross-tabulation, such as Kendall's tau coefficient, a measure of the association between two ordinal variables. Although sometimes researchers use ordinal data in statistical procedures designed for interval-level data (to be described next), this should always be done with caution.

The third level of measurement is *interval*. Interval data have the same qualities as nominal and ordinal, with the added characteristics that the distance between two consecutive numbers is meaningful and equal. As a consequence, you can subtract numbers in an interval measure. Perhaps the clearest example of this is temperature in Fahrenheit degrees. The distance between 91°F and 90°F is 1°F, the same as the difference between 41°F and 40°F. Subtractions are meaningful, so you can say that the rise in temperature from 20°F to 60°F is the same as the rise from 40°F to 80°F. Therefore, while with ordinal measures we can only rank observations, with interval scales we can both rank *and* quantify the magnitude of difference between two observations.

Unlike ratio measures, however, interval scales have no *true* zero. The zero in interval measures is arbitrarily defined, and it does not indicate the true *absence* of a quantity. For example, 0°F does not mean an absence of heat, whereas for spatial distance in meters (a ratio measure), 0 meters means an absence of distance. Consequently, ratio and proportions are not meaningful with interval measures. For example, it is not meaningful to state that 40°F is half as hot as 80°F, or 80° divided by 2. Whenever the zero does not indicate the absence of a quantity, you are looking at an interval measure. Some interval measures in the social sciences are the time of the day and the calendar year, although the interval level of measurement is actually not very common in social research.

Describing interval data is important because most of the higher-level statistics familiar to us, such as the *t*-test, ANOVA (analysis of variance), and regression models, rely on data that are at least *interval*. Because subtraction is meaningful, interval data allow you to calculate a mean and a standard deviation. These are the fundamental building blocks of most higher-level statistics. This is also the reason some people treat ordinal data as interval.

The last level of measurement is *ratio*. Ratio measures share all of the characteristics of nominal, ordinal, and interval data, with the added characteristic that a real zero point exists, which indicates the absence of a quantity. Ratio and interval variables are also often called "continuous." Spatial distance, age, and income are examples of ratio measures that you may find in the social sciences. Many variables in personal network research are ratio measures too. Typical personal network variables, such as the percentage of your network who are family, the number of times you saw your mother in the past year, or the density of ties in your networks, have a meaningful zero. With ratio data, ratios and proportions are meaningful, so you can make statements such as "Joe is twice as old as Tom," "Ann makes twice as much money as John," or "Jeff has three times as many relatives in his personal network as Paul." Some statistical procedures take advantage of that ability, but they are not very common. Most statistical packages treat interval and ratio data the same.

You can extract lower-level measures from higher-level measures. For example, in some cases you may want to recode age from a continuous variable with many values (typically, from 0 to 100) into a smaller set of response categories (age brackets). This is typically done, for example, to understand how other variables behave in different age brackets. In most countries, people under 18 are considered children and adolescents, those 18 to 64 are adults, and those 65 and older are seniors, who are often retired. So you might want to *recode* age into the categorical variable "Child/Adolescent, Adult, Senior" to analyze the behavior of other variables in these three groups.

### Needle-Sharing and Personal Network Correlates

Carl Latkin and colleagues (1995) conducted a study to determine the extent to which personal network characteristics explained the frequency of needle-sharing among drug users in Baltimore, Maryland. A sample of 330 respondents was interviewed at two different times, on average 5.2 months apart. Respondents were asked to list people they had known at least a month who fit into one of six support domains, such as material assistance or socializing, and they were also asked if each was a drug user. A number of questions about ego were posed, with a special focus on HIV-related behaviors. In particular, respondents were asked about the number of times they had shared a needle and the number of times they had cleaned it (ratio variables in both cases). Respondents who reported sharing needles tended to have larger drug networks and higher density of the total personal network. Lower frequency of cleaning needles was associated with needle-sharing in public places, such as bathrooms and parks.

Similarly, you may want to treat an ordinal variable as a nominal variable. Researchers often analyze ordinal data using the *top-box* approach, where they examine the percentage of respondents who answered at particular levels—for instance, going back to the ordinal question example presented earlier, the percentage of respondents who "Agree" or "Strongly agree" that homosexual couples should have the right to marry one another. To do this, you recode the original ordinal variable into a nominal, dichotomous variable that equals 1 if the respondent answered "Agree" or "Strongly agree," 0 otherwise. You then calculate the proportion of 1's in the new variable.

## 5.3 WORDING A QUESTION

### Common Mistakes in Wording Questions

Now that you know about the types of questions you can ask, let's turn to the way you actually word them. Several issues require consideration in crafting questions. First, it's important to make sure that your question is *valid*. This means the question measures what you think it measures. For example, asking respondents how many days they jog during the week is not a valid measure of exercise because there are many other ways to exercise. Your questions must measure the concept you have in mind as closely as possible.

Invalid questions can be crafted in many ways, a couple of which we have touched on already. Categorical questions are valid only if their response categories are mutually exclusive. A common mistake is to use ranges, such as income ranges, where the same number appears in more than one response category and categories overlap. In Figure 5.1A, a respondent making $40,000 could pick category 2 or 3. This is an example of a categorical question whose response categories are *not* mutually exclusive. When determining numeric ranges for categorical questions, you should also be aware that respondents tend to answer with some numbers more than others, a behavior known as *heaping*. These numbers tend to be divisible by 10 or 5.

In addition to being mutually exclusive, response categories for nominal or ordinal questions also need to be exhaustive. In Figure 5.1B, the response categories do not include all possible choices. This forces the respondent to either skip the question or use a category that is incorrect. The option "Other (Please specify)" is a common way to handle this problem, providing the respondent with the ability to write in an open-ended response.

You should also be careful not to make questions too long or wordy, and you should avoid jargon that might be unknown to respondents. It is quite common for experts to be overly concerned that the survey question represents all the issues currently debated among their colleagues. For example, researchers who want to know if the public will support a new vaccine for children may want to craft a question that includes all of the information debated by epidemiologists. However, respondents are not colleagues. They may not understand a complex and lengthy question, and almost certainly, they will not examine it with the intensity of those who crafted it. In general, survey questions should have no more than three sentences and ideally just a single sentence. Exceptions to this rule should be rare.

Try not to mix more than one concept in your question; otherwise you may end up with a question that is *double-barreled*. Figure 5.1C is a good example of this problem. In such a case, you will not really know what the respondent is rating. The question refers

<table>
<tr>
<td>A</td>
<td>What is your income?<br>1. $20,000<br>2. $20,000–$40,000<br>3. $40,000–$60,000<br>4. $60,000–$80,000<br>5. $80,000–$100,000<br>6. $100,000+</td>
<td>B</td>
<td>Where do you get most of your medical advice?<br>1. My doctor<br>2. TV<br>3. Friends<br>4. Family members</td>
</tr>
<tr>
<td>C</td>
<td colspan="3">Please rate your satisfaction with the amount and kind of care you received while you were in the hospital.<br>1. Very satisfied<br>2. Satisfied<br>3. Neither satisfied nor dissatisfied<br>4. Dissatisfied<br>5. Very dissatisfied</td>
</tr>
</table>

**FIGURE 5.1.** (A) Example of a question whose response categories are not mutually exclusive. (B) Example of a question whose response categories are not exhaustive. (C) Example of a double-barreled question.

to both the amount and kind of care—two different aspects. The respondent could have received a great deal of care but not the right kind of care.

Avoid questions that are *leading*; that is, questions that hint to the respondent that they should answer in a particular way. This admonition may sound obvious, but it is easy to let your own opinions creep into the construction of a question. Remember, you are measuring the attitudes, behaviors, and conditions of a population. You want to know their true responses, not a mirroring of your own opinions and not a reflection of what *you* believe are the attitudes, behaviors, and conditions of that population. Also, try to avoid constructing questions to be "politically correct." Survey questionnaires are an instrument of measurement, not a testament to your beliefs. If your theory suggests that a question should be asked in a particular way, do not worry about the opinions of your peers regarding the way you ask it. (This concern among researchers is more common than you might think!)

Sometimes researchers ask unreasonable questions. In general, respondents who agree to be interviewed want to be helpful. They will try to answer any question you ask. However, be careful not to put respondents in a position of answering unreasonable questions. Some common examples include asking respondents about behaviors that occurred over a long period of time ("How many times did you eat out over the last three years?"), behaviors that occurred too long ago ("How often did you go out during the first year of your marriage?"), or financial questions they may not have accurate answers to ("How much was your taxable income last year, after all deductions?"). Also, be wary of asking respondents their opinions about a current event or debate without first finding out if they're familiar with it, and possibly asking them to rate their level of familiarity. Not all people follow current events.

Along the same lines, most questions should allow the respondent to reply, "Don't know" or "Refuse." Sometimes, respondents simply do not understand a question. Allowing them to answer, "Don't know," can be informative to you as a researcher, letting you know they do not understand a concept well enough to answer. Similarly, some respondents do not want to answer certain questions, such as their age and income. Institutional Review Boards (also called IRBs and human subjects review boards) and Research Ethics Committees are units within universities and government agencies that make sure you recognize the rights of respondents. They typically require you to let the respondent refuse to answer questions they do not want to answer. We'll talk more about ethical issues of this type in Chapter 14.

Most Questionnaire Authoring Software that lets you program survey questions includes some form of *skip logic*. The purpose of skip logic is to reduce respondent burden by skipping questions that are irrelevant based on previous answers. For example, you don't want to ask a respondent without children "How old is your first child?" Skip logic is also very important for the integrity of your data. It prevents respondents from providing answers to questions that do not pertain to them. Once your data are collected and you are working with them in a statistical package, it becomes difficult to sort out this kind of mistake. Skip logic lets you avoid these mistakes in the first place. Table 5.1 summarizes the general principles to follow and the common mistakes to avoid when writing survey questions.

**TABLE 5.1. General Principles and Common Mistakes to Keep in Mind When Wording Survey Questions**

1. Questions capture the *general concept* you want to measure (e.g., physical exercise). They shouldn't focus on a single, specific aspect of it (e.g., jogging).
2. Response categories are *mutually exclusive*, not overlapping.
3. Response categories are *exhaustive* of all possible responses you might collect.
4. Some response categories do not *tend to attract responses* more than the others (e.g., this is referred to as *heaping*).
5. Questions are *not too wordy* (ideally, one to three sentences long).
6. Questions are *not double-barreled* (i.e., they don't ask about two different things at once).
7. Questions are *not leading* (i.e., they don't suggest the response that should be given).
8. Questions do not ask for information *the respondent can't reasonably know* (e.g., not too much detail, not about events/situations too far in the past).
9. Questions should have a *"don't know"* option.
10. Questions are *consistent with previous answers* the respondent provided in the survey (use skip logic).

## Using Standardized Questions

In many cases, it is a good idea to borrow existing questions from widely used surveys. By using standardized questions when possible, your results can more easily be compared to findings from existing studies, and you can be more confident that your questions are valid and reliable. Topics such as depression, smoking behavior, or acculturation have long been studied in different disciplines, so standard survey instruments exist for them. In our personal network study on immigrant acculturation in Spain, for example, depression was measured using the short form of the Beck Depression Inventory (see Section 5.2). To measure smoking behavior, we used a question from the Behavioral Risk Factor Surveillance System implemented by the Centers for Disease Control and Prevention. To measure obesity, we asked for height and weight so that we could calculate a body mass index (BMI), a standard measure to assess weight problems.

Sometimes standardized questions exist about the variables you want to measure, but in practice, you have to adapt them to your population, or they might not be appropriate for your respondents. For example, in the acculturation study, we needed to measure a number of demographic variables that are known to affect acculturation as well as personal networks. Although standard ways of asking many demographic questions exist (particularly from the U.S. Census and related surveys such as the Current Population Survey), some of them do not make much sense in the case of migrants. For instance, many migrants are undocumented; therefore, standard questions about income were difficult or impossible for them to answer.

To measure other concepts, we had to *readapt* standardized questions to the specific characteristics of our population. One aim of the acculturation project was to test whether personal network measures of acculturation explain more variability than standard acculturation scales in use. Therefore, we had to collect a standard acculturation scale on the respondents. Acculturation scales are a series of questions used to capture the abstract and complex concept of acculturation. They are typically designed for the specific language and geography of a migrant group, such as Mexicans residing in the United States. We needed to use an acculturation scale, but by their very nature none are intended for use across languages and geographies. Moreover, no existing acculturation scale is designed for Moroccan migrants to Spain, one of the populations in our study. As a consequence, we were forced to modify an existing scale. The most widely used acculturation scale is the Acculturation Rating Scale for Mexican Americans (ARSMA-II; Cuellar, Arnold, & Maldonado, 1995). The ARSMA-II consists of 30 questions covering a wide range of topics such as the tendency to speak Spanish more than English, food preferences, ethnic identity of friends, and language preferences for reading, viewing TV and other media. Each item is phrased as a statement (e.g., "I write letters in Spanish"), and the respondent evaluates the statement using a set of five responses (e.g., Extremely Often, Very Often, Moderately, Not Very Much, Not at All). This is a typical question format called a *Likert scale*. With Likert questions, respondents rate their level of agreement to a statement.

Because the ARSMA-II is not designed for cross-cultural purposes, we faced problems in adapting it to certain cultural groups and geographies in our study. For example, one of the ARSMA-II items is "I like Spanish TV"; another is "I like English TV." These items were crafted to be asked of Mexican immigrants in the United States, where there's a choice between Spanish and English TV. In our study, one of the immigrant groups was Senegalese migrants in Spain, and many of our Senegalese respondents spoke a language called Wolof. In adapting the ARSMA-II to this group, the obvious modification to the TV-related items would be "I like Wolof TV" and "I like Spanish TV." However, this was problematic, as Wolof TV is not available in Spain. Moreover, while the ethnic majority in the United States speaks a single language, English, the ethnic majority in our field site, Catalonia in Spain, spoke two different languages, Spanish and Catalan.

## Open-Ended Questions

Some people opt to use open-ended questions. Although there is nothing wrong with this kind of question, they tend to be overused in surveys. An open-ended question is justified in a survey in two specific situations. The most common circumstance in a survey occurs when you have no idea what the response categories should be. You may be measuring a concept that has never been measured before. An open-ended response allows you to code the responses later based on the answers you get back. However, coding open-ended responses into a fixed set of response categories is time consuming and prone to error. Therefore, if you know what many of the response categories will be, you are better off mixing closed-ended responses with open-ended responses. This is typically done by providing some fixed response categories for a question, but adding "Other (please specify)" as a final category. If respondents are not satisfied with any of the response categories provided, they'll provide their own category in the text box:

In which of the following places do you spend most time hanging out with your friends? (select only one)

1 – Somebody's house

2 – Bar/restaurant/club

3 – Mall

4 – Park

5 – Other (please specify): ____________________

The other circumstance in which you may want open-ended responses is when you want to incorporate a qualitative analysis approach or when you want to use the results as quotes in your report or article. In both cases, the open-ended option is well justified.

If a personal network study contains a semistructured interview module with many open-ended questions, you will probably record the narration and transcribe and code it afterward with a program different from the one you use (if you use software) for collecting the data about the network. If the open-ended questions form part of a survey, just be aware of the potential downside of using open-ended responses and having to enter open-ended data after collection. In many cases, survey researchers collect open-ended data but never use them because they prove difficult to recode.

## CHAPTER SUMMARY

This chapter dealt with common issues and problems in formulating questions about respondents (egos), which typically constitute Module 1 of a personal network survey. We considered what types of questions are relevant, important, and appropriate to ask respondents. The other topics covered in the chapter apply to all the modules of a personal network survey—not just Module 1: how to identify the right questions, knowing the levels of measurement produced by your question, and wording survey items appropriately. These are very important topics when designing any survey, not just personal network surveys (see Further Reading in this chapter).

### FURTHER READING

Bernard, H. R. (2006). *Research methods in anthropology: Qualitative and quantitative approaches.* Lanham, MD: AltaMira Press.

Fowler, F. J., Jr. (2013). *Survey research methods.* Los Angeles: SAGE.

Latkin, C., Mandell, W., Vlahov, D., Knowlton, A., Oziemkowska, M., & Celentano, D. (1995). Personal network characteristics as antecedents to needle-sharing and shooting gallery attendance. *Social Networks, 17*(3), 219–228.

Moore, D. S., McCabe, G. P., & Craig, B. A. (2009). *Introduction to the practice of statistics* (6th ed.). New York: Freeman.

Schweizer, T., Schnegg, M., & Berzborn, S. (1998). Personal networks and social support in a multiethnic community of southern California. *Social Networks, 20*(1), 1–21.

**6**

# Delineating Personal Networks

## *Alter Elicitation*

---

### *What Is This Chapter About?*

This chapter describes ways to delineate personal networks that are appropriate for your research (Module 2 of personal network research). The chapter starts with reflections on the people who make up a personal network and the important issue of accuracy when reporting social ties (Sections 6.1 and 6.2, respectively). Next, Section 6.3 focuses on network boundaries and how to make decisions about what portions of the personal network are of greatest interest to you. Section 6.4 provides an in-depth review of six types of name generators for eliciting intentional subsets of personal networks (affective, role-related, exchange, interactive, domain-specific or contextual, and freelist), and discusses when and how to use them. Section 6.5 presents strategies for eliciting a random subset of personal networks, and Section 6.6 discusses additional qualifiers often used in personal network studies to refine the process of alter elicitation. Finally, Section 6.7 makes recommendations about how to administer the chosen name generators.

---

## 6.1 WHAT IS A NAME GENERATOR?

The last two chapters described the first steps of a personal network study, which are very similar to any social science study. For the most part, personal network studies are just a special form of research, and so all the principles of social science research are important. In this chapter, we will discuss the first aspect of personal network data collection that makes it different from other kinds of social science research, namely, the way that we get respondents to tell us whom they know.

This is not an easy task because, as we indicated in Chapter 1, there are no clear boundaries for a personal network. In principle, a personal network includes everyone a person knows, and they can live anywhere. People have a great diversity of relationships, ranging from very intimate and enduring ties to people individuals barely know or people they only recently met. Personal networks include hundreds or even a few thousand people (see Chapters 2 and 10), so it would not be feasible to create an exhaustive list of someone's alters. In the past, some researchers have tried to do just that. Jeremy Boissevain (1974) for example, opted to turn to two Maltese teachers he already knew as informants (Pietru, a village teacher with whom he had worked, and Cecil, a city teacher he met one year earlier). Each made out lists of all people over 14 years of age whom he knew (1,751, and 638 persons, respectively). After all acquaintances were listed, the informants provided information about social background, number of shared role relations, frequency of contact, and so on. Obviously, this is an impractical, expensive, and invasive way to collect data beyond case studies. It is also questionable to what extent each of these people has a real effect on individuals' lives.

Typically, no predefined list exists to tell us which people make up someone's network. Some researchers have suggested using lists of email contacts, phone contacts, or contacts on social-networking sites, such as Facebook and Google+, to represent individuals' personal networks. Although those are valid representations of those social contexts, they may not be representative of the subset of the network that you are interested in, and they are hardly representative of the entire social context within which most people live. Although the people you interact with through your job or university are very likely people you email, your family and friends are often not people you would email. You may email them occasionally, but most people still maintain contact with a large portion of their network in person or by telephone. By limiting the personal network to email contacts, you are selecting a particular subset of the personal network. This does not mean that it is not a valid social context to study, but it is very specific. Also, many populations we tend to study as social scientists, such as economically disadvantaged groups, may not use email.

Social media sites are yet another social context for which a list of network members can be obtained with relative ease. Many people certainly have online contact with

### *Contact Lists in Phones and Personal Networks*

Markku Lonkila (2004) analyzed his own personal phone notebook and mobile phone contacts from 1993 to 2000 in order to understand how these resources might be used in personal network analysis. He noted that some people who were included in these lists did not make sense as part of his personal network, while others were not included, even though they were part of his personal network. The self-analysis of the lists was instructive because it suggested that phone notebook lists may not be representative of the personal network. Comparisons with mobile phone contacts suggest that these may be more reliable representations, particularly with access to the number and length of phone calls.

many of their important alters. Nevertheless, with few exceptions, even those who have large numbers of alters on social-networking sites also have alters who are not on those sites. In 2011, in the Pew Research Center's Internet and American Life Project, Keith Hampton and colleagues (Hampton, Sessions Goulet, Rainie, & Purcell, 2011) estimated that Facebook users maintain contact on the site with about half of the people in their lives. Furthermore, about 7% of the online contacts were people whom the users had never met in person. Social media sites allow you to selectively follow and befriend people you know or unfollow and unfriend them. Another issue is that people on social-networking sites may exhibit behavior that is quite different from their behavior in person or over the phone. Some people assume different personalities online, simply because they can. Again, while studying this social context may be relevant for some research, for example, for studies investigating online sociability, it is often not a substitute for the social contexts we as personal network researchers are interested in. Just because they are easily available does not make them substitutes, although they can be valuable complementary information.

For all these reasons, if we want to study personal networks, we have to ask individuals to identify the people with whom they have the type of social ties we are interested in. When we do conduct such a study, we usually do not try to capture the whole personal network. Rather, we either estimate specific characteristics of the network without generating an exhaustive list of network members (see Chapter 10) or we focus on a specific subset of the larger network that is of relevance to our research question (this chapter). In most cases, this is an intentional subset. For example, we may only be interested in the people who are important to the respondents, the people who help them out in certain situations, the people with whom they interacted in the last week, or the people who fulfill certain roles for the respondents, depending on our research questions. In some cases, we are truly interested in that larger (total) personal network, and then we may try to get a subset of alters that is a random representation of the wider network. As each subset may refer to partially or entirely different people in one's personal network, it is important to think about what information to extract and how to extract it. This chapter addresses how to do that.

## 6.2 HOW SOCIAL TIES ARE STORED IN MEMORY AND HOW THEY ARE RECALLED

Before we turn to the questions we can ask respondents about their social ties, we should return to an important issue: Can respondents accurately report whom they know? We need to consider this issue so that we can construct instruments for eliciting personal networks that minimize bias in reporting. As we already indicated in Chapter 3, a self-reported network is a cognitive representation of the network, which may sometimes diverge from what we could call the "actual" or "behavioral" network. When asked to give a list of people they know, respondents mention those whom they perceive to be part of their network. As discussed in Chapter 3, that is often fine, as many individuals' decisions are based on the perceived rather than the actual network, but other times we want to measure the behavioral networks. We must therefore be aware of the cognitive schemas that can affect individual responses and decide whether or not we should worry about that.

As is true of any other information, the names of people we know are stored in our memories in a structured way. Human memory makes use of organizational structures, or schemata, to store as much information as possible, so that it can be extracted efficiently. Alters are stored in our memories in clusters of social groups, contexts, or roles, and "*chunked substructures*" (Brashears & Quintane, 2014, 117), rather than, for example, on the basis of individual attributes such as gender, age, or education (Brashears, 2013; Fiske, 1995). Furthermore, our mental maps represent long-term social structures, or routinized ties, rather than actual interactions (e.g., Freeman & Romney, 1987).

Because of the way our network members are stored in memory, it is easier for respondents to list, for example, their family members (or anyone within a particular context or social group) than it is to list all people they know who have a university education (or another characteristic that can occur across all the social groups they engage with)—unless this is a relatively rare but salient quality in their network. Furthermore, as our mental maps represent routinized ties, it is more complicated for people to recall a small interaction with the waiter (especially if it is not a daily routine) than to recall recurring interactions with close colleagues. Recall problems are typically larger for network members with whom respondents feel less close, whom they see less frequently, whom they've contacted less recently (Brewer, 2000), or who are less central in their networks (Marin, 2004). Nevertheless, some researchers have found that respondents also tend to forget to name others they take for granted, like their neighbors and even their spouses (e.g., Fischer, 1982a). It may be good to sensitize interviewers to this latter problem, for example, by asking them a posteriori whether their partner also helps them with some tasks or by asking them explicitly to include them in the alter list, if that is logical for the research. Despite these findings, there is also some evidence that the number of forgotten alters is proportional to the number of recalled others, so that the number of recalled others may still be a good indication of how many people respondents could list (Brewer, 2000).

When respondents are asked to freely list any series of items (animals, food, and also people), they do so in different, typically organized ways. For animals, some may begin with domesticated animals and then move to animals in the wild. Others may begin with small animals and then move to large ones. Lists of foods may start with meats, then move to vegetables and fruits. People do not exhaust a category before they jump to another group, and they may switch between methods, but their listing typically shows some sort of organization. Listing people works more or less the same way. Studies of *freelisting*, where alters are listed by respondents as they recall them, demonstrate order effects. Many people will start by listing people who are important to them such as the partner and family, but others may start by listing the people whom they have seen most recently or whom they see in a typical week. And no matter what method of starting is used, respondents often diverge from their original strategy as names come up. They may list a family member named John, who makes them think of their friend named John, who makes them recall other friends like John. When given no specific instructions, names can be listed in a variety of ways. Although some respondents will use similar strategies, not all respondents will freelist in the same way (Unsworth, 2017).

The network-elicitation task presents an added problem for some populations. Some people often studied by social scientists, such as drug users or senior citizens, may have compromised memories, so that memory storage and name retrieval are not as efficient as they once were. Also, depending on the types of alters we want to elicit, respondents may have a difficult time remembering them. For example, we may want to study prostitutes in the social context of their clients as a way of understanding sexually

### *Probing*

Carl Latkin and his colleagues (Latkin, Kuramoto, Davey-Rothwell, & Tobin, 2010) investigated whether the personal network structure was associated with HIV risk behavior among more than 800 injection drug users. The researchers delineated the drug networks of respondents by asking them the following question: "Now, I am going to ask you about another group of people, those who you do drugs with." ("Do drugs with" was defined as being in the same room when using drugs.) "These individuals may be close friends or casual acquaintances. Who are the people that you do drugs with? These might be people you have listed before, or they could be new names. (This question pertains to all drugs, not just injection drugs, but it does not include alcohol or marijuana.)"

They used a list of probes to have respondents remember more members of their networks, starting with the unspecific probe. "Is there anyone else you can think of?" Specific probes included the following questions:

- "When you use drugs with [name of alter], who else is usually there?"
- "Who do you consider your running buddy?"
- "Who did you do drugs with last month?"
- "How about three months ago, who were you doing drugs with then?"
- "Think about the place where you copped last week and the people who you were with. Who are the people that you regularly buy or use drugs with?"
- "Think about all the different places where you used last week. These might be friends' places, abandoned houses, your place, or galleries. Was there anyone there who you do drugs with on a regular basis?"
- "Sometimes the people you list are not available; they may be sick, locked up, or just not around. So can you think of anyone else that you did drugs with in the last couple of months?"

transmitted disease. In all of these cases, names will almost certainly not be retrieved without recall errors.

Apart from the cognitive schemas and related recall problems that are specific for lists of social relationships or lists in general, network surveys also share all the concerns of common survey research. Respondents can misinterpret questions. For example, they can misunderstand the minimum requirements for listing a network member. They may vary in the number of names they list as a function of their willingness to cooperate or their fatigue. The size of the elicited network may also be influenced by the qualities of the interviewer (Marsden, 2003) and by the interview mode.

When you design a network survey, you need to try to minimize these possible biases. It is advisable to ask solid, practical questions that minimize distortions and to pre- and pilot-test your survey thoroughly. If you make use of interviewers, careful interviewer training helps to standardize the administration of the survey and to avoid interviewer bias (Marsden, 2003). With respect to recall problems, you may consider repeating a question at a later stage or use multiple questions to activate different areas in our cognitive schemas. You may also consider implementing specific and nonspecific ("Anyone else?") prompts (Brewer, 2000). In order to increase cooperativeness and attention, researchers should endeavor to keep respondent burden within acceptable limits. This effort involves keeping the number of questions as low as possible and making the survey attractive, which can be challenging in a personal network survey, as we will see in the following chapters. One way to increase the attractiveness of a survey is to introduce greater participation in the ways of eliciting alters (more on this later). As a control, it is a good idea to have interviewers rate the cooperativeness of respondents at the end of the interview or to indicate the parts of the survey they didn't understand well. This information can later be used to disqualify a case or a response to a question, if necessary.

## 6.3 DEFINING THE BOUNDARIES OF PERSONAL NETWORKS

With the cognitive schemas and recall issues in mind, we will now explore different ways of eliciting lists of network members from respondents, using surveys or interviews. The most prevalent method for compiling these lists is the *name generator*, which is a question that aims to elicit a list of names of alters with whom the respondent has a certain type of relationship. Researchers either use a single name generator or multiple name generators to elicit such a list. The questions typically provide a specific criterion for defining a relationship, and respondents are often asked to recall as many people as they can who fit the description. Sometimes however, the number of people respondents are asked to recall is fixed, and other times upper or lower limits to this number are established (see Section 6.6).

Typically, researchers are not interested in all the relationships an individual has, but rather in a specific subset of ties relevant to the research questions. Therefore, to develop our name generator(s), we should first articulate our research questions. If, say, we wish to collect data in order to test whether personal networks have an effect on a certain outcome variable, we should think about how that effect may take place (see Chapter 3). What social mechanism produces this effect? For example, if we study feelings of loneliness among the elderly, we may wish to find out with whom respondents feel particularly close and to ask a bit more broadly about people they socialize with rather frequently. It is not necessary that they inform us about all the people they know by name or all the people they have interacted with in the past two years. Rather, it would be sufficient that they limit themselves to the set of ties that are most important to them or with whom they socialize frequently.

If, however, we study starting entrepreneurs and we wish to predict whether a startup will survive the initial phase, it may be less informative to focus on close personal relationships. Entrepreneurs can have a large circle of good friends and a loving family, but prior research might have shown that what really counts for running a business is whether some of them, or others they don't feel close with at all, are willing and able to help the person out with this endeavor. Chances of survival may increase when respondents have someone who is willing to help out in the enterprise for free, when respondents can rely on neighboring enterprises to share some resources, when the entrepreneur's soccer club mates all spread information about the startup, or when an acquaintance happens to be an accountant. So for this study, we would rather focus on the people who have provided or who could provide different types of help (labor, advice, material help, spreading information, etc.) to our respondents than on people they feel close with, or we could combine the two. We may translate these different types of help in different name generators that give us insight into the informal support that the entrepreneur receives or that is available to him or her.

We might also be interested in the extent to which broader interaction patterns in society are structured by, say, socioeconomic class. If not only the core networks of individuals but also their wider personal environments are characterized by homophily in terms of class (DiPrete et al., 2011), this may have implications for people's perceptions about, say, the severity of a crisis or their trust in the government. In this case, we are interested not only in emotionally close ties, but also in weak ties, regardless of the precise exchanges that go on in these relationships. We are also not particularly interested in the consequences for the individual, so in this case, we might opt for obtaining a random selection of the alters in the larger personal network, which will give us both weak and strong ties. This method may miss out on some ties that are important for the respondent. In this case, however, it doesn't really matter, since we are interested in drawing conclusions about patterns of sociability in society at large and representation at the individual level may be a secondary issue.

Whatever your research question may be, you need to clearly define who is and who is not included in the network we are interested in. This fundamental question is called *network boundary definition* (Marsden, 1990). The boundary definition must truly represent the social context that interests you. It is very important to think about this issue because how you define the boundary of the network will determine the type of data you end up with. The definition of whose name you want to elicit must also be clear

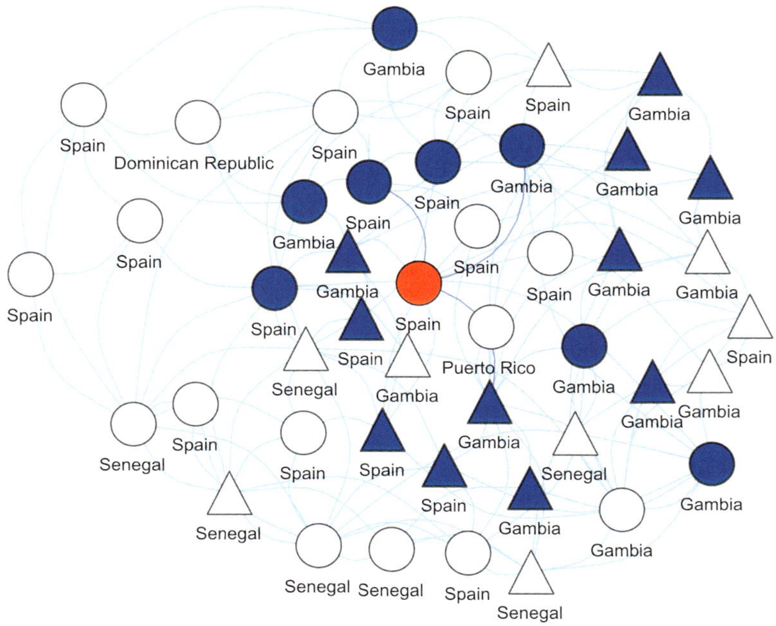


**PLATE P.1.** Personal network visualization for Mariama.

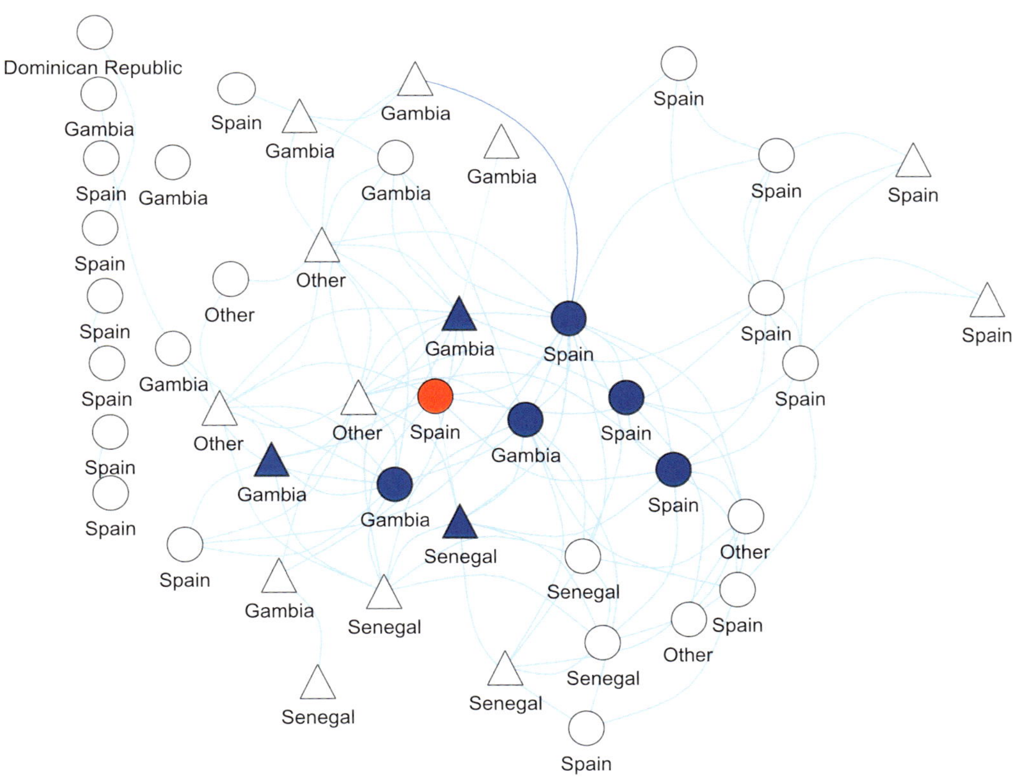


**PLATE P.2.** Personal network visualization for Awa.

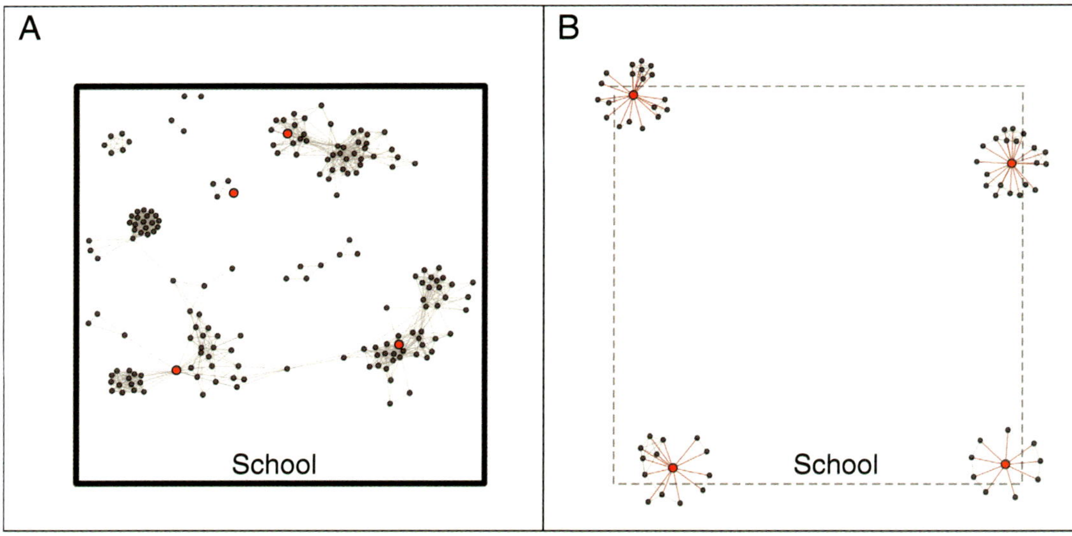


**PLATE 1.1.** Whole versus personal network approach. (A) In the whole network approach you set a boundary of a group and collect the networks among all actors within that boundary. For example, that could be the network among all students in a high school. (B) In the personal network approach, you start from focal individuals, or egos (the red nodes in the figure), and for each ego you collect the network among their contacts, or alters. You typically do not set a boundary or group to which alters must belong. If your egos are high school students, alters might be both people within the high school (e.g., other students) and people outside the high school (e.g., family or neighbors).

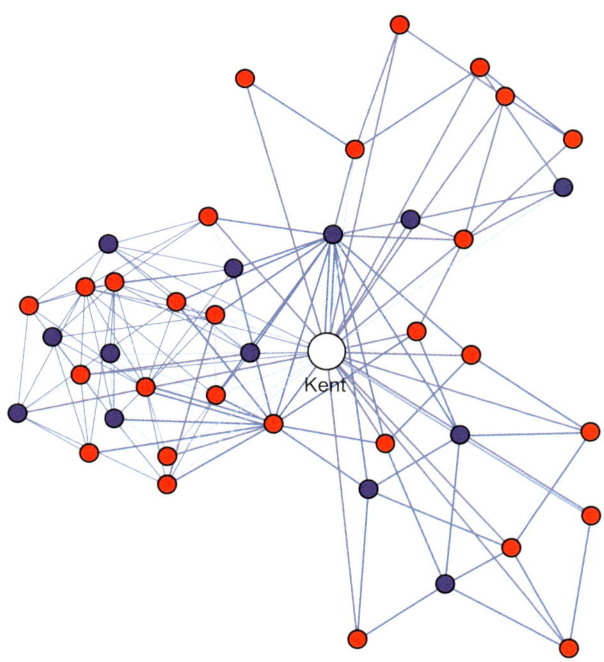


**PLATE 1.2.** A personal network visualization. Kent is the ego, while blue and red nodes are the alters. Blue nodes are men and red nodes are women in Kent's personal network. The first 12 rows and columns of this network's adjacency matrix are shown in Table 1.2.

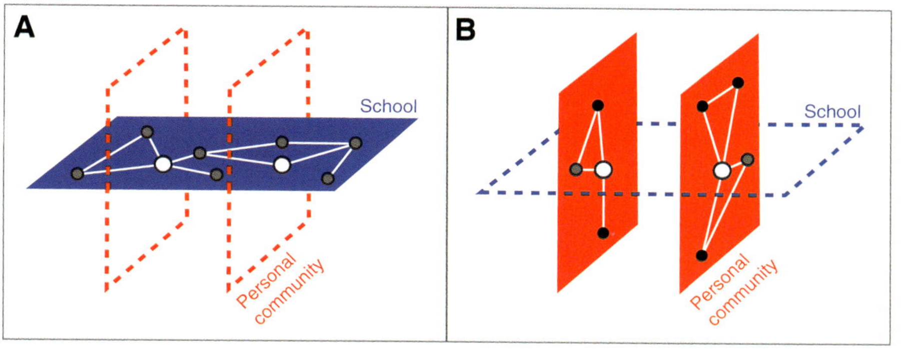


**PLATE 1.3.** Whole networks (A) and personal networks (B) as different "slices" or dimensions of social reality. White nodes are particular individuals of interest in a study. Note that the direct contacts of white nodes in the school (gray nodes in panel B) are captured in both designs as they are both part of the school and of the egos' personal communities. In panel A, the white nodes have a contact in common, while in panel B they are assumed not to share any alter or be directly connected.

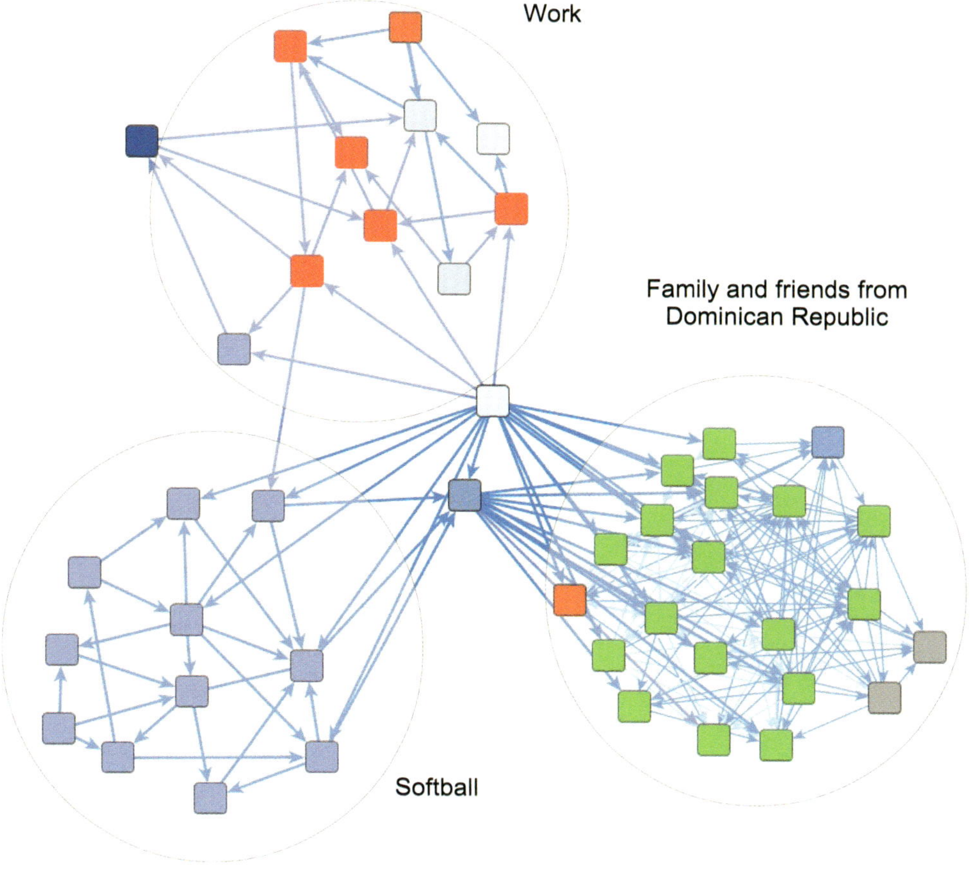


**PLATE 9.1.** Personal network of a Dominican male living in Barcelona.

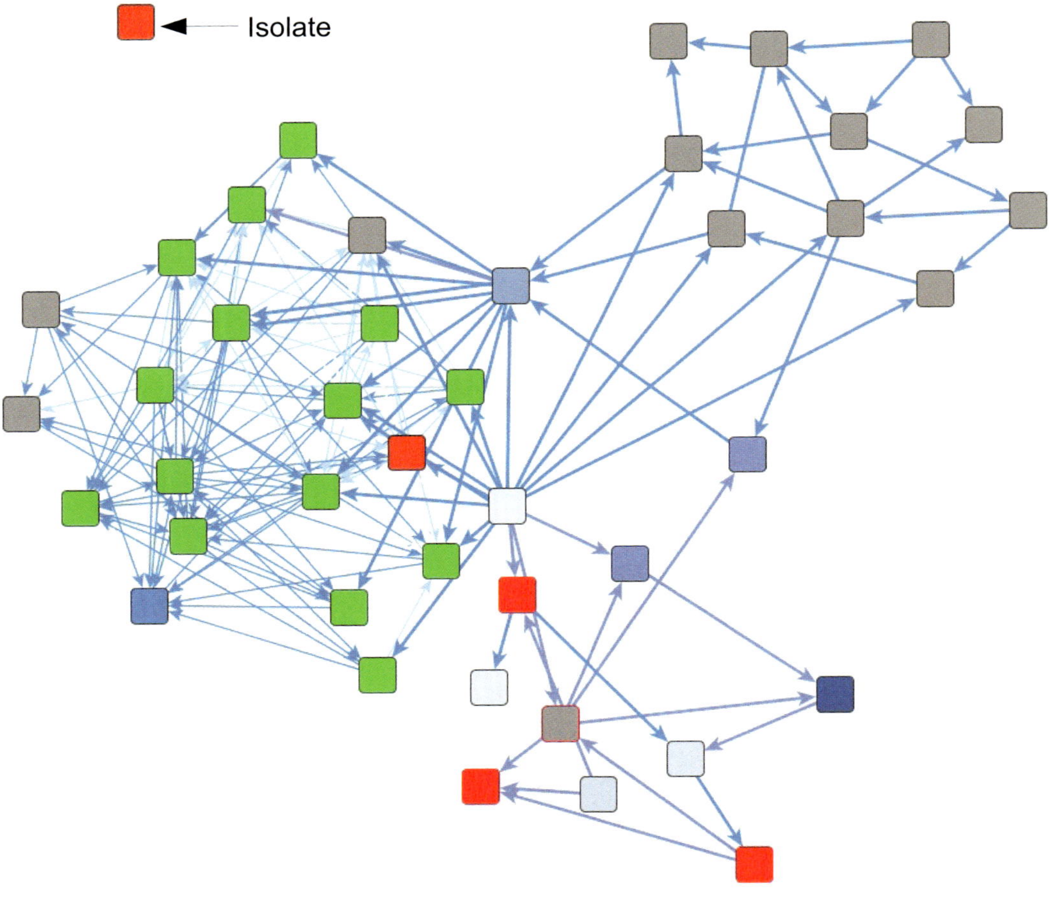


**PLATE 9.2.** Personal network of the same Dominican male of Plate 9.1 some years earlier.

and meaningful for the respondent. It must be a reasonable question. Asking someone to name all the people they called on the telephone in the past year is not reasonable. Asking IV drug users to name all the people they shared needles within the past 12 months may also be unreasonable.

In most cases, we are interested in intentional, nonrandom subsets of relationships (the closest ties, the more frequently contacted ties, the most supportive ties, and so on). We will discuss these relationships in Section 6.4. In some occasions however, we are actually interested in the entire set of social relationships, both weak and strong. While it may not be feasible to elicit a complete list of names, we may be able to draw a random sample of alters (see Section 6.5). Alternatively, if we are only interested in knowing a particular characteristic of that entire set, we may measure it without eliciting a list of names. Chapter 10 describes methods that measure a specific aspect of the personal network often without eliciting list of names. In some cases, we may also opt for methods other than name generators; these are discussed in Section 6.7. For the sake of clarity, we have treated each type of name generator as a distinct method, highlighting their strengths and weaknesses. In reality, the boundaries between the different methods are often less clear, as researchers mix methods or use them in a way that best serves their interests.

## 6.4 NAME GENERATORS FOR ELICITING INTENTIONAL (NONRANDOM) SUBSETS OF ALTERS

Researchers have defined relationships using one of four analytical approaches to delineate intentional, nonrandom subsets of network members: the affective, role, exchange, and interactive approaches. We will first describe each of these approaches, giving examples of research for each type. Subsequently, we will discuss two methods that combine different approaches to delineate larger networks, together with name generators for ties with a negative content, so-called negative ties.

### The Affective Approach

Many researchers have been interested in the personal network subset of "strong ties." In his foundational work, Mark Granovetter (1973, p. 1361) defined tie strength as "a (probably linear) combination of the amount of time, the emotional intensity, the intimacy (mutual confiding), and the reciprocal services which characterize the tie." Peter Marsden and Karen Campbell investigated various possible indicators of the concept, such as frequency and duration of contact, emotional intensity or closeness, and specific roles, and concluded that emotional closeness is the best indicator of tie strength.

The affective approach intends to elicit the names of people with whom respondents feel emotionally close, in terms of affection, trust, intimacy, or importance. It consists in asking respondents to name those people with whom they feel closest or most intimate or who are most important to them. For example, for his famous East York

Study in Toronto, Barry Wellman (1979) formulated the following name generator: Will you list here, please, the initials of the people outside your household that you feel closest to. These could be friends, neighbors or relatives. Start with the one you feel closest to, then next closest, and so on.[1] Wellman used an upper limit of six names in his study.

Another well-known and often replicated method based on the affective approach was designed by Robert Kahn and Toni Antonucci (1980) for their work on the social convoy theory (see Chapter 2). The method consists in drawing three concentric circles on a paper centered around a smaller circle with the word "You" (see Figure 6.1). Respondents are asked to look at the diagram. They are told that the three circles should be thought of as including "people who are important in your life right now" but who are not necessarily equally close. The inner circle refers to "those people to whom you feel so close that it is hard to imagine life without them." The second circle refers to "people to whom you may not feel quite that close but who are still important to you," and the outer circle, "people whom you haven't already mentioned but who are close enough and important enough in your life that they should be placed in your personal network." They are then asked to fill in the names of these people. The circle diagram provides respondents with a framework for the description of their network that is comprehensible. Using cognitive probing, researchers have shown that respondents obtain a good understanding of the hierarchical construction of the name generator (Nadoh, Podreberšek, & Hlebec, 2004). The method is highly interactive, reducing respondent burden.

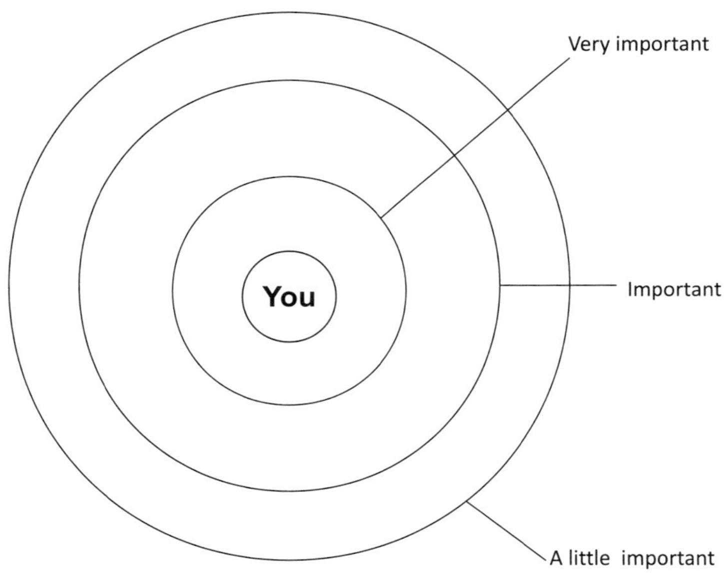


**FIGURE 6.1.** A circle diagram similar to that used by Kahn and Antonucci (1980).

[1] See *http://groups.chass.utoronto.ca/netlab/wp-content/uploads/2012/05/First-East-York-Survey.pdf*

Later research has used this approach with many variations (e.g., Bellotti, 2015; Ryan, Mulholland, & Agoston, 2014; Spencer & Pahl, 2006). For example, Laura Bernardi (2011) adapted the technique by placing two boxes outside the circles with the texts "not important at all" and "problematic (important in a negative sense)." Also, she extended the number of rings to six. Bernie Hogan and colleagues (Hogan, Carrasco, & Wellman, 2007) also used the technique for delineating personal networks with paper-and-pencil techniques, but they extended the technique to measure network structure as well (something Kahn and Antonucci did not do). For this aim, they showed a similar circle diagram to respondents and asked them to write the names of network members on sticky notes and paste them in the circles. The sticky notes allowed the researchers to reorganize the names later on with the respondents, so that alters connected with each other could be placed closer together. After the reorganization, it becomes relatively easy to draw circles around cliques of people and lines between two people who are connected. The method has also been used in qualitative research, either as described or with different colors of post-its to distinguish between different types of relationships.

The circle diagram has been implemented in the software VennMaker and the app Network Canvas for interactive computer-assisted personal interviewing to collect personal network data, including network structure (see the Appendix). In addition, Paola Tubaro and colleagues (Tubaro, Casilli, & Mounier, 2013) implemented the circle diagram in a web survey allowing self-administration, which she used in a study of girls with eating disorders who participated in online communities.

Name generators following the affective approach tend to measure relatively long-term, strong ties. They let respondents determine for themselves who is important to them, rather than making assumptions of who should and should not be a network member. This can be favorable, but for some studies it may also have the disadvantage that different people can use different criteria for inclusion. It may help to use follow-up questions to clarify what "close" or "important" means to the respondents, allowing researchers to compare the criteria that individuals use. In general, this approach yields high test–retest reliability.

## The Role Relation Approach

The role relation approach assumes that people are influenced by others who have culturally circumscribed role relationships that are accompanied by a set of norms and expectations (e.g., Broese van Groenou & van Tilburg, 1996). Examples are family members, colleagues, or church members. In this case, researchers ask respondents to name people who fulfill such roles.

For example, Eduardo Marques (2009) studied the role of personal networks for coping with urban poverty in two Brazilian cities. In a two-step name generator, he first asked respondents to list up to five names of people in each of eight spheres of sociability (family, friends, work, neighbors, religion, associations, leisure, and other spheres). In the second step, he extended the research to the second order zone by asking respondents to name, for each alter, up to three other persons the alter was associated with.

In the Framingham Heart Study, famous among social network researchers for the work of Nicholas Christakis and James Fowler (e.g., Christakis & Fowler, 2013; Fowler & Christakis, 2008), social network information was derived from the tracking sheets that respondents were asked to fill in order to keep track of them for follow-up waves of this longitudinal study. So, even if the respondents moved at some point, this formation could help the researchers track their current addresses. On the tracking sheet, respondents were asked to give the names of relatives and close friends who might be able to tell where they would be in two to four years' time, and respondents also gave their place of residence in Framingham (which could identify current neighbors within the whole network of the town) and their place of work (which could identify coworkers within the whole network). Also, the respondents gave the name of their spouse, if they had one. While the role approach was not intentionally applied to the study, the resulting data are role-dependent.

The role approach is particularly suitable for investigating social participation or social integration. If the aim is to study the supportive exchanges or interactions, the approach is less well suited. A major advantage of this approach is that our cognitive schemas make it relatively easy for us to answer this type of question. It also makes sure that a diversity of roles or spheres are studied and that the relationships are relatively stable, at least on a short-term basis. Furthermore, for many roles, people are thought to use more or less similar criteria, such that the networks are roughly comparable. A clear exception is the category of friends: research has shown that some people use far looser criteria than others (Burt, 1983). Indeed, Liz Spencer and Raymond Pahl distinguish many types of friendship, ranging from soulmates and confidants to fun friends and useful contacts (Spencer & Pahl, 2006). For other categories, no investigations have been launched to determine whether they are similarly interpreted across individuals. However, anthropologists have observed that the kinship category often includes "fictive kin" or "chosen kin" (e.g., Ibsen & Klobus, 1972): ties identified as kin that are based neither on blood nor on marriage. This category includes godparents and "aunts" and "uncles" who are close friends of the parents rather than actual relatives. So, perhaps the category of family members is not homogeneously interpreted either. Again, if such distinctions are important for the research, you can either better specify the name-generating question or add a follow-up (name interpreter) question about the precise nature of the relationship that allows you to distinguish between alters and even discard alters for analysis.

Even when people use more or less similar criteria of inclusion, however, it is questionable whether people are equally influenced by each role. In other words, the relevance of certain roles in people's networks may differ across individuals. For example, on one hand, neighbors may be more important for individuals in rural areas than for residents of large cities. Also, coworkers may be more important for people who work longer hours and who are more dependent on their coworkers in their jobs than for others. On the other hand, respondents may have important relationships with people they met through atypical relationships that have no formal role category or are difficult to predict. For example, some people have friends and acquaintances they know through other people, for example, their practitioner (Pinfold et al., 2015), the wife of a coworker, or the friend of a spouse. These people are typically not identified using a role approach.

Typically, researchers employing this approach ask about multiple roles. The use of multiple cues implies that a person can fit more than one category. For example, someone from work may also be your neighbor. Or someone you met at school may now be a member of the same club or social organization you belong to. You should therefore be careful to check for duplicate alter entries, which indicate "role multiplexity." All this means that the role approach, as all other approaches, is more suitable for some studies than for others.

## The Exchange Approach

In many investigations, it is assumed that network effects are produced through some form of exchange, flow, or transmission (e.g., flow of money, information, or control) from person to person. If that is the case, one may try to identify the subset of ties in which such exchanges take place. That is what the exchange approach is about: identifying those alters with whom certain exchanges take place.

A well-known example of this approach can be found in the classical Northern California Community Study conducted by Claude Fischer (1982a; see Section 2.1). To understand how urban life affects personal relationships, he asked approximately 1,000 respondents to nominate people with whom they exchanged certain types of support: those they could talk to about personal problems, lend them money, help them with household chores, take care of their house if they were out of town, share recreational activities, and a number of other questions. In total, there were 10 questions, including 2 questions related to roles and affection (whether the person had a partner or a best friend and who else was important to them). Respondents gave an average of 18.5 names to the set of questions: 12.8 names to the first 9 questions and 5.7 to the "anyone else who is important" probe. On average, 42% of the alters were family members (Fischer, 1982a; McCarty, Bernard, Killworth, Shelley, & Johnsen, 1997). As we already mentioned in Section 2.1, the questionnaire was replicated and adapted in other countries and settings.

The exchange approach is quite common in studies on social support and social capital (see Section 2.3). Both concepts are multidimensional. For example, social support includes emotional, instrumental, and informational support, as well as social companionship. Therefore, these network studies often use multiple name generators to cover the different dimensions (e.g., 8–12 questions in total; 2–3 questions per dimension). For example, with regard to material help, one could ask respondents who helps them with household chores or who could lend them a substantial amount of money. For emotional support, one could ask who respondents go to for advice on personal problems and important life decisions.

Researchers must adapt the instruments to the realities of the specific populations under investigation. Social support would be operationalized differently in different kinds of studies. For example, these would be the type of questions in a study about entrepreneurs (Berrou & Combarnous, 2012):

> "Who could give you financial backing in times of crisis, or for an investment, through loan or gift?"
>
> "Who could give you support in administrative or bureaucratic relationships with local institutions, to obtain favors concerning tax payments, local placement, or conflict resolution?"

Whereas these might be the kinds of questions in a study on parents of young children (Hennig, 2007):

> "If you or your child is sick, is there someone who could help you at that time? Is there someone you could contact?"

Or on injection drug users (Latkin et al., 1995):

> "Who could you talk to about issues related to drug use?"
>
> "Who would let you stay at their place?"

When asking about social support, researchers must further decide whether they focus on *available help*, which is a prospective question ("Who could/would help you with . . . ?") or on actually *mobilized help* over a certain time period (e.g., "Who has helped you with . . . in the past six months?"), which is a retrospective question. Questions about available help refer to imaginary scenarios that may never have occurred and that may show a poor fit with actual help if the need ever arises. However, if the feeling of being supported affects outcomes more than actual support, then questions about available help may be appropriate. For example, on the one hand, the feeling of having a supportive network may boost self-esteem more than the help the network has provided lately. If, on the other hand, it is the actual support that matters, questions about mobilized support are more appropriate. For example, a person's ability to cope with poverty in the last year may depend on the extent to which family members and others have really provided help during that time.

If researchers opt for focusing on actual help, they must further decide about the time frame they select. The time period specified must be long enough for the need to have occurred, yet short enough for people to remember. Some researchers also ask about satisfaction with the provided help. Other researchers distinguish between received help and help that the respondents provided to others in order to understand whether norms of reciprocity govern the exchanges. Because only the ego is asked about these exchanges, the answers may be biased by his or her perception. This explains why, on average, people tend to report that they give more help than they receive (e.g., Taylor, Mouzon, Nguyen, & Chatters, 2016).

### *Multiple Name Generators for Social Support*

The method Manuel Barrera has developed for measuring social support, the Arizona Social Support Interview Schedule (ASSIS), has become a standard. Barrera (1980) identified six types of social support:

1. *Material aid.* Providing material aid in the form of money, food, clothes, and so on
2. *Physical assistance.* Sharing tasks
3. *Intimate interaction.* Sharing or communicating about important problems and worries
4. *Guidance.* Offering advice and guidance
5. *Feedback.* Providing individuals with information about themselves
6. *Positive social interaction.* Engaging in social interaction for leisure, relaxation, and diversion from demanding conditions

Two questions were prompted for each category in order to elicit the names of network members. First, respondents were asked who they regarded as providers of *each* support type. Second, respondents were asked to indicate which of the individuals who were named in response to the first question had *actually* supplied that type of support during the past month. In this way, it was possible to assess both available and enacted social support. For each question, respondents could name new persons or repeat persons who were already mentioned in response to an earlier name generator question, so the multiplexity could also be assessed.

As we have already indicated when presented with multiple name generators, respondents may nominate the same persons on multiple generators. This happens, for example, when your mother helps you with household chores and she is also the one you go to for advice on important life decisions. This is called *multiplexity*, meaning that people fit more than one category. A *multiplex* (or *multistranded*) relationship is a relationship in which multiple types of support have been exchanged. In *uniplex* or *specialized* relationships, however, only one type of support is exchanged. This multiplexity is of substantive interest in social support research. Therefore, in the data collection phase, it is important to explain to respondents that on the second and later name generators, they can nominate not only new people, but also people they had already mentioned. When respondents give a first name or a nickname that was already given on an earlier question, interviewers must make sure it is the same alter. When entering the data, each unique network member should only be entered as a single case, and the types of support that this person has provided or could provide should appear as (binary) variables. So, the interviewer writes down the new names on a list and checks the type of support provided, but if an alter name is repeated, and the name indeed refers to a repeated alter, the name is not entered again. Instead, the interviewer checks another box behind the name of the alter. An example of how to enter this information using paper-and-pencil techniques is given in Table 6.1. Software for the collection of personal network data such as EgoNet and VennMaker also allow you to do this in Computer Assisted Personal Interviews (CAPI) methods, and they save the links with the specific name generators.

The use of multiple name generators provides more reliable measurement (e.g., Marin & Hampton, 2007), but of course it also increases respondent burden. To reduce this burden, some researchers have suggested using minimal modules of three to five name generators that best capture the variability of social support (e.g., Bernard et al., 1990; Van der Poel, 1993). In any case, when you combine different name generators (be it 3 or 12), you must make sure that together they have an overall logic. Claire Bidart and Johanne Charbonneau (2011) warned that combining name generators with vastly different contents may give you a "patchwork" of networks that are difficult to interpret as a whole. Also, multiple name generators may lead to *question order effects*; that is, the order in which you ask the questions may affect the answers (Pustejovsky & Spillane, 2009). Pilot tests can help you find out whether that is the case.

Although name generators based on the exchange approach usually consist of multiple name generators, this is not necessarily the case. One of the most widely used examples of the exchange approach is the "discussing important matters" question designed by Ronald Burt and included in the General Social Survey (GSS; Marsden, 1990). Respondents were asked, "From time to time, most people discuss important matters with other people. Looking back over the last six months, who are the people with whom you discussed matters important to you? Just tell me their first names and initials." If fewer than five names are given, the interviewer probes: "Anyone else?." While the survey collects up to eight names, only five are used for analyzing the network. On average, respondents nominated three persons in the GSS of 1984 and two in the 2004 survey. This name generator can be easily implemented in large surveys using conventional techniques such as telephone interviewing, and it has therefore become

**TABLE 6.1. Example of a Table for Filling in Multiple Name Generators**

| First name or initials of alter | Who could help with household chores? | Who could look after the house when you are out of town? | With whom do you talk about personal problems? |
|---|---|---|---|
| 1 Mary S. | x | | |
| 2 Alice | x | | x |
| 3 John | | x | |
| 4 Wilma | | x | |
| 5 Mary V. | | | x |

*Note.* x, nominated on this question.

### *Single and Multiple Name Generators*

Alexandra Marin and Keith Hampton (Marin & Hampton, 2007) compared the social support network measures obtained from single name generators to measures obtained from a six-item multiple name generator. Although some single generators provided passable estimates of some measures, no single generator yielded reliable estimates across a broad spectrum of network measures. Marin and Hampton then evaluated two alternative methods of reducing respondent burden: (1) the Modified Multiple Generator (MMG), a multiple generator using the two most robust name generators, and (2) the Multiple Generator Random Interpreter (MGRI), a six-item name generator administered for a random subset of alters. Both the MMG and the MGRI were more reliable than single generators when measuring size, density, and mean measures of network composition or activity, though some single name generators were more reliable for measures consisting of sums or counts.

quite a standard in social sciences all over the world (Boase & Ikeda, 2012; Mollenhorst, Volker, & Flap, 2011; Ruan, 1998; van Tubergen, 2015). The "important matters" question is believed to capture one's *core discussion network*, and although it focuses on an exchange, it has long been thought to elicit affective ties.

With regard to the latter assumption, there is reason to doubt the presumed strength of the ties reported to this name generator (Small, 2013, 2017). First, respondents may have very different criteria about what constitutes an "important matter." Some studies delved deeper into the response patterns by asking respondents to cite the last important matter they talked about with the mentioned network members. Those studies found that important matters included a variety of issues, ranging from highly political and moral topics to topics that may seem more like small talk, such as a new haircut, care for the neighbor's lawn, or the new traffic lights installed in town (Bearman & Parigi, 2004). But even for issues that may be generally believed to be important, Mario Small observed that approximately half of the time, respondents discuss such matters with people they don't personally care about. He showed that they chose to discuss these matters with weak ties, either because they believed that these people were knowledgeable about the subject (such as doctors or spiritual leaders), because they expected the particular person could empathize with the topic, because they avoided confiding in stronger contacts with incompatible role expectations, or simply because these people were available when the issue arose. In conclusion then, while the core discussion network question is a standard measure in the social sciences, it is not a representation of our strong ties (Small, 2013). To improve on the question, some have suggested indicating specific conversation themes. In this line, the National Social Life, Health and Aging Project (NSHAP; Cornwell, Laumann, & Schumm, 2011, p. 189) asked the following question:

> From time to time, most people discuss things that are important to them with others. For example, these may include good or bad things that happen to you, problems you are having, or important concerns you may have. Looking back over the last 12 months, who are the people with whom you most often discussed things that were important to you?

In general, exchange name generators are easy to understand for respondents, and they typically have high test–retest reliability. They tend to tap into strong ties, but they also include moderately strong and sometimes weak ties. A possible limitation is that the approach typically focuses uniquely on positive exchanges, but negative tie generators can be added to the list (see the subsection "Negative Tie Generators" later in this chapter).

### The Interactive Approach

Of greater concern to some outcomes is not the strength or the role of the tie or what is exchanged through it, but rather the actual contact. In that case, it may be appropriate to identify the subset of ties with whom a respondent has been interacting over a specified amount of time. The interactive approach does just that. Typical questions in this approach are: "With whom have you been in contact today [/ over the last week/ month/ six months]?" or "With whom do you interact on a typical day?" You may also ask respondents to think about the people with whom they interacted just prior to the interview and going backwards. The method will intentionally bias the list toward people whom the respondent tends to see daily or weekly and against less frequent interactions. In other words, it captures social activity rather than a set of strong ties, and it may even miss out completely on some significant others. For example, adult respondents may see parents and siblings less regularly, particularly if they are mobile professionals who have moved far away from home. Name generators that use an interaction approach may therefore miss out on these people. Depending on the type of study, this may be appropriate.

The interactive approach is cognitively demanding. As we indicated before, respondents tend to report on typical (routinized) network ties when asked about interactions, and they tend to be highly inaccurate when reporting retrospectively on interactions that take place within highly specific time frames. Researchers may help respondents a bit by giving them specific clues. For example, Robert Milardo (1989) called people to ask them about their interactions in a 24-hour period that ended earlier that day. In order to give them a better frame of reference, he first asked them about the activities they carried out at the beginning and end of that period. Asking about activities or events that happen in the time period can help respondents remember whom they saw or talked to at the time. Still, with the possible exception of personal network studies of interactions within bounded groups or organizations, researchers interested in "daily contacts" are probably better served by *contact diaries* (Dávid, Huszti, Barna, & Fu, 2016; Fu, 2007; Gurevitch, 1961; Huszti, Dávid, & Vajda, 2013; Lonkila, 1997; Pachur, Schooler, & Stevens, 2014) or other procedures where respondents repeatedly report on interactions shortly after they occur, during a certain period of time (e.g., each day during one week or during three months). Contact diaries are described in Section 6.7.

## The Domain-Specific or Contextual Name Generator

Apart from the four basic approaches described so far, two other approaches have blended several aspects of the four approaches: The domain-specific or contextual name generator, and the freelist name generator. The domain-specific or contextual name generator asks respondents to list alters in a number of formal roles or types of relationships (domains or contexts) and then poses further requirements of affection or regular interaction. For example, van Tilburg (1992), in his investigation of the social involvement of the elderly, asked respondents the following, for each of seven domains (household members, children and partner, other relatives, neighbors, persons from work or classes, members of organizations, others): "*Name the persons [in domain X] with whom you are in touch regularly and who are important to you.*" Respondents named on average 13 people on these seven questions.

A second example is the contextual name generator that was developed for the study "Sociability and Social Integration: Processes of Entry into Adult Life, Transition to Work and Evolution of Social Networks" in Caen, France. Claire Bidart and her colleagues (e.g., Bidart & Lavenu, 2005) were interested in socialization processes at the transition into adulthood. For this aim, they designed a set of name generators to capture the relationships that have originated in all social contexts in which respondents have participated. The first stage of the technique consists of a systematic review of all possible life contexts (past and present) in which respondents might have participated. These include not only the usual suspects, such as school, family, and workplaces, but also contexts that might not occur to us so quickly, such as the military service, romantic attachments, all sorts of clubs, holidays and travels, and parents' friends, to name just a few. In the second stage, name generators are linked to each context in which the respondents reportedly participated: "In [context X], are there any people whom you know a little better, with whom you talk a little more often?"

In total, up to 50 questions could generate names. Not all of them were equally productive, but the method intended to facilitate the best possible reconstitution of all the social worlds that have provided their respondents with relationships that remained active at the time of interviewing. In a third stage, additional questions (name interpreters; see the next chapter) were introduced only for the significant alters in each context.

In the Caen study on young adults, the size of the delineated networks varied from 14 to 122 significant alters. The approach blends aspects of the role approach with aspects of the affective approach. Since the organization of the name generators closely resembles the organization of our contacts in our brain, it is easy for respondents to respond to them. Of course, there is a large respondent burden to produce the larger networks.

## The Freelist Name Generator

Another method that does not fit well within any of the four basic approaches is the freelist name generator, which aims to delineate the active personal network. It focuses on a broader subset of the whole personal network, including both strong and weaker ties. Christopher McCarty (2002) proposed measuring the active personal network with a single broad question: "Please, give us the names of [*n*] persons you know and who know you by sight or by name, with whom you have had some contact in the past two years, either face-to-face, by phone, mail or email, and whom you could still contact if you had to." Respondents are asked to include people whom they felt closest to or people they do not feel so close to but whom they happen to see frequently, and then to fill out the remaining number of names with friends, family, and acquaintances who fit the definition.

The number of names is fixed in this approach for the following reason. When you are trying to get respondents to list all the people they know in a certain, large subset, you never truly know if they have done so. Respondents will stop listing alters for a number of reasons. They may stop because they have listed all of the ones they know, or because they cannot remember any more. In some cases, respondents stop listing alters because they are tired, or worse, uncooperative. Also, some interviewers may be more successful than others in having respondents name as many alters as apply. These problems are likely bigger when the subset to which the question refers is bigger.

An even greater problem is that, with variable network size, structural measures of the network such as its density or the number of cliques are not comparable. Suppose that two people each have about 20 friends and acquaintances, but one of them nominated only 3 friends, restricting the response to the strongest ties, while the other named all 20. In that case, it is, for example, much more likely that the network of the person who named 3 people has a density of 1 (i.e., all the people in the network know each other) than the network of the person who named 20 people.

Given that the researcher likely cannot know which of these reasons made a respondent stop listing alters, and given that structural measures are not comparable across networks of different size, our preference for questions referring to generally larger alter sets is to have respondents list a fixed number of alters. This way, each respondent has the same amount of work to do. Some respondents will have difficulty listing the required number of alters, and others will not. This difficulty will in all likelihood be reflected in the variability of the alter characteristics when you do your analysis. For example, you may see that some respondents have a larger number of strong ties than others. This variability, incidentally, is precisely the type of data you are trying to capture.

If you decide to specify a fixed number of alters, the next question is, how many alters should you elicit? Previous studies have used a fixed number that varied from 20 (Roman et al., 2012; Wenzel, Tucker, Golinelli, Green, & Zhou, 2010), to 25 (Tucker et al., 2009), 30 (Cachia & Maya Jariego, 2018; Martí, Bolíbar, & Lozares, 2017; Rodríguez-García, Lubbers, Solana, & de Miguel-Luken, 2015), 40 (Negrón, 2012), 45 (Lubbers et al., 2010; McCarty & Killworth, 2007; Molina et al., 2015; Vacca et al., 2018), to 60 (McCarty, 2002). McCarty and Killworth (2007) have recommended a minimum number of 25 alters. This number is large enough to represent the overall network structure accurately. Of course, higher numbers of names imply a higher respondent burden. The elicitation of names itself goes fast, but the respondent burden lies in the name interpreters (see Chapter 7) and edge interpreters (see Chapter 8); ways to reduce respondent burden will be discussed in those chapters.

This method elicits networks of the desired size combining strong and relatively weaker ties. Of course, respondents who have larger networks may reach the required number of names quite easily, while others with smaller networks may struggle to come up with the last names, particularly when higher numbers of names are asked for. If the researcher later asks about the closeness that the respondent feels toward each of the alters, then this difference can be observed in the composition of the networks in terms of emotional closeness. The respondents who struggled to come up with the required number of names will have a larger number of weaker ties in the delineated network than respondents who did not have such problems, corresponding with real-life differences. So even though network size cannot be used as a variable in this approach since it is fixed, if the fixed network size is large enough, the individual variability in tie characteristics, especially in emotional closeness, might give you the precise information you were seeking.

The name generator can be implemented among others in the software EgoNet or Vennmaker, which allows computer-assisted personal interviewing and the visualization of the networks immediately upon completion of the interview. This is particularly interesting if researchers wish that the interviewers can ask questions about the resulting network to the respondents.

Benefits of the method, as we have indicated above, are that it makes it possible to represent both strong and relatively weaker ties and that it maximizes comparability of network structural measures. A possible disadvantage is that the weaker ties typically form a small selection of a large pool of weak ties and the particular selection may influence the overall composition strongly. However, if the strength of tie with each alter is also measured, then one can easily control to what extent the weaker ties affect the overall composition.

## Negative Tie Generators

Personal network studies are predominantly focused on strong and supportive ties. However, social network researchers are increasingly recognizing that unsupportive, conflictive, forbidden, absent, lost, or broken ties can be equally relevant for understanding individual outcomes (Ferrand, 2014; Hosnedlová, 2017; Leffler, Krannich, & Gillespie, 1986; Neal, 2009; Offer & Fischer, 2018; Plessard, 2014). For example, the absence of unsupportive or conflictive ties may be more crucial than the presence of supportive or positive ones for individual well-being. If negative ties are potentially important for your study, you may decide to add one or multiple name generators that elicit those ties.

For example, the UC Berkeley Social Networks Study (UCNets) asked respondents to nominate persons whom they "sometimes find demanding or difficult" (Offer & Fischer, 2017). Ann Leffler et al. (1986) elicited the names of people whom respondents found "overly demanding," and "most likely to let you down," and who "make you angry or upset." In contrast to common belief, the in-laws were less often mentioned on such name generators than blood and work ties.

The diversity of ties that are typically grouped together as "negative" are not always necessarily negative, nor do they need to have a negative effect on individual outcomes. For example, Anand Sokhey and Paul Djupe (2014) claimed that the typical name generators for political discussion networks tended to elicit relatively homogeneous networks. In order to test whether Americans are indeed so little exposed to disagreement, they proposed various name generators, asking respondents not only to name those people with whom they discussed government, elections, and politics, but also those people with whom they disagreed about these matters. Among the people with whom respondents disagreed about politics, many were friends.

Another type of tie that is not typically included in name generators is the zero-quality or absent tie (Ferrand, 2014; Plessard, 2014). For example, it can be of interest to ask whether people whom respondents had expected to give help did not do so, for various reasons. An example is provided by Miranda Lubbers and Hugo Valenzuela-García in their study about the relevance of informal support for households in poverty (2018). Apart from various questions about received, provided, and available material, financial, and intangible support, they added the following question: "Are there any people you went to for economic or material help who could not help you?" Some of the nominees were people who wanted to help but were not economically able to do so.

Of course, questions about negative or absent ties may be more sensitive than questions about positive ties. Therefore, the wording and place in the order of questions are particularly important.

## 6.5 A NAME GENERATOR FOR ELICITING A RANDOM SUBSET OF ALTERS

Most research on personal networks focuses on individuals' primary relationships, and therefore they intend to delineate the subset of alters with whom respondents have more intimate, more supportive relationships. Some research, however, may be interested in understanding the broader social landscape surrounding an individual. Weak ties have both similar and complementary functions to strong ties, and we still know very little about these ties. Even if it is practically undoable to delineate personal networks of size 300, say, we can attempt to take a random sample of the larger personal networks. In other words, we can try to delineate a subset of the larger personal networks that is representative of those larger networks.

McCarty and colleagues (1997) attempted to use first names as a way to randomly elicit names from respondents. Using a U.S. Census website that listed the proportion of all male and female first names, they read a list of 50 first names proportionate to their representation in the population, alternating male and female names to eliminate a gender bias. They asked respondents to tell them to stop reading when they recognized a first name as the name of someone they knew. Then, the researchers would ask them to explain how they knew this person. They further explained:

> For the purposes of this study, the definition of knowing someone is that you know them and they know you by sight or by name, that you could contact them (even though we will not do that), that there has been some contact (either in person, by telephone or mail) in the past two years, and that they live within the United States. We will be selecting 14 names.

Devon Brewer (1997) examined the resulting data for order effects and found none where ordinary freelists introduced extensive order effects. Tyler McCormick et al. (2010) provided further guidance to avoid alter selection biases. In particular, they recommended using a combination of names that together represent a truly scaled-down version of the sociodemographic composition of society in terms of gender, ethnicity, and birth cohort. For this aim, researchers can use census data (if they exist) regarding the frequency of names for different birth cohorts and so on. They further recommended choosing names that compromise 0.1%–0.2% of the population. This latter recommendation is useful because if too common names are used (such as "Robert"), a respondent may know several people with those names, and when asked about only one, they may still select the person (named Robert) who is closest to them.

The unbiased selection of network alters from memory is one of the most important and understudied areas of personal network research. By understanding how names are stored in memory, we may ultimately be able to drastically reduce the bias associated with name generators and elicit a much more representative sample of alters, giving us a better picture of the social environment that surrounds an individual respondent. Several methods have also been developed for understanding the characteristics of this broader social environment without delineating the underlying network. These methods will be discussed in Chapter 10.

## 6.6 ADDITIONAL QUALIFIERS OF THE NETWORK BOUNDARY

The name generators that we have introduced delineate specific subnetworks within the respondents' larger networks (e.g., close ties, ties with whom a respondent exchanges information, or a random subset of the larger personal network). Apart from defining the content of the relationship, researchers tend to specify additional qualifiers of the network boundary in terms of time, geographical location, and number of alters.

These examples make it clear that part of the boundary definition for personal network research should often be some decision about a *maximum amount of time since the respondents had their last contacts* with the alters, or the maximum amount of time passed since a type of support was exchanged. Researchers should decide how far relationships can go back in time for them to still be meaningful in terms of the research question.

In most studies of personal network research, we are interested in people *with whom the respondent still communicates*. What about people the respondent knew very well, even recently, but who are now deceased? In terms of information transmission, these alters may be viewed in the same way as people the respondent no longer talks to and could not contact if he or she wanted to. An argument can be made, however, for including someone who is deceased, particularly if the person died recently and we want to understand how the composition and structure of that network alter affect the individual. This is particularly the case in mental health studies, where we may want to capture the effect of the loss of a loved one on the respondent, but we have no data on the personal network before the alter deceased. Allowing respondents to include the deceased alter then allows us to observe with whom the person was connected. But while it may be valid for some studies to include deceased people or former acquaintances, in most cases we will probably want to exclude them. Ultimately, the purpose of the study will determine this.

In some cases, researchers may also specify the *minimum age* an alter should have. For example, while parents talk a lot with their toddlers, these conversations may not be as useful for your investigation into information exchange.

Another issue that often comes up in the elicitation of personal network alters is the listing of *famous or even fictitious people (or pets)* whom the respondent wants to list as network members. It is not uncommon for respondents to list "Jesus" as a network member, adamant that he is a big influence in their lives. Others may list a pop star or the president, claiming that they know who these people are and that their lives are influenced by them. Typically, we want respondents to exclude these kinds of people because, even though they may have influenced respondents' lives, the respondents do not have a bidirectional communication with them. Many things influence attitudes and behavior, especially books, TV shows, and personal observations about the world. But while influential, they are not the same as relational influences and should be studied differently. You may stimulate the elicitation of bidirectional relationships by explicitly including it in the question, for example: "Please give us the names of [*n*] persons you know *and who know you* by sight or by name."

Sometimes *geographical qualifiers* have been added to the boundary definition. In some cases, we may be particularly interested in the number of persons a respondent knows within a specific geographical area, for example, within the country or abroad. Also, some studies focus explicitly on people who are not part of the respondent's household.

Despite clear instructions, you may not be able to completely prevent respondents from naming people below a minimum age; deceased people; and famous, fictitious, and other nonqualifying contacts. In this case, your best course is to let them do so during the interview and to separate such alters only after data collection. It is their social world they are talking about, and they should be allowed to do so in a way that makes sense to them.

Finally, let's consider the consequences of limiting or fixing the number of alters. Most name generators do not specify how many names a respondent should give, although many specify a *maximum number of names*, usually for logistic reasons. If there are multiple name generators, researchers can either set *a maximum for the total set of names* or a *maximum for the number of names returned on each name generator.* When you limit the total number of alters for multiple name generators, having respondents exhaust all members from a list of cues may bias the results toward the earlier cues. For example, cued elicitation may start by asking the respondent to list family members. Depending on the size and level of contact with their family, some respondents may achieve the desired sample size of alters before getting to other cue categories. An alternative is to ask for a maximum number of alters from each cue category. For example, you could ask to name maximally five family members, five friends, five workmates, and five neighbors. However, this may lead to a different type of bias. Maybe one person socializes primarily with his extensive family. He has about 30 family members he sees frequently, but he is only allowed to list five. He does not work, he does not socialize with his neighbors, and he has only one friend he considers close, so his observed total network size will be six, even though the real network size for these roles is 31. Another respondent may have four family members, five friends, three neighbors, and three workmates she socializes with. In this case, both her observed network size and her real network size is 15. So the real network size is half the number that our first respondent had, yet her observed network size is 2.5 times larger. In this case, the observed network size is to some extent a proxy for network heterogeneity rather than a reflection of network size itself. In either case, using a maximum number of names on a set of name generators will compromise any analysis that depends on the proportion of the network of the specific relations specified in the name generators.

In the case of the freelist name generator, researchers have specified a fixed number of names using a single name generator. As we explained earlier in this chapter, observed network size is not a good estimator of the true network size. The number of names people freely list depends not only on their network size, but also on their willingness to cooperate, their energy, and their memory, and probably even on interviewer skills. The larger the subset of the personal network that the name generator refers to, the larger we think this problem is. An additional problem is that with variable network sizes, networks are not comparable with each other in terms of their structure. For these reasons, we recommend that respondents list a *fixed number of alters* for questions referring to generally larger alter sets. Variability in alter characteristics, such as emotional closeness, will still allow you to perceive differences in the underlying network size.

Of course, this is possible only when you ask about a general set of people "you know," and it is not possible with all types of questions. If you ask parents of young children to list the names of those who have helped them with child care in the past year, you cannot ask them to "name exactly five persons." Some people simply didn't have five persons taking care of their children, either because they didn't need child care very often or because they didn't have five persons they could turn to for help with child care. Forcing them to name five alters, then, only introduces error. One might probe a little further ("Anyone else?") or ask, in addition, whether there are others who haven't helped in the past year but could have been relied on for help had the respondent needed it.

Researchers try to get respondents to list all of their alters in a specific subset in order to estimate the respondent's network size. Although network size is an important personal network attribute, for the above reasons it is debatable whether it can be measured by asking the respondent to list them. Other methods exist for estimating network size, which, again, requires each respondent to do the same amount of work and less work than listing all their alters (see Chapter 10).

If you decide to specify a fixed number of alters, the next question is how many alters should you elicit? Again, this will depend on your research questions, your time, and your resources. As you will see, the number of alters also determines the respondent burden in providing information about the alters and the relations between them. Asking respondents to freelist very few alters (such as 10 or fewer) will result in a set of alters who are very close to the respondent. Longer lists will include a larger variety of groups and acquaintances. Assuming you do not want a list biased toward very close alters, one approach is to ask respondents to list a relatively large number of alters. With larger samples, some bias is probably removed.

## 6.7 ALTERNATIVE APPROACHES TO NAME GENERATORS

Apart from name generators, a variety of other approaches have been used to elicit lists of network members, such as contact diaries (Dávid et al., 2016; Fu, 2007; Lonkila, 1997); retrieval from specific contact modes such as social media (but see our thoughts about that above; Brooks, Hogan, Ellison, Lampe, & Vitak, 2014); qualitative methods (Armitage, 2016; Boissevain, 1974; Reyes, 2016); archival records in the case of historical research (e.g., collections of letters; Edwards & Crossley, 2009); and experiments (Killworth & Bernard, 1978). In this section, we discuss the first three, the most prevalent ones, in more detail.

### Contact Diaries

Researchers interested in interaction networks have also used *contact diaries* (Dávid et al., 2016; De Sola Pool & Kochen, 1978; Freeman & Thompson, 1989; Fu, 2005, 2007; Gurevitch, 1961; Huszti et al., 2013; Lonkila, 1997, 1999; Pachur et al., 2014) instead of interaction name generators. A contact diary is a research instrument in which informants record all the people with whom they have had contact in their lives in a diary log, on a daily basis, for a preestablished period of time. The diary, which usually consists of a small booklet with a page for every day, typically records the names of the contacts. It also records detailed information about the characteristics of each individual (e.g., gender, age, education), interaction (e.g., location, duration), and relationship (e.g., closeness, duration).

### *Keeping Diaries of Contacts during Three Months and Beyond*

Yang-chih Fu has conducted several studies using contact diaries in Taiwan (Fu, 2005, 2007; Fu, Ho, & Chen, 2013; Yen, Fu, & Hwang, 2016). In one of these studies (Fu, 2007), 62 participants were asked to keep a diary at the end of the day of their interpersonal contacts for three months. After three months, 54 participants had completed this task. The log diary contained detailed information about (1) the demographic characteristics and socioeconomic status of alters, (2) the context of the interaction, and (3) the ego–alter type of relationship. These 54 participants elicited 103,016 interpersonal contacts (an average of almost 2,000 per participant) and 26,503 unique individuals (with an average of almost 500 per participant). Fu suggests that the three-month interval captures approximately 50–70% of the extant personal network and that a combination of diary and surveys methods could be introduced in order to extend the area of coverage to one year. On average, participants devoted approximately 20–40 minutes per day to record their interactions. Although diaries imposed a heavy burden on participants, Fu contended that this method is the most comprehensive measurement of extant personal networks and that it can be taken as the yardstick of other measurements.

Diaries have been provided for a single day (e.g., Mossong et al., 2008), a week (Huszti et al., 2013), two weeks (Lonkila, 1997), and three months (e.g., Fu, 2007; Gurevitch, 1961; Pachur et al., 2014). The particular example of the single-day diaries is presented with the aim of understanding the contact patterns relevant for airborne and direct contact infections. For this case, resembling a normal survey, Joël Mossong and colleagues (2008, p. 0382) defined a contact as "either skin-to-skin contact such as a kiss or handshake (a physical contact), or a two-way conversation with three or more words in the physical presence of another person but no skin-to-skin contact (a nonphysical contact)."

With diaries that are held for a longer period of time, researchers try to obtain in-depth information about the larger personal networks of individuals, including strong and weak ties. In these cases, researchers tend to focus on all kinds of contact, sometimes specifying a lower threshold for the duration of contact (e.g., at least 10 minutes) and at other times including all one-on-one contact.

As a result, the interactions are more accurately represented in diaries than in interviews, assuming that the respondent diligently enters them into the diary and it produces a particularly rich dataset about personal networks. It also has the disadvantage, however, of an extremely high respondent burden. Diary keepers may spend 20 to 40 minutes a day detailing the individual characteristics of the people they had contact with, the type, length and situation of each interaction, and so on. Consequently, a certain level of attrition can be expected. In order to stimulate continuing participation, most studies use monetary incentives or gifts, enough to make the exchange feel equitable to participants. Constant contact with the researchers is also necessary to motivate diary keepers and check the consistency of their reporting. The method tends to generate very large alter sets, but it does not produce data about network structure.

## Online Social Networks

As we indicated in Chapters 2 and 3, among the numerous studies of online social networking sites such as Facebook and Twitter, there is a growing number of studies on the ego networks of the users of these platforms (e.g., Brooks et al., 2014; Dunbar et al., 2015; Ellison, Steinfield, & Lampe, 2011; Hofstra et al., 2017; Hogan, 2009; Park, Lee, & Kim, 2012). Studies of online social networks tend to collect egocentric network data directly from the websites, using Application Programming Interfaces or web scraping tools, and sometimes purchasing the data. Before researchers collect data, they must delineate their strategy by defining the appropriate platform for data collection (a single or multiple platforms), establishing criteria to delimit users, topics, time frames, language, or geographical locations, and specifying how much data they will need (Mayr & Weller, 2017). Whatever the preferred data collection method, researchers are often limited by legal, ethical, and technical restrictions that must be taken into account.

Although these data are currently not substitutes for personal network data for the reasons stipulated earlier in this chapter (see Section 6.1), they are valuable for describing the characteristics of computer-mediated personal communication. They are also important for exploring whether the structure of online networks is similar to that of offline social networks (either by comparing it with the literature of offline social networks or by interviewing social media users directly using name generators, allowing comparisons at an individual level of their social media network and their personal network) and for investigating processes of diffusion of information on these social network sites. To characterize these new forms of communication, new concepts have been introduced, such as media multiplexity, hyperconnectivity, and virtual locality (e.g., Quan-Haase & Wellman, 2005; Wellman & Haythornthwaite, 2002).

## Qualitative Approaches

Not all qualitative research into personal relationships and networks intends to chart or map those networks explicitly. Among the qualitative and mixed-methods researchers who do, many also use the name generators discussed before (e.g., Bernardi, 2011; Ryan, 2016; Sommer & Gamper, 2018; Wissink & Mazzucato, 2018). Often, they choose relatively open and participatory methods to elicit the networks, mostly the concentric circle diagram presented in Section 6.4, with either paper-and-pencil methods or software that allows constructing the network on screen. This method still allows informants relative freedom in discussing their networks. Qualitative researchers are often interested in how informants organize their network in the process and in what they explain while they do so. Semistructured questions are often integrated or used as a follow-up to further contextualize the network, to investigate subjective perceptions of the network and practices of networking, and to explore relatively unknown aspects of networks such as their temporal dimensions (Hollstein, 2014b).

Some researchers, however, use qualitative approaches to elicit a set of alter names. One such method is the biographical network approach proposed by Neil Armitage (2016), a method that mixes the life history approach with social network analysis. Armitage also used multiple name generators, but in addition, he performed life history interviews, which he states are "ideal to explore the numerous contexts that people engage in through life." The interviews are structured by the different "chapters" of life that the researcher asks participants to suggest, in order to structure the narration. While they talk about their lives, informants often mention individuals who have been important and who are thus placed in a specific spatiotemporal context. Some of these alters were also elicited by the name generators, but others were not. Subsequently, Armitage had informants place all the alters they deemed important in a concentric circle diagram, following the paper-and-pencil procedure of Bernie Hogan and colleagues (Hogan et al., 2007; see "The Affective Approach" in Section 6.4). In his case, the circles did not represent levels of closeness, but rather the stages of life as proposed by the informant. While the list of alters named during life history interviews may not represent current networks well, or in a directly comparable way across informants, they do give some insight into people who are retrospectively considered important over the course of life, which can include ongoing as well as currently dissolved relationships.

Researchers have also used free-style drawings to elicit networks (e.g., Cachia, 2014; McCarty, Molina, Aguilar, & Rota, 2007; Reyes, 2016). For example, Cornelia Reyes (2016) proposed the method of hand-drawn network maps for her research into the online sociability of creative professionals. These professionals often had large social media networks, including hundreds of people, many of whom were not well known to them (not even their real names), so they did not engage well with name generators. Therefore, Reyes used the visual method to better understand the sometimes ephemeral practices of networking on social media sites and informants' processes of meaning-making. In this approach, the participants are asked to draw their social network on a large, blank sheet of paper, after being provided with color pencils, markers, and sticky notes. The process is completely unstructured so as to have the best chance for eliciting information that is novel or difficult to verbalize; it shifts the focus from actors to situations. However, at least in the context of this particular research, it elicited clusters of alters (e.g., "suppliers," "art friends") rather than those clusters being broken down into discrete individual alters. Therefore, further questions should be added if the method is to be used to elicit names.

## 6.8 FINAL REMARKS

Simply put, there is no one correct question to elicit network alters. The method you choose depends on several factors, such as the purpose of your research and your resources. No matter which question or set of questions you use, you should take into account the general guidelines for the construction of survey questions. For example, questions should be clear, and they should not be leading or double-barreled (see Section 5.3). Also, if you want to be able to compare the networks later on, make sure each respondent receives the same cues. One of the biggest mistakes you can make in the elicitation of alters is using different cues for different respondents. The list of alters is the basis for all subsequent data collection and analysis. If the way the lists are generated is biased across respondents, the data will not be comparable. Indeed, all network elicitation is biased; we just want to control what kind of bias we introduce.

Sometimes respondents may do things that bias the elicitation as well. It is not uncommon for respondents to pull out a Personal Digital Assistant (PDA), address books, or smartphones during the interview process to retrieve the names of people they know. This is a problem for three reasons. First, if only some of the respondents use these resources, their data may be substantially different from those who do not. Second, like email, not everyone in a person's network is necessarily listed in a PDA, smartphone, or address book. These media may be biased toward particular types of relations, such as work. Finally, the way names are listed in these media may be biased. Names may be entered chronologically or alphabetically. It is unlikely they are entered in the same way they are stored in human memory. Indeed, that is why we use these devices—to store names, addresses, and phone numbers using systems that make retrieval easy—something that we cannot easily do with our minds.

We must also note that some IRBs and Research Ethics Committees do not approve of asking respondents to list the real names of alters, even if they will be encrypted in the database (see also Chapter 14). To avoid problems, researchers can ask respondents to use initials or nicknames. With many alters, however, respondents need to be able to recognize alter names later on in the interview. Therefore, it is wise to use a few more letters. For example, they can reduce William Shakespeare to "WilSha." For longitudinal personal network studies, it is even important that respondents still recognize the names a couple of years later. In research designs that link interconnected personal networks—for example, to make a whole network of the personal networks of connected individuals, or to combine the personal networks of a duo (e.g., husband and wife)—it is even more important that alters can be identified sufficiently for researchers to connect the networks among them.

The list of names in itself is of course not the information we are after (or not all information we are after). What we really want to know is who the listed people are. For example, we may want to know where they live, what they do for a living, how strong their relationship is with the respondent, how long the respondent has know them, or how they met. When aggregated over all the network members, this gives us an understanding of the composition of the network. Typically, we are also interested in how the listed members are related to each other. This gives us an impression of the structure of the networks. The type of compositional and structural information to collect and the way to collect it will be discussed in the next two chapters.

## CHAPTER SUMMARY

In this chapter, we first reviewed the question of recall bias and how to address it, and then we presented the variety of name generators that have been used in past research. Many issues have been treated along the line: First, we should define if we want to collect an intentional subset of relationships based on closeness, roles, exchanges, or interactions, or a random set of the larger network. For larger networks, we can also consider a domain-specific or freelist name generator. Second, we should make a decision about using a single or multiple name generators. We also have to choose whether we want to focus only on positive or on negative exchanges as well. As we tried to show, the term "negative ties" includes a wide variety of relationships. Third, we should assess whether it is best to let the number of names vary across respondents or to fix the number of names (or at least the minimum or maximum of names). Fourth, we saw what kind of prompts we can use to elicit additional names. And, finally, we should reflect on the convenience of restricting the elicitation of alters temporally, geographically, or otherwise. As we already noted, there is not a single correct strategy but a variety of strategies to elicit network alters for reaching different research goals.

### FURTHER READING

Bidart, C., & Charbonneau, J. (2011). How to generate personal networks: Issues and tools for a sociological perspective. *Field Methods, 23*(3), 266–286.

Fischer, C. S. (1982). What do we mean by "friend"?: An inductive study. *Social Networks, 3*, 287–306.

Fu, Y.-C. (2007). Building archives of actual and comprehensive personal networks. *Field Methods, 19*(2), 194–217.

McCarty, C. (1995). The meaning of knowing as a network tie. *Connections, 18*, 20–31.

Pustejovsky, J. E., & Spillane, J. P. (2009). Question-order effects in social network name generators. *Social Networks, 31*, 221–229.

Wellman, B. (2007). Challenges in collecting personal network data: The nature of personal network analysis. *Field Methods, 19*(2), 111–115.

# 7

# Collecting Alter Attributes

---

*What Is This Chapter About?*

This chapter describes so-called name interpreters—questions aimed at collecting information about each of the alters and/or the relationship or shared characteristics between ego and each alter (Section 7.1). This is what we called the third module of a personal network study in Chapter 5. We will first discuss what type of information the ego knows about alters (Section 7.2), which needs to be taken into account when constructing questions about alters. Section 7.3 presents measures for the attributes of the alter, and Section 7.4 presents measures of the relationship that the ego has with the alter. As this module of the study is typically the lengthiest part of the interview, the last section discusses methods to reduce respondent burden without compromising the reliability of the data (Section 7.5).

---

## 7.1 WHAT IS A NAME INTERPRETER?

Now that you have a list of names of people the respondent knows, you will want to know some things about them. In most cases, you will rely on the respondent to tell you that information. In this chapter, we will talk about questions researchers often ask respondents about their network members. These questions are known in social network research as "name interpreters," and they are classified in two types: questions about alters' individual *attributes* (such as alters' gender, age, attitudes, or behaviors) and questions about the properties of the *dyad*, that is, the relationship between the ego and alters (such as the ego's closeness to the alter and the duration or type of relationship). We can simply refer to these as *alter attributes* and *dyadic attributes*, respectively. Sometimes, researchers also use the term "name interpreters" for questions about *ties between alters*, but we think it is more appropriate to use a distinct term: *edge interpreters*, as it interprets the values of pairs of already generated alters. (Borgatti et al., 2013, introduced the term "name interconnectors" for this type of information.) In this chapter, we will focus on alter attributes and dyadic attributes, while Chapter 8 will describe edge interpreters, questions about ties between alters.

Ultimately, what you want to know about the alters is determined by your research question, for example, by which attitude, behavior, or condition of the respondent you want to estimate or predict. As you will see in Chapter 11, the information gleaned in this part of the study may be the most important data you will collect. In Chapter 5, you already learned about some of the types of questions you can ask about the ego, how you might analyze the data, and how to go about constructing the questions. Everything in that chapter also applies to questions about alters.

Reporting alters' attributes or relationships is a complex and time-consuming task that provides rich information about respondents' social environments but that has some limitations and accuracy problems as well. The first point to keep in mind may seem obvious, but you should remember that you are asking respondents to report things about people they know. Respondents will know some people better than others, so a question may be reasonably asked about one alter, such as a confidant or family member, and not reasonably asked about others. In this vein, you certainly want to avoid having respondents make uninformed guesses about people they know. Most respondents who agree to do an interview try to be helpful. They may be inclined to attempt to answer questions about their alters, even if they don't know the answer. So what can we expect people to know about all of their alters?

## 7.2 WHAT WE REALLY KNOW ABOUT ALTERS

The number of things we can say with certainty that people know about their alters is small. Generally, research into pairs of close friends finds high rates of agreement between respondents' reports of the alter's sociodemographic characteristics and the alter's direct reports (Marsden, 1990). Respondents know if alters are male or female, although they may not be sure about alters who were met over the Internet whom the respondent never talked to face to face or over the phone. People typically have some idea about the age of alters, as long as the age categories are wide enough. It is often more problematic to ask a respondent to report an alter's exact age. They typically know where the person lives, particularly if you make the ability to contact them part of the boundary definition. They often know the race and/or ethnicity of alters, although this information may not be reliable. Bear in mind that the respondent may define an alter's race or ethnicity differently than the alter would him- or herself.

Respondents may have information about some behaviors of their alters. For example, they may know whether or not alters smoke, use IV drugs, or are homeless. These behaviors or conditions may be difficult to hide or are not typically hidden. It is more difficult to be certain about attitudes (Laumann, 1969a), such as political affiliations or opinions about specific consumer products and about more hidden behaviors (White & Watkins, 2000). Respondents may know these things about some people but not others. Or they may *think* they know these things about an alter but may be inaccurate. Some researchers have argued that in many cases it is not so important that respondents report incorrect information about an alter, as often it is the respondents' perception of the alter that influences their own attitudes and behaviors, not their real attitudes and behaviors (see Section 3.3). Other researchers, however, have suggested that when people are uncertain about their alters' attitudes or preferences, they project their own attitudes or preferences on them (Laumann, 1973; Montgomery & Chung, 1999; Udry & Billy, 1987; White & Watkins, 2000). You want people you like to think like you. In addition, people selectively disclose their political preferences, in the sense that they only reveal them when they are certain others agree with them, adding to an experience of network homogeneity (Cowan & Baldassarri, 2018). Do you know with certainty how the people around you vote? And how many of them vote? Have you ever been surprised when somebody told you they voted for this or that party? (If you live in a country with multiple-party systems, this may be especially difficult.)

If a tendency to assume similarity exists, it is problematic to establish a causal connection between the perceived behaviors of others and respondents' own behaviors: Do the attitudes you perceive around you influence your own attitude, or does your own attitude affect your perceptions? If you expect such difficulties to occur, it is a good idea to include a response category "I don't know" or "I don't know with certainty." You could also try to formulate a measurement model that allows you to distinguish between alternative mechanisms. For example, you could ask not only about the political preferences of alters but also whether respondents tend to talk with alters about politics. That is an aspect of the relationship between respondents and their alters, a dyadic attribute.

### *Alters' Real Attributes or the Ego's Perception of Their Attributes?*

Thomas Valente et al. (Valente, Watkins, Jato, van der Straten, & Tsitsol, 1997) wanted to explain contraceptive use among women in Yaoundé, Cameroon. Their hypothesis was that respondents' perceptions of their network alters' contraceptive use explained more of the variance in their own use than personal characteristics, such as age, education, and wealth. They conducted 495 interviews with women under the age of 45 who were members of 10 different women's associations. Women reported on alters whom they regularly talked to, including other members of their women's group. Most respondents thought they knew the behavior of their alters regarding contraceptive use, and because they collected data from group members, in many cases the researchers knew the behavior of alters as well. The researchers found that even when the respondent's perception of alters' contraceptive use was wrong, it still predicted the ego's contraceptive use.

So far, we have talked about individual characteristics of alters that might somehow influence the attitude, behavior, or condition of the respondent that you want to understand or predict. Another set of items the respondent can tell you about each alter are aspects of her relationships with them. These relationships are the vehicle by which the alter characteristics might influence the respondent. Respondents can tell you how long relationships exist, what role people have in their network, or how frequently they contact them. On the one hand, studies that compared responses of pairs of people about each other have revealed a high agreement among two persons about these characteristics (e.g., Hammer, 1984). On the other hand, agreement is lower for emotional closeness and for specific exchanges (Shulman, 1976). However, lower agreement does not necessarily indicate a lack of accuracy in reporting about relationships; it can also indicate asymmetries in relationships. In the case of emotional closeness, this is to be expected, as two people do not have to feel equally close to each other. In other words, closeness is not an undirected relationship. You can ask how close the respondent feels toward an alter, but you will not know how close the alter feels toward ego. Questions about exchanges are often directional (who provided you with [type of support]?), but on average, respondents believe they give more help than they receive (e.g., Shulman, 1976).

## 7.3 QUESTIONS ABOUT THE ATTRIBUTES OF ALTERS

What we want to know about the network members of our respondents depends fundamentally on our research questions. For example, in a study on the adaptation of migrants to their new country of residence, we might want to know the alters' country of origin and country of residence. With this knowledge, we can deduce what proportion of the relationships migrants maintain are with people in the country of origin, with co-nationals in the country of residence, and with natives of the country of residence. In a study about the impact of informal support on coping with poverty, however, we may not be interested at all in that information. Rather, we would like to know what economic resources alters have or, more simply put, what their economic situation is. Maybe it is easier to do that in a comparative way: Does the ego perceive the economic situation of the alter to be better, more or less equal, or worse than his or her own situation? In a study about the impact of the personal network on the decision to have children, researchers may expect that the underlying mechanism is social pressure or social comparison, maybe particularly with people of the same sex. If so, we would like to ask about the gender and age of alters and whether they have young children themselves.

Gender and age are two attributes of alters that are included in many personal network studies. In the case of age, as indicated earlier, we recommend using broad categories (e.g., comprising 10 years) rather than asking for the exact age, since respondents might not know the exact age, but they may know approximately what age an alter has. For most characteristics, it may be a good idea to include a category, "I don't know," to prevent respondents from guessing.

## 7.4 QUESTIONS ABOUT RELATIONSHIPS BETWEEN THE EGO AND THE ALTER

Personal network studies also tend to include various characteristics about the ego's relationship with his or her alters. Most personal network studies ask respondents to evaluate how well they know each alter or how close they are to them emotionally. These questions evaluate *tie strength*, which relates to the concepts of *strong and weak ties* introduced in Chapter 2. You may use, for example, a 4- or 5-point ordinal scale ("How close are you to [alter X]?": not close at all, a little close, quite close, very close). The wording of the question is also important. Asking "How well do you know Mary?" may not be the same as "How close are you to Mary?" Past research suggests that the second question about *closeness* captures the concept of tie strength better than knowing.

"Closeness" may be a better word for measuring tie strength partly because it reflects the type of interaction the respondent has with the alter. Most people have both positive and negative relationships in their lives. No matter how pleasant and amenable we may be, we will always get along better with some people than with others.

The term "closeness" seems to capture that better than the term "know" because people tend to be less close to people they do not like, even though they may know a lot about them. In most cases with personal network research, we are interested in the variability of the interaction between the respondents and their alters. Therefore, closeness is likely to be a better measure of tie strength. You can imagine cases in which you are more concerned with how well the respondent knows the alter; in this event, knowing may be a better term to use. There is no perfect measure of tie strength. It should be measured in a way that best accommodates your particular research.

Other basic relational characteristics are the *duration* of the relationship—that is, how long the respondent has known the alter, which you could measure as a ratio variable in years or, ordinally, in broader categories—and the *frequency of contact* with the alter. Although some have suggested that these are also indicators of tie strength, do not

### *Tie Strength: Closeness, Duration of Relationship, or Frequency of Contact?*

Peter Marsden and Karen Campbell (1984) analyzed data from three cross-sectional surveys that had gathered data on personal networks: (1) Laumann's Detroit Area Study data from 1964 to 1966 on 1,013 males in Detroit; (2) an Aurora, Illinois, study on 496 residents from 1974 to 1975; and (3) an Altneustadt, Germany, study on 820 residents from 1971. Each survey focused on the three closest alters of the respondent. They all concluded that frequency and duration of contact may not be reliable indicators of tie strength. Duration may be biased toward kin, and frequency of contact toward neighbor relations and coworkers. The term "closeness" may be the best all-around term to use with respondents when asking about tie strength, and it also appears to be free of contamination from any kind of relationship category.

### *Level of Knowing, Duration of Relationship, and Frequency of Contact*

Christopher McCarty (1995) conducted three studies to understand what dimensions were represented by the term "knowing." He collected the personal networks of 47 respondents in Gainesville, Florida, each listing exactly 60 alters. He also completed two telephone surveys, one of 233 respondents selecting 8 alters and another of 747 respondents selecting 14 alters. Both telephone surveys used first names as cues for selecting alters. Respondents reported several characteristics for each alter, including how well they knew them on a scale from 1 to 5, the duration of their relationship, and how frequently the respondent/ego had contact with them. McCarty found that for all three studies, the level of knowing increased as the duration of the relation increased. Furthermore, the reported level of knowing an alter increased with frequency of contact, until the highest category of knowing was reached. This level is the one typically reserved for family and very close friends. Alters known the longest and rated the highest on the level of knowing could often be those the respondent saw least frequently.

assume that duration of relations or frequency of contact are strongly correlated with assessment of the strength of a tie. We often have alters we have known for a long time whom we fall out of touch with, or others whom we regularly see at work but do not feel close to at all. The duration of the tie is biased toward kin relationships, whereas the frequency of contact is biased toward work and neighbor relationships.

The duration of the relationship is related to the level of knowing each other, but the frequency of interaction does not have that relation, as Christopher McCarty (1995) showed. So, all of these indicators reveal different pieces of information about the relationship. Even though they may not measure the same dimension of tie strength, these variables capture meaningful aspects of personal relationships, and they are often included in personal network research.

Another common piece of information collected about each alter is the type of relation the respondent has with him or her, that is, the *role* that the alter has in the ego's network or the *social context* where they met. This is probably the most important characteristic explaining modularity or clustering in networks, at least in larger personal networks, as clusters in the personal network are often produced by common contexts.

To collect that information, researchers often ask whether alters are family, friends, or acquaintances. This classification may work for some research, but in other cases, you may want more detail. This additional information is often generated by asking the respondent how he or she knows the alter. Common categories include family (sometimes broken down into biological versus family-by-marriage, or even further into parent, sibling, child, other biological family, and inlaws), work (sometimes broken down by hierarchical position at work, such as coworker, supervisor, or employee), church, school, organization, known through someone else, and other. Sometimes the category "professionals" is added (e.g., for when alters include their practitioner, psychiatrist,

### *The Friendship Label*

As noted earlier, Claude Fischer (1982a) conducted a face-to-face survey of 1,050 adults living in northern California, known as the Northern California Community Study. Respondents provided the names of people with whom they were involved in supportive social exchanges and reported some attributes of each, including whether they were a "friend." On average, respondents reported 18.5 alters, with a total of 19,417 alters across all respondents. Of these, 59% were labeled as "friends." Analysis of the data revealed a lack of consistency in the application of the label. Friend was typically applied to nonrelatives, non-neighbors, non-coworkers, and people near them in age. Other personal characteristics varied widely. The application of the label "close" was not strongly correlated with the label "friend." Respondents tended to associate long-term relationships and sociability with friends. Fischer concluded that the term "friend" is applied so loosely that it imparts little information. He advised researchers against using "friend" as an indicator of social involvement of intimacy.

teacher, or lawyer). Some researchers include the category "friend" in this list. Some of us consider that a mistake, for many alters from a variety of social settings will fall into that category, which ultimately provides little detail about the social context. A better question may then be, "How did you meet?" This captures the social context of virtually every relationship, and few people meet immediately as friends.

We need to consider that current roles or contexts may differ from past roles. You may know someone from school who is now your brother-in-law. Or maybe you knew someone through someone else, but now you are coworkers. You need to decide whether or not that information is important for you. Also, some people have multiple roles, which may explain why they form a bridge between two subgroups in the networks. Do you want to allow for multiple roles or not?

Another set of potentially important variables is the *mode of contact* between ego and alter: How often do ego and alter contact each other face to face, by phone, email, instant messaging, or social media? Computer-mediated communications have different affordances, facilitating social interactions regardless of time and space. Since people often combine different modes of contact for each alter, inquiring about mode of contact at an alter level usually involves adding a set of name interpreters to the study, one question for each contact mode (e.g., "How often do you contact [alter X] in person?" Broad response categories may be Daily, Weekly, Monthly, and Yearly). Therefore, including these questions adds a weighty respondent burden, especially for larger networks. Therefore, you need to ask yourself if it is important to ask these questions for each alter, or whether having such information at the ego level, or for a subgroup of alters, will be sufficient. Bernie Hogan (2009) showed how the different contact modes employed for each alter in a network can be visualized by using radial pie charts for each node. On the basis of the responses to this set of name interpreters, he also proposed a *particularity score* for each ego, to measure whether individuals fine-tune their modes of contact to each specific alter or whether they adopt a general strategy that is more or less the same for all alters. He used this score to test Barry Wellman's theory of networked individualism (see Chapter 2).

The characteristics we have mentioned so far are the most common attributes of ego–alter relationships (ego–alter dyads) captured in personal network research. However, you can measure a host of other characteristics of ego–alter dyads, but again this depends on your research questions. You might ask about the *exchanges* that take place in relationships, for example, whether you can talk with each alter about personal problems. Another frequently used name interpreter is the geographical *proximity* of the alter: Instead of asking where the alter lives (which is an alter characteristic) and then calculating the distance between the ego's and alter's place of living, we can simply ask respondents how far away the alter lives from the ego, for example, in terms of miles/kilometers or travel time. Be aware that people may never meet at each other's home.

In some cases, dyadic characteristics can also be calculated from the name generators or from the ego and alter characteristics. If we have multiple name generators, we can calculate the *multiplexity* of each relationship as the number of types of support that is exchanged between the ego and alter. If we have asked for provided support and received support, we can create a variable *reciprocity* and assign the value 1 (reciprocal) if the ego both provided and received support from the alter, and 0 if he or she only provided or only received support. We can also create dyadic characteristics on the basis of the *similarity* of alter and ego characteristics. For example, based on the gender of the ego and alter, we can create the variable "gender similarity," assigning the value 1 if the alter has the same gender as the ego and 0 if he or she does not. We can do the same thing for similarity in age.

If you collect your data using paper questionnaires, you can make a table where you can fill in the attributes of alters and ego–alter dyads, as is shown in Table 7.1. Software for the data collection of personal networks with computer-assisted personal interviewing, such as EgoNet and VennMaker, allows you to specify these questions and repeat them for each alter. In these networks, the program fills in the names of alters in the question itself.

**TABLE 7.1. Example of a Table for Filling in Name Interpreters**

| Name | Gender<br>Is ______ male or female? | Smoking<br>Does ______ currently smoke? | How close are you to ______?<br>1 = Not close at all<br>2 = A little close<br>3 = Quite close<br>4 = Very close<br>9 = NA | How long have you known ______? (in years) |
|---|---|---|---|---|
| 1. | Male/Female | Yes/No/Don't know | 1/2/3/4/9 | |
| 2. | Male/Female | Yes/No/Don't know | 1/2/3/4/9 | |
| 3. | Male/Female | Yes/No/Don't know | 1/2/3/4/9 | |
| 4. | Male/Female | Yes/No/Don't know | 1/2/3/4/9 | |

### Name Generator or Name Interpreter?

You may have noticed that many of the tie characteristics we have mentioned so far (closeness, roles, exchanges, and frequency of interaction) are the same ones we use to define the boundaries of the network (see Section 6.4). So, these characteristics can be used to generate names or to know more about the network you have generated. For example, you can ask people to nominate alters they feel close with and then ask with whom of these people they exchange support (so the name generator is based on closeness and exchange is a name interpreter). You can also ask people to name a list of others who give them support and then ask how close they feel to each of them (in this case, the name generator is based on exchanges, and closeness is a name interpreter). However, if you think about it, this is not the same. There is a fundamental difference in the type of data you collect. In the first case, you will know the characteristics of the people a respondent feels close with and to what extent they provide him or her with support, but you may miss out on supportive people with whom the respondent does not feel close. Therefore, you can draw conclusions about the supportiveness of the affective network, but not about the availability of social support per se. You cannot conclude, for example, that the respondents receive a lot of emotional support, but they have nobody who can take care of their house. You simply don't know that. In the second case, where you generate the network on the basis of support, you will know the characteristics of the support network and how close the respondent feels toward these people, but you may miss out on a number of people with whom the respondent feels close, just because they don't give social support. You can therefore draw conclusions about the strength of the support network but not about the number or type of people with whom the ego feels close. You cannot conclude, for example, that the people respondents feel closest with are those who live near them.

A good example of this is given by William Eveland, Osei Appiah, and Paul Beck (2018). The literature about political discussion networks tends to find that agreement in networks is relatively high, in the sense that the ego tends to prefer the same candidate for president as her alters. Eveland et al. argued that the degree of agreement might be due to the name generator, which asks respondents about who in their network they discuss politics with. A name interpreter would then inquire about the perceived presidential vote choice of the resulting alters. Yet when Eveland et al. added a second name generator to probe for political disagreement in the network, over half the respondents who had had a homogeneous network on the former name generator were able to name an alter who supported a different candidate. So, agreement can be measured as a name interpreter or as a name generator, with different results.

## 7.5 HOW MANY QUESTIONS ABOUT ALTERS?: RESPONDENT BURDEN

Asking respondents to provide detailed information about each alter is typically the lengthiest and most burdensome part of the interview. Although you may be able to skip some questions about alters based on their answers to other questions (see Section 5.3 on skip logic), in general, you should think in terms of the respondent having to answer each question about every alter. With 10 alters and 10 pieces of information, that is 100 questions. With 40 alters and 10 questions that is 400 questions. This can be incredibly time consuming (Golinelli et al., 2010, estimated 5 seconds per question in this part), and few ways exist to shortcut the process. This is the biggest reason to think carefully about how many alters you want to elicit and how much information you want to know about each one. You must balance these two to best address your research question. Be careful not to add unnecessary questions.

To reduce respondent burden, you can also ask some questions only for a sample of alters (Golinelli et al., 2010). You can either randomly select a subset about which to collect detailed alter data, or you can select a purposive sample of alters (e.g., only for strong contacts or contacts with the highest frequency of interaction).

Something else that often comes up when thinking about respondent burden is how to present alter-information questions to the respondent. Generally, two methods are used: The same list of questions is asked about each alter; or a question is asked and the respondent lists the alters about whom the question is true, or to whom the question pertains. Researchers disagree about which method is less burdensome. However, in the latter case, you may replace alter questions with a yes/no format ("Did Harry help you find a job? Did Sally help you find a job?") by listwise questions ("Who of these people helped you find a job?"), which may be quicker but also a little more inaccurate as it is easier to forget someone.

Sometimes it can also help to build in some interactivity to keep the data interview more fun to do. In this aspect, participatory methods to draw networks are more interactive, but they can sometimes be less systematic. Also, the alter information part can still be burdensome.

In very special circumstances, some researchers try to verify information about an alter by interviewing him or her as well (e.g., Green, Hoover, Wagner, Ryan, & Ssegujja, 2014). This process has sometimes been referred to as *alter chasing* (Killworth, McCarty,

### *Ordering Questions about Alters Alterwise or Questionwise*

Tina Kogovšek et al. (Kogovšek, Ferligoj, Coenders, & Saris, 2002) conducted surveys to test whether alter attribute data are more reliable when asked by alter (all questions for each alter), or by question (all alters for a single question). A total of 1,033 respondents from Ljubljana, Slovenia, were interviewed twice. The design was to vary the survey mode (telephone vs. face-to-face) and interview method (by alter vs. by question). Respondents were randomly assigned to three groups, which varied these approaches across the two waves of interviews, and reliability was measured by the similarity of the alter attribute data collected. Overall, the telephone mode by *alter* (compared with the telephone mode by question and the face-to-face mode by alter) was the most reliable for measuring closeness and importance. The face-to-face by alter mode was the most reliable for measuring contact.

Johnsen, & Bernard, 2006). As you can imagine, alter chasing is typically time consuming, expensive, and impractical. Some studies of respondents, however, are interconnected by a link-tracing sampling design, which means that selected alters of egos are interviewed and become egos themselves. These designs may allow the study of agreement in respondent pairs about their relationships (e.g., Mouw et al., 2014).

Finally, in many cases, we also want to know how the alters are related to each other, which tells us something about network structure. This network structure can have an impact on the flow of information, social control, and mobilization of social support, which can affect respondents' outcomes. How to measure relationships among alters will be discussed in the next chapter.

## CHAPTER SUMMARY

We started this chapter reflecting on the issue of what egos really know about alters. This knowledge helps us to ask appropriate questions about alter attributes. In addition, the chapter showed that we can ask questions about *alter attributes* and *dyadic attributes* (i.e., ego–alter relationship or characteristics). This is normally the lengthiest part of the interview, and we have described some methods to reduce respondent burden.

### FURTHER READING

Eagle, D. E., & Proeschold-Bell, R.-J. (2015). Methodological considerations in the use of name generators and interpreters. *Social Networks, 40,* 75–83.

Kogovšek, T., Coenders, G., & Hlebec, V. (2013). Predictors and outcomes of social network compositions: A compositional structural equation modeling approach. *Social Networks, 35*(1), 1–10.

Marsden, P., & Campbell, K. (1984). Measuring tie strength. *Social Forces, 63,* 482–501.

Vehovar, V., Lozar Manfreda, K., Koren, G., & Hlebec, V. (2008). Measuring ego-centered social networks on the web: Questionnaire design issues. *Social Networks, 30*(3), 213–222.

8

# Collecting Data about Ties between Alters

---

*What Is This Chapter About?*

This chapter explains how to collect information about indirect ties, that is, alter–alter ties, in order to understand the network structure. This is what we called the fourth module of a personal network study (see Chapter 5). As Section 8.1 explains, this information has proven to be important for understanding the ego's personal network constraints and opportunities and its consequences. Section 8.2 addresses the issue of what type of information we know about alter–alter ties. As in the case of alter attributes, the perceived network and the bias on recall of social ties are key issues to take into account. Section 8.3 covers the different types of questions you can ask for collecting alter–alter ties, and Section 8.4 suggests ways to reduce the burden of participants reporting alter–alter ties, a task that grows exponentially with the number of alters.

---

## 8.1 WHAT IS AN EDGE INTERPRETER?

The last module of a personal network study concerns asking the respondent about the ties between his or her network members. In contrast to the ego's direct relations with alter, the ties between the network members have also been called "indirect relations." Questions about the relationships between alters can be called *edge interpreters* (usually they have also been called "name interpreters" [see Chapter 7] and sometimes "name interconnectors"; Borgatti et al., 2013). Past personal network studies have often skipped this module because they often relied on the analysis of personal network composition only to test their hypotheses. Researchers who limit their approach to network composition are assuming that the effects of social context on attitudes, behaviors, and conditions are more about who occupies the personal network than about how they are structurally arranged around the respondent. In many cases, this assumption works. However, researchers are increasingly asking about ties between alters to expand the set of variables they have available for making predictions.

To understand why structure may matter, look at Figure 8.1. The figure shows two personal networks of two different egos (the black nodes in the center of the graphs), each of whom has 21 alters in four different contexts—work, family, peers known since childhood, and friends from university. As far as we can see in the graphs, the network size and composition are completely comparable. However, the structure is quite different. In the first graph, we see that the ego is the only person who connects these different groups. Family, workmates, peers, and friends never meet independently of the ego with people from other contexts. In the second graph, this is different. Here, we see that relationships between people from the different contexts exist. Maybe this is because the ego is still living in the town where she was born, a small university town, and all people in her network have lived in that town since her childhood. Maybe the ego works in a family business, so the borders between different contexts are less clear. Or maybe it is because the ego likes to throw dinner parties, and people at his or her parties now meet independently.

Whatever the reason is, the way these people are structured around the ego may have consequences. Consider that the ego is ill one day. She calls her workmate to say that she won't come in and to ask whether they can cancel her meetings that day. In the first graph, people from other contexts won't know about the ego's illness if the ego doesn't tell one of them herself. In the second network, however, it may happen that the

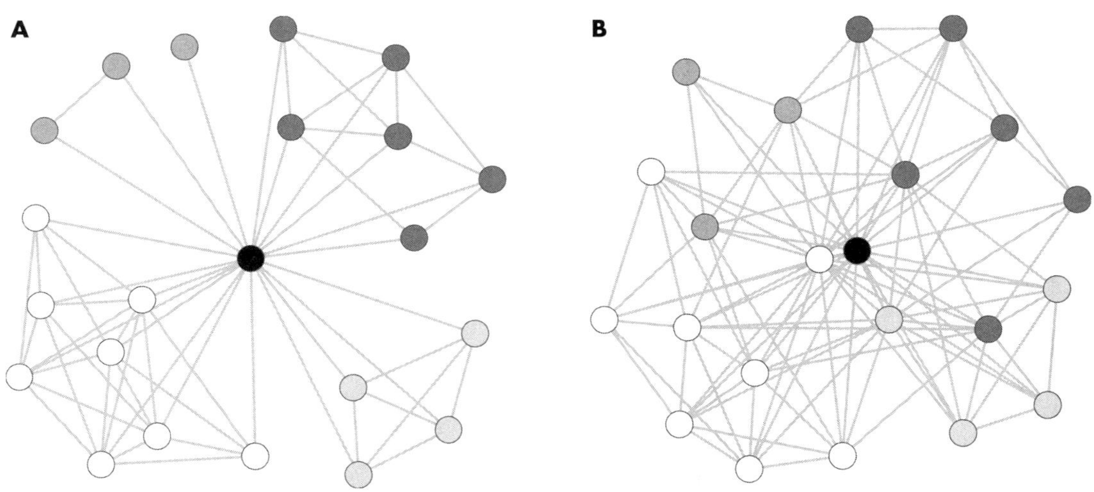


**FIGURE 8.1.** An example of two personal networks with similar network composition but different structural arrangements. *Note.* The black node represents the ego, who is connected to everyone else; the white nodes are family members. The light gray nodes are university friends, the darker shade of gray represents peers known since childhood, and the darkest shade of gray represents people from work.

ego's workmate runs into the ego's sister and tells her that she is ill. Having heard that the ego is ill, the sister may decide to stop at the ego's house to bring chicken soup or to check if she needs anything. Social support is more easily mobilized if alters are connected to each other.

Now imagine that the ego went out for drinks with her university friends, and she drank a tad too much that night. In the first network, that stays among the friends. In the second network, however, it is possible that one of her friends runs into one of the workmates, whom he also personally knows, and asks laughingly how the ego is doing that day. In other words, social control is also stronger in networks that are more connected. And if the ego is seeking employment or housing, the second network is thought to give more redundant information than the first network, where the ego knows people who are unrelated to each other and who may therefore have access to information that others don't have.

This is the type of information we are after when we study personal network structure. We want to know about the network structure because we assume that it influences flows of information, social control, or the mobilization of social support. We believe that it matters whether the ego has different groups of people that only she bridges, that her network has a densely connected core surrounded by peripheral relations, or that, for example, only her husband or partner also bridges all these groups of people. We assume this has effects, for example, in case of a rupture of the relationship with her husband. Some researchers also focus on the micro level in processes of transitivity: If the ego is related to two alters, what are the chances that these two alters know each other? Are these chances lower when the tie crosses categorical boundaries of social class, race, or sex? Are boundary-crossing relationships more frequent when people know persons in common? At the micro level, these are questions about *triadic closure*, given that the ego is by design related to both alters. The question now is, how can we collect that type of information?

## 8.2 WHAT WE REALLY KNOW ABOUT ALTER–ALTER TIES

As shown in the previous chapters, alter–alter tie data is information you can only get from the respondent; usually, there are not other ways of observing the interactions between a respondent's alters. The same rules as in the previous chapters apply for formatting the questions and ensuring they are reasonable. The questions' being reasonable is particularly important. In the last chapter, we saw that you must not ask respondents a question about their alters that they cannot know. The risk of asking such questions is higher for ties between alters. The ability of respondents to report on the ties between their alters is constrained if the question is too detailed.

Some researchers do not believe respondents can report alter–tie data with any accuracy at all. They cite research that compares observations of persons' interactions with interactions reported by the observed persons themselves (Bernard & Killworth, 1977), and they show that informant accuracy is generally very low. The assumption is that if respondents cannot report accurately on their own interactions with others, they cannot possibly be reliable in their evaluations of interactions between their alters. However, as we discussed in Chapter 6, people have trouble remembering their real-time interactions, but they are much better able to report on routinized ties. If we ask about alter ties in personal networks, we do not ask which alters have had contact with which alters in the previous 24 hours. Rather, we ask much simpler questions about routinized ties, for example, about whether two alters know each other.

Researchers who do not believe that respondents can report alter–tie data with accuracy may also cite research on cognitive social networks in bounded groups—that is, studies where everybody in a bounded group is asked to rate the relationships that exist between group members, for all pairs of group members. Researchers who compared the cognitive structures of members of the group with a consensus structure of the group have shown that people tend to simplify distal relationships by imposing a balance scheme (Krackhardt & Kilduff, 1999). So, if they don't know persons A and B too well, but they know that A is close with C and that B is also close with C, they simply assume that A and C must get along well. Researchers use this evidence to support their argument that people cannot report reliably about relationships among their network members. The comparison with personal networks, however, is invalid. In a whole network, such as a fraternity or an organization, there may be many members whom the respondent does not know well. For example, someone in a fraternity does not necessarily know everybody else in the fraternity. They are part of the same group by definition (i.e., the researcher has assigned them to that boundary), not necessarily by social interaction. In addition, respondents in whole network research are asked to report on sometimes subtle interactions within a constrained social domain. This is clearly the source of at least some of the inaccuracy.

In a personal network, respondents typically report on the interactions among a set of people who, by definition, they know reasonably well. These network alters may come from a variety of social domains, such as family, work, or church. It is much easier for respondents to report on the existence of ties between members whom they know well but who are of different social domains (e.g., their family and their work) than it is to report on ties between people they may not know well but who fall within a single domain (a fraternity). As personal network researchers, we are far more interested in the larger structures reflecting different groups and bridging between groups than subtle interactions within groups, so our questions about alter–alter ties are usually quite simple. In personal networks that have multiple social domains, many of the tie evaluations will be null: that is, no tie will exist between two given alters. It is relatively easy to tell whether people in the family interact with people from work.

Apart from this consideration, sometimes the perceived network structure is precisely what you would like to know. This may be the case if you study some behavior of individuals and you believe that individuals act upon the cognitive network rather than the network we could observe. For example, if on one hand, a respondent believes that her acquaintance, Ann, knows her coworkers, she may not ask Ann whether she knows about job opportunities, just to make sure that her colleagues don't get to know she is thinking of leaving. If, on the other hand, she does not know that Ann knows them, she might not be that careful with this question. So, the respondent mobilizes the network for obtaining information about jobs on the basis of whom she perceives to be connected with her work environment, rather than on the basis of the "real" network structure.

## 8.3 ALTER–ALTER PROMPTS

The limited ability of respondents to report about alter–alter ties implies that we should ask simple questions to respondents about these relationships that they can actually report on. We should not ask them to report how often two people in their networks have contacted each other lately. We typically do not ask either whether the relationship that alter A has with B is different from the relationship that B has with A. This is difficult to assess. Rather, we ask about symmetrical relationships. Of course, if we focus on core networks (say, on the respondent's five closest ties), our questions can be a little bit more complex than if we focus on somewhat broader networks (say, of 45 people), where the connection may be weaker. But still, it is advisable to limit your questions about alter–alter relationships to a minimum (to one question, usually) and also to use a limited set of response categories.

A critical question to consider in both personal and whole network data collection is how to define the tie or ties you will ultimately use to measure network structure. Not all tie questions are the same, and the way you ask the question will determine the structure you are measuring. Let's consider an example. Say you have a friend named Ken. A year ago, you introduced Ken to your brother, Tom, who came for a visit. They spent some time socializing, and then Tom returned home. He never contacted Ken again. If you were asked to report whether Ken and Tom knew each other, you might say yes. Many examples just like this exist of people who have met and would recognize each other by sight or by name, but in the absence of an artificially imposed opportunity like the one above, would never actually talk to each other. Just having met (and therefore "knowing") someone is not necessarily the type of social interaction that interests social network researchers.

As network researchers, what typically interests us is the potential for (or lack of) interaction. Having met in the past is not enough. Our preference for a general alter–alter tie question is to ask the respondent about the likelihood that the two alters would be talking when the respondent is not present. In other words, do the two alters have a relationship independent of the respondent? If so, then the tie contributes to the social context in which the respondent lives. If not, then any interaction must go through the respondent or somebody else. An example of such a question is given by Caterina Gouvis Roman and colleagues (2012, p. 39) for their study with young people:

> "What is the likelihood that [alter X] and [alter Y] talk to each other or hang out with each other without your involvement or independently of you? Think about any kind of interaction, even if the two don't get along. Would you say not at all; they might, but not sure; or definitely?"

Having used both questions (knowing each other and talking when the respondent is not present), we see that the question about talking reveals a less dense network with more interesting structural features than the knowing network. That is not to say that using "knowing" or having been in contact as a tie definition is incorrect.

For some studies, the subject matter may be more specific, requiring a different question. A study about the professional personal networks of researchers may want to ask whether two alters have collaborated in projects or publications in the past. Respondents may not always know that. A study about creativity may benefit from a question about whether two alters tend to bounce ideas off each other. And in some cases you may want to ask more than one tie question, using skip logic to keep the number of questions to a minimum. In such cases, it is best to ask one question about all alter–alter ties and then to go back and ask a second question about the ties for which it is relevant. Otherwise, some respondents may change their answers to avoid answering more questions.

Finally, let's look at the response categories you will use for the tie question. Unlike the question in which you ask the respondent to report about his or her tie with each alter where, by definition, the respondent has at least some tie to each alter, when evalu-

### *Detailed Answer Categories for Smaller Personal Networks*

In the Survey of the Social Networks of the Dutch (SSND; Mollenhorst et al., 2011), respondents were asked to nominate others with whom they discussed important personal matters in the past six months. The vast majority of respondents named between one and five people, with a mean of 2.4 and only 8% of the respondents naming more than five. So, in this case, the number of alter–alter ties to evaluate is low, mostly from no tie (for one alter) to 10 ties (for five alters). Also, since the respondent feels close to the alters, she or he should be better able to evaluate their ties, so the response categories can be a little bit more elaborate. The question to elicit alter–alter ties was as follows: "Finally, I would like to know whether some people you know also know each other. How well do the following persons know each other? Do they know each other, and if yes, do they get along well, or do they avoid each other?" Interviewer: hand over CHART "network members among each other."

1 – They avoid each other.

2 – They do not know each other.

3 – They hardly know each other.

4 – They know each other well.

5 – They know each other well and get along.

Only 0.1% of the alter pairs avoided each other, and more than a third of the alter pairs knew each other well and got along well.

ating alter–alter ties, many may be null. Recall that you are asking about a symmetric relationship between the two alters. This could be something very specific, such as "Have Alter A and Alter B ever had sex?," or something more general, such as "How well does Alter A know Alter B?" In either case, do not expect too detailed an evaluation from the respondent. Although you could use a scale ranging from 0 to 10 for the respondent to assess how well the two alters know each other, it is doubtful that respondents have that level of knowledge about any of their alters. Our preference is to use no more than three levels (e.g., a 0–2 scale) for alter–alter tie evaluations, as in the example given above ("not at all," "they might, but not sure," "definitely"). However, in some cases you may extend this, for example, to include negative alter–alter ties (e.g., Hosnedlová, 2017).

If you collect personal network data with paper-and-pencil techniques, you can use a lower triangle of a matrix to fill in the data (as is shown in Table 8.1) in that example for a network of maximally five alters. You can also collect these data with computer-assisted personal interviewing, using software that has been developed for collecting personal network data. This type of software allows you to specify one or multiple alter–alter questions, and during the interview, it will repeat the question for all pairs of alters, implementing the names of alters until all pairs are evaluated.

In our experience, even if you collect data about network structure with special software in a structured way, it still helps to write down the complete list of alters on paper during the name-generating process, especially if the list is large. This paper serves as a visual aid for the respondent at the moment he or she is asked to evaluate alter–alter pairs. It will quickly become clear that the interviewer first asks if alter 1 is related to alter 2, 3, 4, 5, and so on, and then goes to alter 2 and goes through the list again (alter 2 with alter 3, 4, 5 etc.; alter 3 with alters 4, 5, etc.; alter 4 with alter 5, etc.). Being able to anticipate the questions accelerates the process and makes it cognitively less demanding than when pairs of alters are "fired" at the respondent without him or her knowing which pair comes next.

Similarly, others have experimented with rearranging the alters by context before asking about network structure (Vacca, 2013). For example, regardless of the order in which alters were originally mentioned by the respondent, the alter list to elicit network

**TABLE 8.1. Example of a Matrix for Filling in Data Resulting from a Name Interconnector**

| Do ______ and ______ know each other? | | | | | |
|---|---|---|---|---|---|
| | Name 1: | Name 2: | Name 3: | Name 4: | Name 5: |
| Name 1: | | | | | |
| Name 2: | Yes/No | | | | |
| Name 3: | Yes/No | Yes/No | | | |
| Name 4: | Yes/No | Yes/No | Yes/No | | |
| Name 5: | Yes/No | Yes/No | Yes/No | Yes/No | |

ties might present first, family contacts, second, coworkers, third, church friends, and so on. The respondent is then asked to evaluate the ties between a given alter and all family members first, second between the same alter, and all coworkers, and so on. This makes the process cognitively less demanding because, for each alter whose ties are being evaluated (the "row" alter), the respondent is presented with all other alters grouped in a meaningful and recognizable order of social contexts (family, work, church, neighborhood, etc.). Thus, the respondent does not have to cognitively "jump" back and forth between different contexts when evaluating ties. Because context switching requires the respondent to refocus on a new context each time, minimizing context switching should decrease respondent burden.

## 8.4 RESPONDENT BURDEN

If we ask the respondent to report on all possible ties between alters, there will be many to evaluate. However, unlike whole network research, where the ties may be asymmetric (I may think my tie with my coworker is a 4 out of 5 when he only thinks it merits a 3 out of 5), in personal network research we typically ask only about symmetric ties. Even if the ties are asymmetric, it would be unusual to ask the respondent to make that sort of assessment. For example, it may be difficult for a respondent to assess whether the tie between two coworkers is unequal. As a result, we typically only ask the respondent to report on the existence of a tie between the two alters, without characterizing its strength.

Although this helps in terms of respondent burden, there may still be many ties to evaluate. The number of symmetric ties to evaluate is given by the formula $N(N-1)/2$, where $N$ is the number of alters in the network. A graph of this formula is depicted in Figure 8.2. The figure shows that the respondent burden increases geometrically as alters are added. For a personal network with 10 alters, the respondent reports on $10 \times 9 / 2 = 45$ ties. For a network with 20 alters, there are 190 ties to evaluate. For a network of 50 alters, the respondent needs to report on 1,225 ties. While we believe that this is the most accurate procedure for measuring network structure, it is a tedious task for respondents, even if it goes pretty fast (at 2 seconds per evaluation; Hogan et al., 2007; McCarty et al., 2007). Therefore, as a researcher, you must balance what you want to get from respondents against the burden it places on them.

People wonder if a respondent can answer so many questions reliably. If respondents had to evaluate more than a thousand ties twice, would they provide the same answers each time? Again, in a personal network where several social domains are represented, many ties will be null. It is not unusual for no social connections to exist between family and work or between work and church. By defaulting the tie to null, this process becomes less burdensome to the respondent.

Also recall that with freelists, respondents tend to list people in groups (Fiske, 1995). Typically, you will ask respondents to evaluate the ties of the first alter with all other alters, the second with the rest, and so on. This means they are evaluating a mem-

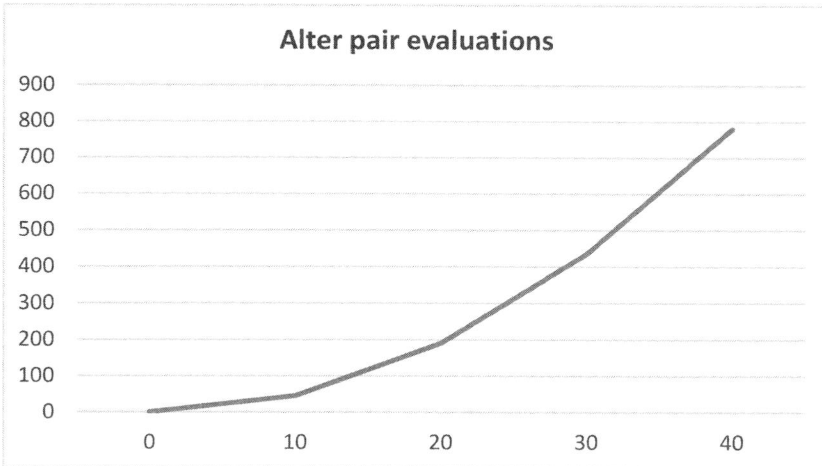


**FIGURE 8.2.** Increase in the number of tie evaluations as alters are added.

ber of a constant group with all other groups; and in many cases this will involve a long string of null evaluations, particularly if the alter is an isolate. This is why respondents can make a thousand such evaluations in around 30 minutes. It is also why respondents can evaluate ties reliably.

We briefly mentioned methods for reducing respondent burden in the previous chapter. These typically involve asking fewer questions. This can be done in different ways: You can (1) select a subset of alters randomly (e.g., 12 out of 20; Golinelli et al., 2010); (2) select a subset of alters based on purposive sampling (e.g., only the closest ties); (3) select a subset of alter pairs randomly; and (4) select a subset of alter pairs based on purposive sampling. Research (McCarty & Killworth, 2007) has shown that the best option to reduce respondent burden is to randomly select a sample of alters from a larger list and ask about the relationships only among those alters (method 1). This method works well when analyses are planned only at the network level, to estimate network structural characteristics. Even so, it has the problem that individuals typically are not interchangeable among them, and for example, a spouse normally shares with the ego a

### *The Reliability of Respondents' Evaluations of Alter–Alter Ties*

Christopher McCarty (2002) tested the reliability of respondent evaluations with 47 respondents, each of whom had generated a 60-alter network and completed 1,770 tie evaluations on a 0 to 5 scale. Every 30th tie evaluation was presented to the respondent for evaluation a second time. Of the 59 reevaluations per respondent, 93% were recoded exactly the same way the second time and 97% were recoded within ± 1 point.

larger proportion of contacts than a neighbor. If the spouse is not selected in the sample, the personal network of the given individual can be inaccurate.

Some researchers have suggested using a visual interface as a way to engage respondents during this part of data collection and make it more fun. Bernie Hogan and colleagues (Hogan et al., 2007), for example, had respondents write the names of alters on tags that they placed on a paper circle diagram (see Chapter 6), where the tags could be moved to other locations to accurately reflect closeness to the ego and the relations they had to each other (Figure 8.3). After that, they measured the network structure. Cliques of very close ties had a circle drawn around them; very close ties between two alters (but from different cliques) had a line drawn between them; cliques of somewhat close ties had a dashed circle; and somewhat close ties between two alters had a dashed line between them. This method allows for some shortcuts: about dense clusters it may be said that "everybody knows everybody else."

Software for the computer-assisted collection of personal network data, such as Vennmaker, also provides participatory methods to draw the network structure. Using this type of software, we can represent alters using dots and labels, and respondents can create the ties between alters by clicking on one dot and dragging the mouse toward the other. This method begins with all ties being null, and respondents supply the non-null ties. This method is quicker than evaluating each alter–alter tie individually, but it may introduce bias, depending on the user interface.

First, respondents often get to choose the ties they supply, and therefore they also choose the level of effort. Some respondents may choose to stop listing ties before all are listed. Second, the visualization itself may introduce biases. If the software does not redraw the visualization after each tie is introduced, it may be difficult for respondents

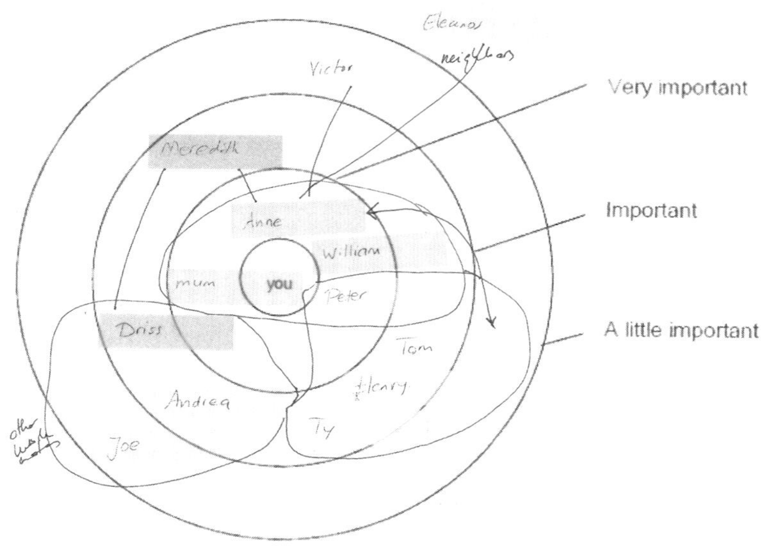


**FIGURE 8.3.** An example of a personal network drawn using paper-and-pencil techniques.

### *A Different Way to Explore Network Structure and Composition*

In a research study concerning smoking behavior, Christopher McCarty and Sama Govindaramanujam (2005) designed an interactive tool (EgoWeb) to assess the accuracy of personal network elicitation methods and try to discover ways to reduce the respondent burden when evaluating all alter–alter pairs. This tool forced respondents to list a single alter but not one who was closest to them. They were then asked to name someone they knew who also talked to that alter. As these alters were added to EgoWeb, a dot was placed on the screen with the alter's name below it and a line was placed between the alter and the dot representing the respondent, indicating a network tie. Next, respondents were asked to name an alter whom they knew, but who did not talk to any of the other two alters already depicted. They were then asked to name an alter who talked to the one just mentioned. If they couldn't think of someone who talked to that alter, that alter was an isolate. This process of naming pairs or singles that were unrelated continued until the respondent couldn't name any more. Finally, they were asked to complete the list until 45 alters.

This method, compared with the freelisting of 45 alters collected with EgoNet, captured the same core of individuals but rendered different composition and structural measures, especially because respondents decided what relationships to report.

to see the possibility that certain ties exist, especially in larger networks. If the software does redraw the graph, it may bias respondents toward adding to groups and not linking groups together. This is an area that needs further investigation and software development. From our experience, we prefer not to do the alter–alter tie evaluations visually in larger networks.

## CHAPTER SUMMARY

When we collect data about personal networks using interviews, we collect four types of data: data about the respondent (Chapter 5); a list of names of alters (Chapter 6); the characteristics of these alters and the relationships respondents have with them (Chapter 7); and the structure of relationships among alters (this chapter). Although some studies do not use edge interpreters for collecting alter–alter ties, this structure, measured typically without ego, gives unique insight into the social pressures and resources embedded in personal networks. The perceived personal network is real for the ego in all its consequences, but it can entail systematic bias that researchers have to take into account. Actually, the ego does not know too much about alter–alter ties, with the exception of close ties, and this is why alter–alter prompts should be simple, easy to answer, and have few response categories. A way to reduce the exponential burden upon ego when reporting many alters pairs is to use lists or drawings combined with computer-assisted personal interviewing. Especially in the case of smaller networks, we can even do interviews by phone or Web survey. Once this information has been collected, we can start to visualize and analyze the personal networks. This is what we will discuss in Chapters 9 and 11–13.

## FURTHER READING

Bernard, H. R., & Killworth, P. D. (1977). Informant accuracy in social network data II. *Human Communication Research, 4*(1), 3–18.

Hogan, B., Melville, J. R., Phillips, G. L., II, Janulis, P., Contractor, N., Mustanski, B. S., et al. (2016). Evaluating the paper-to-screen translation of participant-aided sociograms with high-risk participants. In *Proceedings of the 2016 CHI Conference on Human Factors in Computing Systems,* Chicago, IL.

McCarty, C. (2002). Measuring structure in personal networks. *Journal of Social Structure, 3*(1), 1–29.

McCarty, C., & Killworth, P. D. (2007). Impact of methods for reducing respondent burden on personal network structural measures. *Social Networks, 29*(2), 300–315.

# 9

# Visualizing Personal Networks

*What Is This Chapter About?*

So far we have been looking at how to collect data about personal networks, mostly by asking questions. In this chapter, we will see how personal network visualizations are not just a way of illustrating compositional and structural measures or a combination of both, but a basic approach for collecting, analyzing, and developing new insights about the ego's social environment. With this aim, in the next section (Section 9.1), you will learn the basic principles typically used in personal network visualization. Next (in Section 9.2), you will see what kind of visual displays have been used for collecting and interpreting personal network data so far. Finally, you will be introduced to the clustered graph method, which is intended to enable the comparison of personal networks at both the individual and community levels. This will be done in Sections 9.3 and 9.4, respectively.

## 9.1 PERSONAL NETWORK VISUALIZATION: BASIC PRINCIPLES

Let us start this account about personal network visualization with a motto: data visualization is not just illustration but also *discovery* (Brandes, Kenis, & Raab, 2005). In this vein, Linton C. Freeman, in his account of social network analysis, pointed out that network visualization was one of its four basic features (Freeman, 2004). What is true for social network analysis in general is also true for personal network analysis in particular, but, as you will see soon, with some specific features.

The first principle governing the display of personal networks is the use of a "target diagram" or "concentric circle diagram" that we introduced in Chapter 2. A target diagram is a succession of concentric circles that places in the center the most important nodes/relationships. This idea goes back to 1940 when Mary Louise Northway published her influential paper "A Method for Depicting Social Relationships Obtained by Sociometric Testing" (Northway, 1940; see Figure 9.1A). This method was intended for depicting sociocentric choices, but in 1969, anthropologist Arnold ("Bill") Epstein (1969) of the Manchester School used the method to depict a gossip network in an African city. He placed the focal individual and his wife at the center. He placed the alters who were involved in the gossiping either in the inner circle or in the periphery (the "extended network"), using a combination of typical anthropological kinship symbols with communication flows (see Figure 9.1B). In 1980, Robert Kahn and Toni Antonucci (1980) also used paper diagrams with three concentric circles around a smaller circle with the word "You" (see Figure 6.1) in order to elicit a set of network members that provided social support to the respondent (see Section 6.4). Since then, with small variations and dubbed with different names, this way of displaying personal networks has been widely used (Wellman & Berkowitz, 1988; see Figure 9.1C), both on paper and on interactive screens, and either for data collection or for analysis.

The first lesson learned from this tradition is that many personal network visualizations place relevant alters in the core and less relevant alters in the periphery of the network, with the ego either present at the center of the circle or absent in the visualization. In this regard, in Chapter 11 you will see that adding the respondent to the adjacency matrix for calculating network structural metrics is problematic, as the respondent is

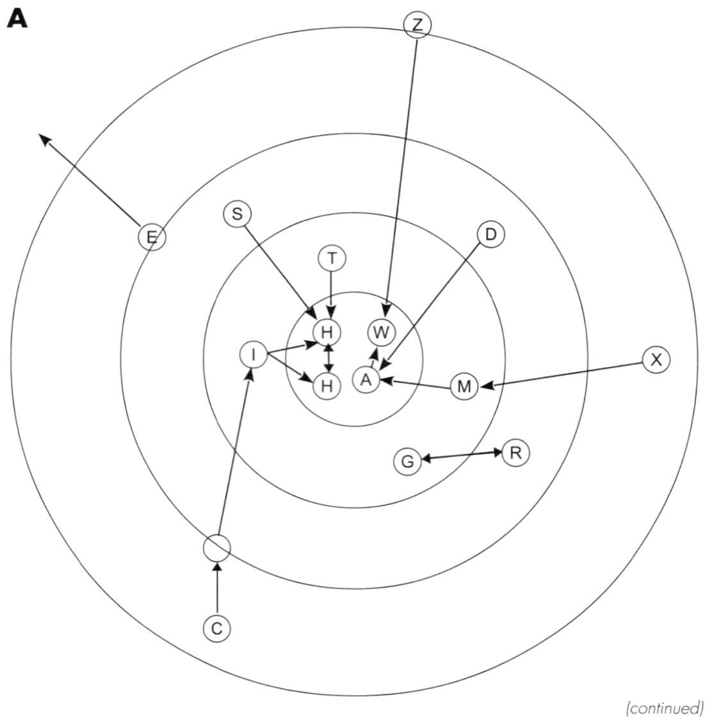


*(continued)*

**FIGURE 9.1.** Free adaptations of target diagrams published by (A) Northway, 1940; (B) Epstein, 1969; (C) Wellman & Berkowitz, 1988.

B

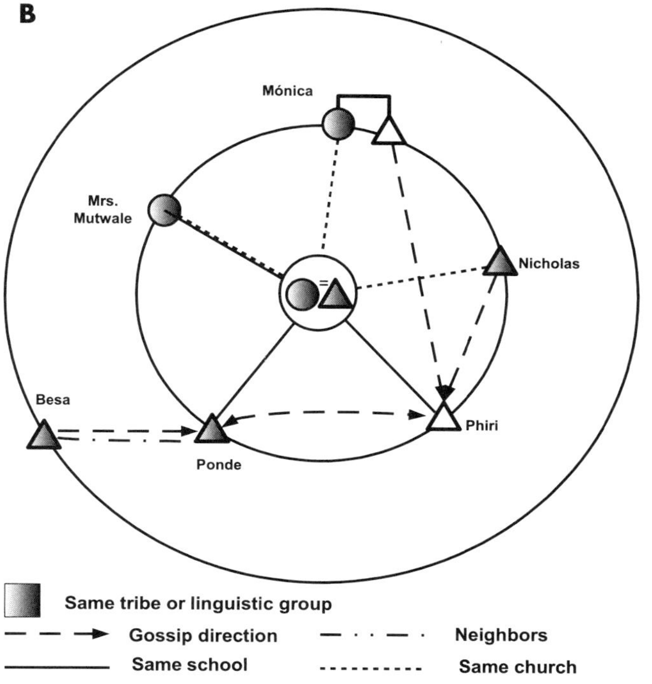


C

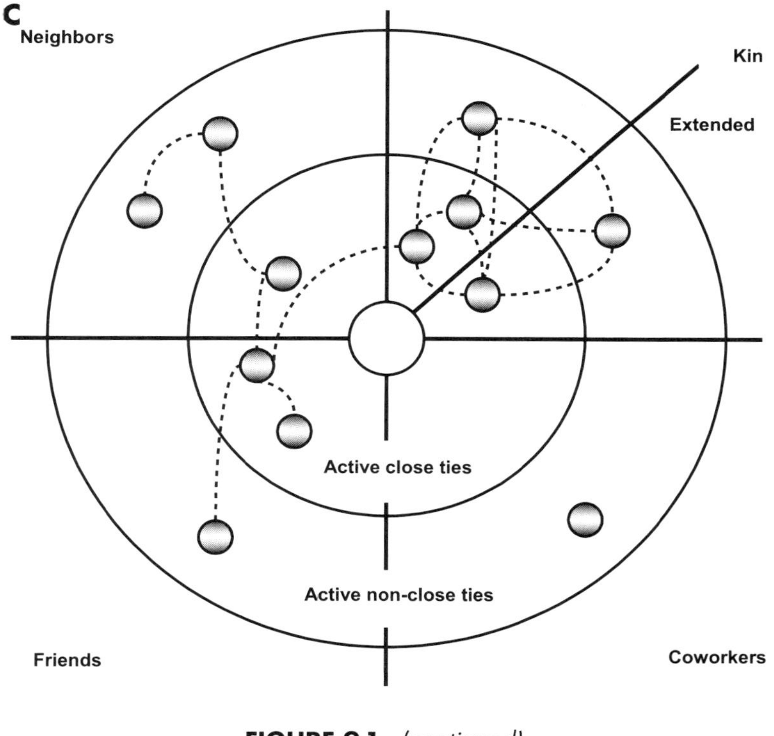


**FIGURE 9.1.** *(continued)*

by definition tied to everybody. Although adding the respondent to a personal network visualization does not cause as many problems, it does not add much to the analysis either. Consider Figure 9.2. The addition of the respondent (Figure 9.2B) does not change the structure of the graph much, yet it does not add any value either. Our preference, particularly in larger graphs where the addition of ego implies many extra lines, is to exclude the respondent from personal network visualizations.

The second principle is arranging connected alters into clusters. Typically, alters are clustered in social settings, that is, family, work, studies, leisure activities, or other groupings that are meaningful for respondents. This setup makes those alters that connect different groups more visible. Plate 9.1 presents the personal network of a Dominican male interviewed in Barcelona. From the picture, it is clear that his personal network is organized in three big clusters: family and friends from the Dominican Republic, the softball competition, and work, with two central persons connecting the different groups, among other features.

Once we have placed alters in a meaningful way, we may consider using visual variables for representing name interpreters. These variables are size, color, shape, and label for nodes, and color and width for edges. Table 9.1 summarizes the main recommendations for using visual variables with both nodes and edges. These variables can be combined in the same visualization.

In this vein, *node size* is typically used for displaying ordinal or interval/ratio variables, such as, for instance, the emotional closeness that the ego feels toward a given alter using a Likert scale.

*Node color* can efficiently show either binary variables like Yes/No variables, using, for example, black and white, or nominal variables, such as country of origin, assign-

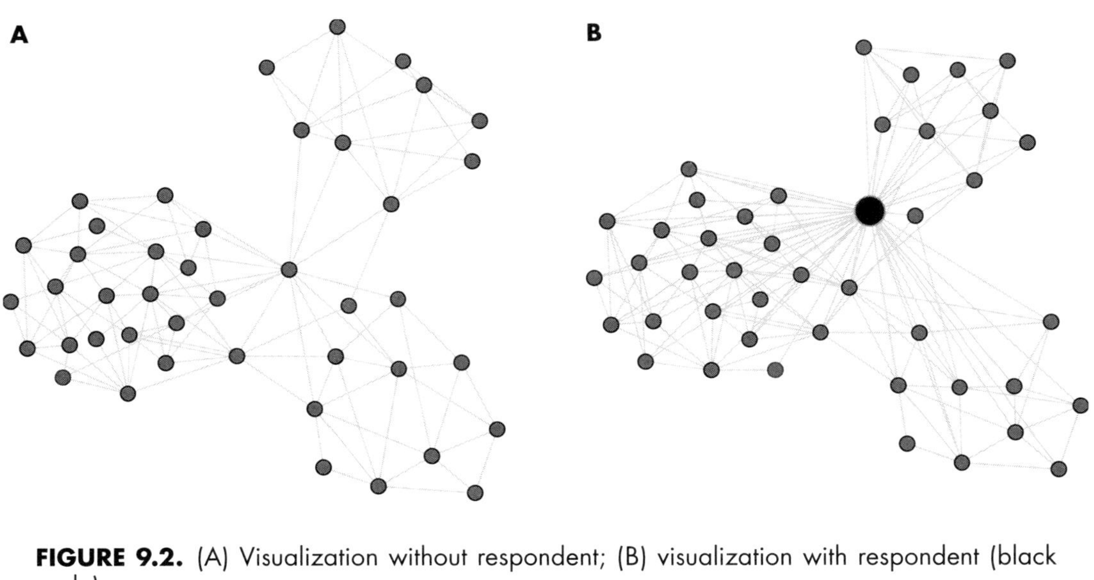


**FIGURE 9.2.** (A) Visualization without respondent; (B) visualization with respondent (black node).

**TABLE 9.1. Visual Variables for Nodes and Links**

| Visual variables | When to apply | Example |
|---|---|---|
| Nodes | | |
| Color | Nominal variables (set of colors) or ordinal/interval/ratio variables (color gradation) | Country of residence or type of relationship with ego (coworker, family member, client, etc.), duration of tie |
| Size | Ordinal/interval/ratio variables | Emotional closeness using a Likert scale or duration of tie |
| Shape | Nominal variables | Gender or profession |
| Label | ID/nominal variables | Name or place of residence |
| Edges | | |
| Color | Nominal variables | Character of alter-alter relationship (e.g., positive, negative) |
| Width | Ordinal/interval/ratio variables | Tie strength or frequency of relationship |

ing a different color to each country. It is also helpful to use colors for the type of relationship that the ego has with each alter. When using colors, it is important to keep the number of choices as low as possible in order to make the picture easily readable. Another option is to use a gradation of colors, which allows the representation of ordinal or interval/ranking variables.

*Node shape* is another meaningful way of representing nominal variables (e.g., men and women, smokers and nonsmokers), but again, if we choose shape to represent many options, the drawing can be difficult to understand.

*Node labels* are typically used for unique identifications (i.e., alter name, when showing the network to respondents, or an ID, in publications) or nominal variables, such as the place of residence. When the label is a number or a short ID, it can be placed inside the node. Otherwise, it is recommended that labels be placed outside the node, adapting the actual position to the available space. Personal network drawings with labels showing personal data should be used carefully for ethical reasons. Chapter 14 contains several recommendations in this regard.

At the relation level, *edge color* can be used to distinguish different types of relationships among alters. Since it is not easy to interpret a colored web of crossing lines, it is wise to highlight one type of relationship at each time. In addition, *edge width* can be used for representing tie strength or the flow of communication or resources among alters. As in most cases the alter–alter matrix is reported by the ego, links are often collected in a nondirected way; therefore, they are represented as lines rather than arrows. Most of these basic principles are implemented by computer algorithms in the visualization modules of personal analysis software (see the Appendix).

## 9.2 COLLECTING PERSONAL NETWORK DATA THROUGH VISUAL DISPLAYS

Compared with systematic questionnaires about alter–alter ties and name interpreters, collecting personal network data using visual displays has the advantage of reducing respondent burden without losing reliability in some key measurements, as you will see in this section. In addition, visualizations enact unique narratives about personal networks that enlarge our understanding of the phenomenon under study. Another important feature of visual methods is the ability to enable collaborative processes. In this regard, participatory research has shown the usefulness of paper-and-pencil-based methods like Net-map (Schiffer & Hauck, 2010) for identifying egocentric networks of people and organizations at the local level. Apart from paper drawings, web-based interfaces and graphic software have been used for collecting personal networks as well. Let's start with paper drawings.

One of the easiest ways to collect data is to ask the respondent to draw his or her personal network. This function is sometimes carried out in a completely free style, such as in the style Romina Cachia (2014) asked of her respondents, who represented their networks mostly in groups of people but sometimes in concentric circles or truly artistic forms, such as in the shape of trees or in spirals. Mostly, however, respondents are given some instructions. Figure 9.3 shows a drawing that a respondent from Vic (Barcelona) made of his network, along with his network visualized using questionnaire data, as described earlier (McCarty et al., 2007). For the drawing, the respondent was asked to represent people with dots and to draw circles around groups of people who were related to each other.

We certainly see some similarities between the two visualizations. This brings up the first important issue to keep in mind: overall social structures depicted by visual means may be comparable to those generated by questionnaires (Hogan et al., 2007; von der Lippe & Gamper, 2016). However, the visualization on the right of Figure 9.3 (generated by a computer on the basis of questionnaire data asking about individual alter ties) shows a level of detail not depicted in the visualization on the left. For example, unlike the hand drawing, the computer graph shows different overlaps among the groups and an isolate. We will come back to these differences later. The drawing may conform to the way the respondent cognitively organizes people.

Another instrument for collecting personal network data using a drawing is the *genogram,* a visual representation of an individual's family relationships. Mental health counselors have used genograms for many years as a way to quickly understand the family and the client's medical history. By using a *stemma* (a system invented by anthropologists to depict kinship diagrams), therapists are able to guide their initial interviews with patients and explore whether existing or past family relationships are contributing to the problem. Genograms can be adapted for personal network interviews as well.

Apart from (relatively) free-style drawings and kinship diagrams, there is the *hierarchical mapping technique,* which we have already mentioned (for a version of the target diagram, see Figure 6.1). This technique makes use of three or more concentric

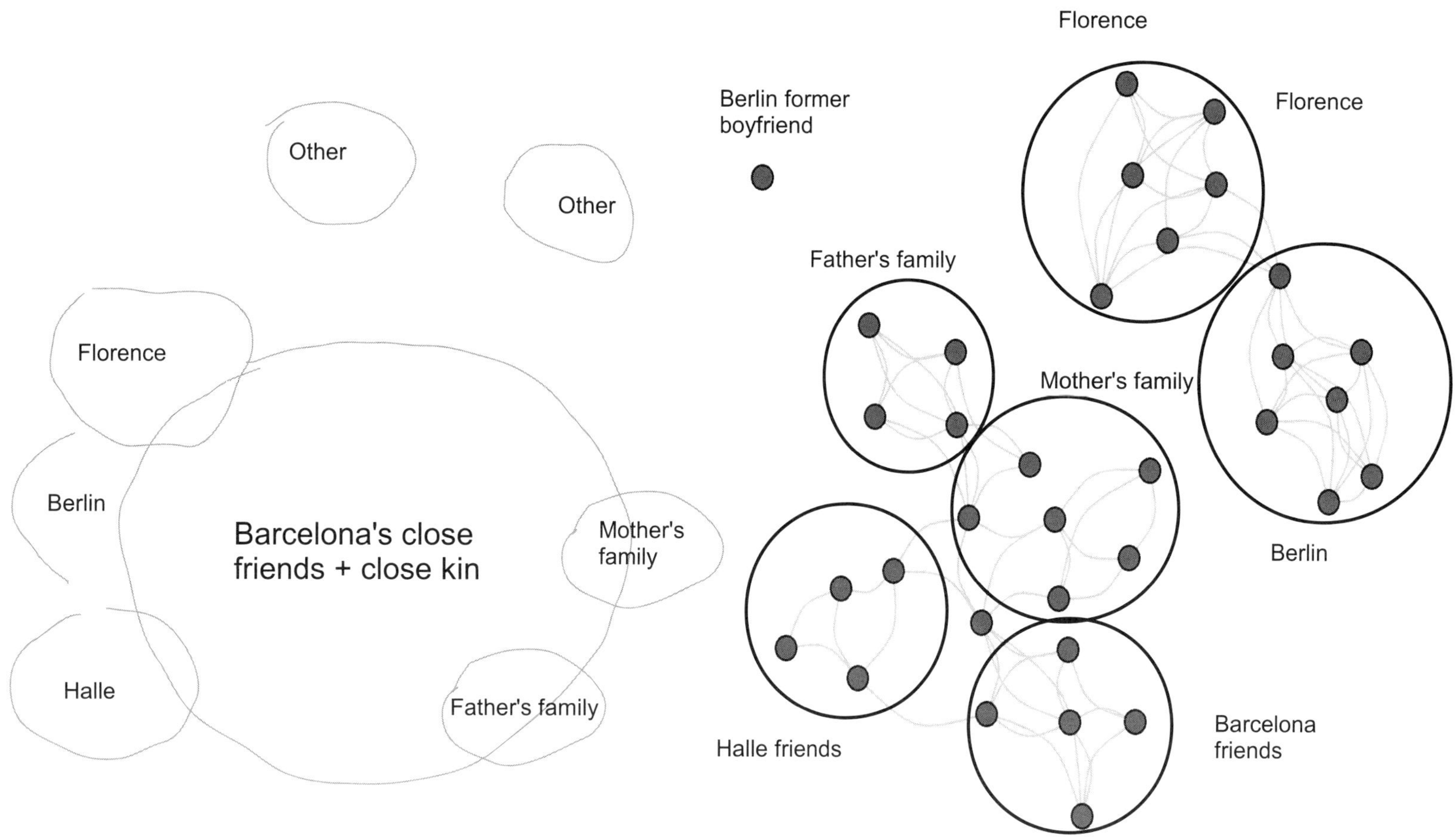


**FIGURE 9.3.** Free-style drawing versus structural visualization for respondent from Barcelona.

circles to represent the personal network of the respondent. The resulting map gives the researcher some sense of the size of the network and the distribution of their network based on closeness. However, such techniques are not always helpful in collecting data on who is tied to whom, making it impossible to calculate network structural metrics. These limitations were overcome with the approach developed by Hogan et al. (2007), and Carrasco et al. (Carrasco, Hogan, Wellman, & Miller, 2004), which uses an A2 sheet of paper with a target diagram and separate tags for writing down alter names (see also Chapter 6). Those tags can first be placed on the diagram and later can be rearranged in groups, which can also be labeled. The respondent then draws circles around groups of alters who are all interconnected, as well as lines between two alters who are connected to each other when they are not part of the same larger group.

Graphic interface programs, such as VennMaker and the forthcoming Network Canvas (see the Appendix), have been developed to simulate this visual method of collecting personal networks. VennMaker, for example, can visualize a circle diagram with the desired number of circles on screen, and it can also divide the diagram into sectors that represent different roles (family, friends, workmates), places of living, or another categorical alter attribute. The people respondents nominate are represented as nodes and placed in the appropriate circle and sector, and they can be rearranged at any time. Once the nodes have been placed, the respondent and the interviewer can draw links between nodes. Network Canvas, which is currently in the design phase, also aims at collecting personal network data in a coproduction environment. It is visually appealing and comprehensible, and it has a touch-optimized interface. Systematic comparison of the results achieved by using VennMaker with standard questionnaires (von der Lippe & Gamper, 2016) shows that the network size and structure generated with this method are reliable and reduce respondent burden. However, compared with questionnaires, this method produces less dense networks, as it is easier to forget drawing a line between close and slightly less close ties. In this vein, when social networking sites like Facebook generate personal networks, the density is typically higher due to the service's systematic attempts to confirm as many connections as possible (Mastrandrea, Fournet, & Barrat, 2015).

While VennMaker is typically used in face-to-face interviews, other programs have been designed to collect personal network data in a visual way using self-administered Web surveys. Such programs are particularly useful for engaging with hidden or sensitive populations, as is the case for the program ANAMIA Egocenter, which Paola Tubaro, Antonio Casilli, and colleagues (2013) developed for individuals with eating disorders. Similarly, the tool EgoWeb 2.0 developed by David Kennedy has been used successfully in intervention programs with homeless individuals (Kennedy, Wenzel, Brown, Tucker, & Golinelli, 2016) and other vulnerable populations. However, they can also be used for general purposes. For instance, the software GENSI collects personal networks online (Stark & Krosnick, 2017; see also the Appendix).

In general, when talking about visual interactive methods, researchers observe that participants enjoy the task and that they are even prone to continue nominating alters beyond the minimum number initially required (von der Lippe & Gamper, 2016). It needs to be noted, however, that use of a Web interface such as EgoWeb has consequences for structure and composition that questionnaires administered by computer, such as EgoNet, do not (McCarty & Govindaramanujam, 2005).

## 9.3 NETWORK VISUALIZATIONS AS CUES IN QUALITATIVE INTERVIEWS

Once the visualization has been generated, either in a visual, interactive way or through a computer-assisted interview based on a questionnaire, it can be used as a cue for conducting a qualitative interview with respondents. Consider Figure 9.4, the personal network of a 77-year-old woman with a score of zero on a seven-item Beck Depression Scale, indicating that this respondent is not at all depressed. The visualization has been color-coded by the respondent's report to indicate whether the alter is someone she can talk to about health problems: the darker the color is, the more likely she is to confide in a particular alter. The nodes are sized by how close the ego is to the alter, and they are shaped by whether or not they live locally (circles are local). This respondent was interviewed about the potential to experience depression and how her network might either prevent or cause depression. She immediately identified Cluster 1 as her family, Cluster 2 as her church group, and Cluster 3 as volunteers and medical professionals at

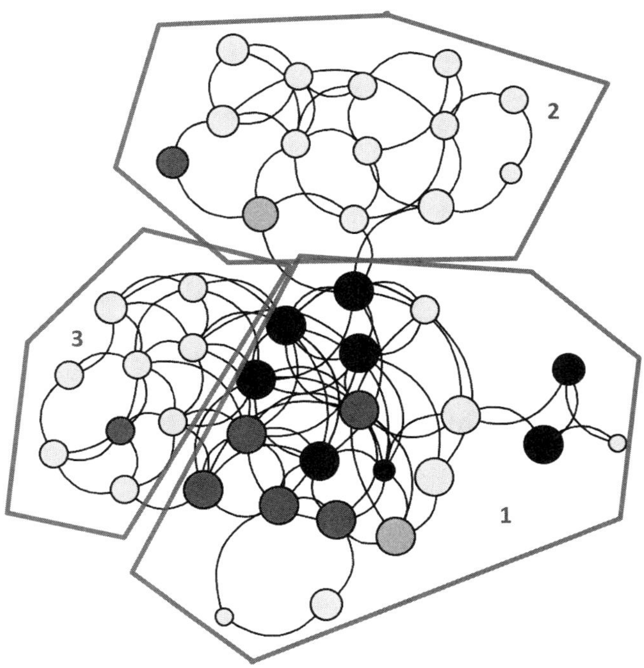


**FIGURE 9.4.** Personal network of a 77-year-old woman with a score of zero on the depression scale.

the hospital where she volunteers. However, until she saw the graph, she had not given any thought to the alter in the middle's central role in bridging Clusters 2 and 3 and serving as a confidante.

By visualizing different aspects of the network in one or in different visualizations, you can ask respondents questions about their social context that would otherwise be impossible to consider. For example, when interviewing the respondent in Figure 9.4, you might ask about the distribution of confidantes within the groups. You can select an alter that is not a confidante and ask why the respondent does not confide in that person. You can also ask if the respondent would ever consider introducing an alter from one group to another. This is a good way to explore whether different norms make the groups incompatible. This is also a useful technique when you are trying to understand the role of isolates. In some cases, there is a reason why isolates are not tied to anyone. In other cases, isolates can be interpreted either as the remnant of a past group (i.e., school mates) or as the seed of an emerging group. This latter case can be observed in Plate 9.2 and comes from the same person depicted in Plate 9.1 but some years *before*. The former isolate became part of a dense group of coworkers some years later, showing the importance of workplaces for personal network dynamics.

In general, visualizations can serve as a cue for asking further, semistructured questions about the network. These questions prompted by visualizations allow the researcher to delve deeper into the meaning of the respondents' relationships and the precise contents of ties or interactions that take place. Thus, it is possible to further understand the context in which such ties are formed or broken, the specific clusters in which the ties emerge or dissolve, the temporal dimensions of the network, and the way it may affect personal well-being or other variables (Herz, Peters, & Truschkat, 2015; Hollstein, 2014b; Molina et al., 2014). Visualizations not only allow participants to enact narratives or even discover new insights about themselves, but also enable researchers to provide feedback, a good practice of social research (see the discussion of research ethics in Chapter 14). Finally, visualizations allow participants and researchers to check possible errors. In this regard, Figure 9.5 depicts three nodes called *pendants*; these nodes have just one relationship in the personal network (apart from their relationship with the ego).

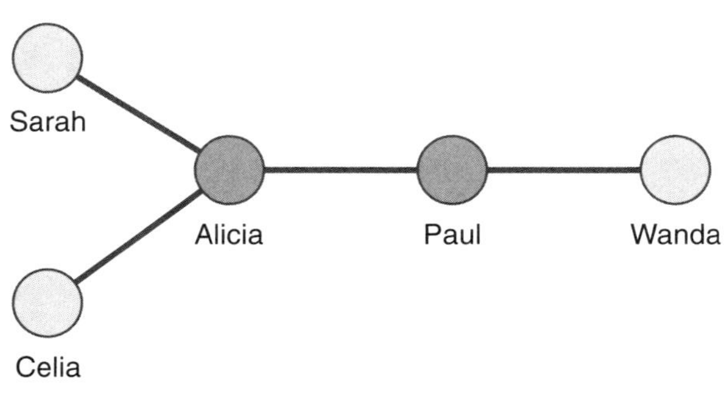


**FIGURE 9.5.** A personal network with three pendants (light gray nodes).

This type of structure is less common in personal networks. In this case, it implies that Alicia knows Paul and Wanda knows Paul, but Wanda and Alicia do not know each other. While this is possible in a personal network, multiple pendants or long paths can be a sign that the respondent may have made a mistake in reporting alter–alter ties or may be using a strict definition of what a tie entails. Respondents usually recognize their mistakes when they see the visualization. This underscores the power of visualization. Our minds, and the minds of our respondents, can make sense of the data very quickly and can also swiftly identify cases that do not make sense.

## 9.4 COMPARING PERSONAL NETWORKS THROUGH VISUALIZATIONS

Visualization allows the combination of multiple visual variables for displaying multiple versions of the same personal network, but at the same time, it hinders its comparative capacity. Several strategies may be used to solve this problem. One technique is to present different visualizations of the same personal network to participants in order to discover what visualization fits better with the research purposes. In this vein, Isidro Maya-Jariego and Daniel Holgado (2005) designed two different visual representations of the personal networks of 173 undergraduate students and compared their reactions and interpretations to the graphs using a set of 25 alters. Participants showed a preference for the graph that emphasized the role of the social support network.

A second and more common option is to keep the visual variables constant across different personal networks—that is, to have node size, shape, and color represent the same variables across different networks and to use the same algorithm for the layout. In some software (e.g., EgoNet), it is possible to create templates for this aim. Standardizing the visualization facilitates comparison. When observing many networks, researchers can more easily detect some common patterns. For example, they may observe that some people have homogeneous networks that consist of a single, dense component, whereas others bridge different social groups with few ties among them, and so on.

An additional complexity emerges when the same personal network is compared at different times. When that is the case, we may be interested, not only in comparing the overall structural and compositional features of a network over time, but also in following particular alters or dyads. In that event, we choose whether to maintain the positions of nodes that are equal across the time points or to allow the individual position to change over time. Fixing the node positions would make it easier to track changes regarding specific alters or dyads over time, whereas allowing positions to change facilitates evaluation of the overall network structure at any given point in time but makes it difficult to track individual alters. The software visone (*www.visone.info*; see also the Appendix), a powerful visualization and analysis tool designed for social networks in general, also allows an intermediate solution, where users can indicate the extent to which the positions may change over time. Also, it is possible to create network movies in visone that show the changes between successive networks.

Although these strategies facilitate comparison, it may still be challenging to go beyond dyadic comparisons, especially when the personal networks are large and different visual variables are combined. An alternative strategy for comparing a set of networks, especially larger ones, was developed by Ulrik Brandes and colleagues (2008). This approach, employing clustered graphs, was implemented in the software EgoNet2GraphML (*http://algo.uni-konstanz.de/software/egonet2graphml*) developed by Jürgen Lerner, which imports personal networks collected with EgoNet for producing clustered graphs. (A tutorial is available at *http://visone.info/wiki/index.php/Personal_networks_(tutorial)*; tutorials in Spanish are also available at *www.redes-sociales.net*, in videos.)

The basic idea is to reduce the set of nodes of a personal network into a limited number of mutually exclusive alter classes or clusters (e.g., "clients," "coworkers," and "family") and to represent the network of alter classes. The number of alters in a cluster can be expressed by varying the node size, the density of relationships within the clusters can be represented by the gradation of a color (where the darker colors represent higher density), and the density of relationships between clusters can be displayed by varying the width or the color of the tie between the clusters. Standardizing the layout of this minimal representation allows systematic comparison of some essential characteristics of networks across different people or over time. Figure 9.6 represents the clustered graph layout that was used for comparing the personal networks of migrants in Spain and the United States (Lubbers et al., 2010).

Figure 9.7 shows the clustered graph of one of the respondents at two different time points. Among others, the figure shows that this respondent nominated more Spaniards on the first time point (left-hand) than on the second time point (right-hand).

Clustered graphs can also be applied to collections of personal networks in order to allow comparisons across groups of people (e.g., countries of origin, men and women, fishermen and ship owners; Maya-Jariego, Holgado Ramos & Florido del Cor-

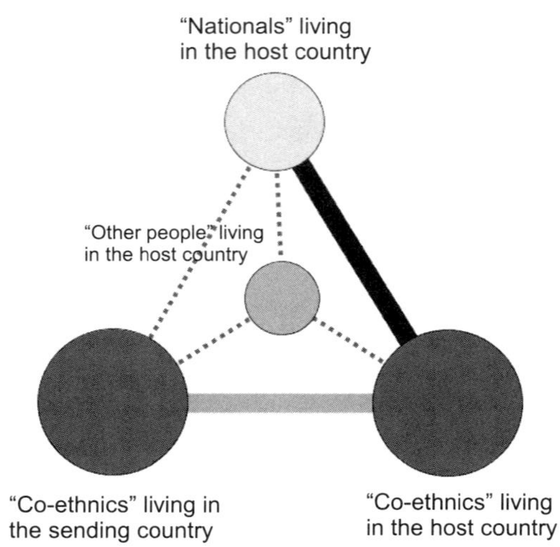


**FIGURE 9.6.** Clustered graph layout.

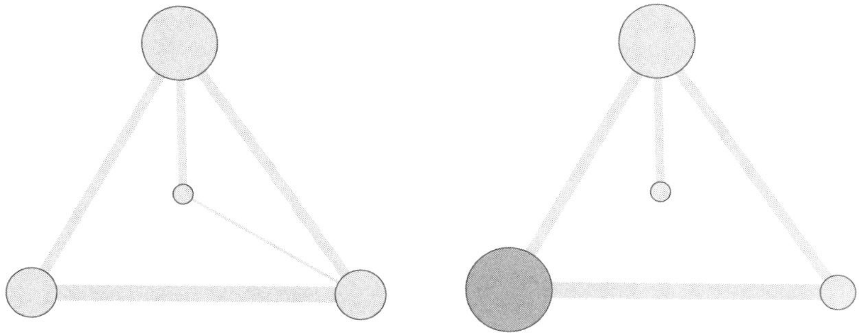

**FIGURE 9.7.** Clustered graph of an Argentinean woman at two different moments. Note that the proportion of active contacts in Argentina (*bottom left of each graph*) increased over time, while the proportion of "nationals" (*right*) decreased at the same time.

ral, 2016; same type of families in different neighborhoods; Maya-Jariego, Holgado, Márquez, & Santolaya, 2018; and so on). In these cases, the node size, node color, and edge width and color represent the average number of alters and density of relationships within and between clusters. The dispersion of (1) the number of alters, (2) the density of relationships within a cluster, and (3) the density of relationships between clusters can be visualized respectively by (a) highlighting a segment of the node proportional to two standard deviations (representing the average plus or minus the standard deviation), (b) coloring two wedges in the upper part of the nodes in the gradations corresponding to the mean plus and minus one standard deviation, and (c) highlighting a small part of the tie proportional to two standard deviations. Following the layout of Figure 9.6 and this approach to showing average tendencies and variability, three migrant communities in Barcelona were compared (Molina, Petermann, & Herz, 2015) showing the different network composition and structure of each community (see Figure 9.8).

The comparison shows how Sikhs maintain strong transnational ties, while Filipinos appear to form an ethnic enclave in Barcelona. The Chinese people in the sample

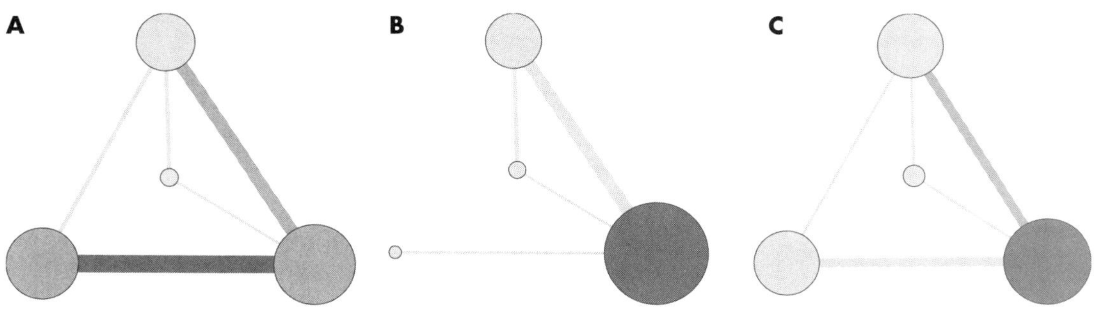


**FIGURE 9.8.** Clustered graph of 25 personal networks in each group. (A) Sikh (Pakistan/ India). (B) Chinese. (C) Filipinos.

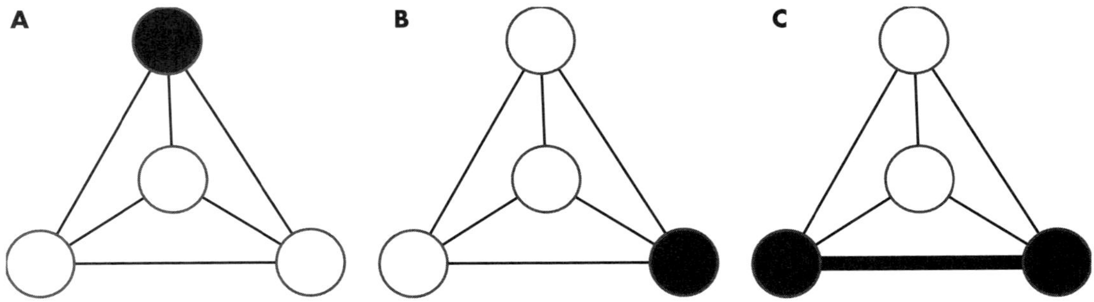


**FIGURE 9.9.** Ideal models of (A) assimilation (all contacts are natives of the country of residence); (B) ethnic enclave (all contacts are co-ethnics living in the ego's country of residence), and (C) transnationalism (all contacts are co-ethnics, and they are located in either the country of origin or the country of destination).

have more ties with native Spaniards, in part because of their higher entrepreneurial orientation.

Finally, the use of clustered graphs allows the development of visual typologies (Molina et al., 2014). Following the same layout used so far, we can easily develop visual models of migrant adaptation, such as complete assimilation, ethnic enclave, and transnationalism (see Figure 9.9). In this way, we can easily compare our empirical data with such ideal models and assess the explanatory power of theories at stake.

## CHAPTER SUMMARY

In this chapter, we explained that personal network visualizations are not only a way to illustrate personal network data, but also a fundamental tool for interacting with participants, reducing the burden of data collection, gaining new insights, and even developing new analytical frameworks. Personal network visualization has used a set of basic principles such as the "target diagram" as layout, placing central or close alters in the center, clustering alters by social contexts, and using visual variables for displaying name interpreter information. These visualizations can be used to generate new narratives from the ego about her personal network in an interview. Also, we discussed clustered graphs, which allow comparison among different personal networks (from different egos or from the same ego at different times) or different groups of personal networks.

### FURTHER READING

Freeman, L. C. (2000). Visualizing social networks. *Journal of Social Structure, 3*(1). Retrieved from *www.cmu.edu/joss.*

Hogan, B., Melville, J. R., Philips, G. L., Janulis, Patrick, et al. (2016). Evaluating the paper-to-screen translation of participant-aided sociograms with high-risk participants. In *Proceedings of the 2016 CHI Conference on Human Factors in Computing Systems*, Chicago, IL.

Molina, J. L., Maya-Jariego, I., & McCarty, C. (2014). Giving meaning to social networks: Methodology for conducting and analyzing interviews based on personal network visualizations. In S. Domínguez & B. Hollstein (Eds.), *Mixed methods in social network research: Design and applications* (pp. 305–335). Cambridge, UK: Cambridge University Press.

Schiffer, E., & Hauck, J. (2010). Net-map: Collecting social network data and facilitating network learning through participatory influence network mapping. *Field Methods, 22*(3), 231–249.

Tufte, E. R. (1990). *Envisioning information*. Cheshire, CT: Graphic Press.

von Der Lippe, H., & Gamper, M. (2016). Drawing or tabulating ego-centered networks?: A mixed-methods comparison of questionnaire vs. visualization-based data collection. *International Journal of Social Research Methodology, 20*(5), 1–17.

# 10

# Measuring Personal Network Characteristics without Generating Names

## *What Is This Chapter About?*

This chapter describes methods for measuring the size, cohesion, and content of the networks in terms of social capital and social support without delineating the network. In these cases, typically we only collect data about respondents and the general characteristics of the networks, without adding questions about the alters, although in some cases those are also included (see Section 10.1). Specifically, Section 10.2 presents two methods for estimating personal network size: the known population method and the summation method. An interesting application of the known population method for describing segregation in acquaintance networks is presented in Section 10.3. Next, Section 10.4 reviews measures of social capital: the position generator and the resource generator. Finally, Section 10.5 presents measures of social support.

## 10.1 CHARACTERISTICS OF LARGER PERSONAL NETWORKS

So far, we have treated the delineation of personal networks of a limited size (say, up to 50 network members), which can be seen as subsets of the larger personal environment—either intentional (e.g., the closest ties, the most frequently contacted, or the most supportive ones) or random subsets. Quite often, however, we are interested in measuring characteristics of the broader personal environment. We might want to estimate the number of people whom individuals know—not just the number of close or supportive ties, but the total number of people with whom they are somehow acquainted. Sometimes we might also wish to know something about the composition of their broader interpersonal environments. For example, we might wish to know whether individuals know people with a broad array of occupational statuses or whether they primarily know people like themselves. Again, we might not just be interested in the social capital accessible through individuals' most intimate relationships, but in the social capital accessible through a larger array of people they know, including their weak ties.

One way to estimate the compositional characteristics of the larger personal networks is to take a random subset of alters and measure their attributes (see Section 6.5). However, when we are only interested in a specific characteristic of the composition (e.g., social capital), we could more efficiently measure it by targeting our questions directly at that characteristic. Also, the cost of using name generators is quite high, and for many research questions it may retrieve superfluous information. Furthermore, some aspects of networks—such as network size—may not be reliably captured by name generators. For some of those questions, more efficient methods have been developed in which the networks themselves are not delineated.

## 10.2 PERSONAL NETWORK SIZE

How many people does a person know? As we briefly discussed in Chapter 2, many researchers have tried to answer this question. Evolutionary anthropologist Robin Dunbar (1993) hypothesized that the number of people a person can know as individuals and with whom he or she can maintain contact is related to the size of the neocortex, the part of the brain most involved in social interaction. Indeed, Dunbar found that the neocortex ratio of primates was related to their average group size. Using the regression line of group size on the neocortex ratio for the subgroup of hominoids to predict the average group size of humans, he found a number close to 150—which is now dubbed "Dunbar's number." On the basis of this finding, he suggested that the human brain capacity limits the number of personalized, reciprocated relationships to about 150. Exploring historical data, Dunbar further observed that 150 is a typical size for premodern communities. Nevertheless, he suggested that the number of faces a person can recognize can be around 10 times as high. Curiously, H. Russell Bernard and Peter Killworth, in their classical study on the social network structure of an ocean-going research vessel (1973), had hypothesized a similar number in 1973, that is, 140 as the threshold of a cohesive subgroup and 2,460 for the size of the maximum group without a central organization.

A wide variety of other methods have been used to estimate broader personal network size, including a year-long observation of two individuals (Boissevain, 1974), contact diaries (Dávid et al., 2016; Fu, 2007; Lonkila, 1997) and experiments (the so-called Reversed Small World Experiment; Killworth & Bernard, 1978; The Telephone Book Studies, Freeman & Thompson, 1989) to estimate the number of people known to an individual. Researchers using these methods generally came up with much higher numbers than 150, ranging from 250 to more than 5,000, depending on the method. The large divergence in the estimated size can be explained at least partially in terms of differences in the underlying conceptualizations of "knowing." Contact diaries and observation, methods that capture the largest networks, might record interactions such as a little chat with the cashier at the grocery store that other methods typically do not capture—for example, when asking respondents about whether they know people with certain family names selected from a telephone guide (Freeman & Thompson, 1989) or about who they send Christmas cards to (Hill & Dunbar, 2003).

Researchers, however, concur that individuals vary greatly in their network sizes, following a log-normal distribution (DiPrete et al., 2011; McCormick et al., 2010). Whereas most individuals have between roughly 400 and 800 ties, a few individuals have thousands of ties, who can thus be considered *hubs* (high-degree nodes) in the overall network of society. So far, little is known about why people have varying acquaintanceship network sizes, but it will be relevant to study this issue in more detail.

Most of the methods for estimating network size are quite time intensive, so in this chapter we only discuss two methods that can be easily included in surveys. These methods aim to estimate the number of persons known to individuals, which can then be related to, for example, sociodemographic characteristics.

## The Known Population Method

The first method is called the known population method and was developed by Christopher McCarty, Peter Killworth, and colleagues (McCarty, Killworth, Bernard, & Johnsen, 2001) as a by-product of the so-called network scale-up method (NSUM). The NSUM method estimates the size of populations for which no reliable official estimates exist (so-called hard-to-count populations), such as the number of people killed in an earthquake. Among other things, it assumes that on average, the personal networks of individuals are representative of the society in which they live (the assumption of random mixing). Consequently, if in a sufficiently large, random sample of a population we find that individuals know on average 300 people of that population and that they know on average 2 people who have disappeared in an earthquake, then we can estimate that 2/300 of the population has disappeared. When we combine this proportion with the total size of the population, which can be known, for example, from a census, we can estimate the total number of people who disappeared in the earthquake. This method has been widely validated and has been used to estimate the size of hard-to-count populations in many countries, particularly subpopulations most at risk for contracting HIV (i.e., IV drug users, men who have sex with men, and female sex workers).

The difficulty is that to estimate this, we need to measure two types of information from survey respondents. The first is the number of people the respondents know with the characteristic of interest (e.g., having disappeared in an earthquake). This information can be easily obtained by asking respondents "How many people do you know [with characteristic X]?" after defining what is understood by "knowing." Knowing could, for example, be defined as "you know the person and they know you by sight or by name; you can contact them in person, by telephone, or by mail; and you have had contact with the person in the past 2 years."

The second type of information we need is the personal network size for each respondent. Obviously, this is not a characteristic that respondents can estimate with even minimal precision (although they will be happy to try if you ask them). Therefore,

### *The Random Mixing Assumption in the Network Scale-Up Method*

More formally expressed, the assumption of random mixing expresses the idea that the proportion of personal networks with a certain characteristic is on average equal to the proportion of the total population with a certain characteristic. We can express this assumption as

$$\frac{\sum_i \frac{k_i}{K_i}}{m} = \frac{n}{N}$$

where $k_i$ is the number of people the respondent $i = (1, \ldots, k)$ knows in a certain population, $K_i$ is the total size of the personal network of respondent $i$, $m$ is the number of respondents, $n$ is the number of people in a population of interest, and $N$ is the total size of the population. From this assumption, it follows that the size of a certain population of interest can be estimated as

$$\hat{n} = \frac{\sum_i \frac{k_i}{K_i}}{m} \times N$$

if the size of the personal network size is known. When the size of a subpopulation is known, the size of the personal network of respondent $i$ can be estimated as:

$$\hat{K}_i = k_i / n \times N$$

When using multiple populations $j$ of known size, an estimate of personal network size is computed as

$$\hat{K}_i = \sum_j k_{ij} / n_j \times N$$

McCarty, Killworth, and colleagues suggest estimating this size using a similar method in which respondents are asked to indicate how many people they know in various populations of *known* size. As the fraction of the total population who have a certain characteristic is known in this case, we can estimate personal network size by asking respondents how many people they know in that population, assuming random mixing. For example, we could ask respondents in Egypt to report how many men they know named Ahmed. This is a subpopulation of known size, since birth registration data reveal how many men have that name. If an Egyptian respondent reports that he knows 5 men named Ahmed and we know there are about 2 million so-named men, we estimate that the respondent knows about 5/(2,000,000) = 0.0000025 of all Egyptians.

Census data show that there are approximately 90 million Egyptians and we estimate that this respondent has a personal network size of 225.

Of course, the personal network will not be a perfectly scaled-down version of each subpopulation, and small variations can lead to large differences in estimated size (had our respondent known 4 people named Ahmed, his or her network size would be estimated at 180). Therefore, we do not ask about a single subpopulation but about a number of subpopulations of known size, say 20. Then, we can estimate the personal network size of each respondent as an average over the 20 questions, to reduce the variance of a single estimate.

The NSUM method has caught the attention of various other statisticians, and this type of data (How many Xs do you know?) is now also known under the term "aggregated relational data." In order to improve estimations of personal network size based on known subpopulations, Tyler McCormick, Matthew Salganik, and Tian Zheng (2010) have proposed a latent nonrandom mixing model. Also, they have offered a set of specific recommendations about the selection of the subpopulations—or characteristics of network members. First, they stressed the importance of using characteristics that people can actually know about all of their network members. It may be difficult to report on the number of diabetics in your network, the number of people who have had a divorce, or people who have a twin brother or sister. Maybe some of the people you know have never told you about that characteristic, either because it is not something they would like you to know or simply because it never came up in conversation. McCarty et al. (2001) used 29 subpopulations of known size, of which 12 referred to people with a particular first name. McCormick et al. (2010) recommended the use of first names if there are official statistics about the size of these name subpopulations, as you would typically know the names of the people you "know." Second, as people may underreport the number of people in larger populations, McCormick et al. further suggested using names that comprise 0.1–0.2% of the overall population to minimize recall errors. Third, they recommended using a combination of names that together reflect a scaled-down version of the population. Names are usually associated with a gender, ethnicity, and birth cohort (e.g., "Dorothy" may generally refer to older women than "Zoe"). Therefore, selecting a set of names that together represent the overall population helps to ensure that everyone has an approximately equal chance to know someone in the combined set. For example, if 50% of the population is female, then half of the names should represent female names. Last, McCormick et al. warned against selecting names that are typically associated with nicknames. When asked, "How many people do you know named Joseph?", you might simply not think of people you have always known only as Joe.

Using the latent nonrandom mixing model and different databases, researchers have estimated that the median size of acquaintanceship networks is about 550 people (DiPrete et al., 2011; Lubbers, Molina, & Valenzuela-Garcia, 2019; McCormick et al., 2010), with considerable interquartile variation. This number is almost four times higher than the number initially predicted by Dunbar. The variation further shows that people differ quite a lot in the number of others they know by their names and with whom they would stop and talk for a moment if they ran into them.

This method can be easily implemented in large-scale surveys and can be embedded into a statistical framework to quantify variance. However, statistics for populations of known size (people's first names, commercial pilots, etc.) may not be available in some countries, and in this case alternative methods should be used.

## The Summation Method

An alternative to the known population method is the *summation method*, as proposed by Christopher McCarty and colleagues (2001). For this method, respondents are asked to enumerate the people they know in a list of specific relationship types or categories, such as family, neighbors, and coworkers, after defining what is meant by knowing. The summation of these responses yields an estimate of the total personal network size. Table 10.1 gives an example of the 16 relationship types used in their study (McCarty et al., 2001).

To use this method, it is essential to construct a list of relationship types that are ideally *mutually exclusive*, which means that they do not overlap with each other. In addition, the list needs to be *exhaustive*, which means that all relationships that would fit the definition of "knowing" should fit into one of the categories. It is quite difficult, however, or maybe even downright impossible, to construct a list of perfectly mutually exclusive categories. For example, someone who is a member of the same church may

**TABLE 10.1. An Example of a List of 16 Relationship Types Used in the United States**

| Relationship Type |
|---|
| • Immediate family |
| • Other birth family |
| • Family of spouse or significant other |
| • Coworkers |
| • Other people at work |
| • Close friends/confidantes |
| • People known through hobbies/recreation |
| • People known through faith-based organization |
| • People from other organizations |
| • School relations |
| • People you know from your neighborhood |
| • Just friends |
| • People known through others |
| • Childhood relations |
| • People who provide a service |
| • Other |

*Note.* From McCarty, Killworth, Bernard, and Johnsen, 2001.

also be a neighbor, and therefore this person could be included in both categories. This is a source of overcounting, which could lead to overestimations of network size. Conversely, undercounting could occur if the list of relationship types is not exhaustive, that is, if a substantial group is omitted from the list. The authors of the method further indicate that relationship categories are culturally relative, so it is important that the set of relationship types be chosen on a country-by-country basis to match the categories that inhabitants of the country actually use to organize relationships. If a relationship category is too large, it is likely that respondents no longer count, but rather guess, the number of persons they know in the category. It is therefore advisable to create smaller categories, for example, by adding alter characteristics (e.g., gender, to divide the larger category "relatives" into "female relatives" and "male relatives").

To develop a list of relationship categories in a given cultural context, Christopher McCarty, H. Russell Bernard, and Dimitri Fazito (2011) proposed a so-called two-mode approach, which they first tested in Thailand. The protocol involves a number of steps. First, they proposed that a number of native speakers of the language in which the survey is administered (in their case 21 persons) freelist the words in their language describing how people can know each other. The terms listed by more than three participants are retained in a draft list of categories. To study whether these relationship categories are mutually exclusive and exhaustive, they then ask each of the participants to list 30 alters using a flexible name generator. Once the participants have given a list of names, they ask them to indicate, for each nominee, which relationship categories of the draft list applied to them; multiple answers are allowed. If none of the categories apply to an alter, it means that the list is not exhaustive; if multiple categories apply, it means that the list is not mutually exclusive. The answers of each respondent are written down in a so-called two-mode network (an alter by a relationship-type matrix; see the example on the left-hand side of Figure 10.1). In the simplified example in Figure 10.1, the first alter of Person 1 was a colleague, while the second alter qualified as both a colleague and a neighbor. These matrices can then be transformed into a one-mode network for each respondent (a relationship type by relationship type network; see the one-mode matrices in the middle of Figure 10.1). The entries on the diagonal of this matrix indicate the total number of times a relationship of this type was mentioned, and the off-diagonal entries indicate the number of times two categories overlap. To obtain an overall view of all participants, these one-mode matrices are then summed over the participants into an aggregate one-mode matrix (see the one-mode matrix on the right-hand side of Figure 10.1). This matrix shows which categories were most often double counted. Categories that show a high degree of overlap should then be collapsed into a single, more inclusive category. The protocol is useful for developing a set of culturally salient and mutually exclusive relationship categories that can then be used as a basis for the summation method instrument in a survey.

The great advantage of this method over the known population method is that it can be applied if statistics for populations of known size (e.g., name statistics) are not available in a certain country. Furthermore, an advantage of the summation method is that it is cognitively easier for respondents to provide answers to these questions since,

Person 1: Two-mode matrix

| | Colleague | Household member | Direct relative | Neighbor |
|---|---|---|---|---|
| Alter 1 | 1 | 0 | 0 | 0 |
| Alter 2 | 1 | 0 | 0 | 1 |
| Alter 3... | 0 | 0 | 1 | 0 |

Person 1: One-mode matrix

| | Colleague | Household member | Direct relative | Neighbor |
|---|---|---|---|---|
| Colleague | 2 | 0 | 0 | 1 |
| Household member | 0 | 0 | 0 | 0 |
| Direct relative | 0 | 0 | 1 | 0 |
| Neighbor | 1 | 0 | 0 | 1 |

Person 2: Two-mode matrix

| | Colleague | Household member | Direct relative | Neighbor |
|---|---|---|---|---|
| Alter 1 | 0 | 1 | 1 | 0 |
| Alter 2 | 1 | 0 | 0 | 0 |
| Alter 3... | 0 | 0 | 0 | 1 |

Person 2: One-mode matrix

| | Colleague | Household member | Direct relative | Neighbor |
|---|---|---|---|---|
| Colleague | 1 | 0 | 0 | 0 |
| Household member | 0 | 1 | 1 | 0 |
| Direct relative | 0 | 1 | 1 | 0 |
| Neighbor | 0 | 0 | 0 | 1 |

Aggregate one-mode matrix

| | Colleague | Household member | Direct relative | Neighbor |
|---|---|---|---|---|
| Colleague | 3 | 0 | 0 | 1 |
| Household member | 0 | 1 | 1 | 0 |
| Direct relative | 0 | 1 | 2 | 0 |
| Neighbor | 1 | 0 | 0 | 2 |

**FIGURE 10.1.** Illustration of the two-mode approach for developing a set of relationship types.

as indicated earlier, relationships are stored in our memory in clusters of relationship types or social contexts. Also, it is quicker to estimate personal network size with this method than with the known population method. A disadvantage of the method is that it is difficult to quantify the uncertainty in the estimate, as the summation approach is not embedded within any statistical framework, although future developments may provide a solution to this problem.

## 10.3 SOCIAL DISTANCE

Apart from the size of the broader acquaintanceship network, researchers are interested in the features of these larger networks. For example, past research shows that core networks are characterized by a strong homophily on various dimensions—that is, a strong tendency to associate with similar others (nicely illustrated by the proverb "birds of a feather flock together"). However, much less is known about the larger acquaintanceship networks. It is generally assumed that those wider networks are more heterogeneous, as they include people from various contexts with whom we interact now and then, and yet little research exists on this topic.

Thomas DiPrete and colleagues (2011) extended the known population method described in Section 10.2 to study precisely this topic. Their idea was as follows: The known population method departs from the assumption of random mixing, that is, the idea that the composition of personal networks reflects the composition of the larger population. For example, if immigrants make up. 10% of the population, then we would expect that 10% of the people respondents know are also immigrants. Of course, we would expect that this percentage would show some variance across people. However, DiPrete et al. argued that the extent to which this assumption holds can be estimated from the data. If the observed variance in these proportions is larger than the variation we would expect on the basis of random mixing, we have a case of *overdispersion*. Overdispersion in the proportion of people from certain races or social classes can tell us whether there is segregation, or nonrandom mixing, in these aspects. If overdispersion is detected, we can further investigate it by relating the residuals to respondents' characteristics. That allows us to explore whether, for example, people are more likely to associate with others from their own race or social class than with others across categorical boundaries.

This method was applied to the data of the U.S. General Social Survey (GSS) of 2006, and DiPrete and colleagues found that acquaintanceship networks are at least as segregated as people's core networks. This was particularly the case for race and for perceived religiosity and political beliefs. Miranda Lubbers and colleagues reported that acquaintanceship networks displayed overdispersion in economic variables (Lubbers et al., 2018).

## 10.4 SOCIAL CAPITAL

Social capital is one of the most popular concepts in the social sciences, but different disciplines have emphasized different aspects of the concept and have assigned different definitions and uses to it. At the individual level, however, considerable consensus has been reached about its central meaning: that is, social capital refers to the resources that an individual can access through his or her personal network. These resources can be instrumental (money, information) or expressive (companionship). Two methods have been used to measure this individual or "network social capital" in survey research: the position generator and the resource generator.

### The Position Generator

The most widely used method to measure social capital is the *position generator*, originally developed by Nan Lin and colleagues (Lin, 2001; Lin & Dumin, 1986). Lin assumed that a person's occupational prestige is a good indicator of the financial and cultural resources he or she controls. Consequently, the composition of the network in terms of occupational prestige may be regarded as a proxy for the array of potential instrumental resources (money, information, influence, etc.) that can be accessed through the personal network.

The method involves presenting a list of occupations with different levels of occupational prestige to the respondents and asking them whether they know someone in each of these occupations. On the basis of this information, various measures of social capital can be obtained:

1. *Extensity*: The number of different positions that can be accessed.
2. *The total prestige*: The sum of the prestige scores of the occupations to which the respondents have access.
3. *The average prestige*: The total prestige divided by the number of different positions that can be accessed.
4. *The range in prestige*: The span in prestige scores between the highest and the lowest positions that can be accessed.
5. *The maximum prestige*: The value of the prestige score of the highest position that can be accessed.

In the case of a positive response to an occupation, respondents are typically also asked to qualify whether this person is a family member, a friend, or an acquaintance, as it is assumed that the type of relationship influences the willingness to provide resources to the focal individual. Usually, if the respondents know multiple persons in an occupation, only the strongest relationship is recorded. Some of the five measures can be weighed by type of relationship (kin, friend, acquaintance). Other attributive variables of the alters can be collected as well, such as place of residence, frequency of contact, or duration of the relationship.

The position generator has been widely used internationally, which implies that validated instruments are already available in many cultural contexts, allowing the reuse of these instruments and enabling cross-cultural comparisons. When an instrument is not available, it is relatively easy to construct a position generator, since the structure of occupations can be objectively drawn from existing national and international scales of job prestige.

The list of occupations that is selected needs to form a sample of the professions, occupations, or authorities of a given society, reflecting the hierarchical distribution of professions in society (see Figure 10.2). These positions can be ranked on the basis of the socioeconomic status attached to them following national surveys or internationally standardized scales of occupations such as the Standard International Occupational Prestige Scale (SIOPS) or the International Socio-Economic Index of Occupational Status (ISEI); these prestige scores are taken as proxies of the resources accessed by these occupations.

The questionnaire can be administered quickly, and it is highly standardized, allowing for comparison across studies and contexts. Martin van der Gaag, Gert Jan Appelhof, and Martin Webber (2012), however, observed that, while the respondents liked the questions in general, they indicated that recalling alters according to their occupation was counterintuitive to how they memorize relationships. This finding is in line with what we mentioned earlier about the cognitive organization of relationships. The authors further found that respondents do not know the occupations of all of their network members, which may lead to an underestimation of social capital. A further possible disadvantage is that the interpretation of the position generator depends on the theoretical importance of job prestige for the dependent variable a researcher considers.

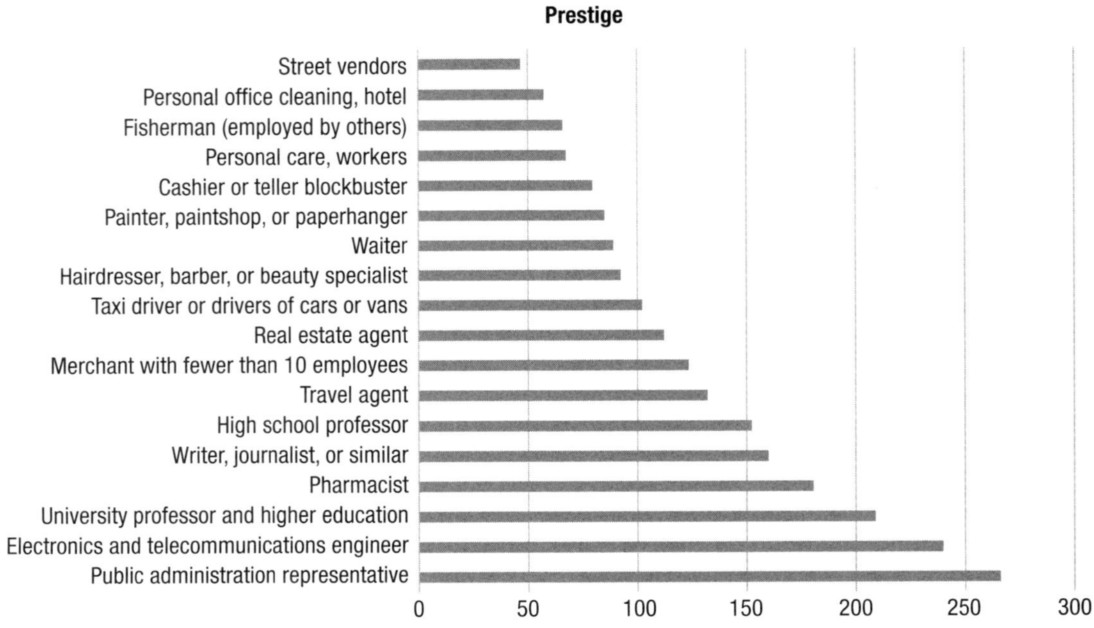


**FIGURE 10.2.** An example of a selection of occupations (used as items in the position generator) and their occupational statuses on the Escala de Prestigio Profesional in Spain (PRESCA, a Spanish scale measuring prestige, Molina et al., 2015).

For some variables, other aspects of social capital than position-related aspects may be more dominant, in which case other measures should be selected.

## The Resource Generator

The *resource generator* was originally developed by Martin van der Gaag and Tom Snijders (2005). In contrast to the position generator approach, this method directly measures the individual's capability to obtain access to diverse resources embedded in social networks. Although it has the same structure as the position generator, in this method, respondents are presented with a roster of *resources*, which together represent the various dimensions of social capital, and they are asked for each resource whether they know somebody who possesses that resource. Example items may be "Do you know someone who can build a website?"; "Do you know someone who knows a lot about governmental regulations?"; " . . . someone who owns a car?", " . . . someone who has good contacts with the media?"; and so on. (The latter three example items stem from the Social Survey on the Networks of the Dutch, performed in 1999–2000.) Again, the respondents should be informed about the minimum criterion of "knowing" someone. From this information, we can calculate the total social capital (as the number of items accessed) as well as scores on each of the underlying subdimensions of the instrument. Again, we might in addition ask about the closeness to the person who has the capability to provide these resources.

The resource generator can be administered quickly, and the questions are easy to understand and interpret. This approach is particularly helpful when we are interested in the usefulness of resources for specific goals, such as escaping long-term unemployment or increasing productivity on the work floor. The items can then be adapted to this specific context. For generic purposes, the list of possibly valuable social resources can be very large, and again, they are culturally relative. As a result, it can be cumbersome to select a short list of items that together represent a coherent and complete picture of social capital; the problems are comparable to constructing a list of multiple name generators described earlier. It is therefore advisable to reuse an already developed and tested instrument, if the context of application is comparable. If reuse is not possible, van der Gaag recommends that the construction of a resource generator should be theoretically guided. He further suggests also including a number of position generator items along with the resource generator items, in order to increase the comparability with other research.

## 10.5 SOCIAL SUPPORT

As we have indicated in Chapters 2 and 6, many personal network studies focus on describing an individual's support network: those people with whom an individual exchanges support of different dimensions. Those studies are interested in finding out *who* gives support to individuals, in terms of their sociodemographic characteristics (such as gender) or in terms of their relationship with ego (such as the strength of their relationship or the type of relationship). They may also be interested in understanding how this network changes over time as individuals experience different life events. However, in some cases a researcher may be interested not in who gives social support, but rather in the availability of social support, regardless of its origin. In these cases, a network study is not necessary: There are social support questionnaires that do not delineate the network itself.

One example of such a questionnaire is the Duke-UNC Functional Social Support Questionnaire (FSSQ), which was developed by W. Eugene Broadhead and colleagues in 1988 (Broadhead, Gehlbach, de Gruy, & Kaplan, 1988). The questionnaire consists of 14 items, which were later reduced to 8. The respondents are presented with a list of "things that other people do for us or give us that may be helpful or supportive," such as "I get chances to talk about money matters" or "I get help when I am sick in bed." Responses are given on a 5-point scale ranging from "much less than I would like" to "as much as I would like." The psychometric properties of the scale are satisfactory, although the internal consistency is not high; this indicates that different types of support have little relation to each other.

## CHAPTER SUMMARY

In this chapter, we have reviewed several methods available for measuring characteristics about alters without the need to go through the whole process described so far. Those methods are important because they can be applied more easily to large national samples. Section 10.2 reviewed the methods intended to estimate the size of personal networks, either using known populations or adding acquaintances from different social contexts. These methods can be considered by-products of the NSUM method, which assumes that personal networks capture on average societal diversity (or "random mixing"). In this regard, Section 10.3 showed how this assumption is problematic but also of substantive interest. Section 10.4 presented two measures of social capital, the position generator and the resource generator. In the two cases, the participant reports on her relationship with either people occupying different occupational positions along the social structure or people able to access a list of resources. Thus, these approaches provide measures about the access to resources embedded in the ego's personal network. Finally, Section 10.5 briefly discussed measures of social support.

### FURTHER READING

Berkman, L. F., & Glass, T. (2000). Social integration, social networks, social support, and health. In L. F. Berkman & I. Kawachi (Eds.), *Social epidemiology* (pp. 137–173). Oxford, UK: Oxford University Press.

Burt, R. S. (2000). The network structure of social capital. *Organizational Behavior, 22,* 345–423.

DiPrete, T. A., Gelman, A., McCormick, T., Teitler, J., & Zheng, T. (2011). Segregation in social networks based on acquaintanceship and trust. *American Journal of Sociology, 116*(4), 1234–1283.

Lin, N., & Erickson, B. (2010). *Social Capital. An international research program.* Oxford, UK: Oxford University Press.

McCarty, C., Killworth, P. D., Russell, H. B., Johnsen, E. C., & Shelley, G. A. (2001). Comparing two methods for estimating network size. *Human Organization, 60*(1), 28–39.

McCormick, T. H., Salganik, M. J., & Zheng, T. (2010). How many people do you know?: Efficiently estimating personal network size. *Journal of the American Statistical Association, 105*(489), 59–70.

Van Der Gaag, M., & Snijders, T. A. B. (2005). The resource generator: Social capital quantification with concrete items. *Social Networks, 27*(1), 1–29.

# 11

# Analyzing Personal Network Composition and Structure

*What Is This Chapter About?*

In this chapter, we will focus on the creation of aggregate or summary variables of personal network composition and structure, using the data generated by the name interpreters and/or edge interpreters, so that they can be employed for further analysis. After an introduction (Section 11.1), we will explain how to create simple (Section 11.2) and more advanced compositional variables (Section 11.3), simple structural variables (Section 11.4), and measures that combine multiple variables (Section 11.5 for composition only and Section 11.6 for measures that combine structure and composition). These measures will then be added to the data file for subsequent analysis (Section 11.7).

## 11.1 SUMMARIZING NAME INTERPRETERS AND EDGE INTERPRETERS BY RESPONDENTS

As you will recall from Chapter 7, respondents are asked a set of questions about the attributes of each alter (e.g., their age or sex). These questions generate nominal, ordinal, or interval/ratio data at the relation level. Often, we want to summarize those questions at the network level. The summary of those data over the set of all the alters that a respondent named in the personal network elicitation gives us information about the personal network composition. Chapter 8 described the types of questions you can ask about the relations among alters. These questions generate nominal or ordinal data that can be dichotomous or dichotomized after data collection. The summary of those data over all the alter–alter pairs gives us information about network structure. These are the real structural data, which can be combined with compositional variables. The aggregated or summary variables can be used to describe the personal networks of people in your sample. The variability in these measures can also be related to respondent-level variables such as those we discussed in Chapter 5, as either the dependent or explanatory variables.

Let's consider an example. Assume that we asked three respondents (Pam, Allen, and Helen) to tell us their sex, age, and income. We then elicited five alters from each of them, using the prompt "Name five people you talked to recently." After that, we asked the respondents to report each alter's sex, age in years, and closeness the respondent feels toward the alter on a scale from 1 (not close at all) to 5 (very close). Last, we asked the respondent to indicate, for each pair of alters, whether the alters knew each other (1) or not (0).

Table 11.1 shows the data we collected about the attributes of each of the three respondents. This data format represents the way the data would be entered into a statistical package (such as R, SAS, SPSS, or STATA) for analysis. The columns represent the variables, and the rows represent the individual observations. This is an *ego-level* dataset because variables are observed for each ego and each ego occupies one row in the matrix. These are typical survey data about respondents. Now consider the data about the respondents' alters in Table 11.2.

You can see that each respondent has five alters and has reported information on each of them. Therefore, each respondent now occupies five rows in the matrix, one for each alter. For example, the respondent Pam listed an alter named Bill who is male, 34 years old, and has a closeness level of 3 to Pam. Helen has an alter named Celia who is female, age 31, and has a closeness level of 2 to Helen. This is an *alter-level* dataset, since variables are observed for each alter and each row corresponds to one different alter.

Last, we have a table with the relationships among alters. This may be in the edge list format, as shown in Table 11.3, or in the adjacency matrix format, as shown in Tables 11.4A, B, and C. For each respondent, there were $N(N-1)/2$ ties to evaluate ($N$ being the number of nominated alters), which in the case of 5 alters amounts to 10 relationships. In Table 11.3, we see the evaluation of all 10 relationships among Pam's alters. For each pair of alters, Pam indicated whether or not the two people knew each other. For example, she reported that Bill knew Cynthia, Lydia, and Janet, but not Joe. In Table 11.4, we see the same data, but in the format of individual adjacency matrices. The edge interpreter questions implied undirected (symmetric) relationships, so the 10 evaluations in the lower triangle of the matrix (below the diagonal) are the same as the 10 evaluations in the upper triangle. Here we can see clearly that Bill, Cynthia, Lydia, and Janet are all connected to each other, but none of them knows Joe.

**TABLE 11.1. Example of a Data File of Attributes of Respondents**

| Respondent | Sex | Age | Income in $ |
|---|---|---|---|
| Pam | F | 32 | 22,000 |
| Allen | M | 46 | 76,000 |
| Helen | F | 28 | 52,000 |

**TABLE 11.2. Example of a Data File of Attributes of Alters**

| Respondent | Alter | Alter Sex | Alter Age | Alter Closeness |
|---|---|---|---|---|
| Pam | Bill | M | 34 | 3 |
| Pam | Cynthia | F | 30 | 5 |
| Pam | Lydia | F | 28 | 3 |
| Pam | Janet | F | 41 | 3 |
| Pam | Joe | M | 35 | 2 |
| Allen | Rick | M | 45 | 4 |
| Allen | Steve | M | 50 | 4 |
| Allen | Art | M | 46 | 3 |
| Allen | Denise | F | 40 | 5 |
| Allen | Sam | M | 38 | 3 |
| Helen | Wendy | F | 28 | 5 |
| Helen | Celia | F | 31 | 2 |
| Helen | Paul | M | 32 | 4 |
| Helen | Sarah | F | 40 | 1 |
| Helen | Alicia | F | 24 | 3 |

**TABLE 11.3. Example of a Data File of Evaluations of Alter–Alter Ties in the Format of an Edge List**

| Respondent | Alter1 | Alter2 | Alter–alter tie |
|---|---|---|---|
| Pam | Bill | Cynthia | 1 |
| Pam | Bill | Lydia | 1 |
| Pam | Bill | Janet | 1 |
| Pam | Bill | Joe | 0 |
| Pam | Cynthia | Lydia | 1 |
| Pam | Cynthia | Janet | 1 |
| Pam | Cynthia | Joe | 0 |
| Pam | Lydia | Janet | 1 |
| Pam | Lydia | Joe | 0 |
| Pam | Janet | Joe | 0 |
| Allen | Rick | Steve | 1 |
| Allen | Rick | Art | 1 |
| . . . (etc.) | . . . | . . . | . . . |

**TABLE 11.4A. Example of a Data File of Evaluations of Alter–Alter Ties in the Format of Adjacency Matrices for Each Respondent (Pam)**

| Pam | Bill | Cynthia | Lydia | Janet | Joe |
|---|---|---|---|---|---|
| Bill | 0 | 1 | 1 | 1 | 0 |
| Cynthia | 1 | 0 | 1 | 1 | 0 |
| Lydia | 1 | 1 | 0 | 1 | 0 |
| Janet | 1 | 1 | 1 | 0 | 0 |
| Joe | 0 | 0 | 0 | 0 | 0 |

**TABLE 11.4B. cont. (Allen)**

| Allen | Rick | Steve | Art | Denise | Sam |
|---|---|---|---|---|---|
| Rick | 0 | 1 | 1 | 1 | 1 |
| Steve | 1 | 0 | 1 | 1 | 1 |
| Art | 1 | 1 | 0 | 1 | 1 |
| Denise | 1 | 1 | 1 | 0 | 1 |
| Sam | 1 | 1 | 1 | 1 | 0 |

**TABLE 11.4C. cont. (Helen)**

| Helen | Wendy | Celia | Paul | Sarah | Alicia |
|---|---|---|---|---|---|
| Wendy | 0 | 1 | 1 | 1 | 1 |
| Celia | 1 | 0 | 0 | 0 | 0 |
| Paul | 1 | 0 | 0 | 0 | 0 |
| Sarah | 1 | 0 | 0 | 0 | 0 |
| Alicia | 1 | 0 | 0 | 0 | 0 |

How can you use these data to say something about the personal networks of the respondents? For each respondent, we first need to create a summary of each characteristic of his or her alters and their relationships to each other. In other words, the data each ego has generated in matrix 11.2, and either 11.3 or 11.4, somehow need to be summarized into a single row, which represents the aggregate characteristics of that ego's personal network. This will be an ego-level dataset, similar to Table 11.1. If needed, this dataset can then be merged or joined to the data in Table 11.1, or even to Table 11.2, if we want to use the aggregate variables to predict characteristics of the alters or the ego–alter ties. How to create such ego-level summary data is what we will discuss in this chapter.

## 11.2 CREATING SIMPLE COMPOSITIONAL VARIABLES FROM PERSONAL NETWORKS

Our first question involves how to summarize alter characteristics and ego–alter tie characteristics, such as those represented in Table 11.2, into ego-level compositional characteristics of personal networks. Of course, we can summarize any characteristic in a variety of ways, depending on our research questions and/or interests. For example, we can summarize the alter variable "age" into a network variable that represents the average age of the alters, the median age, the proportion of alters above or below a certain age threshold (say alters over 40), the number of alters in a specific age range, such as alters between 25 and 35, or even the minimum or maximum age. We can also look at the diversity or heterogeneity of the network in terms of age by taking, for example, the standard deviation of age among the alters of a network as a summary variable. This may show us that some people have very diverse networks, including a variety of very young and very old people, while others have networks that consist primarily of people in a limited age range.

Instead of describing the age of alters per se, we could also summarize the extent to which the age of the alters matches that of the respondent. We call this "ego correspondence" or similarity. Such correspondence is often used to measure homophily, that is, the ego's tendency to maintain ties with alters who are similar to those of the ego (e.g., alters of the same sex or with similar age as the ego). Age correspondence might be measured by calculating the average *difference* in age between the respondent and each of his or her alters. Alternatively, we could look at the proportion of alters who are exactly the same age as the respondent, or who do not differ more than, say, five years from the respondent. Apart from the proportion of (approximately) same-age alters, we may further distinguish between the proportion of alters who are older (or younger) than the respondent. As you see, for each variable there is a whole range of options of aggregation, and which one you choose depends on your research hypotheses or interests, together with theoretical considerations or findings from previous research.

To decide which measure is most suitable for your goals, you also need to recall the discussion in Chapter 5 concerning levels of measurement. In the preceding example, we have collected three alter-level variables: one nominal (sex), one ordinal (closeness), and one interval/ratio (age). We need to consider the level of measurement when creating a summary variable. Table 11.5 summarizes various possibilities for describing the central tendency, specific locations, and the heterogeneity or dispersion of the characteristic in the network.

For *nominal alter variables*, such as Sex, you could use the mode (the category that was most frequently observed) as a summary, as indicated in Table 11.5. However, you will most likely create a separate summary variable for each or for one of the possible values (e.g., for "Male" and/or for "Female"; see the column "Specific Locations"). This is the easiest thing to do. It involves using some form of *array statement* to loop through the alter data for a respondent and count the number of alters that have a particular value (Sex="Male" or Sex="Female"), while keeping a count of the total number of alters. Ultimately, you will end up with a distinct summary variable for each value (or category) of the original nominal attribute. For Sex, for example, you will end up with two summary variables, one for "Male" and one for "Female." Each summary variable measures the number of alters whose attribute is equal to a specific value, for example, the number

**TABLE 11.5. Summary Variables of Network Composition**

| Level of measurement | Central tendency | Specific locations | Dispersion or heterogeneity |
|---|---|---|---|
| Nominal | Mode | Number or proportion of alters with a specific value (i.e., in a specific category) | IQV, for example, Agresti's Index of Diversity, Generalized Variance, Entropy; in some cases, the number of categories with nonzero values |
| Ordinal | Mode, median | Number or proportion of alters above or below a certain threshold value or within a certain range of values, minimum, maximum | For example, range, interquartile range |
| Interval/ratio | Mode, median, mean | | For example, standard deviation, range |

of alters whose Sex is equal to "Male" in each ego's personal network. In addition to the number (or absolute frequency), it is also common to calculate the proportion (or relative frequency) of alters who match a condition (e.g., male alters) over the total number of alters in an ego's personal network. When you force all respondents to nominate the same number of alters, this calculation is easier because the denominator is always the same.

In this example, respondents reported the sex of each alter. In Table 11.6, you see two variables, one the proportion of males in the network and the other the proportion of females. In this case, 60% of Pam's network is female, while only 20% is female in Allen's network. You could also create a variable equal to the *number* of alters who are male and the number who are female. Again, remember that you will typically have a variable for each value of the nominal variable. So if you ask respondents to report the relation type of alter, such as family, work, or church, you can create a variable for each of these. If you sum these proportion variables, they will add to 1.0.

**TABLE 11.6. Compositional Data from Table 11.2 Summarized at the Respondent Level**

| Respondent | Proportion of male alters | Proportion of female alters | Average age of alters | Standard deviation of age of alters | Proportion of alter closeness to the ego, 4 and 5 (strong ties) | Average alter closeness to the ego |
|---|---|---|---|---|---|---|
| Pam | .4 | .6 | 33.6 | 5.0 | .2 | 3.2 |
| Allen | .8 | .2 | 43.8 | 4.8 | .6 | 3.8 |
| Helen | .2 | .8 | 31.0 | 5.9 | .4 | 3.0 |

If you are interested in the heterogeneity of the network in terms of a categorical attribute like sex, you may calculate an index of qualitative variation (IQV) such as Agresti's Index of Diversity. The formula for this index is:

$$\left(1-\sum_{i=1}^{k}p_i^{\,2}\right)/\left(1-\frac{1}{k}\right)$$

where $p_i$ is the proportion of alters in category $i$, and $k$ is the total number of categories of the attribute. The numerator $(1 - \Sigma p_i^2)$ can be interpreted as the probability that two randomly extracted alters in the network belong to different categories of the variable of interest; in other words, it is a measure of diversity. The denominator $(1 - 1/k)$ is the maximum value that this measure can have, given the number of categories. For example, in the case of sex, there are only two categories, so the maximum probability we could observe that two randomly extracted alters belong to different categories is (1 – 1/2) = 0.5, which would occur in a personal network in which half the alters are male and half are female. If a variable has three categories, however, that maximum probability increases to (1 – 1/3) = 0.67. By dividing the probability that two alters belong to different categories in the actual ego network by this maximum value, the index conveniently runs from 0 to 1, regardless of the total number of categories in the nominal alter attribute. The value 0 will be observed if there is complete homogeneity (namely, when all alters belong to the same category of the variable). The value 1 will be observed when there is complete heterogeneity (i.e., when the alters are spread evenly over the different categories). In the case of Pam, the index has the value of $(1 - 0.4 \times 0.4 + 0.6 \times 0.6) / 0.5 = 0.96$, a value that is very close to 1. This indicates that Pam's network is very diverse in terms of gender. In the case of Allen and Helen, the index has the value of $(1 - 0.2 \times 0.2 + 0.8 \times 0.8) / 0.5 = 0.64$, which indicates that their networks are more homogeneous than Pam's. In this case, the simple proportion of men or women in the network gives us a good indication of how heterogeneous the network is in terms of sex. We would probably not calculate Agresti's IQV in this case. For variables that have more than two categories, however, the IQV index is a useful measure for dispersion.

In some cases, for example, when we have asked respondents to indicate the roles of alters or the contexts in which they met them, we may also be interested in the total number of roles or contexts observed in the personal network. In this case, we can simply count the number of categories of a nominal variable for which at least one alter was found—that is, the number of categories with a nonzero number or proportion of alters. We can easily calculate this once the data have been aggregated into proportions. One person may have a network that is entirely composed of family members and colleagues (only two roles have nonzero counts of alters), whereas another may also have nominated neighbors, members of the same church, parents of their children's classmates, and so on. This second person, then, has a greater role diversity than the first.

We also asked the respondents to report their level of closeness to each alter on a scale from 1 to 5. This is clearly an *ordinal variable*. If we wish to say something about the central tendency of an ordinal variable, we could use the *median*, the value with half of the alters above it and half below. We could also calculate the number or proportion of alters above a certain threshold of the variable. In Table 11.6, we actually created a variable that adds together the proportions for closeness levels 4 and 5, which have been arbitrarily labeled "strong ties." As we mentioned in Chapter 5, some people treat ordinal variables as interval variables and calculate the mean. Although this approach is not statistically valid, it is not that unusual. This has been represented in the last column of Table 11.6.

We also asked respondents to report the age of each alter in years. This is a *ratio variable*, so a good summary of that will be the mean (for the central tendency) and the standard deviation (for dispersion). For nominal variables, you can use an array to represent the count or proportion of different values. For interval and ratio variables, you will simply calculate the mean. You see the result of this in Table 11.8. The average age of Pam's alters is 33.6, while for Allen it is 43.8. We have also calculated the standard deviation, which captures the degree to which the ages of alters cluster around the average age. Table 11.8 (on page 166) shows that Pam and Allen have a standard deviation of around 5, whereas Helen has a higher standard deviation of 5.9. Thus, Helen's network is the most diverse in terms of age.

Keep in mind that the described procedures to create compositional summary variables can be conducted either in standard software for statistical analysis, or in one of the specific programs for personal network analysis listed in the Appendix. In SPSS, for example, you can aggregate sets of variables of all measurement levels to the network level selecting the command "Aggregate" in the Data menu. When you do so, you will need to use the respondent ID (in our example, the variable "Respondent") as the grouping or "break variable," and then indicate which variables you wish to summarize to this grouping level—that is, the personal network level. Each alter variable can be summarized multiple times, using different functions of aggregation. For example, you can take the median, mean, minimum, maximum, standard deviation, or the number or proportion of alters below or above a certain threshold or within or outside a certain range of values. In R, you can easily obtain summary variables on ego-network composition by applying functions from the *plyr* package (e.g., the *ddply* function) and in the *dplyr* package (in particular, the *group_by* and *summarise* functions) to a data frame of alter attributes, in which each row is an alter and one of the variables (columns) indicates the ID of the respondent (ego) who nominated each alter.

Before you calculate compositional summary variables, be sure that you have properly declared the missing data categories or codes in your file. If some networks have many missing data points, your best option might be to create an additional summary variable that indicates the proportion of missing data for the respondent's alters in the variable. In this way, you can later decide to declare if the summary variable is missing or is based on too few values.

You can save the new ego-level summary measures to a separate file that will have the respondent ID as one of its variables. The respondent ID can then be used as a key to merge the resulting ego-level file (comparable to Table 11.6, where the name is the respondent ID) with the file that contains the respondent-level characteristics (comparable to Table 11.1). In SPSS, for example, this can be done with the command "Match

> **How to Use SPSS for Working with Personal Network Data**
>
> Christoph Müller and colleagues (Müller, Wellman, & Marin, 1999) proposed ways to use SPSS with ego-centered social networks. They showed how analysis of the composition of ego-centered networks is most effective when starting with two data files: (1) individuals and their egocentric networks, and (2) members of the network and their links with central individuals. They also showed how to tie together these two files: providing general information on each ego-centered network and combining the central individuals, relationships, and data network.

Data—Add Variables" in the Data menu. In R, you would join data frames with the *merge* function from base R or with the **_join* family of functions in the *dplyr* package.

In SPSS, some of the summary variables we proposed in Table 11.3 cannot be selected in the "Aggregate" function, but they can be easily calculated manually. This is the case for the mode and for Agresti's IQV. For these variables, you need to summarize the nominal variable into a set of variables that give the proportions of alters in each category, as we explained before. Once you have aggregated this information to the network level, you can simply use the "Compute Variable" command in the Transform menu to create your variables on the basis of these proportions. In R, you can write your own function to calculate any compositional measure on a personal network, which you would typically store as a data frame of alter attributes if you are analyzing composition. You can easily write your own function to calculate Agresti's IQV on a variable in a data frame, but there are often specialized packages that offer pre-written functions for popular measures (for example, the *qualvar* package provides several functions to calculate qualitative variation indices). Once you have written or retrieved a function that calculates a compositional measure of interest, you can apply this function to all your ego-networks at once using the *plyr*, *dplyr*, or *purrr* packages. If the ego-networks are stored as separate data frames in a list, you would use *plyr::ldply* or *purrr::map* to apply your compositional measure to every list element. If the ego-networks are stored in a single data frame of alter attributes, which includes all alters nominated by all respondents, you would first "group" this data frame by ego ID (*dplyr::group_by*) and then apply your measure to all ego ID's with *dplyr::summarise*.

## 11.3 MORE ADVANCED COMPOSITIONAL VARIABLES

### Ego Correspondence

The measures we have looked at so far account for the majority of uses in personal network analysis. But we can look at network composition in another way. Rather than just summarize the alter characteristics, we can measure the extent to which the alter characteristics match those of the respondent. This is called *ego correspondence*. Correspondence is a typical measure of *homophily*, the tendency of people to establish relationships with people who are similar to them.

To create an ego correspondence measure with respect to a certain variable, such as sex, you should first calculate the match between the ego and alter—*before* aggregating the variable to the network level. To do that, you will have to merge your respondent-level data onto your alter-level data. In SPSS, you can do this with the command "Match Data—Add Variables," indicating that the file that contains the respondent-level data is a table with keys, so that the program understands that each case in this table will be merged onto multiple cases in the alter-level dataset.

In the case of nominal variables, such as sex, the match measure between the ego and alter should simply indicate whether the ego and alter have the same or a different sex. Therefore, the measure will be a new alter-level variable that equals 1 for alters whose sex is the same as the respondent's and 0 for alters whose sex is different from that of the respondent. Then, we can aggregate this variable as we did with sex, simply taking the proportion (or number) of same-sex alters in the network.

In the case of interval or ratio variables, such as age, the match measure can be a simple difference between the ego's and alter's age. For this, we first need to subtract the ego's age from the alter's age. Once we have calculated these differences at the alter level, we can aggregate this information to the network level, for example, by averaging the differences over all the alters of a respondent. The result will be the *average* age difference between an ego and that ego's alters. If we are not interested in the precise age differences, but rather in whether alters have the same age as the ego (or, for example, not more than five years older or younger), we need to dichotomize the age differences before aggregating the information. We can then summarize the dichotomized scores by taking, for example, the proportion of same-age alters.

In R, you can join ego-level variables (e.g. ego's age) into a data frame of alter-level attributes (e.g., alter's age) using *merge* (base R) or the **_join* functions from *dplyr*. You can then use *dplyr::mutate* to obtain any new alter-level variable indicating the match or similarity between each alter and that alter's ego: for example, an alter-level binary variable indicating if each alter has the same age as ego. Finally, you can use *dplyr::summarise*

### *The Power of Homophily*

Social scientists have pointed out that similarity (sharing the same attributes) is a powerful predictor for socialization, a tendency that is called homophily. Miller McPherson and colleagues (2001) showed that people's personal networks tend to be homogeneous with regard to many sociodemographic, behavioral, and intrapersonal characteristics. Geographic propinquity, families, organizations, and isomorphic positions in social systems all create contexts in which homophilous relations form. Ties between dissimilar individuals also dissolve at a higher rate, which sets the stage for the formation of niches (localized positions) within social space.

(after *dplyr::group_by*) to aggregate the alter-level similarity variable by ego, for example, generating the proportion of same-age alters for each ego.

By looking at ego correspondence variables, we are assuming that the variability in the match between respondents and alters affects respondents in some way. Consider Table 11.7, which contains the ego correspondence variables for sex and age. As Pam and Helen are female, the proportions of alters of the same sex are the same as the proportions of female alters for them (see Tables 11.4A and 11.4C). But for Allen, the proportion of alters of the same sex is the same as the proportion of alters who are male (see again Table 11.4B). By looking at the correspondence with the ego's sex, we can now see that both Allen and Helen have networks that are made up mostly of alters of the same gender.

The age correspondence variable is a sum of the squared differences between the ego's age and that of their alters. Since in our example all networks have the same size, it is not necessary to divide the sum of squares by the number of alters minus one. We see that Helen shows a much wider variability of ages in her network compared to her own age than Pam or Allen. These differences may be important in explaining the characteristics, attitudes, or conditions of the respondent.

## Geographical Dispersion

Some researchers are interested in the spatial dimension of personal networks, for example, in the effects of distance on the functioning of social relationships, particularly in comparison to times when maintaining contact over larger distances was less easy. Social geographers are also interested in the effects of the spatial dispersion of the individual's personal networks on mobility patterns.

Of course, you can capture those dimensions by simply asking how far the alters live from the respondent (e.g., in terms of kilometers or travel time) or whether alters live in the same neighborhood, town, province, state, or country as the ego. The result is an alter-level distance variable that can be summarized in any of the ways discussed earlier. If you have asked respondents more precisely where they and their alters live (or where they meet), you can use geographic information system (GIS) or spatial analysis software to transform this information into distances.

Two measures are particularly useful for averaging spatial distances over a personal network: the average distance between the ego and his or her alters; and the average

**TABLE 11.7. Ego Correspondence Summaries**

| Respondent | Proportion of alters who are the same sex as the respondent | Sum of squared age differences |
|---|---|---|
| Pam | .6 | 114 |
| Allen | .8 | 117 |
| Helen | .8 | 185 |

distance among the alters (Molina, Bolíbar, & Cruz, 2011). The first measure can be calculated using this formula:

$$\frac{\sum_{j=1}^{N} \log\left(\text{distance}\left[\text{ego}, j\right]\right)}{N}$$

where $j$ indicates the alter ($j = 1, \ldots, N$). The measure takes the averaged natural logarithm of the distances to weigh down longer distances. This measure only takes into account the distances between the ego and his or her alters. But consider the following two situations. One respondent may live approximately 1,000 km away from all alters, who all live in the same place. Another respondent may also live approximately 1,000 km away from all alters, but in this case some alters live 1,000 km to the north, some 1,000 km to the east, some 1,000 km to the south, and others 1,000 km to the west of the ego. While both respondents would have the same value on the first measure, reflecting the respondent's distance from his or her network members, obviously the two situations are quite different and may have different implications for the structure and functioning of the network. To capture that second idea, a complementary measure of the *spatial dispersion* of the network is given by

$$\frac{\sum_{j,k=1;j<k}^{N} \log\left(\text{distance}\left[j,k\right]\right)}{N\left(N-1\right)/2}$$

where $j$ and $k$ indicate the alters (with $j$, $k = 1, \ldots, N$). This measure is an average of the spatial distances in each (unordered) pair of alters. Because each pair is only considered once ($j < k$, so we count the distance from Alter 1 to Alter 2, but not the distance from Alter 2 to Alter 1), we have $N(N - 1)/2$ such distances, which explains the denominator of the average. Together, these two measures give good insight into the spatial distance and dispersion of the network.

## 11.4 CREATING SIMPLE STRUCTURAL VARIABLES FROM PERSONAL NETWORKS

So far we have discussed the creation of compositional variables, which measure different aspects of the distribution of *alter attributes* in the personal network (*who* the ego knows). However, if you have collected data about ties among alters (see Chapter 8), you will also be able to create structural variables, which quantify different aspects of the *connectivity* among personal network members (how the ego's contacts *know each other*). Note that the same structural measures used on whole networks can be applied to personal networks, and vice versa. Tables 11.3 and 11.4A, B, C show the two most typical formats of your structural data: an aggregate edge list (including all alters from all egos) and individual adjacency matrices (one for the alters of each ego). The two formats can be easily converted into one another using statistical software.

**To Include or to Exclude the Ego?**

Christopher McCarty and Amber Wutich (2005) studied the effect of keeping the ego in or leaving the ego out from personal network adjacency matrices. They found that a number of important structural measures, including density, degree, structural equivalence, and betweenness, did not change materially when the ego was included in the matrix, whereas for other measures, such as closeness centrality or the number of components, the difference was meaningful. Personal network visualizations also looked very similar in both cases. The authors concluded that there is no single rule for this issue, but the ego can be kept or removed from the analysis depending on the research focus (e.g., the impact the ego has in brokering their network).

The analysis of edge lists or adjacency matrices is far more common in sociocentric network research. However, with a few exceptions, most of the structural measures applied to whole networks can be applied to personal networks as well. Keep in mind that the adjacency matrix you use to calculate these metrics for a personal network should, in most cases, *not* include the ego. In other words, the network you are using to measure structure should represent the interactions among the people to whom the respondent is tied (see Figure 11.1B), but not these people's ties to the respondent (as in Figure 11.1A). This is because the respondent, by definition, is tied to all of the alters. Thus, including the respondent would just add one node (the ego) and $N$ ties between

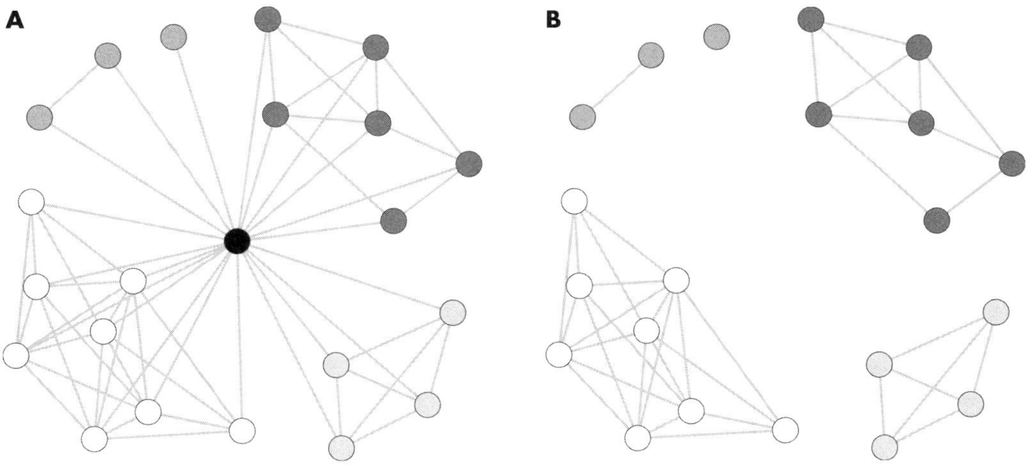


**FIGURE 11.1.** An example of a personal network (the left-hand network of Figure 8.1), where the ego is (A) included (left-hand) and (B) excluded (right-hand). *Note.* The black node represents the ego, who is connected in the left-hand figure to everyone else. The white nodes represent family members, the light gray nodes university friends, the darker shade of gray peers known since childhood, and the darkest shade of gray people from work.

that node and all other nodes (the *N* alters). This is redundant information, and most network-structural measures are functionally the same when ties between the respondent and the alters are introduced.

There are many aspects to personal network structure. Structural metrics are each designed to capture a specific aspect of that structure. One of the most basic and widely used structural metrics for social networks is *density* (in personal network analysis, this is also called the ego's *clustering coefficient*), which is a measure of overall network cohesion or connectedness. Density is simply the percentage of ties that exist out of all possible ties, and it ranges from 0 (no actor is connected to any other) to 1 (every actor is connected to every other). In a personal network, density measures how many alters know each other or, more precisely, how many ties among alters do exist out of all the ties that could potentially exist, given the number of alters. Note that the total number of ties that could potentially exist depends on the number $N$ of alters: it is $N(N-1)/2$ if alter–alter ties are undirected (therefore, each unordered pair of alters is counted only once because only one tie is possible in the pair), which is the most common case; and $N(N-1)$ if alter–alter ties are directed (therefore, each pair of alters is counted twice because two ties are possible in the pair: Alter1 → Alter2 and Alter2 → Alter1). For the data in Table 11.4, the densities are 0.6 for Pam (60% of the possible ties exist), 1.0 for Allen (all possible ties exist, meaning that all of his alters know each other), and 0.4 for Helen (40% of the possible ties exist). This means that Allen's network is much denser than Pam's and that Pam's is denser than Helen's. We can now attach a new variable to the dataset we had before (Table 11.6), as depicted in Table 11.8, and use it for our analysis.

Notice that the numbers in Tables 11.3 and 11.4 are all zeros and ones. These numbers simply indicate whether or not a tie exists. But in Chapter 8, we also described procedures where we ask respondents to report the likelihood that the two alters know each other or talk to each other on a three- or even five-level scale. Although we could collect data where we ask the respondent to report whether or not a tie exists, frequently we ask the respondent to give us more detail than that. In other words, the data are often not *binary* (zeros and ones) but *valued*, with at least three levels. However, for the pur-

**TABLE 11.8. The Structural Metric Density Added to the Dataset Represented in Table 11.6**

| Respondent | Proportion of male alters | Proportion of female alters | Average age of alters | Standard deviation of age of alters | Proportion of alter closeness to the ego, 4 and 5 (strong ties) | Average alter closeness to the ego | Density |
|---|---|---|---|---|---|---|---|
| Pam | .4 | .6 | 33.6 | 5.0 | .2 | 3.2 | .6 |
| Allen | .8 | .2 | 43.8 | 4.8 | .6 | 3.8 | 1.0 |
| Helen | .2 | .8 | 31.0 | 5.9 | .4 | 3.0 | .4 |

pose of measuring network structure, we often dichotomize those data first. If desired, we can use different dichotomizations of the same data and calculate network structural measures for these different dichotomizations.

## Graph-Based Procedures

Some network structural metrics are graph-based; that is, they are based on *graph theory*, a branch of mathematics that studies graphs, which are objects representing the relations (edges) among entities (nodes). Graph-based measures can sometimes use valued (weighted) data as we described earlier. But most graph-theoretic measures you will typically use rely on binary data. For those measures then, you will have to recode valued alter–alter tie data into zeros and ones. For example, you may decide that you only want to consider strong ties in the analysis. In this case, you would recode ties that the respondent is unsure about to zero. Keep in mind that the structural properties of the network are not only determined by the question you ask, but also by decisions about what counts as a tie. By recoding weak ties to zero, you will end up with a less dense network.

Many graph-based measures have been studied in social network analysis over the last few decades; these are described in detail in a variety of textbooks and articles on whole social networks. They include node-level measures, which are calculated for each network node, such as the centrality scores; and network-level measures, which are calculated for each network, such as density. Keep in mind that in personal networks nodes are alters, so node-level measures are calculated for each alter, and network-level measures are calculated for each personal network or, equivalently, for each ego. Also note that, just like compositional alter-level measures, every structural alter-level measure can be aggregated at the ego level, for example, by taking the average, maximum, or minimum.

Following is a list of commonly used graph-based structural metrics besides density. These metrics typically have a particular meaning and interpretation when applied to personal networks, especially if the ego is excluded. These meanings are different from their sociocentric network meaning.

- *Degree centrality* of an alter $i$ is the number of other alters to whom $i$ is directly connected. In other words, this is the number of the ego's contacts or acquaintances that alter $i$ also knows. The most degree-central alter is the one who is tied to the most alters. Average degree centrality is a measure of overall cohesion and is directly proportional to network density. In fact, if $\bar{d}$ is average degree, then density is $D = \bar{d}/(N - 1)$, $N$ being the number of alters. In Figure 11.1B, the degree centrality of alters varies from 0 for the isolated node to 7 for one of the family members who is connected to all other family members. The average degree centrality is 3.7; that is, the average alter is connected to 3.7 other alters. And 3.7 divided by 20 other alters (the total number of alters is 21) is 19%, which is the density of the network.

- *Degree centralization* is the extent to which the network structure is dominated by a single alter in terms of degree.

- *Closeness centrality* of an alter *i* is a measure of how close *i* is to all other alters. Formally, it is the inverse of the average of the *distances* from that alter to all other alters—if the ego were not present. Personal networks can (and often do) have network isolates if the ego is removed, such as in Figure 11.1B: alters that are only connected to the ego but who do not know other alters in the network. Closeness centrality is not meaningful with unconnected graphs, that is, in the presence of isolates or multiple components. Some computer routines get around the problem of isolates by assigning them the maximum distance.

- *Closeness centralization* is the extent to which the network structure is dominated by a single alter in terms of closeness.

- *Betweenness centrality* of alter *i* quantifies how often *i* appears on the shortest paths between all other nodes (when the ego is excluded from the network, and usually it is only calculated for larger personal networks). The most central alter in terms of betweenness is the one that "bridges" the most pairs of other alters. Highly between-central nodes in social networks are often considered to control the flow of information or resources in the network. However, you should keep in mind that in personal networks all pairs of alters are also bridged by the ego, who is connected to everyone. Therefore, in personal networks highly between-central alters are actors who connect separate circles of people and control resource flows *together with* the ego. Often these are very important people in the ego's life, such as spouses or intimate friends, who know people in all the different circles or contexts of the ego's social world.

- *Betweenness centralization* is the extent to which the network structure is dominated by a single alter in terms of betweenness.

- *Connected components* or simply *components* are subgraphs (subsets of network nodes and edges) in which all alters are *reachable* from each other through at least one path. This path can be direct (A is connected to B) or indirect (A is connected to C who is connected to B, or A is connected to C who is connected to D who is connected to B, etc.). Note that because the ego is connected to all alters, the personal network is always a single component if the ego is included (Figure 11.1A). However, when the ego is removed, multiple disconnected components may emerge. In Figure 11.1B, we can see five components when we exclude ego, including four components of size 2 or higher (nonisolate components) and one component of size 1—an isolate. Components often reveal separate settings, environments, or contexts in the ego's social life. For example, a respondent may have a group of coworkers in her network, including some who talk to each other and some who do not. As long as they are all either directly or indirectly connected, they still form a single component. In addition, the same respondent might also be connected with old friends from college, who are all directly or indirectly linked to each other. If no network path exists (in the network without the ego) which connects this group to the coworker group, then the two sets of alters are two disconnected components. Respondents who have many components in their network have a high betweenness centrality in their own network. Often, they must spend time and effort to maintain the separate groups.

- *Cliques* are maximally complete subgraphs, that is, subgraphs in which every alter is directly connected to each other. While components are mutually exclusive (no alter can be part of multiple components), cliques can overlap, with the same alters being part of multiple cliques. With personal networks, cliques often share multiple alters and differ by only one or a few alters. Less strict definitions have been proposed as well, for example, *n-cliques* and other types of cohesive subgraphs. In Figure 11.1B, if we focus only on the darkest gray nodes, we see that they form one clique of four nodes and five partially overlapping cliques of three nodes.

- *Number of isolates.* Isolates are alters who are not tied to anyone other than the ego. As with many components, maintaining many isolates takes time and effort for the ego. A personal network with many isolates may indicate that the respondent does not tend to belong to larger groups. Figure 11.1B has one isolate.

- *Core-periphery* refers to network structures in which some alters form a densely connected core, whereas others, the periphery, are more sparsely linked with the core and with each other. This is one of the network structures we frequently see in personal networks, with the core representing the central and dense group of contacts with whom the ego has the strongest ties and highest frequency of interaction, such as family members and intimate friends. Various software packages can be used to identify core-periphery structures.

- *Size, effective size, and efficiency.* The size of the network is simply the number of alters. The effective size of the network, a measure proposed by Ronald Burt (2000) for measuring the nonredundancy of contacts, is the size minus the average centrality of alters (excluding ego). So, if the ego has a network of 15 persons and on average these alters are related to 5 others, then the effective size is 10. Efficiency is the effective size divided by the real size and is a measure of the relative impact that the ego can obtain from his or her network. In the example mentioned earlier, efficiency is 10/15 = .67.

- *Constraint* is another measure that Burt introduced for network redundancy, that is, the extent to which the ego concentrates his time and energy in a single, densely connected group of alters. Constraint is higher in smaller networks, in more densely connected networks, and in networks where one alter is highly central).

All these structural measures can be calculated using special software for social network analysis, such as UCINET,[1] visone,[2] or Pajek.[3] Specific software for the collection of personal network data, such as EgoNet and Vennmaker (see the Appendix),

[1]See *https://sites.google.com/site/ucinetsoftware/home.*

[2]See *www.visone.info.*

[3]See *http://mrvar.fdv.uni-lj.si/pajek.*

**Personality and Personal Network Structure**

Yuval Kalish and Garry Robins (2006) studied the effect of individual psychological traits on personal network structures and found that psychological predispositions explained a significant proportion of the variance of egocentric structures. They suggest that, on the one hand, people who see themselves as vulnerable to external forces tend to inhabit closed networks of weak connections. On the other hand, people who seek to keep their strong-tie partners apart, and thereby bridge structural holes, tend to be individualists, to believe that they control events in their lives, and to have higher levels of neuroticism. Finally, people with strong network closure and "weak" structural holes tend to categorize themselves and others in terms of group memberships. They also tend to be more extraverted and less individualistic.

also allows you to calculate several basic structural measures. In R, structural measures can be calculated with functions from packages such as *igraph*,[4] *network* (*statnet*),[5] *egonet*[6] and *egor*.[7] If you use the popular *igraph* or *network* packages, it is a good idea to store all your ego-networks as elements (igraph or network objects) of a single *list*. This allows you to easily apply the same structural measure at once to all the elements (ego-networks) in the list using tools from the *plyr* or *purrr* packages.

## Statistical Procedures

Some network measures are not graph-based, but instead use *statistical procedures* that are commonly used in many other disciplines. These procedures were not specifically developed for network data, and, unlike graph-based measures, they are used to analyze the variability of the valued tie data. Keep in mind that, technically, the alter–alter tie evaluations are usually binary or ordinal data. However, it is quite common for researchers to treat ordinal alter–alter tie evaluations as interval/ratio data for this part of the analysis. Several procedures are available for this type of data. You should consult a good statistics text and/or statistical software package for further information. Here are a few procedures commonly used with network structural data.

- *Multidimensional scaling* is a procedure used to determine the number and type of dimensions in a dataset. It is often used in network visualization, which we discussed in Chapter 9. These visualizations help to determine what combinations of alter attributes are associated with alters being tied to each other.

[4]See *igraph.org*.

[5]See *statnet.org*.

[6]See *https://cran.r-project.org/web/packages/egonet/egonet.pdf*.

[7]See *http://tilltnet.github.io/egor*.

- *Cluster analysis* is a family of statistical procedures designed to group similar objects into categories.
- *Quadratic Assignment Procedure (QAP)* is a bootstrap method that generates a high number of permutations from the actual network and uses them as a simulated sample to construct probability distributions. QAP can be used to determine whether two networks are correlated (similar) or uncorrelated (different). The QAP procedure can also be used on matrices constructed from alter compositional characteristics, for example, matrices whose $(i, j)$ cell is 1 if alters $i$ and $j$ have the same value of an attribute (e.g., they are both male), and 0 otherwise.

Personal network structural data are sensitive to the question used to represent the alter–alter tie and the way that you recode the data. So even assuming that all respondents approach the task of providing structural data in the same way, the alter–alter tie question you use may still introduce variability. In addition, variability may also be introduced by the way in which different respondents approach the task. Some researchers try to reduce the burden of structural data collection on respondents by introducing shortcuts. These shortcuts often include some variation of letting respondents answer a subset of all possible alter–alter tie evaluations. Christopher McCarty (2002) reviewed a few of these techniques. Be careful with such procedures, however, as they may dramatically affect the structural data. Ideally, you want each respondent to do the same amount of work.

## 11.5 CREATING COMPOSITIONAL VARIABLES BASED ON MORE THAN ONE ATTRIBUTE

So far we have focused on the creation of summary variables based on a single alter-level characteristic. For example, the proportion of females in the network summarizes the sex of alters, the average age in the network summarizes the age of alters, and the proportion of strong ties (closeness level equal to 4 or 5) summarizes closeness. For many applications, however, we may be interested in creating compositional variables that combine more than one alter attribute. For example, when we use personal network data to predict a migrant's level of acculturation, the average closeness with his or her network members may be a poor predictor. Perhaps instead it is the average closeness with locals that increases acculturation, whereas the average closeness with transnational contacts has no effect on a person's acculturation. To test this possibility, we would first need to construct new ego-level variables based on the interaction of two alter attributes: alter's closeness with ego and alter's place of residence. One variable summarizes the ego's closeness with alters who live locally (local alters); the other variable summarizes the ego's closeness with alters who live abroad (transnational alters). The two variables, for example, can indicate an average closeness score of local and transnational alters; or the proportion of strong ties (with a closeness level equal to 4 or 5) among local and transnational alters. These can then be entered as predictors in a regression analysis of migrant acculturation. In some statistical programs, to obtain these interaction variables, you might need first to create a new alter-level attribute that is nonmissing only for the relevant alters (e.g., a new closeness column that is nonmissing only for local alters), and then summarize this new attribute.

In many situations, compositional summary variables need to be created by combining multiple alter attributes. Let's consider the following example. A researcher who wishes to predict childbearing intentions among young married females may ask her respondents which of their network members are themselves expecting a child or have children under a certain age, believing that the presence of such people in the ego's social environment can have a social diffusion effect on respondents. However, maybe respondents are not equally influenced by members who have childbearing plans or already have children. Having friends with babies may be more influential than having colleagues or neighbors with babies, or maybe the women are only influenced by other women (as opposed to their men friends) who have children. To test these propositions, we again need to create ego-level summary variables that combine various alter-level variables, such as the number of friends (not colleagues or neighbors), or the number of contacts with the same sex as the ego, who have childbearing intentions or children under a certain age. In this case, we are combining the "childbearing/number of children" alter attribute with alter role or alter sex.

## 11.6 CREATING VARIABLES THAT COMBINE COMPOSITION AND STRUCTURE

A special situation arises when you want to combine compositional and structural data into a single network-level measure. For example, you may want to summarize the extent to which closure or openness exists between different groups of alters in the personal network. If the ego is an immigrant and has relationships with natives and other immigrants, to what extent are these groups interrelated in the network, rather than forming separate clusters? To measure this, you could use the *E – I index*, a metric developed by David Krackhardt and Robert Stern (1988) to compare the relative density of ingroup ties vis-à-vis outgroup ties. The $E - I$ index is calculated as follows:

$$\frac{E-I}{E+I}$$

where $E$ represents the number of edges between alters of different classes or categories and $I$ the number of edges between alters who are from the same alter class or category (categories must be mutually exclusive). The index has a theoretical range from –1, in the case that all relationships are internal (i.e., there is complete separation between the two alter classes) to +1, in the case that all relationships are external (i.e., there are no ties between people of the same alter class). The $E - I$ index is 0 when the numbers of external and internal ties are exactly the same. Keep in mind that the $E - I$ index is sensitive to differences in network size and the number of groups and their relative sizes, so it cannot be compared across networks that differ on those characteristics. To make those comparisons, you would have to normalize the measure first by dividing it by the total number of possible external edges. The $E - I$ index can be calculated with the software UCINET separately for each network, at both the network level and the group and individual levels. UCINET further allows you to test whether the $E - I$ index has a significantly different value from what one might expect on the basis of random mixing.

Several other scenarios are possible in which we need to combine compositional and structural information into single network-level summary variables. For example, we might want to measure the structural importance of a specific social setting or environment in the ego's network. A common way of doing so is to calculate average centrality indices for alters in a specific social setting or type of relationship with ego. These variables answer questions such as: What is the average degree centrality of family members in the ego's personal network? What is the average betweenness centrality of coworkers in the ego's network? The average degree or betweenness centrality of family members in a personal network, for example, provides a measure of the family's structural importance in the ego's social life. Such variables combine structural information (alter centrality) with compositional information (the alter's social context or type of relationship with the ego).

Instead of taking a specific social context, such as the family, and calculating its structural centrality, we might want to do the inverse operation: identify the most central alter (e.g., according to betweenness centrality) and find that alter's social context. The result would be a categorical variable that takes the value "Family," for example, if the most central alter for that ego is a family member; "Coworker" if the most central alter for that ego is a coworker; and so on. This would be a way to identify the structurally more important social setting, according to centrality, in the ego's personal network.

Similarly, we might want to construct a variable that returns the level of closeness between the ego and her most between-central alter. This could be used as a measure of "social consonance" (vs. dissonance) in the ego's personal network: the most between-central alter occupies a structurally very important and powerful position in the ego's network; low levels of closeness associated with this alter would indicate that the ego does not feel close to, or does not trust, such a central contact in his social life. Such a measure could explain levels of social conflict or chronic stress in the ego's life. In all these examples, we are generating variables that incorporate compositional and structural information at the alter level: for example, alter centrality and the social context in which the ego interacts with the alter; or alter closeness and alter centrality.

In addition to centrality metrics, we can also combine measures of structural cohesion with compositional information to obtain new network-level variables. We might want to assess, for example, to what extent a certain attribute-based category of alters, such as family members or coworkers, represents a consistent and cohesive social group in the ego's social life, or if it is rather a collection of separate alters from separate circles. In this case, we can take the subgraph of alters with a certain attribute value in the personal network (e.g., alters whose type of relationship with ego is "family" or "coworker") and calculate a measure of overall cohesion in that subgraph. Raffaele Vacca and his colleagues (2018) apply a similar procedure to personal networks of international immigrants. Their goal is to measure the extent to which native alters (social contacts who were born in the immigrant's host country) form a single cohesive group in the immigrant's personal community. This measure can be used as an index of the immigrant's embeddedness in the host society, that is, his structural or social assimilation. Vacca and colleagues calculate this index by taking the subgraph of native alters in each ego's personal network and then using a cohesion metric called connectivity (Moody & White, 2003) to measure the social cohesion in this subgraph. In this case, the nationality of alters is the compositional information, while the subgraph connectivity is the structural information extracted from the personal network.

Sometimes we may also combine various *network-level variables* into a single, new network-level variable. This is very much like standard survey research, where we also combine, for example, various educational, job status, and income variables of the respondent into a single socioeconomic status index. In personal network research, multiple network-level variables are often combined into one single variable, especially if they are correlated, with the aim of obtaining network *profiles*. Section 12.3 discusses this type of analysis in greater depth.

## 11.7 ADDING COMPOSITIONAL AND STRUCTURAL VARIABLES TO THE DATASET

Once you have created the summary variables of your interest, you can attach them to the respondent-level data represented in Table 11.1. This would be done by *merging* the summarized variables into the respondent-level data. In SPSS, for example, this can be done with the command "Match Data—Add Variables," where you use the unique ID of the respondent as a key for matching the data in the two files correctly. (In our case, the variable "Respondent" would be the key to match Table 11.8 with Table 11.1, the result being Table 11.9.)

At this point, the network-level variables can be used like any other variable in an analysis at the respondent level. You can describe the variables numerically, for example, using frequencies, cross-tabulations (for nominal variables), or correlations (for interval/ratio variables), or you can present them graphically. At this point, you can also relate the network variables to respondent-level data and analyze their relationships using statistical models. Chapter 12 illustrates some of the models you can use on this type of data.

You can also use the network characteristics in an analysis of ego–alter relationships. To do so, you would merge the dataset, including respondent-level and network-level characteristics (exemplified by Table 11.9), with the dataset including characteristics of the ego–alter ties (exemplified by Table 11.2). The result would look like Table 11.10. You can see that some data are repeated for all alters of the same ego, namely, the

**TABLE 11.9. Respondent-Level Data and Network Characteristics Combined in One Data File**

| Respondent | Sex | Age | Income | Proportion of male alters | Proportion of female alters | Average age of alters | Standard deviation of age of alters | Proportion of alter closeness to the ego, 4 and 5 (strong ties) | Average alter closeness to the ego | Density |
|---|---|---|---|---|---|---|---|---|---|---|
| Pam | F | 32 | 22,000 | .4 | .6 | 33.6 | 5.0 | .2 | 3.2 | .6 |
| Allen | M | 46 | 76,000 | .8 | .2 | 43.8 | 4.8 | .6 | 3.8 | 1.0 |
| Helen | F | 28 | 52,000 | .2 | .8 | 31.0 | 5.9 | .4 | 3.0 | .4 |

first ten columns, whereas other data (the alter ID and name interpreters) are unique for the case. Chapter 13 discusses some of the *multilevel* statistical models that can be used to analyze this type of variable at the level of ego–alter ties.

## CHAPTER SUMMARY

This chapter reviewed the ways personal network data can be summarized, combined, and analyzed. Typically, you will start with an ego-level dataset of the ego's attributes. This dataset can be enhanced with compositional variables about the alters (e.g., the proportion of women in the personal network). These compositional variables are related to the name interpreters of the study. Next, structural measures can be computed at the personal network level and added to the dataset, based on edge interpreters (i.e., the alter–alter matrix), such as degree and betweenness, using R, UCINET, EgoNet, or other programs. Finally, it is possible to compute indices based on a combination of both structural and compositional variables (e.g., the E – I index). Some of these operations can be performed automatically using popular programs such as R or SPSS.

### FURTHER READING

Field, A. P., Miles, J., & Field, Z. (2012). *Discovering statistics using R*. Thousand Oaks, CA: SAGE.

Knoke, D. H., & Yang, S. (2007). *Social network analysis* (2nd ed.). Los Angeles: SAGE.

McCarty, C., & Wutich, A. (2005). Conceptual and empirical arguments for including or excluding ego from structural analyses of personal networks. *Connections, 26*(2), 82–88.

McPherson, M., Smith-Lovin, L., & Cook, J. M. (2001). Birds of a feather: Homophily in social networks. *Annual Review of Sociology, 27*, 415–444.

**TABLE 11.10. Example of a Data File at the Alter Level, with Respondent and Network Characteristics Added**

| Respondent | Sex | Age | Income in $ | Proportion of male alters | Proportion of female alters | Average age of alters | Standard deviation of age of alters | Proportion of alter closeness to the ego, 4 and 5 (strong ties) | Average alter closeness to the ego | Density | Alter | Sex of alter | Age of alter | Alter closeness to the ego |
|---|---|---|---|---|---|---|---|---|---|---|---|---|---|---|
| Pam | F | 32 | 22,000 | .4 | .6 | 33.6 | 5.0 | .2 | 3.2 | .6 | Bill | M | 34 | 3 |
| Pam | F | 32 | 22,000 | .4 | .6 | 33.6 | 5.0 | .2 | 3.2 | .6 | Cynthia | F | 30 | 5 |
| Pam | F | 32 | 22,000 | .4 | .6 | 33.6 | 5.0 | .2 | 3.2 | .6 | Lydia | F | 28 | 3 |
| Pam | F | 32 | 22,000 | .4 | .6 | 33.6 | 5.0 | .2 | 3.2 | .6 | Janet | F | 41 | 3 |
| Pam | F | 32 | 22,000 | .4 | .6 | 33.6 | 5.0 | .2 | 3.2 | .6 | Joe | M | 35 | 2 |
| Allen | M | 46 | 76,000 | .8 | .2 | 43.8 | 4.8 | .6 | 3.8 | 1.0 | Rick | M | 45 | 4 |
| Allen | M | 46 | 76,000 | .8 | .2 | 43.8 | 4.8 | .6 | 3.8 | 1.0 | Steve | M | 50 | 4 |
| Allen | M | 46 | 76,000 | .8 | .2 | 43.8 | 4.8 | .6 | 3.8 | 1.0 | Art | M | 46 | 3 |
| Allen | M | 46 | 76,000 | .8 | .2 | 43.8 | 4.8 | .6 | 3.8 | 1.0 | Denise | F | 40 | 5 |
| Allen | M | 46 | 76,000 | .8 | .2 | 43.8 | 4.8 | .6 | 3.8 | 1.0 | Sam | M | 38 | 3 |
| Helen | F | 28 | 52,000 | .2 | .8 | 31.0 | 5.9 | .4 | 3.0 | .4 | Wendy | F | 23 | 5 |
| Helen | F | 28 | 52,000 | .2 | .8 | 31.0 | 5.9 | .4 | 3.0 | .4 | Celia | F | 36 | 2 |
| Helen | F | 28 | 52,000 | .2 | .8 | 31.0 | 5.9 | .4 | 3.0 | .4 | Paul | M | 32 | 4 |
| Helen | F | 28 | 52,000 | .2 | .8 | 31.0 | 5.9 | .4 | 3.0 | .4 | Sarah | F | 40 | 1 |
| Helen | F | 28 | 52,000 | .2 | .8 | 31.0 | 5.9 | .4 | 3.0 | .4 | Alicia | F | 24 | 3 |

# 12

# Statistical Modeling with Personal Network Data

## *The Level of Egos*

---

### *What Is This Chapter About?*

The previous chapter showed you how to calculate quantitative measures that describe the composition and structure of personal networks. This and the next chapter take a step further and discuss how to use these measures to build statistical models that can test hypotheses and theories about the social world. Chapter 12 focuses on statistical models for outcomes observed for each respondent. We start by reviewing the different levels of analysis that exist in personal network data and general notions in statistical modeling as applied to personal networks (Sections 12.1 and 12.2). Then we examine statistical models for individual, non-network dependent variables, such as depression or occupational status (Section 12.3). Finally, we consider models for individual, network dependent variables, such as the number of family contacts or network density (Section 12.4). We also touch on the use of multivariate methods to combine multiple personal network variables into fewer indices, such as principal component analysis and cluster analysis. While part of the chapter introduces well-known statistical models that might already be familiar for some readers (such as linear and logistic regression models), our aim is to discuss them with a particular focus on their specific applications and issues in personal network research.

---

## 12.1 PERSONAL NETWORK DATA AND STATISTICAL MODELING

As you learned in Chapter 11, personal network databases include different levels of analysis: the level of egos or networks, the level of alters, the level of ego–alter ties, and the level of alter–alter ties (Figure 12.1). By level of analysis, we mean the level of the units on which a variable is observed and measured. An ego-level variable is observed

| Unit of analysis | Example variables | |
|---|---|---|
| Ego | • Ego's yearly income: 0 to 1,000,000 (continuous)<br>• Ego is a smoker: 1 = Yes, 0 = No (binary)<br>• Ego's transportation preference: 1 = Walking, 2 = Bicycle, 3 = Public transport, 4 = Car (categorical) | 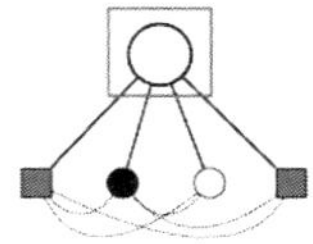 |
| Alter | • Alter's age: 0 to 90 (continuous)<br>• Alter is employed: 1 = Yes, 0 = No (binary)<br>• Alter's education level: 1 = No education, 2 = Primary, 3 = Seconday, 4 = More than secondary (categorical) | 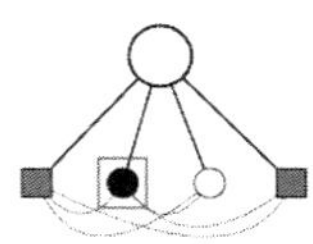 |
| Ego–alter tie | • Alter provides financial support to ego: 1 = Yes, 0 = No (binary)<br>• Frequency of interaction between alter and ego: 1 = Less than monthly, 2 = Monthly, 3 = Weekly, 4 = Daily (categorical) | 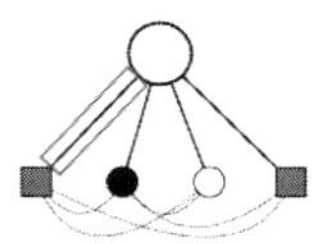 |
| Alter–alter tie | • Alter1 knows Alter2: 1 = Yes, 0 = No (binary)<br>• Alter1 talks with Alter2: 0 = Never, 1 = Rarely, 2 = Frequently (categorical) | 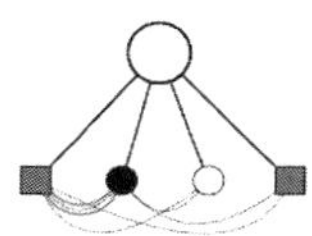 |

**FIGURE 12.1.** The different levels of analysis in personal network data.

on egos: it includes a different observation or measurement for each ego and therefore varies across egos. The ego's yearly income and the number of cigarettes ego smokes are examples of ego-level variables. Note that, in typical personal network data, the ego level is the same as the (personal) network level. This is because there is a one-to-one correspondence between egos and networks: we have only one network for each ego and only one ego for each network. Therefore, any measure that varies across networks is also varying across egos and vice versa. We can talk equivalently of ego-level or network-level variables.

By contrast, an alter-level variable is measured on alters: it comprises a measurement for each alter, and it varies across alters. The alter's age and educational level, for example, are alter-level variables. We then have variables observed at the level of ego–alter ties, which include a measurement for each tie between an alter and an ego, such as whether the alter provides support to the ego, how often the ego and alter talk to each other, or how similar they are in age. Finally, a variable observed at the level of alter–alter ties is one that we observe for each tie between two alters, such as whether two alters know each other or how likely two alters are to talk to each other (as reported by the ego). Note that, just as egos and networks are really the same level, alters and ego–alter ties are the same level too. There is a one-to-one correspondence between alters and ego–alter ties, with each alter corresponding to one and only one ego–alter tie (assuming that personal networks do *not* overlap). Therefore, whatever is measured for each ego–alter tie is also measured for each alter; any variable that varies across ego–alter ties also varies across alters. Figure 12.1 provides more examples of variables at these different levels of analysis. This chapter considers models based on ego-level variables, whereas Chapter 13 focuses on models based on variables at the level of alters, ego–alter ties, or alter–alter ties.

## Dependent and Explanatory Variables, Network and Non-Network Variables

By and large, statistical modeling aims to explain variation in a *dependent* variable as a function of variation in one or more *independent* or explanatory variables. Here we refer to the generic dependent variable as $y$ and to the generic explanatory variable as $x$. Chapters 3 and 4 explained the notions of dependent and explanatory variables, and how these are used in personal network research designs. The dependent variable $y$ is a measure of the outcome or phenomenon that we are ultimately interested in explaining. The overall goal of our research is to understand how that phenomenon is produced and what explains, predicts, or causes that phenomenon and its *variation*. Our dependent variable, for example, might be immigrant acculturation to a host society. In this case, our research aims to explain what generates acculturation; why some immigrants are more acculturated than others; what accounts for this variation among immigrants; and what factors or causes predict higher or lower acculturation.

By contrast, explanatory variables (or *predictors*) are the conditions, traits, or characteristics that we hypothesize will cause, explain, or predict the variation in the dependent variable. Our explanatory variables usually correspond to hypotheses, which we derive from one or more theories about the social world. In the acculturation example, we might hypothesize that immigrants who spent more time in the host country are characterized by higher levels of acculturation, which is a classical hypothesis derived from the sociological theory of immigrant assimilation. In this case, $y$ is acculturation, and $x$ is the length of time spent by the immigrant in the host country. Drawing on the same theory, we might also hypothesize that participation in primary social groups of individuals who are native members of the host society leads the immigrant to higher acculturation. In this hypothesis, $y$ is again acculturation, and $x$ is the immigrant's degree of participation in native social groups. We could use personal network variables to measure such participation. In this case, we have formulated a hypothesis about a *personal network* explanatory variable.

In addition to dependent and explanatory variables, another important distinction to be made is between network and non-network variables. Network variables are those that measure the characteristics of personal networks, their alters, or their ties. They can only be calculated using personal network data. By now you have seen many examples of network variables, such as the proportion of alters who are women, the number of connected components, or the average degree centrality of relatives in one's personal network. By contrast, non-network variables measure individual characteristics of the respondents (the egos), which are not inherent in their personal networks. Non-network variables can be extracted without using data about personal networks. These are variables that we could find in any social science study, including one that has nothing to do with personal networks: for example, gender, education, self-rated health, occupational prestige, or degree of agreement with certain statements.

## The Logic of Statistical Modeling

A *statistical model* represents our assumptions about (1) the probability distribution of the dependent variable $y$ and (2) the relationship between some characteristic of this distribution, typically, the expected value or mean and the explanatory variable(s) $x$. For example, a linear model represents the assumption that $y$ has a normal distribution and that the mean of this distribution, $E(y|x)$, is a linear function of the explanatory variable $x$.

We normally assume that the relationship between $y$ and $x$ has a general shape, such as linear or logistic, but we don't know what the exact function is: we try to find this exact function using *regression analysis*. Regression is a procedure for estimating the statistical model, where by "estimating" we mean specifying the exact relationship between the probability distribution of $y$ and the predictors $x$, with specific values for its parameters or coefficients. In other words, regression analysis finds the specific parameters of the function that describes how (the distribution of) $y$ changes when values of $x$ change. Remember that the dependent variable $y$ is always thought of as a random variable with a probability distribution, and we are interested in how certain characteristics of this distribution change with $x$: typically, how the average level of $y$ (i.e., the mean of its distribution) changes with $x$.

Most frequently, regression analysis estimates the function that links $x$ to the *mean* of the distribution of $y$. Intuitively, this means that we compare the average value of the outcome $y$ between groups of individuals with different values of the explanatory variable $x$. For example, we compare the average value of our acculturation score between immigrants with 5 years and immigrants with 10 years spent in the host country; or between immigrants with no alters who are native of the host country and immigrants with 30% native alters in their personal network.

We speak of *multiple* regression when our analysis links the mean of $y$ to *multiple* predictors, which is typically indicated as $x_1, x_2, \ldots, x_k$. The crucial advantage of multiple regression is that it allows us to quantify the specific association between the outcome $y$ and an explanatory variable, say $x_1$, *separately* from the other explanatory variables ($x_2, \ldots, x_k$). For example, we can measure the effect of the proportion of native alters in one's personal network ($x_1$) on acculturation, separately from the effect of the number of years the immigrant spent in the host country ($x_2$). This idea is often expressed by saying that we quantify the effect of $x_1$ on the outcome, "with other characteristics being equal" or "ceteris paribus." In other words, we measure the association between the proportion of native alters ($x_1$) and acculturation ($y$) among immigrants who have spent *the same* number of years in the host country (i.e., with the same value of $x_2$). This analysis answers questions such as: How does acculturation change, on average, when an immigrant's proportion of native alters increases, while keeping constant the number of years an immigrant has lived in the host country? What is the average difference in acculturation between two immigrants who have been in the host country for the same length of time but have a different degree of social integration with people who are native of the receiving society?

Some explanatory variables included in a statistical model might be referred to as *control* variables. Often, we are mainly interested in the relationship between the outcome $y$ (e.g., acculturation) and a specific predictor $x$ (e.g., the proportion of natives in the personal network); however, we might realize that the outcome is likely to also depend on another characteristic of the respondents, say $z$. For example, we might suspect that unemployed egos are more likely to exhibit lower acculturation scores. In this case, the immigrant's employment status is another explanatory variable that might affect acculturation—the control variable $z$. We need to *control for* employment status, in the sense that we need to quantify the effect of our primary explanatory variable $x$, independently or separately from employment status. In other words, we do not want the effect of employment status ($z$) to *confound* our measure of association between acculturation ($y$) and the proportion of native contacts in the network ($x$). In personal network research, control variables are usually individual traits of egos, such as the ego's age, marital status, or employment status; these traits do not represent characteristics of their social world and are not the main focus of the study.

The idea of accounting for control variables is particularly important if, for some reason, there is a correlation between $x$ and $z$—in our example, between the proportion of native alters in the network and the ego's employment status. If that is the case and we exclude the ego's employment status from our statistical model, the estimated association between the proportion of native alters in the network ($x$) and immigrant acculturation ($y$) might, in fact, reflect the association between employment status ($z$) and acculturation ($y$), at least in part. We can avoid this only by including employment status in the model as a control variable. The question we ask, then, is: How do immigrants with lower and higher proportions of native alters in their network differ, on average, in their level of acculturation, when they have the same employment status?

## 12.2 PREDICTING EGO-LEVEL DEPENDENT VARIABLES

Ego-level statistical models predict outcomes that are measured for each ego and vary across egos and use ego-level variables as predictors as well. When the analysis is at the level of egos, the first step consists in aggregating or summarizing all data at that level.

Chapter 11 illustrates different ways of conducting this summarization for personal network characteristics.

On the one hand, ego-level *network* variables quantify the characteristics of personal network composition, structure, or composition and structure combined for each ego. On the other hand, ego-level *non-network* variables measure other individual characteristics of egos, such as age, education, marital status, smoking behavior, or acculturation score. Table 11.9 shows examples of these different variables: ego-level statistical models are fitted using datasets such as those in Table 11.9.

In ego-level analyses, network variables might be treated as dependent variables or as explanatory variables. Certain ego-level studies do both, using some network characteristics as dependent variables and other network characteristics as predictors. Chapters 3 and 4 discuss these different research designs in greater depth, providing several examples.

In most personal network research, ego-level statistical models include network variables as *explanatory* variables, which are used to operationalize various characteristics of the respondents' social world or personal communities. These characteristics are hypothesized to predict non-network outcomes of the same respondents, such as depression, smoking behavior, acculturation, or job performance. Thus, statistical models in this research test theories according to which individual outcomes (such as smoking behavior or job performance) depend, at least in part, on features of the social world in which individuals are embedded.

For example, we might hypothesize that more fragmented personal networks (explanatory variable) are associated with higher depression (dependent variable); that personal networks of youths with older alters on average (explanatory variable) lead individuals to smoke more (dependent variable); that personal networks with a higher proportion of conational contacts (explanatory variable) are associated with poorer acculturation outcomes among immigrants (dependent variable). In all these cases, we are testing hypotheses about the way in which features of a person's social world explain individual characteristics of that person.

In other cases, personal network measures are treated as the *dependent* variable. In this type of research, we try to explain the characteristics of the ego's social world as a function of conditions, preferences, behaviors, or other traits of the ego. For example, we might hypothesize that more extroverted individuals tend to surround themselves with a broader variety of social contacts, including different genders, age categories, and nationalities. In this case, we are hypothesizing that an individual's psychological trait (extroversion, the explanatory variable) predicts a characteristic of that individual's social world (diversity of personal network, the dependent variable).

## 12.3 MODELS FOR NON-NETWORK DEPENDENT VARIABLES

In statistical models for non-network dependent variables, $y_i$ is an individual outcome observed on ego $i$, such as depression, smoking behavior, or acculturation. The main independent variable, $x_i$, is a characteristic of the ego's personal network. Obviously, the model can incorporate multiple characteristics of personal networks as multiple independent variables ($x_{1i}$, $x_{2i}$, . . . , $x_{ki}$). For ease of exposition, however, we only consider models in which a single personal network predictor is included. We then indicate any non-network control variable as $z_i$.

Non-network outcomes can be analyzed using linear or generalized linear models. The choice of the model depends on the nature of the outcome and the probability distribution that can be assumed for it. Continuous dependent variables, for example, can often be assumed to follow a normal distribution. Binary variables are typically assumed to follow a Bernoulli distribution. Count variables normally follow a Poisson distribution. These different distributions correspond to different statistical models. Table 12.1 summarizes the types of ego-level analyses considered in this chapter, providing example references for each.

In a linear model, we have a *continuous* dependent variable, $y_i$, and we assume that it follows a normal distribution with a fixed variance, $\sigma^2$ (which we estimate). We also assume that the mean of $y_i$'s normal distribution, $\mu_i$, changes depending on the values of the explanatory and control variables ($x_i$ and $z_i$), and it does so in a linear fashion. In other words, we assume that the average value of $y_i$ is a *linear* function of the predictors:

$$y_i \sim N(\mu_i, \sigma^2)$$
$$\mu_i \equiv E(y_i | x_i, z_i) = \beta_0 + \beta_0 x_i + \beta_0 z_i$$

What this model means is that, *on average*, individuals with different values of $x_i$ (the personal network characteristic) will show different values of $y_i$ (the individual outcome). Specifically, individuals who are characterized by a value of $x_i$ that is higher by $\Delta x$ will show, *on average*, a value of $y_i$ that is higher (if $\beta_1$ is positive) or lower (if $\beta_1$ is negative) by $\beta_1 \times \Delta x$. For example, suppose that $y_i$ is ego's depression score and $x_i$ is personal network density. If $\beta_1$ is estimated as equal to 2, our model is predicting that respondents whose personal networks have a density value that is 0.1 units higher ($\Delta x$ = 0.1), will show an average depression score that is 0.2 units higher ($\beta_1 \times \Delta x = 2 \times 0.1$) than the average depression score of respondents whose personal network density is 0.1 units lower. Because the model is linear and $\beta_1$ is constant, this effect will remain the same regardless of the actual value of $x_i$, the personal network density.

**TABLE 12.1. Types of Dependent Variables**

| | Method of analysis | | |
|---|---|---|---|
| Type of dependent variable | Linear models | Generalized linear models | Principal components analysis/cluster analysis |
| Non-network variable | Vacca et al. (2017) | Lubbers et al. (2007); Valente and Saba (1998); Latkin et al. (2017) | Brandes et al. (2010) |
| Network variable | Moore (1990); Kalish and Robins (2006); Roberts et al. (2009) | McPherson et al. (2006) | Kalish and Robins (2006) |

### *Using Personal Network Characteristics to Predict Immigrant Assimilation*

Raffaele Vacca and colleagues (2018) used personal network measures to quantify immigrants' structural assimilation and transnationalism—that is, the degree to which immigrants maintain primary social networks with people who are native of their country of destination ("Natives") and with people who live in their country of origin ("Origin Conationals"). The authors hypothesized that these personal network measures are associated with two outcomes: (1) cultural assimilation, as measured by a standard Acculturation Rating Scale and (2) economic assimilation, as measured by net monthly income. Structural assimilation is measured as the number of Natives as well as the structural cohesion among Natives in an immigrant's personal network. Similarly, structural transnationalism is measured as the number of Origin Conationals and the structural cohesion among them in an immigrant's personal network. Using standard linear regression models, Vacca et al. found that the number of Natives and Origin Conationals in a personal network, the structural cohesion within each of these classes of alters, and the structural cohesion between different alter classes are significantly associated with cultural and economic assimilation among immigrants of different African and Asian nationalities in Spain and Italy.

Another example is provided by Raffaele Vacca and colleagues (2018), who measured acculturation of immigrants in Barcelona, Spain, using a continuous Acculturation Rating Scale ($y_i$). They assumed that this scale has a normal distribution and that the mean of this normal distribution (i.e., the average Acculturation Rating Scale of immigrants in Barcelona) is a linear function of different personal network characteristics, including the number of native people (alters who were born in Spain) in the personal network. The linear model in this paper finds that an additional native alter in an immigrant's personal network ($\Delta x = 1$) is associated with an average increase of +0.11 units in the Acculturation Rating Scale ($\beta_1 = 0.11$).

If the dependent variable is not continuous or it does not follow a normal distribution, *generalized* linear models are used instead of linear models. Generalized linear models are extensions of linear models, based on these two assumptions:

1. The outcome $y_i$ has a known probability distribution, which is not normal.
2. The mean of this distribution (i.e., the average value of $y_i$) is a nonlinear function of ($\beta_0 + \beta_1 x_i + \beta_2 z_i$), which is called the "linear predictor."

Probably the most popular generalized linear model in the social sciences is the *logistic model*. This model is used to predict binary (1/0) dependent variables, which represent the occurrence or nonoccurrence of an event: for example, whether an individual is employed ($y_i = 1$) or not employed ($y_i = 0$); married ($y_i = 1$) or not married ($y_i =$

0); a smoker ($y_i = 1$) or not a smoker ($y_i = 0$). Since $y_i$ is binary, it cannot follow a normal distribution; instead, it is assumed to follow a Bernoulli distribution, whose mean is $\pi_i$, that is, the probability that $y_i = 1$, or "response probability" (the probability that the individual is employed, married, or a smoker). This probability is then assumed to change with $x_i$ and $z_i$, according to a logistic function:

$$y_i \sim B(\pi_i)$$

$$\pi_i \equiv E(y_i | x_i, z_i) = \frac{\exp(\beta_0 + \beta_1 x_i + \beta_2 z_i)}{1 + \exp(\beta_0 + \beta_1 x_i + \beta_2 z_i)}$$

The logistic model means that individuals with different values of $x_i$ (and $z_i$) have different probabilities of being employed, married, or a smoker—or whatever $y_i = 1$ represents. The relationship between the response probability and $x_i$ is described quantitatively by the logistic function. This function implies a specific measure for the association between changes in $x_i$ and changes in the response probability: if $x_i$ changes by +1 unit, then the *odds* of the event $y_i = 1$ occurring (i.e., $\pi_i/(1 - \pi_i)$) are multiplied by a factor of ($\beta_1$). In other words, individuals whose value of $x_i$ is greater by one unit show,

### *The Effect of Personal Network Exposure on Reproductive Health Behavior*

Thomas Valente and Walter Saba (1998) studied how changes in contraceptive behavior in Bolivia are associated with exposure to a communication campaign about reproductive health and with personal network exposure to family planning. Two of the dependent variables they studied are binary: interpersonal communication about reproductive health ($y_i = 1$ if the respondent spoke to anyone about reproductive health in the past six months); and current use of contraceptive techniques ($y_i = 1$ if the respondent did report current use of contraceptive techniques). One of their hypotheses was that personal network exposure to family planning ($x_i$) determines higher probability of both interpersonal communication and current use of contraceptive techniques. Valente and Saba measured $x_i$ as an ego-level index of personal network composition: the percentage of the respondent's personal contacts who practice family planning (as far as the respondent knows). Among other results, they found that, in a sample of 1,990 married women in urban Bolivia, personal network exposure significantly predicts increased probability of interpersonal communication about contraceptive use and actual current use of contraception. In other words, women with a higher number of personal contacts who practiced family planning were more likely to talk about family planning themselves and to currently use contraception. More precisely, the odds of talking about family planning increased by a factor of $\exp(\beta_1) = 1.35$ (a 35% increase), and the odds of using contraception increased by a factor of $\exp(\beta_1) = 2.29$ (a 129% increase) for women whose entire personal network ($x_i = 100\%$) practiced family planning, compared to women who had no personal contact ($x_i = 0\%$) who did (a change of $\Delta x = 1$ unit).

on average, higher or lower odds of the event occurring by a factor of $\exp(\beta_1)$. This means higher odds of the event if $\exp(\beta_1) > 1$ (i.e., $\beta_1 > 0$), and lower odds if $\exp(\beta_1) < 1$ (i.e., $\beta_1 < 0$).

More complicated generalized linear models can be used in personal network studies. Miranda Lubbers and colleagues (2010), for example, studied the type of immigrants' self-identification in Spain. Here the outcome $y_i$ is a *nominal* variable that can take three values: 1 = Ethnic-exclusive identification, 2 = Ethnic-plural identification, 3 = Generic identification. Lubbers and colleagues examined the association between personal network characteristics, including the proportion of native and conational contacts in the personal network, network density, and number of cohesive subgroups, on the one hand; and the type of ethnic self-identification (the category or level of $y_i$) on the other. Because $y_i$ is neither continuous nor binary, the authors could not use a linear or logistic model. Rather, they estimated a multinomial logit model. This can be seen as a set of multiple, simultaneously estimated logit models that predict the probability of $y_i$ being in each of the nominal categories (Ethnic-exclusive identification, Ethnic-plural identification, and Generic identification).

## Longitudinal Ego-Level Models

Longitudinal personal network analysis allows researchers to study how personal networks change over time. For example, longitudinal analysis can show, at a relationship level, which ties are created, maintained, and dissolved over time, as well as how persistent ties change in contents. At the ego level, it shows how networks change in size, composition, and structure over time.

As we saw in Chapters 5–8, personal network data collection may be costly and demanding in terms of respondent burden. Collecting personal networks from the same respondents at different points in time is even more costly. This is a major reason why *longitudinal* personal network data are rare, and most personal network studies are based on cross-sectional data collected at a single point in time. However, examples of longitudinal personal network databases do exist in the literature (e.g., Bidart & Lavenu, 2005; Lubbers et al., 2010; Mollenhorst et al., 2014). These data include personal network information, as well as individual data on the egos, collected at different times on the same set of respondents. The same respondents are interviewed on different occasions, at a baseline time and at subsequent follow-up times—typically, months or years later. The same personal network survey, with the same name generators, name interpreters, and edge interpreters, is administered at baseline and follow-up.

Longitudinal personal network analyses might use the characteristics of personal networks to predict non-network outcomes of egos and the way they change over time. However, in addition to more costly data collection, longitudinal studies also require more complicated statistical models. A typical issue with longitudinal data is that observations are not statistically independent from each other, a fundamental assumption required for accurate estimation of standard statistical models. If the same individuals are observed on multiple occasions over time, observations (i.e., rows of

### *A Longitudinal Analysis of Personal Support Networks and Depression*

Carl Latkin and colleagues (2017) examined data from a survey on personal networks and depression that was administered to the same sample of black men who had sex with men in six U.S. cities, at three different time points—baseline, 6-month follow-up, and 12-month follow-up. For each time point, the data included information on the personal support network and a standard depression scale measured on egos. The authors converted the depression scale to a binary dependent variable ($y_i$), indicating whether the individual experienced depressive symptoms in the past week (1 = Yes, 0 = No). This outcome was modeled as a function of personal network characteristics, such as the size of different types of support networks and the frequency of contact with alters; and a number of control variables, including the ego's age, education, and household income. Since $y_i$ was binary, the researchers used a logistic model. However, they estimated a *multilevel* or *mixed-effects* logistic model because observations at different time points were clustered by respondents. Therefore, they were not independent. The cluster or group represented by an individual respondent included between one and three observations (dataset rows), one for each time that the respondent was interviewed. The mixed-effects model did find significant personal network effects on depression over time. Larger emotional support networks, larger financial support networks, and larger medical support networks, as well as a higher number of personal contacts that the ego saw weekly, were associated with lower probability of the ego experiencing depressive symptoms. Network characteristics at baseline, however, were not associated with *changes* in the ego's probability of depression over time—another type of hypothesis that can be tested using mixed-effects longitudinal models.

the dataset) are grouped or clustered by individuals. This means that some of the observations come from the same individual (who is observed at different points in time). Observations coming from the same individual are not independent, but rather they are correlated with each other. For example, the number of family members that an ego nominates in her personal network at baseline is likely to be significantly correlated with the number of family members that the *same* ego mentions six months later. This time-related dependence among observations can be taken into account using multilevel or mixed-effects models for longitudinal data (Singer & Willett, 2003; see also Section 13.1).

## Addressing Multicollinearity between Personal Network Variables

Multicollinearity is a well-known issue in linear and generalized linear models that occurs when two predictors are correlated or, more generally, when a predictor is approximately equal to a linear combination of one or more of the others. If predictors $x_1$ (e.g., the proportion of family members in the personal network) and $x_2$ (e.g., personal network density) are highly positively correlated, then all individuals with high values of $x_1$ (many family members in their personal network) tend to also have high values of $x_2$ (high personal network density), and all individuals with low values of $x_1$ tend to have low values of $x_2$.

Intuitively, this poses a problem for regression because if $x_1$ and $x_2$ always change together, it is impossible to determine whether a certain effect on the dependent variable derives from changes in $x_1$ or in $x_2$. For example, if all individuals with high proportions of family in their network have lower depression scores, but they also always have high network density (because of the positive correlation between the two explanatory variables); and individuals with low proportions of family in their network have higher depression scores, but they also always have low network density, then it becomes unclear if lower depression derives from the high proportion of family members or from the high network density.

Personal network studies encounter the problem of multicollinearity more often than other social science studies. This happens because different characteristics of personal networks are often strongly correlated with each other in real-world data samples. It is often the case, for example, that smaller personal networks are denser because they are composed of intimate family or friends of ego, who tend to know each other. This is due to the tendency toward *transitivity* or *clustering* of strong ties in social networks and is reflected in the negative correlation between personal network size and density. Another example is the typical positive correlation between the proportion of family members in the personal network and network density. With such correlated data, if we find a negative association between, say, network density and ego's depression, we may conclude that denser networks are better able to buffer depression. However, the correlation may just as well be spurious, as both density and depression may be related to the proportion of family ties in the network. The association might really indicate that egos are better able to contrast depression with networks dominated by family members, which also happen to be dense.

Multicollinearity is also likely to occur when the personal network explanatory variables are proportions of mutually exclusive types or categories of alters (e.g., the proportion of family members, the proportion of friends, and the proportion of others). Negative correlations often exist between these variables because they are proportions of the same whole, and if one is higher, the others are necessarily lower. In other words, egos who nominate more alters in a certain category necessarily tend to nominate fewer alters in another, particularly if they can nominate up to a fixed number of contacts. Thus, for example, the proportion of family members in the personal network might be negatively correlated with the proportion of friends simply because egos who mention more family members have fewer slots left to nominate friends, and vice versa.

A common way of dealing with multicollinearity is to summarize the correlated predictors into a single index. Different methods exist to do this. Two popular methods are principal components analysis (PCA) and cluster analysis (Johnson & Wichern, 2007). PCA takes a set of correlated variables and extracts a lower number of new variables that are linear combinations of the original ones, which incorporate the highest proportion of the sample variation on the original variables.

Cluster analysis refers to a set of different methods used to identify clusters or types of observations in the data, which are similar to each other with respect to a number of original (correlated) variables. The resulting clusters are such that two observations in the same cluster are more similar to each other than two observations in different clusters. The partition of observations into clusters can then be used as a new, single categorical variable that represents the variation of the original set of correlated variables. This new categorical variable can often be interpreted as a typology of observations, that is, a classification of observations into different *types* or *profiles*.

When applied to personal network variables, cluster analysis often returns a typology of personal networks into different interpretable types: for example, the "Dense family network" (the type of personal network with many family members and high density); the "School friends network" (personal networks with more friends from school and average values of density); and the "Sparse distant network" (personal networks with lower density and a higher number of distant acquaintances). Eric Giannella and Claude Fischer (2016) provide a recent example of research using cluster analysis to study typologies of personal networks. Claire Bidart, Alain Degenne, and Michel Grossetti (2018) used a structural approach to derive a network typology.

### *Using Cluster Analysis to Find Types of Immigrants' Personal Networks*

Ulrik Brandes and colleagues (2010) employed *k*-means cluster analysis to extract a typology of immigrants' personal networks. *k*-means (or *k*-medoids) cluster analysis refers to a set of algorithms used to identify *k* groups of observations such that each observation is always closer, with respect to the original variables, to the mean or medoid of its own cluster than it is to the mean of any other cluster. Closeness or similarity can be measured using any of several distance metrics. Brandes and colleagues classified immigrants' personal contacts into four national geographical classes, including alters who were born in the ego's host country ("Host") and conational alters who live in the ego's country of origin ("Origin"). For each personal network, the authors calculated the proportion of each alter class in the network (resulting in four variables), as well as a measure of density of alter–alter ties within each class (resulting in four additional variables) and between each pair of classes (resulting in six additional variables). Thus, they obtained 14 network-level variables describing the composition and structure of each immigrant's personal network in terms of the four alter classes. The 14 variables, which were highly correlated, were aggregated through a *k*-means cluster analysis. The resulting clusters or types of personal networks closely reflected four well-known modes of immigrant acculturation traditionally studied in cross-cultural psychology.

## 12.4 MODELS FOR NETWORK DEPENDENT VARIABLES

Although most personal network research uses network metrics as independent variables, a smaller but significant portion of studies view personal network characteristics as the dependent variable in a statistical model. These studies seek to explain the features of individuals' social worlds or personal communities as a function of non-network characteristics. Examples of network dependent variables include the size of different types of personal networks (e.g., kin versus nonkin personal networks), the diversity of the personal network (e.g., ethnic diversity or diversity in the context of socialization between ego and alters), or the density of the personal network. Thus, both compositional and structural characteristics of personal networks may be investigated as dependent variables.

Like the models discussed in the previous section, the models considered here view the egos as the units of analysis. All variables, therefore, are observed (and in some cases summarized) at the level of egos. Table 11.9 still represents the type of dataset on which these models are fitted. The statistical models themselves are no different from those used to predict non-network outcomes, discussed in the previous section. These include linear models, logistic models, and more sophisticated generalized linear models.

The network dependent variables sometimes measure characteristics of personal network *composition*. Gwen Moore (1990), for example, investigated differences between the personal networks of American men and women in terms of "absolute" and "relative" composition, using data from the 1985 U.S. General Social Survey. Twelve dependent variables describing personal network composition were considered, including the number of kin alters, the number of nonkin alters, the number of different kin types, and the number of different nonkin types in the personal network. The author sought to explain gender differences in personal network composition, such as the higher number of kin and the lower number of coworkers and friends who are observed in women's networks compared to men's.

Moore's analysis is based on multiple linear regression. The *multiple* character is crucial here, as the author aims to demonstrate that compositional differences between personal networks of men and women largely disappear when *controlling* for explanatory variables other than gender, such as individuals' family structure, age, education, and employment. Moore found that, in a bivariate analysis, women have significantly different average values of all network dependent variables compared to men. However, for most of these dependent variables, the gender difference disappeared when family, age, education, and employment-related predictors were included in the models. Thus, while women do seem to have different personal networks than men in aggregate bivariate analyses, in fact women do *not* when they are compared to men *with similar* family structure, age, education, and employment status. In other words, the gender-based differences in personal networks that emerge from aggregate comparisons between women and men are not due to different predispositions inherent in the genders, but rather to systematic differences between women and men in terms of family structure, age, education, and employment.

Sometimes personal network *structure*, rather than composition, is the dependent variable. Yuval Kalish and Garry Robins (2006), for example, calculated a number of personal network structural metrics, such as network density, efficiency, and constraint, and showed that these characteristics can be predicted by specific psychological traits of the egos, including extraversion, neuroticism, and self-monitoring.

In other studies, personal network characteristics are used as both dependent and independent variables in the same analysis. An example is provided by Sam Roberts and collaborators (Roberts, Dunbar, Pollet, & Kuppens, 2009), who investigated variation in the size of related and unrelated personal networks. They predicted these two dependent variables using both individual characteristics of egos and features of egos' personal networks. Specifically, they used linear regression to show that the sizes of related and unrelated personal networks are associated with non-network predictors, such as the

### *Predicting Network Dependent Variables with Generalized Linear Models*

Ego-level network dependent variables can be analyzed using generalized linear models as well. In a widely cited and discussed study, Miller McPherson and colleagues (2006) analyzed changes in the core discussion networks of Americans between 1985 and 2004, as observed in GSS data from the two waves. The researchers pooled the 1985 and 2004 GSS data together and fitted two types of generalized linear models, namely, negative binomial models and logistic models. Negative binomial models, which predict count-dependent variables, were used to analyze the number of discussion partners nominated by a respondent. Logistic models, which predict binary dependent variables, were used to analyze the probability of respondents *not* nominating *any* discussion partner. Both dependent variables, which were observed at the level of egos, were modeled as a function of several ego-level predictors, including the ego's education, age, marital status, race, and attitude toward the survey. However, the key explanatory variable in the models was the survey wave the data were from—1985 versus 2004. Coefficients for the survey wave predictor indicated that Americans had significantly fewer confidants in 2004 than in 1985 and were significantly more likely to have no confidant in 2004 compared to 1985, above and beyond the effects of sociodemographic characteristics, attitude toward the survey, and mere chance. The authors concluded that social isolation had significantly increased in America between the 1980s and the 2000s.

McPherson and colleagues' findings attracted much attention in the popular media. However, they were later questioned as a possible data collection artifact owing to differences between the 1985 and the 2004 GSS survey designs (Fischer, 2009; McPherson, Smith-Lovin, & Brashears, 2009; Smith, McPherson, & Smith-Lovin, 2014). Other research has also cast doubt on the extent to which the GSS name generator actually captures strong ties or confidant networks (e.g., Bearman & Parigi, 2004; Small, 2013, 2017).

ego's education, as well as network predictors, such as the average emotional closeness between the ego and alter, and the ratio between male and female alters in the personal network.

## Non-Normality and Multiple Dependent Variables

Two difficulties are typical of the statistical modeling of personal network dependent variables. First, personal network measures often exhibit a distribution that is far from normal. This is especially a problem if these measures need to be treated as dependent variables because a central assumption of the linear regression model is that the dependent variable follows a normal distribution. If the actual distribution is very different from normal, the results from linear regression risk being biased and inaccurate. This problem is commonly addressed by transforming the dependent variable using functions such as the logarithm or the square root, which bring its values closer to a normal distribution. If such transformations are unsuccessful, then the variable may be dichotomized and analyzed using logistic regression instead of linear regression. Yuval Kalish and Garry Robins (2006) and Sam Roberts et al. (2009) offer interesting examples of transformations that convert personal network dependent variables to normally distributed measures.

Second, personal network composition and structure are typically described by *many* variables. However, for ease of computation and interpretation, analysts often prefer statistical models for *single* dependent variables rather than multivariate models for *multiple* dependent variables. The researchers, therefore, face the problem of having to select just one or a few out of several possible personal network indices to examine as dependent variables or having to somehow aggregate multiple personal network dependent variables into one.

Some studies deal with this problem by simply fitting one separate model for each personal network dependent variable. Gwen Moore (1990), for example, estimated as many as 11 different linear models for 11 network dependent variables. Roberts et al. (2009) and Miller McPherson et al. (2006) provide other examples of this approach.

Another approach is to use multivariate methods, such as PCA or cluster analysis, to aggregate several dependent variables into fewer indices. We have briefly discussed such methods in the previous section as a way to address multicollinearity. The main goal here is always the same: to summarize the variation in a set of many (typically correlated) variables through a smaller set of a few variables. This aim is often referred to as reducing the dimensionality of the data.

Kalish and Robins (2006), for example, considered data, including nine network dependent variables, each representing the proportion of a certain type of triad between ego and two alters. Each of these variables could have been modeled with a separate regression, resulting in nine models. However, results would have been more complicated to interpret and report. In addition, the nine triad proportions were correlated with each other, perhaps reflecting variations across fewer latent variables. Therefore, the authors first used PCA to reduce the nine proportions to just three components, which could be interpreted as indices of three major structural features of personal networks, including weak tie network closure, strong versus weak structural holes, and strong-tie network closure. Then, they fitted three (instead of nine) linear regression models to explain each of these structural features as a function of the ego's psychological traits.

## CHAPTER SUMMARY

Personal network data include variables observed at different levels: egos, alters, or ego–alter ties and alter–alter ties. This chapter focused on the statistical modeling of ego-level variables. Ego-level models typically use network variables as predictors to explain individual, non-network characteristics of the respondents, such as smoking behavior, depression, or level of acculturation. However, network variables can also be modeled as dependent outcomes themselves, for example, when we are interested in explaining variation in the size, density, or diversity of the personal networks in our data. Compositional and structural characteristics of personal networks are often correlated, which leads to issues of multicollinearity. This problem can be addressed by summarizing the correlated predictors into a single index with multivariate methods such as PCA and cluster analysis. When personal network characteristics are the outcomes of interest, these techniques can also be used to reduce the number of dependent variables. In this case, you might also have to transform your network dependent variable to make its distribution closer to normal.

## FURTHER READING

Brandes, U., Lerner, J., Lubbers, M. J., McCarty, C., Molina, J. L., & Nagel, U. (2010). Recognizing modes of acculturation in personal networks of migrants. *Procedia—Social and Behavioral Sciences, 4,* 4–13.

Fox, J. (2008). *Applied regression analysis and generalized linear models* (2nd ed.). Los Angeles: SAGE.

Giannella, E., & Fischer, C. S. (2016). An inductive typology of egocentric networks. *Social Networks, 47,* 15–23.

Long, J. S. (1997). *Regression models for categorical and limited dependent variables.* Thousand Oaks, CA: SAGE.

Moore, D. S., McCabe, G. P., & Craig, B. A. (2009). *Introduction to the practice of statistics* (6th ed.). New York: Freeman.

Valente, T. W., & Saba, W. P. (1998). Mass media and interpersonal influence in a reproductive health communication campaign in Bolivia. *Communication Research,* 25(1), 96–124.

# 13

# Statistical Modeling with Personal Network Data

## *The Level of Alters and Ties*

### *What Is This Chapter About?*

Much personal network research uses the ego-level statistical models examined in Chapter 12. A substantial proportion of personal network data, however, is collected at a finer level than egos: it is collected for each alter or for each alter–alter tie nominated by an ego. This chapter focuses on the problem of explaining variation in these finer-level variables, modeling characteristics of alters, ego–alter ties, or alter–alter ties. In Section 13.1, we consider an increasingly popular method among personal network researchers: multilevel statistical models, which are used to explain the characteristics of alters or ego–alter ties. These include hierarchical linear models, hierarchical logistic models, and nonhierarchical models for both cross-sectional and longitudinal personal network data. In Section 13.2, we discuss the problem of modeling the formation of alter–alter ties, which has been addressed using multilevel models as well as exponential random graph models (ERGMs) and stochastic actor-oriented models (SAOMs).

## 13.1 STATISTICAL MODELS FOR ALTERS OR EGO–ALTER TIES

In Chapter 12, we made the distinction between network and non-network dependent variables. This distinction is less relevant in this chapter because in analyses at the level of alters, ego–alter ties, or alter–alter ties, the dependent variable $y$ is always a network variable, as it is always obtained from the personal network data. We obviously need personal network data to measure any characteristic of alters, ego–alter ties, or alter–alter ties. At the same time, the explanatory variables in models for alters or ties may or may not be personal network variables: they might measure characteristics of the personal networks (or their actors and ties), or non-network characteristics of the respondents.

## Personal Network Data as Multilevel Data

Personal network data are always collected, at least in part, at the level of alters and ego–alter ties: they consist of variables that are observed for each alter or ego–alter tie. Alters and ego–alter ties represent a finer, more detailed level of analysis compared to egos, because for each ego there are multiple alters or ego–alter ties. As you know by now, whenever we conduct analyses at the level of egos or networks (such as those described in Chapters 11 and 12), we need to summarize all variables about alters and ego–alter ties into aggregate metrics on egos or networks. Summarizing data is fine when we are interested solely in the characteristics of respondents and overall networks. However, if we wish to understand patterns that characterize alters and ties, summarizing is like zooming out from a finer, more precise view of social reality to a coarser, more approximate one.

With personal network data, as with all types of data, summarization inevitably implies loss of information and detail. The original data points (alters or ego–alter ties) carry more information than averages or other summarizations over groups of data points (egos or networks). Among other things, working with summarizations exposes analysts to the risk of what statisticians call the *ecological fallacy*: making wrong conclusions about individuals based on observations about *groups* of individuals. Consider the following example. Suppose we measure the proportion of foreign-born residents and the average income for several European cities. We might then observe that cities with relatively more foreign-born residents have higher average income—a positive correlation between proportion of foreign-born population and average income *at the city level*. Based on this correlation, we could be tempted to conclude that foreign-born residents have higher incomes. This, however, would be a (probably wrong) conclusion about individuals (residents) based on an aggregate analysis about groups (cities)—an instance of ecological fallacy.

Similarly, we might observe in our data that egos with a higher proportion of alters who provide support tend to also have older alters on average—a positive correlation between proportion of supportive alters and average alter age, two *network-level* variables. We cannot conclude, based on this correlation, that older alters tend to be more supportive. That would also be a fallacious conclusion about individuals (alters) based on an analysis about groups (networks). This example is further illustrated by Table 13.1. An analysis of the network-level averages in this table indicates that the higher the average age of network members is, the higher the proportion of supportive alters. That might suggest that older contacts tend to provide more support. This conclusion, however, would be incorrect. If we use the *individual* alter data in Table 13.1 to fit a logistic regression for the probability of providing support as a function of age, the result is a negative age coefficient: *younger* alters are actually more likely to provide support. This can also be seen from the younger average age of support providers (32 years) vis-à-vis nonproviders (40 years).

Thus, data at the level of alters and ties always include richer information than ego-level data and allow us to draw more detailed conclusions that we could not if simply

**TABLE 13.1. Illustration of an Ecological Fallacy**

| Ego ID | Alter ID | Age of alter | Support given by alter | Average age of alters | Average proportion of supportive alters |
|---|---|---|---|---|---|
| 1 | 1 | 20 | 1 | | |
| | 2 | 60 | 1 | 40 | 1 |
| | 3 | 40 | 1 | | |
| 2 | 4 | 50 | 0 | | |
| | 5 | 20 | 1 | 33 | 0.67 |
| | 6 | 30 | 1 | | |
| 3 | 7 | 20 | 1 | | |
| | 8 | 30 | 0 | 30 | 0.33 |
| | 9 | 40 | 0 | | |

Average age of support providers: 32 ($n$ = 6)

Average age of nonproviders: 40 ($n$ = 3)

based on ego-level analyses. For this reason, much personal network research directly deals with variables that are observed for each alter or ego–alter tie, such as alter age, sex, and nationality; the type of relationship or context of socialization between ego and alter (family, coworker, neighbor, etc.); or the degree of support that each alter provides to the ego. Table 11.10 shows an example of such alter-level data. Each row in the dataset represents an alter or, equivalently, an ego–alter tie. Note that ego-level or network-level variables can also be included in this type of data. However, their values will be repeated across all rows (all alters) that belong to the same ego. You can see this, for example, in the variable "Age" in Table 11.10, which refers to the ego's age. The first value of this variable is repeated across the first five rows, which represent five different alters associated with the same ego, namely, Pam. In other words, the first five observations are all part of the same "group," that is, the same ego or network. We say that these five observations are grouped, clustered, or nested together in the same higher-level unit.

Clustered data such as those in Table 11.10 are very common in the social sciences. Consider, for example, a dataset about students who go to different schools. Each row represents a student, and multiple rows will be associated with the same school. Any school-level variable (e.g., school size) will have repeated values across all students who belong to the same school. Other examples are those of data about patients who are treated by different doctors, residents who live in different cities, or football players who belong to different teams. In Chapter 12, we saw another example, where observations at different time points are nested within an individual. Many aspects of social reality can be represented by such *multilevel* data structures, which are composed of information about multiple levels—students and schools, patients and doctors, residents and cities, observations and individuals. The atomic level, which is the finest or most detailed one, is called level 1. Students, patients, residents, and observations belong to level 1. The higher level, referring to the groups to which the level-1 units belong, is called level 2. Schools, doctors, cities, and, in the latter example, individuals belong to level 2.

Figure 13.1 shows the multilevel nature of personal network data compared to school data, which are the typical example of multilevel structure in the social sciences. In the case of personal networks, alters or ego-alter ties are nested within networks (or egos). Note that the multilevel structures mentioned so far are all *hierarchical* in that each level-1 unit belongs to one and only one level-2 unit. Each student belongs to one and only one school. Similarly, in typical personal network data, each alter belongs to one and only one ego. This is not always the case, however. Certain studies deal with students who take classes in multiple schools or with alters who belong to multiple egos, that is, with *overlapping* personal networks. In these cases, the data are multilevel, but they are not hierarchical. We will talk more about these data toward the end of this section.

## Hierarchical Models for Personal Networks

Hierarchical data structures pose a major problem for traditional statistical modeling. One central assumption of traditional statistical models is that observations are, in the statistical jargon, "identically and *independently* distributed." This means that the dependent variable $y_i$ always has the same distribution for every individual $i$ and that, more critically here, each observation $i$ is independent from every other observation $j$. In other words, $y_i$ and $y_j$ (the values of the dependent variable measured on $i$ and $j$) cannot be correlated. This fundamental assumption is not realistic in multilevel data. In fact, if $i$ and $j$ belong to the same group, their values of $y_i$ and $y_j$ *will* be correlated. Students who go to the same school will tend to be more similar (i.e., positively correlated) to each other than students who attend different schools—for example, with respect to exam scores. Patients who go to the same doctor will be more similar to each other than patients who go to different doctors, for example, in terms of received treatment.

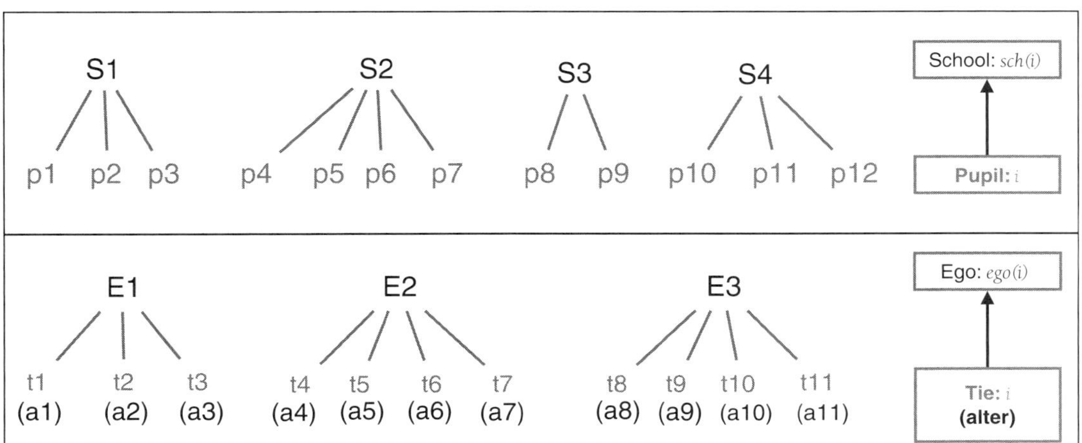


**FIGURE 13.1.** The multilevel nature of personal network data.

And alters, or ego–alter ties, who are nominated by the same ego will be more similar to each other than those who are mentioned by different egos. For example, alters who are named by the same ego will be more likely to have the same educational level or the same smoking behavior compared to alters who "belong" to different egos. In part, this is simply a consequence of the homophily of social networks: people who know each other, or have at most one degree of separation (such as alters in a personal network), tend to be similar (see Section 2.2). Closeness, trust, or support scores of ego–alter ties reported by the same ego will also be more similar to each other, compared to those of ties mentioned by different egos.

Given the lack of independence between observations, clustered data cannot be analyzed using traditional linear or generalized linear models. A different class of statistical models is needed, called *multilevel* or *hierarchical models*.[1] Both linear and generalized linear models have their hierarchical version. The main difference between hierarchical models and traditional models consists in the assumption that model parameters are not fixed quantities, but they are also random variables that include a "random effect" associated with each level-2 group, for example, with each ego. The intercept of a hierarchical linear model, for instance, includes a school random effect or, for personal network data, an ego random effect. The random effect of an ego can be thought of as a random deviation associated with all the ties (or alters) of that ego, which creates the correlation between them. Because they include these random effects, multilevel models are also called random-effects or mixed-effects models in the statistical literature.

## Hierarchical Linear Models

As an example, we show here the multilevel version of linear and logistic models. We adopt the classification notation proposed by Harvey Goldstein (2010), so that $i$ indicates an alter (or ego–alter tie) and $ego(i)$ indicates the ego who nominated that alter. Note the difference from Chapter 12 in which $i$ indicated an ego, not an alter or an ego–alter tie. We call $x$ the explanatory variables measured at the level of alters or ego–alter ties and $w$, the explanatory variables observed at the level of egos. While the following models only include one $x$ and one $w$ predictor, they can be straightforwardly extended to multiple alter-level ($x_1, x_2, \ldots, x_k$) or ego-level ($w_1, w_2, \ldots, w_q$) explanatory variables.

In hierarchical models, the dependent variable $y_i$ is always a level-1 variable—a characteristic of students, patients, residents, alters, or ego–alter ties. In our case, $y_i$ might represent, for example, a continuous measure of closeness between ego and alter, which is a characteristic of each ego–alter tie. We might think that the closeness between alter and ego depends on the context of socialization between them (family,

[1]Note that "multilevel" and "hierarchical" are not synonyms in this context. Multilevel data structures and statistical models can be hierarchical or nonhierarchical. Nonhierarchical models, which we treat more succinctly than hierarchical models in this chapter, include cross-classified, multiple-membership, and Multiple Membership Multiple Classification (MMMC) models (Rasbash & Browne 2008). Snijders and Bosker (2012) and Goldstein (2010) offer a good introduction to both hierarchical and nonhierarchical statistical models.

friend, coworker, neighbor, other), which is also a variable observed for ego–alter ties ($x_1$); on the alter's age, which is an alter-level variable ($x_2$); and on the ego's sex ($w$). To keep the notation simple, we only include one generic $x$ predictor and one $w$ predictor in the following models.

A hierarchical linear model with *random intercept* can be defined as follows:

$$y_i = \beta_{0,ego(i)} + \beta_1 x_i + e_i$$

$$\beta_{0,ego(i)} = \gamma_{00} + \gamma_{01} w_{ego(i)} + u_{0,ego(i)}$$

$$e_i \sim N\left(0, \sigma_e^2\right)$$

$$u_{0,ego(i)} \sim N\left(0, \sigma_{u0}^2\right)$$

where the meaning of symbols is just as it is in traditional linear models, except that the intercept $\beta_{0,ego(i)}$ is random and takes a different value for each *ego(i)*. This value depends on characteristics of ego ($w_{ego(i)}$) and on an ego random effect ($u_{0,ego(i)}$). The random effect, which captures any other unobserved ego characteristic that might systematically affect the intercept, is a random variable. We assume that it follows a normal distribution with zero mean and a fixed variance ($\sigma_{u0}^2$), which is one of the model parameters to be estimated.

By including a random intercept in the model, we are offering the hypothesis that the overall starting level of tie closeness ($\beta_{0,ego(i)}$) is different for each ego, depending on that particular ego's random effect ($u_{0,ego(i)}$). Also, because all the ties $i$ associated with the same *ego(i)* share the same random effect $u_{0,ego(i)}$, the model accounts for the correlation between the ties nested in the same ego. In other words, there is a common deviation ($u_{0,ego(i)}$) that contributes in the same way to the closeness values ($y_i$) of all ties nominated by the same *ego(i)*, making those ties more similar to each other.

We might hypothesize that what changes with each ego is not only the overall value of tie closeness ($\beta_{0,ego(i)}$), but also the *specific effect* of alter or tie characteristics ($x_i$) on that closeness, that is, the slope $\beta_1$. In this case, we adopt a hierarchical model with *random slope*:

$$y_i = \beta_{0,ego(i)} + \beta_{1,ego(i)} x_i + e_i$$

$$\beta_{0,ego(i)} = \gamma_{00} + \gamma_{01} w_{ego(i)} + u_{0,ego(i)}$$

$$\beta_{1,ego(i)} = \gamma_{10} + \gamma_{11} w_{ego(i)} + u_{1,ego(i)}$$

$$e_i \sim N\left(0, \sigma_e^2\right)$$

$$\begin{pmatrix} u_{0,ego(i)} \\ u_{1,ego(i)} \end{pmatrix} \sim N\left\{ \begin{pmatrix} 0 \\ 0 \end{pmatrix}, \begin{pmatrix} \sigma_{u0}^2 & \\ \sigma_{u01} & \sigma_{u1}^2 \end{pmatrix} \right\}$$

In this model, each *ego(i)* is associated with a random deviation in the overall level of closeness of the ego's own ties ($u_{0,ego(i)}$), as well as a random deviation in the effect of $x_i$ on that level of closeness ($u_{1,ego(i)}$), that is, in the slope of $x_i$. Each ego random effect has its own fixed variance ($\sigma^2_{u0}$ and $\sigma^2_{u1}$, respectively) and a (possibly null) covariance ($\sigma_{u01}$). These variances and covariances are parameters to be estimated in the model. Note that while, for simplicity, the model above assumes that the ego-level random intercept and random slope depend on the same ego variable, $w_{ego(i)}$, this need not be the case, and they might depend on *different* ego-level variables (say, $w_{1,ego(i)}$ and $w_{2,ego(i)}$).

## Hierarchical Logistic Models

In many cases, statistical models for ego–alter ties are used to explain binary tie variables. A typical example is social support, with $y_i$ indicating whether the tie between the ego and the alter provides, for example, financial support ($y_i = 1$) or not ($y_i = 0$). We might think that the likelihood of a tie providing financial support to the ego is affected, again, by the socialization context between the ego and the alter (family, friend, coworker, neighbor, other; $x_1$); the alter's age ($x_2$); and the ego's sex ($w$). To analyze variation in a tie-level binary variable, we can use a hierarchical *logistic* model:

$$\pi_i = \frac{\exp\left(\beta_{0,ego(i)} + \beta_{1,ego(i)} x_i\right)}{1 + \exp\left(\beta_{0,ego(i)} + \beta_{1,ego(i)} x_i\right)}$$

$$\beta_{0,ego(i)} = \gamma_{00} + \gamma_{01} w_{ego(i)} + u_{ego(i),0}$$

$$\beta_{1,ego(i)} = \gamma_{10} + \gamma_{11} w_{ego(i)} + u_{ego(i),1}$$

$$\begin{pmatrix} u_{0,ego(i)} \\ u_{1,ego(i)} \end{pmatrix} \sim N\left\{\begin{pmatrix} 0 \\ 0 \end{pmatrix}, \begin{pmatrix} \sigma^2_{u0} & \\ \sigma_{u01} & \sigma^2_{u1} \end{pmatrix}\right\}$$

where, as in the standard, single-level logistic model, $\pi_i$ is the probability of $y_i = 1$.

This model presents the hypothesis that each *ego(i)* is associated with two random effects on all the ego's ties to alters: (1) A random effect on the intercept ($u_{0,ego(i)}$), which changes the overall probability of providing support for all the ties linked to *ego(i)*, in the same direction; and (2) a random effect on the slope ($u_{1,ego(i)}$), which changes the effect of predictor $x_i$ (e.g., the alter's age) on the probability of providing support for all the ties nominated by *ego(i)*, also in the same direction. In addition, certain characteristics of egos ($w_{ego(i)}$) can systematically affect both the intercept $\beta_{0,ego(i)}$ and the slope $\beta_{1,ego(i)}$ (the impact of $x_i$ on the probability of support). Thus, this model can describe a situation in which certain egos (e.g., women) tend to obtain more support from older alters (positive $\beta_{1,ego(i)}$, with $x_i$ being alter age), while for other egos (e.g., men) the alter's age does not affect the likelihood of obtaining support ($\beta_{1,ego(i)}$ equals 0). Note that just like hierarchical linear models, hierarchical logistic models may include only a random intercept and no random slope.

## Research Applications

Since they were first proposed in the mid-1990s (Snijders, Spreen, & Zwaagstra, 1995; van Duijn, van Busschbach, & Snijders, 1999), hierarchical models for personal network data have been widely adopted to explain a broad variety of outcomes at the level of alters or ego–alter ties. They have been used in studies of social support and social capital (De la Haye et al., 2012; Martí et al., 2017; Wellman & Frank, 2001), migration and integration (De Miguel Luken & Tranmer, 2010; Lubbers et al., 2010; van Tubergen, 2015), sexually transmitted diseases (Hoover et al., 2016; Kennedy et al., 2013), mental health and help-seeking behaviors (Fulginiti, Pahwa, Frey, Rice, & Brekke, 2016; Perry & Pescosolido, 2015), substance use (Green, De la Haye, Tucker, & Golinelli, 2013), transportation and communication (Carrasco & Miller, 2009; Carrasco, 2011; van den Berg, Arentze, & Timmermans, 2010), and more. In most multilevel studies, the dependent variable is a characteristic of the ties between egos and alters, but in some cases the characteristics of alters themselves, such as nationality, have been examined with multilevel methods (e.g., De Miguel Luken & Tranmer, 2010).

One reason for this popularity is that multilevel models allow researchers to keep the data at the finer level of alters instead of summarizing them, which enables more detailed analyses relying on more data points. With more data points (larger samples, in a way), more predictors can be included in the models, and standard deviations of parameter estimators are lower—that is, parameter estimates are less variable and more precise.

A second, related reason is that, by maintaining the data at the level of alters, multilevel methods enable social scientists to retain all kinds of predictors in the analysis, including variables on egos, networks, alters, and ego–alter ties. This means that multilevel models can test more research hypotheses compared to single-level models for ego variables. With multilevel regression, researchers can investigate how the outcomes of ego–alter ties (e.g., the level of support obtained from the alter) are affected by:

1. Characteristics of egos, such as the ego's sex or employment status.
2. Characteristics of alters. These can be individual attributes, such as the alter's age, or network properties, such as the alter's degree centrality in ego's personal network.
3. Characteristics of the ego–alter tie, such as the type of relationship or the frequency of contact between ego and alter.
4. Characteristics of the ego–alter dyad. These are typically measures of similarity or dissimilarity between ego and alter, such as the age difference between them, or whether ego and alter are of the same sex.
5. Personal network characteristics. These can be compositional variables, such as the proportion of women in the network or average alter age; or structural variables, such as network density or the number of components in the network.
6. Cross-level interactions between level-2 variables (characteristics of egos or networks) and level-1 variables (characteristics of alters or ego–alter ties).

Figure 13.2 shows examples of dependent and explanatory variables that can be included in a multilevel model for personal network data. Table 13.2 provides examples of specific research hypotheses that can be tested on the basis of each type of predictor and on the interaction between predictors, considering the case of social support as a tie-level binary dependent variable ($y_i = 1$ if the tie between the ego and the alter is supportive; $y_i = 0$ otherwise).

Note that, as we saw in Chapter 11, personal network characteristics are frequently a summarization (e.g., proportions or averages) of alter-level characteristics. Thus, a multilevel model can include the *same* variable as a predictor both in its original, alter-level version ($x$ in the models above) and in its summary, network-level version ($w$ in the models above). For example, the model can include both the alter-level predictor, "Whether alter is female" ($x$), and the network-level predictor, "Proportion of female alters in the network" ($w$); both "Alter age" ($x$) and "Average age of alters in the network" ($w$). In this way, we can ask research questions about both the *individual* and the *contextual* or *network* effects of the same variable. For example, we can ask whether alters who are women, or older alters, tend to provide more support individually; and we can ask if personal networks with a higher proportion of women or with older alters on average are associated with a higher probability of every alter (both men and women, young and old) providing support. This would mean that female-dominated networks or older networks facilitate or encourage *every* alter to provide more support, regardless of the alter's individual sex or age.

### *Testing Theories on Social Support with Hierarchical Models for Personal Networks*

Barry Wellman and Kenneth Frank (2001) used one of the first and most well-known personal network databases, the East York 1968 data (Wellman, 1979), to test a comprehensive set of theoretically grounded hypotheses about social support and social capital. They estimated that hierarchical logistic models would predict a binary variable, namely, whether ego obtains support from alter ($y_i = 1$) or not ($y_i = 0$). Their models include random intercepts, random slopes, and cross-level interactions between characteristics of ego–alter ties (level 1) and characteristics of personal networks (level 2). They found that the provision of social support in both everyday situations and emergency situations (two different dependent variables) were affected by characteristics of the tie between the ego and the alter (e.g., stronger ties provide more support); alter characteristics (e.g., female alters are more likely to provide emergency support); ego characteristics (e.g., female egos are more likely to obtain support); and characteristics of the whole personal network (e.g., networks with a higher average accessibility of alters are associated with higher likelihood of individual alters providing support). Interestingly, they also found that some cross-level interactions were statistically significant. For example, if a personal network was characterized by a higher average accessibility of alters, then single accessible alters were even *more* likely to provide support (compared to accessible alters in networks with lower average accessibility of alters).

| | Measurement unit | Hierarchical level | Example variable | |
|---|---|---|---|---|
| **Dependent variables** | | | | |
| Characteristic of tie | Ego-alter tie | Level 1 | Tie provides support (binary) | 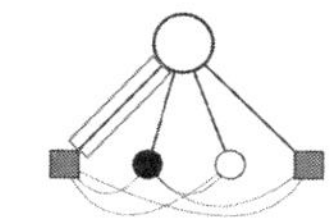 |
| Characteristic of alter | Alter | Level 1 | Alter's smoking frequency (categorical) | 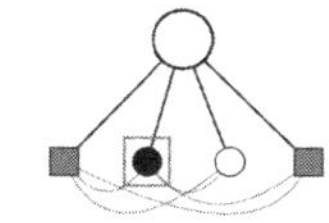 |
| **Explanatory variables** | | | | |
| Characteristic of ego-alter tie | Ego-alter tie | Level 1 | Frequency of contact between ego and alter (categorical) | 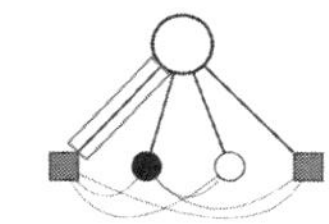 |
| Characteristic of ego-alter dyad | Ego-alter tie | Level 1 | Age difference between ego and alter (continuous) | 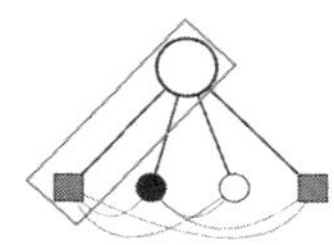 |
| Characteristic of alter | Alter | Level 1 | Alter's sex (binary) | 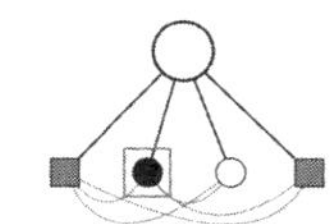 |
| Characteristic of ego | Ego | Level 2 | Ego's age (continuous) | 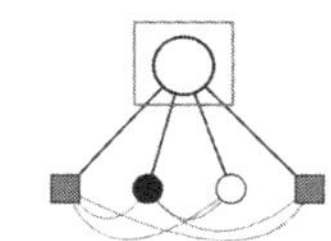 |
| Characteristic of network composition | Network | Level 2 | Proportion female alters (continuous) | 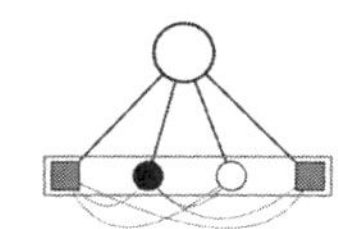 |
| Characteristic of network structure | Network | Level 2 | Personal network density (continuous) | 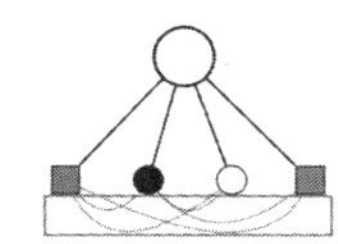 |

**FIGURE 13.2.** Types of dependent and explanatory variables in multilevel models for personal networks.

**TABLE 13.2. Explanatory Variables and Examples of Hypotheses That Can Be Tested**

| Explanatory variable | Measurement unit | Hierarchical level | Example variable | Example of a testable hypothesis |
|---|---|---|---|---|
| Characteristic of the ego–alter tie | Ego–alter tie | Level 1 | Frequency of contact between the ego and the alter (categorical) | Alters who see the ego more frequently are more likely to provide support to the ego |
| Characteristic of the ego–alter dyad | Ego–alter tie | Level 1 | Age difference between the ego and the alter (continuous) | Alters who are about the same age as the ego are more likely to provide support to the ego. |
| Characteristic of the alter | Alter | Level 1 | Alter's sex (binary) | Women alters are more likely to provide support to the ego. |
| Characteristic of the ego | Ego | Level 2 | Ego's age (continuous) | Older egos tend to enjoy more social support overall. |
| Characteristic of network composition | Network | Level 2 | Proportion of female alters (continuous) | All alters (men and women) are more likely to provide support to the ego when there are more women in the network. |
| Characteristic of network structure | Network | Level 2 | Personal network density (continuous) | Alters are more likely to provide support to the ego when they are part of more cohesive (dense) networks. |
| *Interaction:* Characteristic of tie * Characteristic of network composition | Ego–alter tie and Network | Level 1 * Level 2 | Tie is family (binary) * Proportion of family alters (continuous) | Family ties are more likely to be supportive when there are more family members in the network. |
| *Interaction:* Characteristic of the alter * Characteristic of network structure | Alter and Network | Level 1 * Level 2 | Alter's sex (binary) * Personal network density (continuous) | Women are more likely to provide support in more cohesive (dense) networks. |
| *Interaction:* Characteristic of the alter * Characteristic of the ego | Alter and Ego | Level 1 * Level 2 | Alter's sex (binary) * Ego's age (continuous) | Women are more likely to provide support when the ego is older. |

*Note.* The dependent variable is whether the ego–alter tie is supportive to the ego ($y_i = 1$) or not ($y_i = 0$).

We might even examine the effect of the *interaction* between individual (alter) predictors and contextual (network) characteristics. For example, we might test whether individual female alters tend to provide more support only *in female-dominated personal networks*. Maybe this could happen because women feel they play a more important and central role in women-dominated social contexts, resulting in a sense of empowerment or obligation to provide support, whereas, in networks with few women, female and male alters tend to provide the same level of support.

## Special Data and Methods

An interesting application of hierarchical models is the analysis of *longitudinal* personal network data to investigate why personal relationships change over time. The data used in this type of research includes multiple personal networks for each ego, observed at different points in time. Marijtje Van Duijn and collaborators (1999) provide an example. They analyzed data from a three-wave personal network survey with 195 Dutch individuals to test hypotheses on why some social relations remain stable over time while others dissolve. Change in ego–alter relations is measured as change in contact frequency between the ego and the alter from wave 1 to wave 3 (four years later). In these data, the level-1 units of analysis were ego–alter ties, and the dependent variable was calculated as a *difference* between the same measure (contact frequency) observed on the same ego–alter tie at time 2 (the final interview) and at time 1 (the first interview). A number of level-1 explanatory variables were also measured as differences between the time-2 and time-1 values: for example, the difference between "Appreciation" of ego for alter at time 2 and at time 1. The study used hierarchical linear models with both random intercept and random slopes. Elisabeth Terhell and colleagues (2007) showed a similar example of hierarchical regression to examine contact changes between egos and alters over time.

*Overlapping* personal networks are another special type of ego-network data that can be analyzed using multilevel models. With overlapping ego networks, however, the data structure is no longer hierarchical, as it is in the vast majority of existing multilevel studies of personal networks. This is because, if the personal networks overlap, the same alter may belong to more than one network and egos may be nominated as alters by other egos, thus occupying the role of egos for certain networks and alters for others. Therefore, we no longer have a structure in which each level-1 unit belongs to one and only one level-2 unit.

This type of data can be analyzed using *nonhierarchical* multilevel models (Rasbash & Browne, 2008). If the dependent variable of interest is a characteristic of alters, then the model must take into account the fact that the same alter (a row in the dataset) can be a member of *multiple* ego networks. In this case, multiple membership multiple classification or MMMC models can be used (e.g., Tranmer, Steel, & Browne, 2014). If the dependent variable is a characteristic of ego–alter ties, then the model should account for the fact that ties are *cross-classified* between egos and alters: each tie "belongs" to an ego and an alter; the same ego can receive ties from multiple alters; and, unlike in traditional personal network data, the same alter can send ties to multiple egos. These data can be analyzed using cross-classified multilevel models (Vacca, Stacciarini, & Tranmer, n.d.). You should also keep in mind that, whenever personal networks share alters or egos, we can actually construct a *whole* network from the data. Therefore, the researcher also has the option of using statistical models for whole or sociocentric networks, such as exponential random graph models (more on these models below).

## 13.2 STATISTICAL MODELS FOR ALTER–ALTER TIES

The models described in the previous section are used to explain the occurrence and characteristics of ties between egos and alters. We might be interested, however, in modeling the existence or characteristics of ties among the alters themselves. This is what the models considered in this section do, answering questions such as the following: When are ties among alters more likely? Which social contacts of our respondents are more likely to know each other? What are the factors associated with more cohesive or denser personal networks, showing more alter–alter ties? What types of subgroups tend to form in our respondents' personal networks? What social processes shape the formation of the personal network structure? In the most recent research, models based on alter–alter tie data are used to answer a possibly more ambitious question: What can the personal networks in our sample tell us about the structure of the *whole*, underlying the social network of the population that we are studying?

Once we remove the ego, who is connected to every alter by construction, a personal network can be represented as a graph, just like a whole or sociocentric network. In this case, the nodes are the alters, and the edges are the alter–alter ties. We should always keep in mind, however, that major differences exist between this alter–alter network and a whole network, which are related to data collection:

1. The network of alters is not limited by the boundary of a social group, organization, or population, as it is in a sociocentric network, but by the existence of a certain relationship, implied by the name generator(s), between all the alters and the focal ego.
2. Data on the ties in a network of alters are not collected from the actors themselves (i.e., the alters), but rather are reported by the ego—a third party who, like a key informant, provides the data but is not part of the network.
3. Our data presumably include many alter–alter networks (dozens, hundreds, or even thousands), which are typically separate as they are observed on different sets of nodes (alters); unlike sociocentric data, which normally include a limited number of networks, often observed on the same set of nodes.

Provided that we consider these important differences in the nature of the data and their implications for the interpretation of results, virtually any statistical model used to analyze whole networks can be applied to a network among alters as well. We focus here on statistical models whose dependent variable is the network itself or the existence of a tie between actors—in our case, between alters. These are sometimes referred to as "network formation models," as they try to explain why and how networks form. In other words, these models are used to identify the factors and processes that drive actors to establish relationships with each other. Similar to the statistical models seen in the previous section and in Chapter 12, network formation models (1) link their dependent variable to multiple explanatory variables, each representing a factor or process; and (2) quantify the distinct contribution of each explanatory variable to the likelihood of actors forming a relationship, while other conditions are held equal.

In our case, the social network whose formation we want to investigate is a network of ties reported by the ego among her social contacts. These are typically undirected and binary ties, the simplest form of ties, because personal network questionnaires most commonly ask egos the simple undirected question of whether two alters know each other (according to some definition of "knowing"). However, as we saw in Chapter 8, personal network research sometimes uses more sophisticated questions about alter–alter ties, which result in directed or valued networks. Network formation models are usually easier to fit and interpret on binary undirected data, but they can be adapted to valued and directed networks too.

This section briefly reviews three types of network formation models and their application to personal network data: hierarchical logistic models, ERGMs, and SAOMs. This is perhaps the most advanced and cutting-edge statistical topic covered in this book. Because a comprehensive discussion of these models is beyond the scope of this chapter, readers should refer to the works cited in the Further Reading section for a more complete treatment of the methods mentioned here.

## Multilevel Models for Alter–Alter Ties

The existence of a tie between two alters can be seen as a binary outcome. Each dyad between alters is an observation or case $i$, and the dyad may be connected ($y_i = 1$, if the two alters know each other) or not connected ($y_i = 0$, if the two alters do not know each other). At the same time, every alter is also connected to an ego. Therefore, whenever two alters know each other, what we are actually observing is a closed triad formed by an ego and two alters who all know each other; this is as opposed to an open triad, which occurs when two alters do not know each other. For this reason, studies of the determinants of alter–alter ties are often presented as studies of "triadic closure" in personal networks.

As we learned in Chapter 12, a binary outcome such as triadic closure can be modeled using logistic regression. Personal network data, however, present a complication: alter–alter pairs are not independent observations, but they are clustered within personal networks (or egos). Pairs of alters nominated by the same ego are more similar to each other than pairs of alters named by different egos. Therefore, similar to the data described in Section 13.1, here we have a multilevel data structure: alter–alter dyads

**_Modeling Alter–Alter Ties to Study Transitivity and Homophily_**

Hugh Louch (2000) analyzes data on alter–alter ties in the personal networks collected by the 1985 GSS. His paper aims to explain integration in personal networks, which Louch defines as the level of connectedness among alters, that is, the level of triadic closure in the networks. However, Louch does not aggregate information on alter–alter ties to measure connectedness at the network level (e.g., through density)—the type of approach we illustrated in Chapter 11. Rather, the author conducts the analysis at the original level of the ties among alters. He uses hierarchical logistic regression to predict the probability of a triad being closed (i.e., of two alters knowing each other). This probability is expressed as a function of transitivity and homophily. *Transitivity* is stronger if the two alters have multiple contacts in common in addition to ego, that is, if they are both connected to the same other alters. Transitivity is also stronger when the two alters both have strong ties with the ego or share the same role or group membership with the ego (kin, coworker, neighbor, etc.). *Homophily* is higher when the two alters share certain attributes, such as race or age. The analysis finds that a tie between two alters is more likely when transitivity is stronger: that is, when two alters have more contacts in common, have more frequent interactions with the ego, have known the ego for a long time, or share the same role or group membership with the ego. An alter–alter tie is also more likely to occur when the two alters are similar in terms of age, race, education, and religion, which indicates that homophily is also a strong determinant of triadic closure in personal networks.

(the level-1 units) are nested within egos or personal networks (the level-2 units). Louch (2000) proposes using hierarchical logistic models to explain the occurrence of ties among alters while accounting for the hierarchy implied in personal network data. Gerald Mollenhorst and colleagues (2011) take a similar approach. In a subsequent study, however, Mollenhorst, van Duijn, Rydgren, and Edling (2016) reflect on the fact that alter–alter ties are actually first clustered within alters: multiple ties of this type can belong to the same alter, and each alter–alter tie belongs to two alters. Alters, in turn, are nested within the egos. To better account for this complicated nonhierarchical structure, Mollenhorst and collaborators propose a more sophisticated, three-level multiple membership logistic model.

## Exponential Random Graph Models

Exponential random graph models are a more sophisticated class of models for the formation of ties in social networks (Robins, Pattison, Kalish, & Lusher, 2007). In ERGM notation, a network is an adjacency matrix $\mathbf{Y}$, which is seen as a random variable; $\boldsymbol{y}$ is the specific *realization* of that variable, that is, the specific network we observe. The particular tie from actor $i$ to actor $j$ is indicated as $y_{ij}$, where $y_{ij} = 1$ if $i$ sends a tie to $j$, and

$y_{ij} = 0$ otherwise. Note that if a network is undirected, then $y_{ij} = y_{ji}$; while if a network is directed, then $y_{ij}$ and $y_{ji}$ might be different.

ERG models posit that the probability of a specific network $\mathbf{y}$ depends on the number of certain *configurations* of ties that appear in the network. A configuration is a pattern or substructure of ties that reflects a specific social process (Figure 13.3). For example, a typical process in social networks is reciprocity: when actor *i* starts a relation or interaction with *j* (e.g., *i* sends a letter to *j*), then *j* tends to start the same relation or interaction with *i* (e.g., *j* sends a letter back to *i*). A pair of reciprocated ties, such that *i* sends a tie to *j* and *j* sends a tie to *i*, is the configuration that reflects reciprocity. Another recurrent social process in networks is transitivity, the process in which "the friends of my friends become my friends." More generally, when social ties are transitive, if *i* is connected to *j* and *j* is connected to *k*, then *k* tends to become connected with *i* as well. A closed triad of nodes, in which *i* is tied to *j*, *j* is tied to *k*, and *k* is tied back to *i*, is the configuration that reflects the social process of transitivity. Configurations might also involve actor attributes. Homophily configurations, for example, are those in which a tie connects two actors with the same value of a given attribute (e.g., same sex or age).

A network configuration can be seen as a particular set of ties, called *A*. Some configurations, when included in an ERGM, imply an assumption of *dyadic dependence*: the assumption of probabilistic dependence among the ties that are part of the configuration set *A*. This means that, if the social process that generates the configuration *A* (e.g., reciprocity or transitivity) is operating in the network, then the ties in the set *A* are *dependent* on each other in that when one of the ties exists, the others have a higher probability of existing too. For example, in the reciprocity configuration, if tie $y_{ij}$ exists, then tie $y_{ji}$ is more likely to exist, precisely by virtue of reciprocity; in the transitivity configuration, if $y_{ij}$ and $y_{jk}$ exist, then the tie $y_{ki}$ is more likely to exist because of transitivity. Other network configurations do not entail any dyadic dependence assumption. An example is the homophily configuration in which a tie connects two nodes that are similar on a certain attribute and no tie affects the probability of other ties existing.

A network configuration *A* can also be represented as a *network statistic*: $g_A(\mathbf{y}) = \Pi_{yij \in A} y_{ij}$. The statistic $g_A(\mathbf{y})$ is a product of the tie variables $y_{ij}$, which equals 1 if and only if all the ties in configuration *A* exist ($y_{ij} = 1$ for all the $y_{ij}$'s in the configuration). For

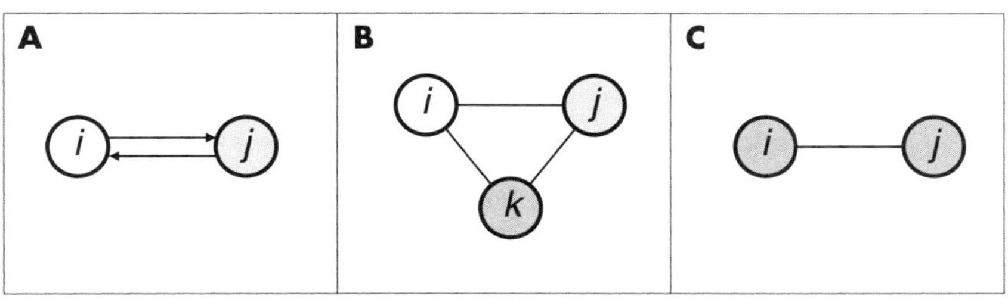


**FIGURE 13.3.** Network configurations reflecting reciprocity (A), transitivity (B), and homophily (C) (nodes of the same color have a similar attribute value).

example, the network statistic associated with a closed triad is $g_A(\mathbf{y}) = y_{ij} y_{jk} y_{ik}$, which is equal to 1 if and only if all the three ties in the triad exist ($y_{ij} = y_{jk} = y_{ik} = 1$). Thus, $g_A(\mathbf{y})$ can be viewed as a dummy variable that equals 1 every time the configuration $A$ appears in the network, and it is 0 otherwise. Clearly, $g_A(\mathbf{y})$ is a function of the observed network, $\mathbf{y}$.

ERGMs model the probability that a specific network arises as a function of certain network statistics $g_A(\mathbf{y})$, and of the parameters associated with each statistic, indicated as $\eta_A$:

$$P(\boldsymbol{Y} = \boldsymbol{y}) = \frac{1}{k} exp\left\{\sum_A \eta_A g_A(\boldsymbol{y})\right\} \tag{13.1}$$

where

$g_A(\mathbf{y})$ is a particular network statistic associated with configuration $A$ (e.g., the reciprocity statistic or the transitivity statistic)

$\eta_A$ is the parameter associated with that statistic

$k$ is a normalizing constant, which makes sure that Equation 13.1 is a proper probability distribution

Note that $\sum_A \eta_A g_A(\boldsymbol{y})$ is analogous to the linear predictor ($\beta_0 + \beta_1 x_1 + \ldots + \beta_k x_k$) that appears in the linear and generalized linear models discussed in Chapter 12: $g_A(\mathbf{y})$ are the "explanatory variables," similar to $x_1, x_2, \ldots, x_k$ in linear and generalized linear models; and $\eta_A$ are the parameters, similar to $\beta_1, \ldots, \beta_k$ in traditional models. The probability of a network, similar to the probability of the event in the logistic models seen in Chapter 12, is assumed to depend on these "explanatory variables" $g_A(\mathbf{y})$, which reflect specific social processes (reciprocity, transitivity, homophily, etc.). In an ERG model, we include only the particular "explanatory variables" $g_A(\mathbf{y})$ that measure social processes that we hypothesize to affect the formation of relationships in our network.

The probability of a network depends on the *summation* over all $g_A(\mathbf{y})$'s, and therefore, on the *count* or the number of times that a certain configuration $A$ is observed in the network. For example, if the reciprocity statistic is included in the model, the probability of the network is assumed to depend on the number of times a tie is reciprocated; if the transitivity statistic is included, it is assumed to depend on the number of times a triad is closed in the network.

As is true of many statistical models, ERGM parameter estimation is based on the principle of maximum likelihood: we find the parameter values that maximize the probability of the observed data *given* the model. In ERGM, this means that we find the parameters $\eta_A$'s that maximize the probability of the observed network, given the social processes whose configurations we have included in the model. Thus, for example, if the observed network contains many closed triads, the estimation procedure will assign a high value to the $\eta_A$ parameter for transitivity (assuming we have included the transitivity configuration in the model), so that the resulting probability distribution (Equation

13.1, i.e., the model) makes our observed network, with many closed triads, very likely. In this way, the estimate for the parameter associated with closed triads will be a measure of the occurrence of closed triads in the network. In other words, the estimate for parameter $\eta_A$, associated with configuration *A*, quantifies the importance or incidence of that configuration in the observed network. A positive and high parameter $\eta_A$ indicates that the configuration *A* is highly recurrent in the observed network: the observed network has a high likelihood of existing if the generating probability function (i.e., the model) places a high weight ($\eta_A$) on the configuration *A*.

Therefore, ERGMs allow us to quantify the incidence of a configuration in the network and to measure to what degree that incidence is statistically significant, above and beyond what we could expect just by chance. Remember that configurations such as reciprocated ties and closed triads are generated even in networks in which ties are created completely at random, without following any social process. This is why we want to assess if and to what extent a specific configuration is occurring *beyond chance*. Because each configuration corresponds to a social process, ERGMs enable us to test hypotheses about the social processes that generated the network we observe. Similar to multiple regression, we include parameters for *multiple* configurations in the model. We can therefore assess the relative strength of each social process in shaping the network, or the effect of each process "with other things being equal."

ERGMs can also be used to *simulate* networks. Once the $\eta_A$ parameters are estimated (or deliberately set), resulting in a specific probability distribution given by Equation 13.1, we can use that distribution to extract random networks, just like we could extract random numbers from a standard normal distribution. Because each $\eta_A$ parameter corresponds to a specific social process with a specific weight, we are effectively generating or simulating networks that are produced by the specified processes, such as reciprocity, transitivity, or certain types of homophily.

We can generate hundreds or thousands of such networks and then measure any of their characteristics, such as average component size, clustering, and average geodesic distance. In this way, we can examine what types of networks are produced, on average, by the social processes incorporated in the ERG model. For example, what is the average component size and geodesic distance of social networks when strong transitivity and sex homophily processes are operating? We can answer this question by simulating networks from the appropriate ERGM.

While most applications use ERGMs to model whole networks, these models can be used to test hypotheses about the social processes that generate personal networks as well. As long as we have data about ties among alters and about alter attributes, we can use ERGMs to measure patterns such as transitivity and homophily in personal networks, and assess the statistical significance and strength of these patterns.

One option is to fit an ERG model to each personal network in our data. However, this is not a common type of analysis because estimation convergence and goodness-of-fit need to be evaluated for each ERGM individually. If our data include hundreds or thousands of ego networks, this is clearly not feasible. A more realistic strategy views our ego networks as samples extracted from a whole, underlying social network. If we

### *Using Personal Networks to Estimate Whole Network Characteristics through ERGMs*

Jeffrey Smith (2012) proposed and tested a method that uses ERGMs to make inferences on a whole network based on a collection of personal networks. The starting idea is that the personal networks in the data are samples extracted from the single, underlying whole network of an entire population. The whole social network is the target of our inference. Smith shows that, given a collection of personal networks, an ERG model can be identified that generates a whole network consistent with the personal networks in the collection. In other words, we can identify an ERGM that simulates a whole network, which contains precisely the types of personal networks actually observed in our data. In particular, ERGMs can be used to simulate whole networks that reproduce the following characteristics of the observed personal networks: (1) Degree distribution, overall and for different categories of egos; (2) the level of homophily between egos and alters; (3) the distribution of ego-network "configurations," defined as combinations of the number of alters, the distribution of alter degree, and the number of closed triads in the alter–alter network. While degree distribution (1) and level of homophily (2) can be extracted from the data simply by using information on the egos' degree (i.e., personal network size), the egos' attributes, and the alters' attributes; the distribution of ego-network configurations (3) can only be measured using data on alter–alter ties. Smith showed that an appropriate value of the parameter for the Geometrically Weighted Edgewise Shared Partner (GWESP) statistic (a network statistic that measures transitivity) can be detected, generating whole networks that reproduce the distribution of ego-network configurations found in the observed data. Once the correct ERG model is identified, which is consistent with the observed personal networks, this ERGM can be used to make inferences on the underlying whole network from which the personal networks were extracted. Pavel Krivitsky and Martina Morris (2017) proposed a similar ERGM-based method, although they did not use data on alter–alter ties.

collected data on 100 personal networks of Sri Lankan immigrants in Milan, Italy, for example, we could think of these as 100 small samples from the whole, bounded social network of the Sri Lankan community in Milan. We can then fit a single ERG model to this network sample in order to make inferences about the social processes that shape the formation of relationships in the social network of *all* Sri Lankans in Milan. This is the approach proposed by Smith (2012).

## Stochastic Actor-Oriented Models for Longitudinal Personal Networks

Stochastic actor-oriented models (SAOMs, also called Siena models; Snijders, et al., 2010) are another class of statistical models that can be used to explain the formation of ties in a social network. While, similar to ERGMs, SAO models have been used mostly to analyze whole networks, they can be applied to networks of ties among alters as well. Unlike ERGMs, SAOMs are mostly used to analyze network dynamics. Therefore, longitudinal network data are needed, which include networks observed at a minimum of two points in time.

SAOMs describe the evolution of networks over time as dependent on network structure, attributes of actors (in our case, alters), and characteristics of dyads of actors. While ERGMs are tie-oriented models, because they view the network as the result of processes based on ties, SAOMs are actor oriented because they assume that network change is driven by actors, who choose which new ties to establish and which existing ties to dissolve at each moment in time. This change happens in continuous time, although we observe the network at a few (at least two) discrete time points.

In the SAO model, actors start new relationships and end existing relationships based on recurrent tendencies or processes, such as reciprocity or homophily, which are represented by specific parameters. These parameters are included in a utility or objective function, and actors are assumed to change their ties over time in a way that increases the value of that objective function. SAOMs are implemented as agent-based

### *Using SAOMs to Examine the Evolution of Alter–Alter Ties over Time*

Miranda Lubbers and colleagues (2010) proposed using SAOMs to conduct what they call the "Type 5" analysis of longitudinal personal networks—that is, an analysis of persistence and dissolution of ties among alters over time. They illustrated the method with data on the personal networks of 25 Argentinean immigrants in Spain, which were collected in two surveys at two different times (between one and four years apart). They estimated an SAO model including parameters for transitivity (two alters who have more contacts in common tend to establish a tie); strength of tie with ego (two alters who have a stronger tie with ego tend to start a relationship); homophily with respect to country of residence and nationality (alters who were born in the same country and alters who live in the same country tend to establish a connection); and shared group membership (alters who share the same type of relationship or socialization context with ego, e.g., they are both kin, coworkers, or neighbors of the ego, tend to connect with each other). Unlike a typical whole network SAOM study, Lubbers and colleagues' data included *multiple* longitudinal networks—the 25 Argentinean personal networks. Thus, the authors completed the analysis in two steps: by first fitting an SAOM to each longitudinal personal network and then conducting a meta analysis that summarized findings over several SAOMs. The study found that, in the aggregate, ties among the alters of the 25 respondents were significantly affected by transitivity, shared group membership, and common residence and nationality. Over time, alters were more likely to start or maintain a relationship if they had multiple contacts in common; if they had a similar group membership with the ego; and if they were born or currently lived in the same country.

simulation models (Macy & Willer, 2002), with a probabilistically selected actor having the opportunity to change one of his or her ties at every given moment in time.

## CHAPTER SUMMARY

This chapter has presented the more advanced statistical models that personal network researchers use to analyze the characteristics of alters, ego–alter ties, or alter–alter ties. This level of analysis is more detailed than the ego level seen in Chapter 12 because for each ego there are multiple alters and ties, and ego-level aggregation hides the variation across them. Zooming in from the ego level to the level of alters and ties, we can test more sophisticated hypotheses on the formation and workings of personal networks, which we could not consider in aggregate ego-level analyses. Because alters and ego–alter ties are clustered within egos, over the past 20 years a growing body of research has used multilevel statistical models for the analysis of variables on alters and ego–alter ties. These include hierarchical linear and logistic models and nonhierarchical models for overlapping personal networks. Multilevel models can also be fitted to analyze longitudinal changes in the characteristics of alters and ego–alter ties in time.

A different problem is the identification of the factors and processes that lead to the formation of ties among alters. This is also known as the question of triadic closure because the occurrence of a tie between two alters implies the existence of a closed triad between those two alters and the ego. Triadic closure has been studied using multilevel logistic models, both hierarchical and nonhierarchical. The formation of alter–alter ties can also be examined with models originally developed for sociocentric networks, such as ERGMs and SAOMs. A very recent and quickly evolving line of research applies ERGMs to personal network data, with the goal of making "macro" inferences on the underlying whole network from which the personal networks are extracted. SAOMs were originally developed for longitudinal whole network data and can be employed to study the formation and dissolution of alter–alter ties over time.

## FURTHER READING

Fox, J. (2008). *Applied regression analysis and generalized linear models* (2nd ed.). Los Angeles: SAGE.

Goldstein, H. (2010). *Multilevel statistical models* (4th ed.). Chichester, West Sussex, UK: Wiley.

Lusher, D., Koskinen, J., & Robins, G. (2012). *Exponential random graph models for social networks: Theory, methods, and applications.* Cambridge, UK: Cambridge University Press.

Rasbash, J., & Browne, W. J. (2008). Non-hierarchical multilevel models. In J. De Leeuw & E. Meijer (Eds.), *Handbook of multilevel analysis* (pp. 301–334). New York: Springer.

Rasbash, J., Steele, F., & Leckie, G. (2008). *LEMMA: Learning Environment for Multilevel*

*Methodology and Applications.* Bristol, UK: University of Bristol, Centre for Multilevel Modelling.

Scott, J., & Carrington, P. J. (Eds.). (2011). *The SAGE handbook of social network analysis.* London: SAGE.

Singer, J. D., & Willett, J. B. (2003). *Applied longitudinal data analysis: Modeling change and event occurrence.* Oxford, UK: Oxford University Press.

Snijders, T., & Bosker, R. J. (2012). *Multilevel analysis: An introduction to basic and advanced multilevel modeling* (2nd ed.). London: SAGE.

Snijders, T. A. B., van De Bunt, G. G., & Steglich, C. E. G. (2010). Introduction to stochastic actor-based models for network dynamics. *Social Networks, 32*(1), 44–60.

Snijders, T., Spreen, M., & Zwaagstra, R. (1995). The use of multilevel modeling for analysing personal networks: Networks of cocaine users in an urban area. *Journal of Quantitative Anthropology, 5,* 85–105.

van Duijn, M., van Busschbach, J. T., & Snijders, T. A. B. (1999). Multilevel analysis of personal networks as dependent variables. *Social Networks, 21*(2), 187–210.

**14**

# Ethics in Personal Network Research

---

### *What Is This Chapter About?*

In this chapter, you will learn how to deal with the ethical issues that arise when you are conducting personal network research. After an introduction (Section 14.1), we will discuss how to gain the consent of respondents (which is comparable to other survey research; Section 14.2), how to protect confidentiality (Section 14.3), what are the caveats you should take into account with data collected from social media and smartphones (Section 14.4), and how to manage and publish personal network data (Section 14.5). These practical tips will be useless if you fail to take the time to reflect on the ethical consequences of your research, anticipating possible (unintended) harm caused to individuals and communities under study. You should particularly reflect on how to deal with eventual incidental findings and how to protect personal data and testimonies collected from the people who agreed to cooperate in the research.

---

## 14.1 PERSONAL NETWORK RESEARCH AND ETHICAL DILEMMAS

All scientific research, basic or applied, inevitably entails ethical dilemmas. This is true whether for astronomical research or for the study of ancient writing. In some cases, when research entails experimentation with animals or humans, these dilemmas become more apparent. These two areas of research have been regulated since World War II by national laws and deontological codes enacted by international bodies, resulting in the formation of Institutional Review Boards (IRBs) in the United States and Research Ethics Committees (RECs) in other countries, in a quite diverse fashion. These regulations, inspired mainly by biomedical research and practice, have extended their reach during the last several decades to the social sciences and the humanities. Now, social researchers have to face the ethical dilemmas natural to their research projects, taking into account not just the traditional disciplinary deontological codes (i.e., social anthropology, sociology, or psychology) but multiple regulations, best practices manuals, and data protection protocols.

In this regard, it is important to keep in mind that compliance with this growing body of regulations does not automatically imply that the researcher behaves ethically. In fact, during the research process, researchers have to solve unanticipated ethical dilemmas for which they must rely on their own ethical integrity.

In short, the basic ethical tenets that all social research should meet are (1) to benefit the population under study (or at least do no harm), (2) to respect the freedom and dignity of participants (informed consent and the right to opt out of the research without reprisal or other consequences), and finally, (3) to acknowledge their right to anonymity.

Social network research in general and personal network analysis in particular pose specific challenges to some of these general principles, as respondents are asked to give information about their alters (Klovdahl, 2005). The first challenge concerns informed consent. Typically, during the personal networks interview, an informed consent is gained from each respondent (ego), and sometimes personalized feedback is provided during or at the end of the interview or some days later. As you saw in Chapter 9, respondents normally appreciate this feedback, and it is indeed an excellent way to balance the costs and benefits that research entails to participants. Nevertheless, most of the time it will be impossible to obtain consent from *alters*. The same concern applies for the attributes collected for each alter and for edge evaluations. This concern is independent of the method of data collection (e.g., face-to-face interviews, Web surveys, or smartphone apps). In the past, most IRBs have not required alter consent, although recently some IRBs have made that suggestion. Realistically, however, in most cases such consent is difficult or impossible to obtain.

A related problem is how to comply with the right to opt out from the research, a principle that was definitively established by the 1964 Declaration of Helsinki (World Medical Association, 2001). A respondent may ask to opt out of a personal network study and to have his or her data removed from the dataset. However, people who do not participate in research are usually not even aware that other respondents have nominated them as alters in their personal networks. Removing them from the dataset can be either ineffective, especially in organizational settings, where the participants can easily be identified (Borgatti & Molina, 2005), or problematic, because this removal can affect the reliability of the data collected.

A further issue concerns the right to anonymity. Participant anonymity is typically reached either by keeping the data *confidential* (protected and accessed just by the research team) or by removing personal identifiers in order to make them *anonymous*, or by a combination of both measures (i.e., having the data split into two halves, with and without personal identifiers and stored separately, or by removing personal data at some point of the research). Unfortunately, when network and geographical data are collected, complete anonymization may simply not be possible. Some authors show how it is possible to identify individuals from anonymous datasets with just a few personal attributes and/or time–space traces (Blondel, Decuyper, & Krings, 2015). The problem of deanonymization is aggravated by the fact that a growing number of funding agencies request the online publication of the raw data collected after a reasonable embargo period. Let's first address the issue of informed consent.

## 14.2 GAINING CONSENT

The basic principle of respect for people involves explaining, in a comprehensible way, the objectives of the study, the voluntary nature of the participation, the type of questions that will be asked, the potential costs (e.g., in terms of time), harm and benefits, and the future use of data. Furthermore, respondents should have an opportunity to ask questions about the research and access to the contact details of the research team in case of further questions or concerns. They should also be informed that they can opt out from the research at any time, without any cost or further explanation. Nowadays, compliance with IRB requirements often involves preparing an information sheet and asking respondents to sign a consent form to show that this practice has been followed.

Templates of information sheets and consent forms are available at the websites of the IRB of the University of Florida (*irb.ufl.edu*), the Ethics Committee of the Autonomous University of Barcelona (in Catalan: *uab.cat/etica-recerca*), and in general in most universities and research center sites. It is possible to find differentiated templates for adults, children, parental consent, and other specific cases. Of course, all information should be translated to the participant language. These measures apply to Web surveys as well, where the respondents' consent is typically collected when they agree to click a button before the data collection starts.

The practice of obtaining informed consent has been criticized in anthropology as an individualistic transposition of "Western biomedical ethics" to social science research (Bell, 2014). During fieldwork, it is often necessary to negotiate access to the community or the group under study before the recruitment process (and consequently the collection of individual consent) can take place. The negotiation of access normally includes contacts with local experts, institutions, associations, and religious or community leaders. During this phase, the research project is presented and discussed, some key contacts are developed, and pilot studies may be conducted.

In the case of ethnographic research, the request for a *written* consent in a given moment can be disruptive as the researcher strives to build trustful relationships with people over time, a rapport that is renewed in every interaction (ASA, 2011). Moreover, for many populations, the simple request of signing a consent form will raise suspicions of surveillance or control by state bodies, seriously compromising the research. This is especially true for research that involves vulnerable populations (including refugees, drug consumers, or nongovernmental organization volunteers in conflictive regions), where having this signed consent can indeed put their safety at risk. Other examples, such as working with illiterate populations or persons with visual deficiencies, could be added (Gordon, 2000). In those cases, it is acceptable to gain an *oral* consent from participants that is either audiorecorded or signed by the researcher.

## 14.3 CONFIDENTIALITY

Personal information about the ego can remain complete and confidential throughout the project when prior consent is given. Completed consent forms should be kept safe in a secure archive (or a secure server if consent was collected electronically). Unless other considerations apply, it is considered good practice to keep this archive, along with the rest of records of the project, for a minimum of five years after the research project ends (UAB, 2013). When data or results are published, the data should be anonymized, unless explicit consent for publishing identifiers is given. This anonymity can be achieved by using numerical IDs or pseudonyms and by removing any variables that alone or in combination can identify a respondent, or coarser variables may be used (e.g., age category instead of precise age).

In personal network research, confidentiality also involves alters. A simple way to collect anonymous alters is to use nicknames given to them by the ego during the interview. To prevent errors, the ego should be able to easily recognize those nicknames in the future. A practical tip is to ask the ego to use the first letters of both the name and surname of nominating alters. The resulting acronym will be meaningful only for the ego. For instance, during the National Science Foundation Acculturation project (#0417429), we used this name generator:

> Please write down a list of 45 people you know by name and vice versa. It can be anyone. Try to include people who are close and important to you. It may also include people who may not be so close but who you usually see a lot. It can help you to think about different groups of people in different places. *Write the name and surname in abbreviated form so that only you can recognize them. It is important that you do not abbreviate too much so that you can recognize them later. For example: "Migcervan" instead of "Miguel de Cervantes."*

Approximately 500 participants (in the United States and Spain) did not have problems eliciting a long list of 45 names and recognizing the names at a later time. In the same vein, Ted Mouw and his colleagues (Mouw et al., 2014) asked approximately 600 Mexican participants living either in the United States or Mexico to mention the first three letters of both the name and surname of their contacts, along with the attached nickname in case they had one.

The same authors collected information about alters' phone numbers, but they only recorded the last four digits of each number, with the aim of identifying unique alters across a larger set of personal networks. In this way, the internal identification of alters across the nominations of different respondents could be made with reasonable accuracy, but without using the full numbers—a personal identifier.

### *Incentives and Respondent-Driven Sampling*

Survey research sometimes uses monetary incentives or compensations. In the case of respondent-driven sampling methods (RDS) (Salganik & Heckathorn, 2004), this practice can sometimes pose important ethical concerns. This method is intended to achieve a quasi-random sample of a hidden or hard-to-count population through a controlled snowball procedure that starts with a limited number of initial respondents ("seeds") and proceeds with four to six waves of referral in order to maximize the reach of the chain of contacts. The process of recruitment involves the same participants through personal invitations (normally through a Web survey or with the aid of coupons). The incentive system is designed so that the recruiter receives a bonus (such as $10) if the recruited alter happens to finish the interview. In general, the incentives given to the respondents are proportional to the time invested in the survey or interview, ranging from $5 to $50 or to as much as $100 if the respondent is asked to fill in diaries or perform other types of time-consuming tasks. But in the case of RDS designs, and despite the fact that the amount of money given is modest, this system can lead to the emergence of a coupon "black market" affecting vulnerable populations. Greg Scott (2008) presents a vivid explanation of how injection drug users deceived other users with false promises and forced them to finish the interview in order to get the bonus, and, in some cases, part of the compensation of the interview. When these methods are used, a close follow-up protocol can prevent some of those problems.

In general, information collected about alters should be as limited as possible, taking into account the research goals. In the case of geographical information (like places of residence or ZIP codes), the anonymization process will take place once the dataset is ready to be released. In this regard, it is important that the consent form clearly show that the data anonymized will be available for reuse by other researchers in the future. Reuse would otherwise be explicitly forbidden by data privacy regulations, at least in most European countries (Hoser & Nitschke, 2010).

## 14.4 SOCIAL MEDIA AND MOBILE PHONES

So far, we have focused mostly on surveys administered face to face or through the Internet. Now we will turn to the collection of egocentric data from social media sites such as Facebook and smartphones or mobile telephone Call Detail Records (CDRs), automatic logs of human-situated communication for billing purposes.

Unfortunately, in some cases, personal data on social media are collected, analyzed, and published or used without gaining anyone's consent. It is ironic that researchers put so much effort into gaining consent and protecting their respondents' right to privacy in comparatively small surveys, such as those we have described so far, while most of the data about social behavior in the world is owned by social-networking sites like Facebook or by Telecom operators. Currently, not all federal or international regulations on IRBs and Ethics Research Committees (ERCs) apply to them, although that may soon change.

Let's start with the CDR datasets from mobile phone logs. These datasets are owned by Telecom companies and contain information about the sender (including her communication space–time details), the recipient, and the duration of the call, among other information. With few exceptions, these datasets are released in anonymized form to researchers through Mobile Data Challenges events organized by the same companies. To obtain access to the data, researchers sign a confidentiality agreement, which includes scrutiny of research results before publication (Saramäki & Moro, 2015).

The release of such data has produced unique insights into human mobility patterns and communication behaviors during daily life (Lambiotte et al., 2008) as well as during catastrophes (Bengtsson, Lu, Thorson, Garfield, & von Schreeb, 2011) around the world. This also applies to the study of egocentric networks, where, for instance, the size and proportion of both strong and weak ties have been estimated from 20 million users by analysis of 9 billion calls (Miritello et al., 2013). This latter research shows the existence of time constraints to the size of personal networks, even in this era of highly mobile technologies. These constraints (possibly along with the cognitive limitations pointed out by Dunbar, 1993), would explain why the pattern of communication is so homogeneously concentrated in a few alters. Moreover, this type of data is one of the main sources of the United Nations Global Pulse Initiative (*www.unglobalpulse.org*), which promotes the use of Big Data for sustainable development and humanitarian action.

These datasets (anonymized basically by replacing telephone numbers with surrogate keys) can be easily deanonymized because mobility patterns are indeed unique (De Montjoye, Hidalgo, Verleysen, & Blondel, 2013), similar to personal networks. Also, one of the rules of scientific research, namely, replicability, cannot be met here because of the private nature of the datasets. In this context, researchers can only rely on their ethical integrity in order to make the right decisions about how to process and protect personal data. One simple measure to adopt in this regard is to explicitly refrain from deanonymizing the dataset.

While phone calls (and their corresponding CDR datasets) will likely be replaced in the future by Internet-based communications, social media services continue attracting growing parts of the world population. For instance, according to Zephoria (*www.zephoria.com*), Facebook had 1.86 billion monthly active users in the beginning of 2017, roughly a quarter of the planet's population, with a 17% increase from year to year. Other services such as Twitter, Instagram, and Google+, among many others, are widely distributed as well. Although Twitter and Facebook, in this order, initially offered ample access to the data, these sites are increasingly restricting access. Data are typically offered to researchers through application programming interfaces (APIs), which theoretically comply with the Term of Service contracts established with users when they agree to create a profile.

We already know that anonymized datasets with social network and/or geographical data can be easily deanonymized, like the famous incident of the project "Tastes, Ties, and Time" (T3) shows. T3 was a longitudinal study of about 1,700 Facebook profiles of students in a "northeastern American university" (Zimmer, 2010). In a short period of time, researchers identified that university as Harvard and proved that participants could be easily identified despite the measures the researchers had taken before publishing the dataset. The lesson learned, from an ethical point of view, is that these datasets cannot be published without the participants' consent, or at least, for a substantial period of time. Research shows that, even with some of the data altered for making the deanonymization more difficult, the identification process is trivial (Narayanan & Shmatikov, 2009).

Facebook is also the site of the famous experiment about emotional contagion through manipulation of the newsfeed of 689,003 users without previous notice (Kramer, Guillory, & Hancock, 2014). The experiment showed how exposing the ego to alters' emotional content (either positive or negative) exerted an influence in the same direction. This influence was present even in the absence of verbal cues. Publication in the *Proceedings of the National Academy of Sciences* (*PNAS*) raised a wave of protests that led the journal to publish an Editorial Expression of Concern. It is illustrative to reproduce a fragment of this document (Verma, 2014):

> Questions have been raised about the principles of informed consent and opportunity to opt out in connection with the research in this paper. The authors noted in their paper, "[The work] was consistent with Facebook's Data Use Policy, to which all users agree prior to creating an account on Facebook, constituting informed consent for this research." When the authors prepared their paper for publication in PNAS, they stated that: "Because this experiment was conducted by Facebook, Inc. for internal purposes, the Cornell University IRB [Institutional Review Board] determined that the project did not fall under Cornell's Human Research Protection Program." This statement has since been confirmed by Cornell University.

This statement can be taken as the epitome of the ethical issues related to social media sites: *users are supposed to give a permanent, multipurpose, and tacit, "informed consent" by accepting the Terms of Service to any kind of research without the need of an IRB or REC approval.*

Nevertheless, it is possible to conduct ethically sound research on social media sites gaining users' consent, as has been shown, for instance, by the study of Brandon Brooks and his colleagues on the egocentric structural correlates of social capital (Brooks et al., 2014). The study recruited 235 employees at a "Midwestern American university" and analyzed data from both an online survey and an online Facebook API network generator. The results showed that traditional views of bonding and bridging social capital at the personal network level had to be adapted to take into account the global cohesive structure of Facebook.

All things considered, it appears that research ethics in Internet research in general and on social media sites in particular rely mostly on the researcher's assessment of the contextual circumstances (Markham & Buchanan, 2017). The Association of Internet Researchers has published a set of guidelines intended to help researchers make decisions in this direction (*https://aoir.org*). In this regard, Jana Diesner and Chieh-li Chin (2015) remind us that the fact that data can be publicly accessible does not mean that it can be analyzed. This is the idea behind the need to respect the "perceived privacy" of Internet users, independently of data availability considerations (Eysenbach & Till, 2001). Bettina Hoser and Tanka Nitschke (2010) frame the issue nicely:

> In ancient Japan, where walls within houses were mostly made of rice paper (shoji), this society created a code of conduct that did not allow to listen to the neighbors' family conversation even if it was clearly audible. Thus, the private sphere was respected.

Finally, let's turn to mobile phone apps for the study of personal networks from an ethics point of view. The advantages of conducting research with an app installed on the participants' smartphones are undeniable: it is theoretically possible to combine pop-up small surveys with logs of activity (calendar, email, social media), while keeping track of mobility patterns. Jürgen Lerner and his associates (Lerner, Lubbers, Molina & Brandes, 2014) pointed out the ability of apps to generate both cognitive and behavioral data. Tetsuro Kobayashi and Jeffrey Boase (2012) conducted research in Japan intended to compare the frequency of mobile phone use as measured by self-report questions of respondents ($N$ = 310) with log data that were automatically collected through an Android smartphone application. The results show a systematic overestimation of the perceived frequency of use in self-reports when compared with activity logs. In another paper (Boase, 2013), the same Jeffrey Boase explains the difficulties that hinder the effective use of this approach. First, smartphones contain multiple applications with multiple configurations, adding another layer of complexity to the data collection process. Second, it is important to collect contextual information about how different affordances are used, which can just be done through observation, focus groups, or other qualitative methods. Finally, privacy issues are in this case of paramount importance because connections, communications, and places are systematically collected. In this regard, it is instructive to present the set of solutions that W. Scott Comulada (2014) applied when facing those concerns in his study about HIV transmission, which included 12 gay men actively giving data through their mobiles phones on a daily basis.

> Phone logs were recorded through SystemSens (*https://github.com/falaki/SystemSens*), an Android application. . . . Once installed, SystemSens automatically encrypted and uploaded phone-log data (including phone numbers, the duration, and date / time stamp of incoming and outgoing calls and text messages) to servers at UCLA whenever the user charged their phone. To protect the identity of phone numbers belonging to individuals who were not enrolled in the study, all phone numbers in the phone log were scrambled using SHA-256, a cryptographic hash function. . . . Hashed numbers appear as unique 256-bit values, e.g. "b8 475260a8bdd4af2984d7d7d8eb9b5a." As a result, one is able to identify if two hashed numbers are of the same phone number. However, it is nearly impossible to recover the original phone number from a hashed number alone. The original phone number is necessary to act as a key that unscrambles the hashed number and verifies the original number.

This research is a good example of how it is possible to collect detailed sensible personal data and at the same time provide reasonable protection to participants.

Another approach to this problem is simply to develop a system that only users can control. The delivery of the data to the researchers would take place as a free personal choice (the Android app "Social Capital Companion" was developed under this concept: *http://algo.uni-konstanz.de/software/scc*).

Before moving on to the next section, it is important to consider the assumption made by some of the authors reviewed in these sections that behavioral data are "true" and "real," whereas cognitive data are "biased" or "incomplete." Although both behaviors and perceptions are valid measurements, depending on what we want to know, we are measuring different domains of human life. Moreover, cognitive data about our personal networks can be as accurate as behavioral-based measures of human interaction, as Rossana Mastrandrea and her associates (Mastrandrea et al., 2015) demonstrate through comparison of the social networks of French high school students obtained by (1) wearable devices and diaries, (2) questionnaires, and (3) Facebook. The results show that, despite the differences between each method, the *overall structure* reported was the same (see also Section 3.3). Clearly, the combination of different sources of information opens new avenues of future inquiry.

## 14.5 MANAGING AND PUBLISHING PERSONAL NETWORK DATA

Most funding agencies now request publication of raw research data after a reasonable period of time. For instance, the National Science Foundation (Award and Administration Guide Chapter VI.D.4.) states:

> Investigators are expected to share with other researchers, at no more than incremental cost and within a reasonable time, the primary data, samples, physical collections and other supporting materials created or gathered in the course of work under NSF grants. Grantees are expected to encourage and facilitate such sharing. Privileged or confidential information should be released only in a form that protects the privacy of individuals and subjects involved.

In Europe, the network OpenAire (*www.openaire.eu*) is the tool of the European Commission for achieving the same goal of open science. This network provides services for storing and anonymizing personal data. This anonymization is normally achieved by replacing direct identifiers by codes, by aggregating variables or reducing the level of detail of existing ones, by using wider geographical identifiers, and so on. In this regard, the Data Management Plan (DMP) contains details about how the research data will be collected, stored, and shared. Many templates are available at universities and research institutes, and some of them offer online tools. For instance, the main DMP sections in the online tool recommended by the network OpenAire are as follows (*https://dmponline.dcc.ac.uk*) (DCC, 2013):

1. Data Collection
2. Documentation and Metadata
3. Ethics and Legal Compliance
4. Storage and Backup
5. Selection and Preservation
6. Data Sharing
7. Responsibilities and Resources

The development of this DMP at the beginning of research will help researchers to inform participants more precisely about the intended uses of the data and the measures adopted for protecting their right to anonymity. In many cases around the world, descriptions of the files containing personal data have to be submitted to a data protection authority. This allows participants in the research to edit, modify, or delete their personal data using the formal procedures set down by the data protection laws. The consent forms grant these rights anyway.

Careful reflection about what data will be collected, stored, and shared is especially important when the research takes place in risky environments. In those cases, researchers have to be aware that confidential data can be eventually requested by a justice court, which can lead to the disclosure of participants' identities. Although conducting scientific research in these environments is totally legitimate (Fitzgerald & Hamilton, 1996), the promise of full confidentiality cannot be sustained because researchers cannot plead to be under a legal confidentiality clause, like other professions can. In these cases, the collection of potentially incriminating data should be reduced to the minimum of the research goals, and the DMP should contain additional data protection measures such as on-site automatic anonymization, encrypted transfer to secure servers, and deletion of local files or documents. In addition, an appropriate incidental findings policy should be developed describing the actions that would be taken in hypothetical cases, such as witnessing a minor crime. Again, the concept of "incidental finding" comes from the biomedical field (Ells & Thombs, 2014), where during the research, patients have the right to know or not know about new or more accurate diagnoses. In our case, this policy implies the definition of a threshold for reporting findings to authorities or appropriate institutions. This threshold should be made clear to participants. The IRB/REC's final approval is a necessary safeguard in this type of research.

Publication and dissemination can be other sources of confidentiality disclosure. Possibly the most famous case in this regard is Carolyn Ellis's *Fisher Folk (1986)* (Kaiser, 2009), an ethnographic research of a small community. Once the book was published and despite the pseudonyms used by the author, the *same participants* could identify the testimonies given by other neighbors in her account, leading to tense relationships within the community. This example shows that this phase of the research also needs careful planning. In this vein, it is useful to distinguish between *internal confidential-*

*ity* (when the recipients are members of the community) and *external confidentiality* (described so far) (Tolich, 2004).

The first issue to be considered is the need to tailor the communication (and the details released) to the different audiences (i.e., the participant, the community, academics, or the society in general) in a way that cannot be considered disruptive or harmful. In this regard, it is important to consult with close insiders previous to the publication or dissemination event. This consultation will detect information that can be considered trivial for the researchers but damaging for specific individuals or the community.

The second issue centers on what can or cannot be published. At the beginning of this chapter, we summarized three tenets of scientific research, the first of which was to benefit or at least do no harm to the individuals or population under study. If researchers, after taking all preventive actions at their disposal, cannot ensure the safety or anonymity of participants, they should refrain from making the details public or they should postpone publication until the conditions allow it.

The third issue concerns ways to deal with verbatim testimonies and personal network visualizations. It is good practice to include an option in the consent form about whether the participants agree that verbatim transcriptions of their interviews can be published in an anonymized way. In this case, and when possible, participants could be consulted about specific fragments of the publication showing these transcriptions. It has been our experience that participants, even when they send minor corrections to the researchers, answer only about half of these types of requests.

### *Doing Network Research in Organizational Settings*

Research in organizations poses specific ethical concerns, which are aggravated by the nature of social network research. Management in organizations (and especially in corporations) are interested in gaining full access to the data collected, especially if the research is conducted as part of an organizational development contract. In practice, this access suspends the right to anonymity and the employee's right to freely participate or opt out. In order to overcome these difficulties, Stephen Borgatti and José Luis Molina (2005) suggested a set of realistic measures for doing network research in organizational settings.

The first measure they presented is to have a Management Disclosure Contract (MDC) signed by the researchers and the organization. This contract stipulates that the company will have access to the full dataset under the following conditions: (1) participants have the right to access and correct, if necessary, their own data; and (2) this data will not be used for individual assessments.

The second measure is to have a Truly Informed Consent form signed, which explains the previous MDC, elucidates how personal names will be available, gives the option of "no participate" (removing the name of the person from the survey rosters), and grants personalized feedback about the ego network. Borgatti and Molina include templates of both documents in their appendix.

Finally, to prevent identifications, personal network visualizations should not include labels with personal names or even detailed geographical information, except when the recipient is the same participant or the research team for analytic purposes. As we mentioned earlier, personal network visualizations are highly valued by all participants, whether they are recent migrants, entrepreneurs, or managers. Nevertheless, in institutional settings, the agreement with the organization should be devised in such a way that no personal network identifiers will be displayed or used for individual assessment purposes.

## CHAPTER SUMMARY

Social research is increasingly being regulated by norms and practices inspired mostly by biomedical principles, such as the obligation to gain individual informed consent and to have contingency plans for "incidental findings." In addition, the new regulations on personal data protection, as well as the wealth of personal data easily available on the Internet, pose new ethics challenges to researchers. In addition, funding authorities are now requesting DMPs in order to manage the whole cycle of research data, ranging from collection, storage, and analysis to publication and reuse. What is true for social research in general also applies for personal network analysis, where egos elicit alters for whom informed consent cannot be gained, nor can they opt out of the research. One way to address this issue is to ask the ego to use nicknames for his or her alters that are easy to remember and to keep information secure, confidential, or anonymized in a nonreversible way after a reasonable period of embargo. Finally, it is ironic that research ethics governance (IRBs and RECs) does not apply to the companies that own most of the personal data of the planet.

### FURTHER READING

Borgatti, S. P., & Molina, J. L. (2005). Toward ethical guidelines for network research in organizations. *Social Networks, 27*(2), 107–117.

Israel, M. (2015). *Research ethics and integrity for social scientists: Beyond regulatory compliance.* London: SAGE.

Kadushin, C. (2005). Who benefits from network analysis: Ethics of social network research. *Social Networks, 27*(2), 139–153.

Scott, G. (2008). "They got their program, and I got mine": A cautionary tale concerning the ethical implications of using respondent-driven sampling to study injection drug users. *International Journal of Drug Policy, 19*(1), 42–51.

**Appendix**

# Software

In this appendix we list some of the software that has been specifically designed for collecting and analyzing personal network data and that we find particularly useful. The list is not exhaustive.

**Anamia Egocenter** (*https://github.com/Bodyspacesociety/ANAMIA-Egocenter*)

ANAMIA Egocenter (Tubaro et al., 2013) is a program for collecting personal network data based on a graphical interface, to be embedded in a computer-based survey. It was developed in the framework of the French ANAMIA (*www.anamia.fr*) project by Paola Tubaro, Antonio Casilli, and colleagues about persons with eating disorders, which needed a name generator that could be easily self-administered.

**EgoNet** (*https://sourceforge.net/projects/egonet*)

EgoNet is a Java-compatible program for the collection and analysis of personal network data, distributed under a general non-profit (GNP) license. It was created by Christopher McCarty at the University of Florida and developed by Martin Smith, with contributions from other researchers. EgoNet includes two modes: (1) The study design tool helps users create a personal network questionnaire, and (2) the interviewing and analysis tool allows users to collect data with computer-assisted personal interviews, to visualize personal networks immediately after completing an interview, and to compute summary network measures. Data matrices can be exported for further analysis by other software. In addition, EgoNet allows users to combine multiple personal networks into a single whole network by fuzzy matching names of alters and egos from different networks. Finally, EgoNet is complemented with a clustered graph and anonymization utility developed by Jürgen Lerner, from the University of Konstanz (Germany) *http://visone.info/wiki/index.php/Personal_networks_(tutorial)*.

**EgoWeb 2.0** (*http://www.qualintitative.com/wiki/doku.php/egoweb_2.0_home*)

EgoWeb is an open-source software for the collection of social network data in surveys and interviews. EgoWeb facilitates egocentric, cognitive, and whole network data collection, and allows for data to be exported into a number of other social network analysis programs. EgoWeb also produces personal network visualizations during interviews to support mixed qualitative and quantitative social network research designs. This feature is also being used as an intervention tool.

The first version of EgoWeb was based on EgoNet. In 2014, researchers of the UCLA RISE-UP project collaboratively developed EgoWeb 2.0, a PHP-based webserver application to facilitate interviewer-assisted interviews using iPad tablets and respondent-driven surveys over the Web with email recruitment invitations. Developers have continued to enhance EgoWeb 2.0 to enable collection of data on Android tablets and local installations on laptop computers. EgoWeb is currently maintained by David Kennedy at the RAND Corporation. EgoWeb data can be imported in R using the *read_egoweb* function in the *egor* package.

**E-NET** (*https://sites.google.com/site/enetsoftware1*)

E-Net is a Windows software program developed by Stephen Borgatti (Kentucky University, USA) for batch analyzing ego network data. The program is freeware and contains tools for efficiently importing network data and analyzing them using procedures taken from the social network analysis software UCINET.

**GENSI** (*www.tobiasstark.nl/GENSI*)

GENSI (Graphical Ego-centered Network Survey Interface) is available in Javascript source code. It was developed by Tobias H. Stark (Utrecht University/ICS, The Netherlands), and provides data collection designs that include a short egocentric module in larger online questionnaires (Stark & Krosnick, 2017). The program facilitates the elicitation of alters, alter characteristics, and alter–alter ties, and presents respondents with a visualization of the resulting network. GENSI is particularly suitable for the collection of relatively small personal networks (up to eight alters) in large online surveys.

**Network Canvas** (*http://networkcanvas.com*)

Network Canvas is an ongoing open-source project led by a team of researchers from the Institute for Sexual and Gender Minority Health and Wellbeing at Northwestern University, with research partners at the University of Oxford, Johns Hopkins University, and Emory University. Network Canvas aims to capture data about both individuals and their social networks through intuitive and engaging interfaces. Through its three components—Architect, Server, and the survey application itself—researchers can design surveys and capture data in an interactive way about both their participants and the people and places with whom participants interact. Windows, Mac, Android and iOS are all supported.

**NodeXL** (*www.smrfoundation.org/nodexl*)

NodeXL is an Excel template for analyzing and visualizing social networks. Currently, NodeXL has two versions: NodeXL Basic and NodeXL Pro. NodeXL basic is a free, open-source template intended for Excel users (from 2007 to 2016) without programming experience. The user has just to introduce a list of edges, and the network visualization will appear on screen or import the data from a variety of sources, including social media sites such as Twitter, YouTube, and Flickr.

NodeXL Pro is a fee version of NodeXL Basic, with enhanced access to social media network data streams, advanced network analysis measures, text, time series and sentiment analysis, programming capabilities with .NET libraries, and assisted report generation.

**OpenEddi** (*www.openeddi.com*)

OpenEddi is a free, open source data collection platform that is being developed by Kate Eddens and Jesse Fagan (cf. Eddens, Fagan and Collins, 2017), with social network data (complete and personal networks) in mind. The program facilitates the elicitation of alters via name generators, their characteristics, and alter–alter ties using network visualization. The web program can be installed on tablets or other mobile devices and caches locally. Data can be synced when connected to wifi. Data can be exported to UCINET and Gephi, and can be imported in R using the *read_openeddi* function in the *egor* package.

**The R Project for Statistical Computing** (*www.r-project.org*)

R is a free, open-source, and cross-platform programming language that is specifically designed for data analysis and statistical modeling. R can be used for any type of quantitative data analysis and has quickly become a major tool for network analysis as well. While R is not used for ego-network data collection, all the analytical methods for personal networks discussed in this book can be implemented with R. The R programming language works by packages. These are collections of functions that users install and load to apply particular analytic tools. The largest repository of R packages is the Comprehensive R Archive Network (CRAN: *https://cran.r-project.org*). Two well-known (collections of) R packages for social network analysis available on CRAN are *igraph* (*http://igraph.org*) and *statnet* (*www.statnet.org*). While *igraph* is a single R package, *statnet* is a suite of interrelated packages, including *network*, *sna* and *ergm*. In many ways, *igraph* and *statnet* are overlapping in that a number of essential tasks and methods can be equivalently performed in either of them; these include importing network data, manipulating networks (e.g., deleting or adding edges and nodes), visualizing networks, and calculating basic measures such as density or centrality indices. In other respects, *igraph* and *statnet* are different and unique. For example, certain algorithms for "community detection" in complex networks are implemented in *igraph* but not in *statnet*; while exponential random graph models can be fitted with *statnet* but not with *igraph*. Although most functions and methods in *igraph* and *statnet* were developed primarily for whole networks, they can be applied to personal networks as well. In addition, measures that are specific to personal networks, such as constraint, are also implemented in these packages. At the same time, R classes such as lists, data frames, and nested data frames offer unique advantages in storing and managing personal network data.

A typical task in a personal network study consists in conducting exactly the same type of analysis on many personal networks in batch. This is particularly useful when we need to calculate network-level summary variables such as those described in Chapter 11. In the R community, this type of analysis has been called "split-apply-combine": We *split* our original data into different pieces (in our case, different ego networks), *apply* the same analysis identically and independently on each piece (i.e., for each ego), and *combine* results back into a single data object (e.g., an ego-level dataset). R offers many facilities to easily perform split–apply–combine tasks on personal network data or any type of data. These include base R functions such as *aggregate* and the apply family of functions (*lapply*, *sapply*, *mapply*, and more), and entire R packages with split–apply–combine resources, such as *plyr*, *dplyr*, and *purrr*. These tools can be used to easily conduct analyses such as those discussed in Chapter 11 on hundreds or thousands of personal networks.

As far as statistical modeling is concerned, standard linear and generalized linear models for personal networks, such as those illustrated in Chapter 12, can be fitted using base R functions like *lm* and *glm*. The more advanced statistical methods considered in Chapter 13 can be implemented with R too. Multilevel linear and generalized linear models for personal networks can be fitted using specialized packages such as *lme4*, *MCMCglmm*, or *R2MLwiN* (the latter, however, requires the proprietary software MLwiN as well). Exponential random graph models can be estimated using *statnet*'s *ergm* package; the *ergm.ego* package allows users to fit ERGMs based on ego-network data and simulate the resulting whole networks—a method examined in Chapter 13. SAO models for whole or personal networks can be estimated with the *RSiena* package.

Finally, the R package *egor* introduces a set of functions that are specifically designed to easily import, handle, and manipulate personal network data. This package allows users to quickly import data collected via other software such as EgoNet and EgoWeb 2.0; to store and easily subset and manipulate the resulting data objects; to calculate summary compositional and structural measures on all the ego networks in a database; and to obtain traditional and interactive visualizations of the imported personal networks.

**UCINET** (*https://sites.google.com/site/ucinetsoftware/home*)

UCINET 6 for Windows is the most popular software for the analysis of social network data, especially whole network analysis. Drawing on early programs developed by Linton Freeman at the University of California at Irvine (UCI), Stephen Borgatti has led the development of the software for decades, leading to the present version. UCINET comes with the NetDraw visualization tool and contains the most thorough set of social network metrics, statistical analysis, social network data management, and import/export tools, including Excel files. UCINET can be downloaded freely during 90 days and offers a student affordable fee. The software has a book companion *Analyzing Social Networks* (2nd ed.) with Internet resources and exercises (*https://sites.google.com/site/analyzingsocialnetworks/home*).

**VennMaker** (*www.vennmaker.com/?lang=en*)

The VennMaker project was led by Michael Schönhuth from the University of Trier (Germany) in collaboration with a group of social scientists and computer scientists. The aim of this project was to develop a software tool that enables the user to interactively collect network relationships from an actor's point of view and render them comparable and quantitatively analyzable by means of a graphical user interface that can be operated intuitively. This makes the program particularly suitable to collect personal network data in a participatory way during personal interviews, but the program can also be used for structured data collection, and users can switch between the participatory and the structured modes. Not only can the resulting network data and the visualization be saved and further processed, but the network creation procedure can also be digitally recorded as a network movie and may be further processed and validated. The tool can be used for both research and consulting purposes.

**visone** (*www.visone.info*)

The first stable version of visone was launched in 2002 as a result of the collaboration between the Algorithms and Data Structures Group and the Domestic Politics and Public Administration Group from the University of Konstanz (Germany), led by Ulrik Brandes and Dorothea Wagner, and since then the program has been evolving continuously. Visone has an interactive graphic interface that allows drawing networks easily, compute structural network measures, and develop powerful visualizations, including movies for temporal series. In addition, visone imports and exports standard formats of social network data, including formats intended for publication like PDF or SVG. From 2010, visone can be used also as an interface with RSiena. Visone is also integrated with EgoNet through the clustered graphs tools (see: *http://visone.info/wiki/index.php/Personal_networks_(tutorial)*) which can be displayed in visone.

# References


Adler Lomnitz, L. (1977). *Networks and marginality: Life in a Mexican shantytown*. New York: Academic Press.

Aldous, J., & Straus, M. A. (1966). Social networks and conjugal roles: A test of Bott's hypothesis. *Social Forces, 44*(4), 576–580.

Alvesson, M., & Sandberg, J. (2013). *Constructing research questions: Doing interesting research*. London: SAGE.

Armitage, N. (2016). The Biographical Network Method. *Sociological Research Online, 21*(2).

Association of Social Anthropologists of the UK and the Commonwealth (ASA). (2011). Ethical guidelines for good research practice. Retrieved from *www.theasa.org/downloads/ASA%20ethics%20guidelines%202011.pdf*.

Axhausen, K. W. (2009). *Social network geographies and travel*. Paper presented at the Third Workshop, Frontiers in Transportation, Niagara on the Lake, Canada.

Barnes, J. A. (1954). Class and committees in a Norwegian island parish. *Human Relations, 7*(1), 39–58.

Barrera, M. (1980). A method for the assessment of social support networks in community survey research. *Connections, 3*, 8–13.

Bashi Treitler, V. F. (2007). *Survival of the knitted: Immigrant social networks in a stratified world*. Stanford, CA: Stanford University Press.

Bearman, P., & Parigi, P. (2004). Cloning headless frogs and other important matters: Conversation topics and network structure. *Social Forces, 83*(2), 535–557.

Beggs, J. J., Haines, V. A., & Hurlbert, J. S. (2010). Revisiting the rural-urban contrast: Personal networks in nonmetropolitan and metropolitan settings. *Rural Sociology, 61*(2), 306–325.

Bell, K. (2014). Resisting commensurability: Against informed consent as an anthropological virtue. *American Anthropologist, 116*(3), 511–522.

Bellotti, E. (2015). Talking ties: Micro-processes of local structures in friendship networks. In *Qualitative networks: Mixed methods in sociological research* (pp. 77–107). New York: Routledge.

Bengtsson, L., Lu, X., Thorson, A., Garfield, R., & von Schreeb, J. (2011). Improved response to disasters and outbreaks by tracking population movements with mobile phone network data: A post-earthquake geospatial study in Haiti. *PLOS Medicine, 8*(8), e1001083.

Berkman, L. F., & Glass, T. (2000). Social integration, social networks, social support, and health. In L. F. Berkman & I. Kawachi (Eds.), *Social epidemiology* (pp. 137–173). New York: Oxford University Press.

Berkman, L. F., Glass, T., Brissette, I., & Seeman, T. E. (2000). From social integration to health: Durkheim in the new millennium. *Social Science and Medicine, 51*(6), 843–857.

Bernard, H. R. (2006). *Research methods in anthropology. Qualitative and quantitative approaches*. Lanham, MD: AltaMira Press.

Bernard, H. R., Johnsen, E. C., Killworth, P. D., McCarty, C., Shelley, G. A., & Robinson, S.

(1990). Comparing four different methods for measuring personal social networks. *Social Networks, 12*(3), 179–215.

Bernard, H. R., & Killworth, P. D. (1973). On the social structure of an ocean-going research vessel and other important things. *Social Science Research, 2*, 145–184.

Bernard, H. R., & Killworth, P. D. (1977). Informant accuracy in Social Network Data II. *Human Communication Research, 4*(1), 3–18.

Bernardi, L. (2011). A mixed-methods social networks study design for research on transnational families. *Journal of Marriage and Family, 73*(4), 788–803.

Berrou, J.-P., & Combarnous, F. (2012). The personal networks of entrepreneurs in an informal African urban economy: Does the "Strength of Ties" matter? *Review of Social Economy, 70*(1), 1–30.

Bidart, C. (2017). *L'amitié, un lien social*. Paris: Éditions La Découverte.

Bidart, C., & Charbonneau, J. (2011). How to generate personal networks: Issues and tools for a sociological perspective. *Field Methods, 23*(3), 266–286.

Bidart, C., Degenne, A., & Grossetti, M. (2011). *La vie en réseau: Dynamique des relations sociales*. Paris: Presses Universitaires de France.

Bidart, C., Degenne, A., & Grossetti, M. (2018). Personal networks typologies: A structural approach. *Social Networks, 54*, 1–11.

Bidart, C., & Lavenu, D. (2005). Evolutions of personal networks and life events. *Social Networks, 27*(4), 359–376.

Bilecen, B., Gamper, M., & Lubbers, M. J. (2018). The missing link: Social network analysis in migration and transnationalism. *Social Networks, 53*, 1–3.

Blau, P. M. (1977). A macrosociological theory of social structure. *American Journal of Sociology, 83*(1), 26–54.

Blondel, V. D., Decuyper, A., & Krings, G. (2015). A survey of results on mobile phone datasets analysis. *EPJ Data Science, 4*(1), 10.

Boase, J. (2013). Implications of software-based mobile media for social research. *Mobile Media and Communication, 1*(1), 57–62.

Boase, J., & Ikeda, K. (2012). Core discussion networks in Japan and America. *Human Communication Research, 38*(1), 95–119.

Boissevain, J. (1974). *Friends of friends: Networks, manipulators and coalitions*. Oxford, UK: Blackwell.

Borgatti, S. P., Everett, M. G., & Johnson, J. C. (2013). *Analyzing social networks*. Thousand Oaks, CA: SAGE.

Borgatti, S. P., & Molina, J.-L. (2005). Toward ethical guidelines for network research in organizations. *Social Networks, 27*(2), 107–117.

Bost, K. K., Cox, M. J., Burchinal, M. R., & Payne, C. (2002). Structural and supportive changes in couples' family and friendship networks across the transition to parenthood. *Journal of Marriage and Family, 64*, 517–531.

Bott, E. (1956). Urban families: Conjugal roles and social networks. *Human Relations, 9*, 325–342.

Bott, E. (1957). *Family and social networks*. London: Tavistock Institute of Human Relations.

Brandes, U., Kenis, P., & Raab, J. (2005). La explicación a través de la visualización de Redes. *REDES—Revista Hispana Para El Análisis de Redes Sociales, 9*(6), 1–19.

Brandes, U., Lerner, J., Lubbers, M. J., McCarty, C., & Molina, J. L. (2008). Visual statistics for collections of clustered graphs. In *IEEE Pacific Visualisation Symposium 2008, PacificVisualisation Proceedings* (pp. 47–54).

Brandes, U., Lerner, J., Lubbers, M. J., McCarty, C., Molina, J. L., & Nagel, U. (2010). Recognizing modes of acculturation in personal networks of migrants. *Procedia: Social and Behavioral Sciences, 4*, 4–13.

Brashears, M. E. (2013). Humans use compression heuristics to improve the recall of social networks. *Scientific Reports, 3*(1513), 1–7.

Brashears, M. E., & Quintane, E. (2014). The microstructures of network recall: How social networks are encoded and represented in human memory. *Social Networks, 41*, 113–126.

Brewer, D. D. (1997). No associative biases in the first name cued recall procedure for eliciting personal networks. *Social Networks, 19*(4), 345–353.

Brewer, D. D. (2000). Forgetting in the recall-based elicitation of personal and social networks. *Social Networks, 22*(1), 29–43.

Broadhead, W. E., Gehlbach, S. H., de Gruy, F. V, & Kaplan, B. H. (1988). The Duke-UNC Functional Social Support Questionnaire: Measurement of social support in family medicine patients. *Medical Care, 26*(7), 709–723.

Broese van Groenou, M., & van Tilburg, T. (1996). Network analysis. In J. E. Birren (Ed.),

*Encyclopedia of gerontology: Age, aging, and the aged.* San Diego, CA: Academic Press.

Brooks, B., Hogan, B., Ellison, N., Lampe, C., & Vitak, J. (2014). Assessing structural correlates to social capital in Facebook ego networks. *Social Networks, 38,* 1–15.

Burt, R. S. (1983). Distinguishing relational contents. In R. S. Burt & M. J. Minor (Eds.), *Applied network analysis: A methodological introduction* (pp. 35–74). Beverly Hills, CA: SAGE.

Burt, R. S. (1984). Network items and the General Social Survey. *Social Networks, 6*(4), 293–339.

Burt, R. S. (2000). The network structure of social capital. *Research in Organizational Behavior, 22,* 345–423.

Cachia, R. (2014). *Connected lives in contemporary mobile societies.* Doctoral dissertation, University of Seville, Spain.

Cachia, R., & Maya Jariego, I. (2018). Mobility types, transnational ties and personal networks in four highly skilled immigrant communities in Seville (Spain). *Social Networks, 53,* 111–124.

Campbell, K. E., & Lee, B. A. (1992). Sources of personal neighbor networks: Social integration, need, or time? *Social Forces, 70,* 1077–1100.

Cantor, M. H. (1975). Life space and the social support system of the inner city elderly of New York. *The Gerontologist, 15*(1 Part 1), 23–27.

Carrasco, J. A. (2011). Personal network maintenance, face-to-face interaction, and distance. *Transportation Research Record: Journal of the Transportation Research Board, 2231,* 120–128.

Carrasco, J. A., & Cid-Aguayo, B. (2012). Network capital, social networks, and travel: An empirical illustration from Concepción, Chile. *Environment and Planning A, 44*(5), 1066–1084.

Carrasco, J. A., Hogan, B., Wellman, B., & Miller, E. J. (2004). Collecting social network data to study social activity-travel behaviour: An egocentred approach. *Environment and Planning B: Planning and Design, 35*(6), 961–980.

Carrasco, J. A., & Miller, E. J. (2009). The social dimension in action: A multilevel, personal networks model of social activity frequency between individuals. *Transportation Research Part A: Policy and Practice, 43*(1), 90–104.

Christakis, N. A., & Fowler, J. H. (2007). The spread of obesity in a large social network over 32 years. *New England Journal of Medicine, 357*(4), 370–379.

Christakis, N. A., & Fowler, J. H. (2013). Social contagion theory: Examining dynamic social networks and human behavior. *Statistics in Medicine, 32*(4), 556–577.

Chua, V., Madej, J., & Wellman, B. (2011). Personal communities: The world according to me. In J. Scott & P. Carrington (Eds.), *The SAGE handbook of social network analysis.* London: SAGE.

Cobb, S. (1976). Social support as a moderator of life stress. *Psychosomatic Medicine, 38,* 300–314.

Cohen, S., Doyle, W. J., Skoner, D. P., Rabin, B. S., & Gwaltney, J. M., Jr. (1997). Social ties and susceptibility to the common cold. *JAMA, 277*(24), 1940–1944.

Cohen, S., & Janicki-Deverts, D. (2009). Can we improve our physical health by altering our social networks? *Perspectives on Psychological Science, 4*(4), 375–378.

Cohen, S., Underwood, G. L., & Gottlieb, B. H. (2000). *Social support measurement and intervention: A guide for health and social scientists.* Oxford, UK: Oxford University Press.

Cohen, S., & Wills, T. A. (1985). Stress, social support and the buffering hypothesis. *Psychological Bulletin, 98*(2), 310–357.

Coleman, J. S. (1988). Social capital in the creation of human capital. *American Journal of Sociology, 94,* 95–120.

Comulada, W. S. (2014). Mobile phone assessment in egocentric networks: A pilot study on gay men and their peers. *Connections, 34*(1), 43–51.

Cornwell, B., Laumann, E. O., & Schumm, L. P. (2011). The social connectedness of older adults: A national profile. *American Sociological Review, 4*(164), 185–203.

Cowan, S. K., & Baldassarri, D. (2018). "It could turn ugly": Selective disclosure of attitudes in political discussion networks. *Social Networks, 52,* 1–17.

Crossley, N., Bellotti, E., Edwards, G., Everett, M., & Koskinen, J. (2015). *Social network analysis for EgoNets.* London: SAGE.

Cuellar, I., Arnold, B., & Maldonado, R. (1995). Acculturation Rating Scale for Mexican Americans—II: A revision of the original ARSMA Scale. *Hispanic Journal of Behavioral Sciences, 17*(3), 275–304.

Dahinden, J. (2005). Contesting transnationalism?: Lessons from the Study of Albanian Migration Networks from Former Yugoslavia. *Global Networks, 5*(2), 191–208.

Dahinden, J. (2009). Are we all transnationals now?: Network transnationalism and transnational subjectivity: The differing impacts of globalization on the inhabitants of a small Swiss city. *Ethnic and Racial Studies, 32*, 1365–1386.

Danchev, V., & Porter, M. A. (2018). Neither global nor local: Heterogeneous connectivity in spatial network structures of world migration. *Social Networks, 53*, 4–19.

Dávid, B., Huszti, E., Barna, I., & Fu, Y. (2016). Egocentric contact networks in comparison: Taiwan and Hungary. *Social Networks, 44*, 253–265.

De la Haye, K., Green, H. D., Kennedy, D. P., Zhou, A., Golinelli, D., Wenzel, S. L., & Tucker, J. S. (2012). Who is supporting homeless youth?: Predictors of support in personal networks. *Journal of Research on Adolescence, 22*(4), 604–616.

De Miguel Luken, V., & Tranmer, M. (2010). Personal support networks of immigrants to Spain: A multilevel analysis. *Social Networks, 32*(4), 253–262.

De Montjoye, Y.-A., Hidalgo, C. A., Verleysen, M., & Blondel, V. D. (2013). Unique in the crowd: The privacy bounds of human mobility. *Scientific Reports, 3*, 1376.

De Sola Pool, I., & Kochen, M. (1978). Contacts and influence. *Social Networks, 1*(1), 5–51.

Degenne, A., & Lebeaux, M. O. (2005). The dynamics of personal networks at the time of entry into adult life. *Social Networks, 27*(4), 337–358.

Diesner, J., & Chin, C.-L. (2015). Usable ethics: Practical considerations for responsibly conducting research with social trace data. In *Workshop: Beyond IRBs: Ethical Review Processes for Big Data Research, Future of Privacy Forum*, Washington DC.

Digital Curation Center (CCC). (2013). *Checklist for a Data Management Plan: Vol. 4.0.* Edinburgh, UK: Digital Curation Centre. Retrieved from *www.dcc.ac.uk/resources/data-management-plans*.

Dillman, D. A., Smyth, J. D., & Christian, L. M. (2014). *Internet, phone,mail, and mixed-mode surveys: The tailored design method*. Hoboken, NJ: Wiley.

DiPrete, T. A., Gelman, A., McCormick, T., Teitler, J., & Zheng, T. (2011). Segregation in social networks based on acquaintanceship and trust. *American Journal of Sociology, 116*(4), 1234–1283.

Dodds, P. S., Muhamad, R., & Watts, D. J. (2003). An experimental study of search in global social networks. *Science, 301*(5634), 827–829.

Dunbar, R. I. M. (1993). Co-evolution of neocortex size, group size and language in humans. *Behavioral and Brain Sciences, 16*(4), 681–735.

Dunbar, R. I. M., Arnaboldi, V., Conti, M., & Passarella, A. (2015). The structure of online social networks mirrors those in the offline world. *Social Networks, 43*, 39–47.

Dunbar, R. I. M., & Sosis, R. (2017). Optimising human community sizes. *Evolution and Human Behavior, 39*(1), 106–111.

Eagle, D. E., & Proeschold-Bell, R.-J. (2015). Methodological considerations in the use of name generators and interpreters. *Social Networks, 40*, 75–83.

Eames, K., Bansal, S., Frost, S., & Riley, S. (2014). Six challenges in measuring contact networks for use in modelling. *Epidemics, 10*, 72–77.

Eddens, K. S., Fagan, J. M., & Collins, T. (2017). An interactive, mobile-based tool for personal social network data collection and visualization among a geographically isolated and socioeconomically disadvantaged population: Early-stage feasibility study with qualitative user feedback. *JMIR Res Protoc, 6*(6), e124.

Edwards, G., & Crossley, N. (2009). Measures and meanings: Exploring the Ego-Net of Helen Kirkpatrick Watts, militant suffragette. *Methodological Innovations Online*, 4, 37–61.

Ellison, N. B., Steinfield, C., & Lampe, C. (2011). Connection strategies: Social capital implications of Facebook-enabled communication practices. *New Media and Society, 13*(6), 873–892.

Ells, C., & Thombs, B. D. (2014). The ethics of how to manage incidental findings. *Canadian Medical Association Journal, 186*(9), 655–656.

Epstein, A. L. (1969). Gossip, norms and social networks. In C. J. Mitchell (Ed.), *Social networks in urban situations: Analyses of personal relationships in central African towns*. Manchester, UK: Manchester University Press.

Ertel, K. A., Glymour, M. M., & Berkman, L. F. (2009). Social networks and health: A life course perspective integrating observational and experimental evidence. *Journal of Social and Personal Relationships, 26*(1), 73–92.

Eveland, W. P., Appiah, O., & Beck, P. A. (2018). Americans are more exposed to difference than we think: Capturing hidden exposure to political and racial difference. *Social Networks, 52*, 192–200.

Eysenbach, G., & Till, J. E. (2001). Ethical issues in qualitative research on Internet communities. *British Medical Journal, 323*(7321), 1103–1105.

Feld, S. L. (1981). The focused organization of social ties. *American Journal of Sociology, 86*(5), 1015–1035.

Ferrand, A. (2014). Les significations des zeros dans les reseaux personnels. *Bulletin of Sociological Methodology/Bulletin de Méthodologie Sociologique, 121*(1), 10–16.

Field, A. P., Miles, J., & Field, Z. (2012). *Discovering statistics using R*. London: SAGE.

Fischer, C. S. (1982a). *To dwell among friends: Personal networks in town and city*. Chicago: University of Chicago Press.

Fischer, C. S. (1982b). What do we mean by "friend"?: An inductive study. *Social Networks, 3*, 287–306.

Fischer, C. S. (2009). The 2004 GSS Finding of Shrunken Social Networks: An artifact? *American Sociological Review, 74*(4), 657–669.

Fischer, C. S., & Shavit, Y. (1995). National differences in network density: Israel and the United States. *Social Networks, 17*(2), 129–145.

Fiske, A. P. (1995). Social schemata for remembering people: Relationships and person attributes in free recall and acquaintances. *Journal of Quantitative Anthropology, 5*, 305–324.

Fitzgerald, J., & Hamilton, M. (1996). The consequences of knowing: Ethical and legal liabilities in illicit drug research. *Social Science and Medicine, 43*(11), 1591–1600.

Fowler, F. J., Jr. (2013). *Survey research methods*. Los Angeles: SAGE.

Fowler, J. H., & Christakis, N. A. (2008). Dynamic spread of happiness in a large social network: Longitudinal analysis over 20 years in the Framingham Heart Study. *British Medical Journal, 337*, a2338.

Fox, J. (2008). *Applied regression analysis and generalized linear models* (2nd ed.). Los Angeles: SAGE.

Fratiglioni, L., Wang, H.-X., Ericsson, K., Maytan, M., & Winblad, B. (2000). Influence of social network on occurrence of dementia: A community-based longitudinal study. *The Lancet, 355*(9212), 1315–1319.

Freeman, L. C. (2004). *The development of social network analysis: A study in the sociology of science*. Vancouver, BC, Canada: Empirical Press.

Freeman, L. C. (2005). Graphic techniques for exploring social network data. In P. J. Carrington, J. Scott, & S. Wasserman (Eds.), *Models and methods in social network analysis* (pp. 248–269). Cambridge, UK: Cambridge University Press.

Freeman, L. C., & Romney, A. K. (1987). Words, deeds and social structure: A preliminary study of the reliability of informants. *Human Organization, 46*(4), 330–334.

Freeman, L. C., & Thompson, C. R. (1989). Estimating acquaintanceship volume. In M. Kochen (Ed.), *The small world* (pp. 147–158). Norwood, NJ: Ablex.

Fu, Y. C. (2005). Measuring personal networks with daily contacts: A single-item survey question and the contact diary. *Social Networks, 27*, 169–186.

Fu, Y. C. (2007). Contact diaries: Building archives of actual and comprehensive personal networks. *Field Methods, 19*(2), 194–217.

Fu, Y. C., Ho, H. C., & Chen, H. M. (2013). Weak ties and contact initiation in everyday life: Exploring contextual variations from contact diaries. *Social Networks, 35*(3), 279–287.

Fulginiti, A., Pahwa, R., Frey, L. M., Rice, E., & Brekke, J. S. (2016). What factors influence the decision to share suicidal thoughts?: A multilevel social network analysis of disclosure among individuals with serious mental illness. *Suicide and Life-Threatening Behavior, 46*(4), 398–412.

Gameiro, S., Boivin, J., Canavarro, M. C., Moura-Ramos, M., & Soares, I. (2010). Social nesting: Changes in social network and support across the transition to parenthood in couples that conceived spontaneously or through assisted reproductive technologies. *Journal of Family Psychology, 24*, 175–187.

Gariépy, H., Honkaniemi, H., & Quesnel-Vallée, A. (2016). Social support and protection from depression: Systematic review of current findings in Western countries. *British Journal of Psychiatry, 209*(4), 284–293.

Giannella, E., & Fischer, C. S. (2016). An inductive typology of egocentric networks. *Social Networks, 47*, 15–23.

Gluckman, M. (1940). Analysis of a social situation in modern Zululand. *Bantu Studies, 14*(1), 1–30.

Gluckman, M. (1958). *Analysis of a social situation in modern Zululand*. New York: Humanities Press.

Goldstein, H. (2010). *Multilevel statistical models* (4th ed.). Chichester, West Sussex, UK: Wiley.

Golinelli, D., Ryan, G., Green, H. D., Kennedy, D. P., Tucker, J. S., & Wenzel, S. L. (2010). Sampling to reduce respondent burden in personal network studies and its effect on estimates of structural measures. *Field Methods, 22*(3), 217–230.

Gordon, E. J. (2000). When oral consent will do. *Field Methods, 12*(3), 235–238.

Gordon, M., & Downing, H. (1978). A multivariate test of the Bott hypothesis in an urban Irish setting. *Journal of Marriage and the Family, 40*(3), 585–593.

Granovetter, M. (1973). The strength of weak ties. *American Journal of Sociology, 78*(6), 1360–1380.

Granovetter, M. S. (1974/1995). *Getting a job: A study of contacts and careers* (2nd ed.) Chicago: University of Chicago Press.

Green, H. D., De la Haye, K., Tucker, J. S., & Golinelli, D. (2013). Shared risk: Who engages in substance use with American homeless youth? *Addiction, 108*(9), 1618–1624.

Green, H. D., Jr., Hoover, M. A., Wagner, G. J., Ryan, G. W., & Ssegujja, E. (2014). Measuring agreement between egos and alters: Understanding informant accuracy in personal network studies. *Field Methods, 26*(2), 126–140.

Grossetti, M. (2007). Are French networks different? *Social Networks, 29*(3), 391–404.

Grossetti, M., Barthe, J.-F., & Chauvac, N. (2011). Studying relational chains from narrative material. *Bulletin of Sociological Methodology/Bulletin de Méthodologie Sociologique, 110*(1), 11–25.

Guiaux, M., van Tilburg, T., & Broese van Groenou, M. (2007). Changes in contact and support exchange in personal networks after widowhood. *Personal Relationships, 14*(3), 457–473.

Gurevitch, M. (1961). *The social structure of acquaintanceship networks*. Cambridge, MA: Massachusetts Institute of Technology.

Hammer, M. (1984). Explorations into the meaning of social network interview data. *Social Networks, 6*(4), 341–371.

Hampton, K. N. (2007). Neighborhoods in the Network Society: The e-Neighbors Study. *Information, Communication and Society, 10*(5), 714–748.

Hampton, K. N., Sessions Goulet, L., Rainie, L., & Purcell, K. (2011). Social networking sites and our lives: How people's trust, personal relationships, and civic and political involvement are connected to their use of social networking sites and other technologies. *Pew Research Center's Internet and American Life Project, 47*(9), 85.

Harris, K. M. (2013). *The Add Health Study: Design and accomplishments*. Chapel Hill: Carolina Population Center, University of North Carolina at Chapel Hill.

Heckathorn, D. D. (1997). Respondent-driven sampling: A new approach to the study of hidden populations. *Social Problems, 44*(2), 174–199.

Heckathorn, D. D. (2002). Respondent-driven sampling II: Deriving valid population estimates from chain-referral samples of hidden populations. *Social Problems, 49*(1), 11–34.

Heidler, R., Gamper, M., Herz, A., & Esser, F. (2014). Relationship patterns in the 19th century: The friendship network in a German boys' school class from 1880 to 1881 revisited. *Social Networks, 37*(1), 1–13.

Hendrikson, H. (2010). Migrant social networks and health care: exploring the relationship between women's social networks and migrant health care access in the United States. *International Journal of Migration, Health and Social Care, 6*(1), 3–14.

Hennig, M. (2007). Re-evaluating the community question from a German perspective. *Social Networks, 29*(3), 375–390.

Herz, A., Peters, L., & Truschkat, I. (2015). How to do qualitative structural analysis: The qualitative interpretation of network maps and narrative interviews. *Forum: Qualitative Social Research, 16*(1), 9.

Hill, R., & Dunbar, R. (2003). Social network size in humans. *Human Nature, 14*(1), 53–72.

Hofstra, B., Corten, R., van Tubergen, F., & Ellison, N. B. (2017). Sources of segregation in social networks: A novel approach using Facebook. *American Sociological Review, 82*, 625–656.

Hogan, B. (2009). From each according to media?: Testing Wellman's theory of networked individualism. In *Conference Papers: American Sociological Association* (p. 1 ).

Hogan, B., Carrasco, J. A., & Wellman, B. (2007). Visualizing personal networks: Working with participant-aided sociograms. *Field Methods, 19*(2), 116–144.

Hogan, B., Melville, J. R., Phillips, G. L., II, Janulis, P., Contractor, N., Mustanski, B. S., & Birkett, M. (2016). Evaluating the paper-to-screen translation of participant-aided sociograms with high-risk participants. In *Proceedings of the 2016 CHI Conference on Human Factors in Computing Systems—CHI'16*, San Jose, CA.

Hollstein, B. (2014a). Mixed methods social network research: An introduction. In S. Domínguez & B. Hollstein (Eds.), *Mixed methods social networks research: Design and applications* (pp. 3 –34). Cambridge, UK: Cambridge University Press.

Hollstein, B. (2014b). Qualitative approaches. In *The SAGE handbook of social network analysis* (pp. 404–416). London: SAGE.

Hollstein, B., & Wagemann, C. (2014). Fuzzy-set analysis of network data as mixed method: Personal networks and the transition from school to work. In S. Dominguez & B. Hollstein (Eds.), *Mixed methods social networks research: Design and applications* (pp. 237–268). Cambridge, MA: Cambridge University Press.

Hoover, M. A., Green, H. D., Bogart, L. M., Wagner, G. J., Mutchler, M. G., Galvan, F. H., & McDavitt, B. (2016). Do people know i'm Poz?: Factors associated with knowledge of serostatus among HIV-positive African Americans' social network members. *AIDS and Behavior, 20*(1), 137–146.

Hoser, B., & Nitschke, T. (2010). Questions on ethics for research in the virtually connected world. *Social Networks, 32*(3), 180–186.

Hosnedlová, R. (2017). Ties that bother—ties that matter. *Bulletin de Méthodologie Sociologique, 133*(1), 29–45.

House, J. S., Landis, K. R., & Umberson, D. (1988). Social relationships and health. *Science, 241*(4865), 540–545.

Huszti, É., Dávid, B., & Vajda, K. (2013). Strong tie, weak tie and in-betweens: A continuous measure of tie strength based on contact diary datasets. *Procedia: Social and Behavioral Sciences, 79*, 38–61.

Ibsen, C. A., & Klobus, P. (1972). Fictive kin term use and social relationships: Alternative interpretations. *Journal of Marriage and the Family, 34*(4), 615–620.

Jackson, P. R. (1988). Personal networks, support mobilization, and unemployment. *Psychological Medicine, 18*, 397–404.

Johnson, R. A., & Wichern, D. W. (2007). *Applied multivariate statistical analysis*. Upper Saddle River, NJ: Prentice Hall.

Kadushin, C. (2005). Who benefits from network analysis: Ethics of social network research. *Social Networks, 27(2)*, 139–153.

Kahn, R. L., & Antonucci, T. C. (1980). Convoys over the life course: Attachment, roles, and social support. In P. B. Baltes & O. Brim (Eds.), *Life-span development and behavior* (pp. 253–286). New York: Academic Press.

Kaiser, K. (2009). Protecting respondent confidentiality in qualitative research. *Qualitative Health Research, 19*(11), 1632–1641.

Kalish, Y., & Robins, G. (2006). Psychological predispositions and network structure: The relationship between individual predispositions, structural holes and network closure. *Social Networks, 28*(1), 56–84.

Kandel, D. B. (1996). The parental and peer contexts of adolescent deviance: An algebra of interpersonal influences. *Journal of Drug Issues, 26*(2), 289–315.

Kennedy, D. P., Hunter, S. B., Osilla, K. C., Maksabedian, E., Golinelli, D., & Tucker, J. S. (2016). A computer-assisted motivational social network intervention to reduce alcohol, drug and HIV risk behaviors among housing first residents. *Addiction Science and Clinical Practice, 11*(1), 4.

Kennedy, D. P., Wenzel, S. L., Brown, R., Tucker, J. S., & Golinelli, D. (2013). Unprotected sex among heterosexually active homeless men: Results from a multi-level dyadic analysis. *AIDS and Behavior, 17*(5), 1655–1667.

Killworth, P. D., & Bernard, H. R. (1978). The reversal small-world experiment. *Social Networks, 1*(2), 159–192.

Killworth, P. D., McCarty, C., Johnsen, E., & Bernard, H. R. (2006). Investigating the variation of personal network size under unknown error conditions. *Sociological Methods and Research, 35*(1), 84–112.

Klovdahl, A. S. (2005). Social network research and human subjects protection: Towards more effective infectious disease control. *Social Networks, 27*(2), 119–137.

Klovdahl, A. S., Potterat, J. J., Woodhouse, D. E., Muth, J. B., Muth, S. Q., & Darrow, W. W. (1994). Social Networks and Infectious Disease: The Colorado Springs Study. *Social Science and Medicine, 38*(1), 79–88.

Knoke, D. H., & Yang, S. (2007). *Social network analysis* (2nd ed.). Los Angeles: SAGE.

Kobayashi, T., & Boase, J. (2012). No such effect?: The implications of measurement error in self-report measures of mobile communication use. *Communication Methods and Measures*, 6(2), 1–17.

Kogovšek, T., Coenders, G., & Hlebec, V. (2013). Predictors and outcomes of social network compositions: A compositional structural equation modeling approach. *Social Networks, 35*(1), 1–10.

Kogovšek, T., Ferligoj, A., Coenders, G., & Saris, W. E. (2002). Estimating the reliability and validity of personal support measures: Full information ML estimation with planned incomplete data. *Social Networks, 24*(1), 1–20.

Kowald, M., Van Den Berg, P., Frei, A., Carrasco, J.-A., Arentze, T., Axhausen, K., et al. (2013). Distance patterns of personal networks in four countries: A comparative study. *Journal of Transport Geography, 31*, 236–248.

Krackhardt, D., & Kilduff, M. (1999). Whether close or far: Perceptions of balance in friendship networks in organizations. *Journal of Personality and Social Psychology, 76*, 770–782.

Krackhardt, D., & Stern, R. (1988). Informal networks and organizational crises: An experimental simulation. *Social Psychology Quarterly, 51*, 123–140.

Kramer, A. D. I., Guillory, J. E., & Hancock, J. T. (2014). Experimental evidence of massive-scale emotional contagion through social networks. *Proceedings of the National Academy of Sciences of the USA, 111*(24), 8788–8790.

Krivitsky, P. N., & Morris, M. (2017). Inference for social network models from egocentrically-sampled data, with application to understanding persistent racial disparities in HIV prevalence in the US. *Annals of Applied Statistics 11*(1), 1–31.

Lambiotte, R., Blondel, V. D., de Kerchove, C., Huens, E., Prieur, C., Smoreda, Z., & Van Dooren, P. (2008). Geographical dispersal of mobile communication networks. *Physica A: Statistical Mechanics and Its Applications, 387*(1), 5317–5325.

Landecker, H., & Panofsky, A. (2013). From social structure to gene regulation, and back: A critical introduction to environmental epigenetics for sociology. *Annual Review of Sociology, 39*(1), 333–357.

Latkin, C. A., Forman, V., Knowlton, A., & Sherman, S. (2003). Norms, social networks, and HIV-related risk behaviors among urban disadvantaged drug users. *Social Science and Medicine, 56*(3), 465–476.

Latkin, C. A., Kuramoto, S. J., Davey-Rothwell, M. A., & Tobin, K. E. (2010). Social norms, social networks, and HIV risk behavior among injection drug users. *AIDS and Behavior, 14*(5), 1159–1168.

Latkin, C. A., Van Tieu, H., Fields, S., Hanscom, B. S., Connor, M., Hanscom, B., et al. (2017). Social network factors as correlates and predictors of high depressive symptoms among black men who have sex with men in HPTN 061. *AIDS and Behavior, 21*(4), 1163–1170.

Latkin, C., Mandell, W., Vlahov, D., Knowlton, A., Oziemkowska, M., & Celentano, D. (1995). Personal network characteristics as antecedents to needle-sharing and shooting gallery attendance. *Social Networks, 17*(3), 219–228.

Laumann, E. O. (1969a). Friends of urban men: An assessment of accuracy in reporting their socioeconomic attributes, mutual choice, and attitude agreement. *Sociometry, 32*(1), 54.

Laumann, E. O. (1969b). The social structure of religious and ethnoreligious groups in a metropolitan community. *American Sociological Review, 34*(2), 182–197.

Laumann, E. O. (1973). *Bonds of pluralism: The form and substance of urban social networks*. New York: Wiley.

Lazer, D., Pentland, A., Adamic, L., Aral, S., Barabasi, A. L., Brewer, D., et al. (2009). Computational social science. *Science, 323*(5915), 721–723.

Lazer, D., & Radford, J. (2017). Data ex machina: Introduction to big data. *Annual Review of Sociology, 43*(1), 19–39.

Lee, N. H. (1969). *The search for an abortionist*. Chicago: University of Chicago Press.

Leffler, A., Krannich, R. S., & Gillespie, D. L. (1986). Contact, support, and friction: Three faces of networks in community life. *Sociological Perspectives, 29*(3), 337–355.

Lerner, J., Lubbers, M. J., Molina González, J. L.,

& Brandes, U. (2014). Social capital companion: Capturing personal networks as they are lived. *Grafo Working Papers, 3*, 18–37.

Lin, N. (2001). *Social capital: A theory of social structure and action*. Cambridge, UK: Cambridge University Press.

Lin, N., & Dumin, M. (1986). Access to occupations through social ties. *Social Networks, 8*(4), 365–385.

Lin, N., & Erickson, B. (2010). *Social capital: An international research program*. Oxford, UK: Oxford University Press.

Long, J. S. (1997). *Regression models for categorical and limited dependent variables*. Thousand Oaks, CA: SAGE.

Lonkila, M. (1997). Informal exchange relations in post-soviet Russia: A comparative perspective. *Sociological Research Online, 2*(2), 1–20.

Lonkila, M. (1999). *Social networks in post-soviet Russia: Continuity and change in the every-day life of St. Petersburg teachers*. Helsinki: Kikimora.

Lonkila, M. (2004). Phone notebooks as data on personal networks. *Connections, 26*(1), 53–61.

Louch, H. (2000). Personal network integration: Transitivity and homophily in strong-tie relations. *Social Networks, 22*(1), 45–64.

Lubbers, M. J., Molina, J. L., Lerner, J., Brandes, U., Ávila, J., & McCarty, C. (2010). Longitudinal analysis of personal networks: The case of Argentinean migrants in Spain. *Social Networks, 32*(1), 91–104.

Lubbers, M. J., Molina, J. L., & McCarty, C. (2007). Personal networks and ethnic identifications: The case of migrants in Spain. *International Sociology, 22*(6), 721–741.

Lubbers, M. J., Molina, J. L., & Valenzuela, H. (2019). When networks speak volumes: Variation in the size of broader acquaintanceship networks. *Social Networks, 59*, 55–69.

Lubbers, M. J., & Valenzuela-García, H. (2018). *Social support networks of households in situations of poverty*. Manuscript submitted for publication.

Lubbers, M. J., Valenzuela-Garcia, H., & Molina, J. (2018). *Whose crisis?: Perceived network exposure to economic distress and institutional trust*. Manuscript submitted for publication.

Lusher, D., Koskinen, J., & Robins, G. (2012). *Exponential random graph models for social networks: Theory, methods, and applications*. Cambridge, UK: Cambridge University Press.

Macy, M. W., & Willer, R. (2002). From factors to actors: Computational sociology and agent-based modeling. *Annual Review of Sociology, 28*(1), 143–166.

Mann, J., Stanton, M. A., Patterson, E. M., Bienenstock, E. J., & Singh, L. O. (2012). Social networks reveal cultural behaviour in tool-using dolphins. *Nature Communications, 3*(1), 980.

Marin, A. (2004). Are respondents more likely to list alters with certain characteristics? *Social Networks, 26*(4), 289–307.

Marin, A., & Hampton, K. N. (2007). Simplifying the personal network name generator: Alternatives to traditional multiple and single name generators. *Field Methods, 19*(2), 163–193.

Markham, A., & Buchanan, E. (2017). Research ethics in context: Decision-making in digital research. In M. T. Schäfer & K. van Es (Eds.), *The Datafied Society: Studying culture through data* (pp. 201–209). Amsterdam: Amsterdam University Press.

Marques, E. (2009). ¿Como son las redes de los individuos en situación de Pobreza en el Brasil urbano? *Revista REDES, 18*(1), 220–251.

Marsden, P., & Campbell, K. (1984). Measuring tie strength. *University of North Carolina Press, 63*(2), 482–501.

Marsden, P. V. (1987). Core discussion networks of americans. *American Sociological Review, 52*(1), 122–131.

Marsden, P. V. (1990). Network data and measurement. *Annual Review of Sociology, 16*, 435–463.

Marsden, P. V. (2003). Interviewer effects in measuring network size using a single name generator. *Social Networks, 25*(1), 1–16.

Martí, J., Bolíbar, M., & Lozares, C. (2017). Network cohesion and social support. *Social Networks, 48*, 192–201.

Maryanski, A., & Ishii-Kuntz, M. (1991). A cross-species application of Bott's hypothesis on role segregation and social networks. *Sociological Perspectives, 34*(4), 403–425.

Mastrandrea, R., Fournet, J., & Barrat, A. (2015). Contact patterns in a high school: A comparison between data collected using wearable sensors, contact diaries and friendship surveys. *PLOS ONE* 10(9), e0136497.

Maya-Jariego, I., & Holgado, D. (2005). Lazos Fuertes y Proveedores Múltiples de Apoyo:

Comparación de Dos Formas de Representación Gráfica de las Redes Personales. *Empiria. Revista de Metodología de Ciencias Sociales, 10*, 107–127.

Maya-Jariego, I., Holgado Ramos, D., & Florido del Corral, D. (2016). Relations between professional groups in the Atlantic and Mediterranean fishing enclaves of Andalusia (Spain): A personal networks approach with clustered graphs. *Marine Policy, 72*, 48–58.

Maya-Jariego, I., Holgado, D., Márquez, E., & Santolaya, F. J. (2018). Behavior settings and personal networks in Jicamarca and Villa El Salvador (Peru): The community role of schools. *Psychosocial Intervention, 27*(1), 1–11.

Mayr, P., & Weller, K. (2017). Think before you collect: Setting up a data collection approach for social media studies. In L. Sloan & A. Quan-Haase (Eds.), *The SAGE handbook of social media research methods*. London: SAGE.

Mazzucato, V. (2008). Simultaneity and networks in transnational migration: Lessons learned from an SMS methodology. In J. DeWind & J. Holdaway (Eds.), *Migration and development within and across borders: Research and policy perspectives on internal and international migration*. Geneva: International Organization for Migration.

Mazzucato, V. (2011). Reverse remittances in the migration-development nexus: Two-way flows between Ghana and the Netherlands. *Population, Space and Place, 17*(5), 454–468.

McCarty, C. (1995). The meaning of knowing as a network tie. *Connections, 18*, 20–31.

McCarty, C. (2002). Measuring structure in personal networks. *Journal of Social Structure, 3*(1), 1–29.

McCarty, C., Bernard, H. R., & Fazito, D. (2011). *A two mode personal network method for creating categories of knowing*. Paper presented at the Sunbelt XXXI International Sunbelt Social Network Conference, St. Pete Beach FL.

McCarty, C., Bernard, H. R., Killworth, P. D., Shelley, G. A., & Johnsen, E. C. (1997). Eliciting representative samples of personal networks. *Social Networks, 19*, 303–323.

McCarty, C., & Govindaramanujam, S. (2005). A modified elicitation of personal networks using dynamic visualization. *Connections, 26*(2), 61–69.

McCarty, C., & Killworth, P. D. (2007). Impact of methods for reducing respondent burden on personal network structural measures. *Social Networks, 29*, 300–315.

McCarty, C., Killworth, P. D., Bernard, H. R., & Johnsen, E. C. (2001). Comparing two methods for estimating network size. *Human Organization, 60*(1), 28–39.

McCarty, C., Molina, J. L., Aguilar, C., & Rota, L. (2007). A comparison of social network mapping and personal network visualization. *Field Methods, 19*(2), 145–162.

McCarty, C., & Wutich, A. (2005). Conceptual and empirical arguments for including or excluding ego from structural analyses of personal networks. *Connections, 26*(2), 82–88.

McCormick, T. H., Salganik, M. J., & Zheng, T. (2010). How many people do you know?: Efficiently estimating personal network size. *Journal of the American Statistical Association, 105*(489), 59–70.

McPherson, M., Smith-Lovin, L., & Brashears, M. E. (2006). Social isolation in America: Changes in core discussion networks over two decades. *American Sociological Review, 71*(3), 353–375.

McPherson, M., Smith-Lovin, L., & Brashears, M. E. (2009). Models and Marginals: Using survey evidence to study social networks. *American Sociological Review, 74*(4), 670–681.

McPherson, M., Smith-Lovin, L., & Cook, J. M. (2001). Birds of a feather: Homophily in social networks. *Annual Review of Sociology, 27*, 415–444.

Menjívar, C. (2000). *Fragmented ties: Salvadoran immigrant networks in America*. Oakland: University of California Press.

Milardo, R. M. (1989). Theoretical and methodological issues in the identification of the social networks of spouses. *Journal of Marriage and Family, 51*(1), 165–174.

Milgram, S. (1967). The small-world problem. *Psychology Today, 1*(1), 60–67.

Miritello, G., Moro, E., Lara, R., Martínez-López, R., Belchamber, J., Roberts, S. G. B., & Dunbar, R. I. M. (2013). Time as a limited resource: Communication strategy in mobile phone networks. *Social Networks, 35*(1), 89–95.

Mitchell, C. J. (1969). *Social networks in urban situations: Analyses of personal relationships in central African towns*. Manchester, UK: Manchester University Press.

Mok, D., Carrasco, J.-A., & Wellman, B. (2009).

Does distance still matter in the age of the Internet? *Urban Studies, 47*(13), 2747–2783.

Molina, J., Bolíbar, M., & Cruz, I. (2011). La dispersión geográfica de las redes personales: Cálculo y significado. *REDES—Revista Hispana Para El Análisis de Redes Sociales, 20*(1), 113–131.

Molina, J. L., Maya-Jariego, I., & McCarty, C. (2014). Giving meaning to social networks: Methodology for conducting and analyzing interviews based on personal network visualizations. In S. Domínguez & B. Hollstein (Eds.), *Mixed methods in social network research: Design and applications.* (pp. 305–335). Cambridge, UK: Cambridge University Press.

Molina, J. L., Petermann, S., & Herz, A. (2015). Defining and measuring transnational social structures. *Field Methods, 27*(3), 223–243.

Molina, J. L., Valenzuela-García, H., Lubbers, M. J., García-Macías, A., & Pampalona, J. (2015). Looking inside the ethnic enclave. In L. Ryan, U. Eret, & A. D'Angelo (Eds.), *Migrant capital: Networks, identities and strategies* (pp. 154–171). London: Palgrave Macmillan.

Mollenhorst, G., van Duijn, M., Rydgren, J., & Edling, C. (2016). Triadic closure in core networks: Disentangling the effects of social distance, national origin similarity and shared contexts. *International Review of Social Research, 6*(4), 146–162.

Mollenhorst, G., Volker, B., & Flap, H. (2011). Shared contexts and triadic closure in core discussion networks. *Social Networks, 33*(4), 292–302.

Mollenhorst, G., Volker, B., & Flap, H. (2014). Changes in personal relationships: How social contexts affect the emergence and discontinuation of relationships. *Social Networks, 37*, 65–80.

Montgomery, M. R., & Chung, W. (1999). Social networks and the diffusion of fertility control in the Republic of Korea. In R. Leete (Ed.), *Social values and fertility change* (pp. 179–209). Oxford, UK: Oxford University Press.

Moody, J., & White, D. R. (2003). Structural cohesion and embeddedness: A hierarchical concept of social groups. *American Sociological Review, 68*(1), 103–127.

Moore, D. S., McCabe, G. P., & Craig, B. A. (2009). *Introduction to the practice of statistics* (6th ed.). New York: Freeman.

Moore, G. (1990). Structural determinants of men's and women's personal networks. *American Sociological Review, 55*(5), 726–735.

Moreno, J. L. (1934). *Who shall survive?: A new approach to the problem of human interrelations.* Washington, DC: Nervous and Mental Disease Publishing.

Morgan, D. L. (1989). Adjusting to widowhood: Do social networks really make it easier? *The Gerontologist, 29*(1), 101–107.

Morgan, D. L., Neal, M. B., & Carder, P. (1997). The stability of core and peripheral networks over time. *Social Networks, 19*(1), 9–25.

Mossong, J., Hens, N., Jit, M., Beutels, P., Auranen, K., Mikolajczyk, R., et al. (2008). Social contacts and mixing patterns relevant to the spread of infectious diseases. *PLOS Medicine, 5*(3), e74.

Mouw, T., Chavez, S., Edelblute, H., & Verdery, A. (2014). Binational social networks and assimilation: A test of the importance of transnationalism. *Social Problems, 61*(3), 329–359.

Müller, C., Wellman, B., & Marin, A. (1999). How to use SPSS to study ego-centered networks. *Bulletin de Méthodologies Sociologiques BMS, 64*, 83–100.

Nadoh, J., Podreberšek, P., & Hlebec, V. (2004). Cognitive evaluation of the hierarchical approach for measuring ego-centered social networks. *Metodloski Zvezki, 1*(2), 379–393.

Narayanan, A., & Shmatikov, V. (2009, May 17–20). *De-anonymizing social networks.* Presented at the 30th IEEE Symposium on Security and Privacy, Oakland, CA.

Neaigus, A., Friedman, S. R., Curtis, R., Des Jarlais, D. C., Terry Furst, R., Jose, B., et al. (1994). The relevance of drug injectors' social and risk networks for understanding and preventing HIV infection. *Social Science and Medicine, 38*(1), 67–78.

Neal, J. W. (2009). Network ties and mean ties: A relational approach to relational aggression. *Journal of Community Psychology, 37*(6), 737–753.

Negrón, R. (2012). Personal networks and migration decision: The case of Jamaican brain drain. *Journal of Identity and Migration Studies, 6*(1), 43–63.

Northway, M. L. (1940). A method for depicting social relationships obtained by sociometric testing. *Sociometry, 3*, 144–150.

Offer, S., & Fischer, C. S. (2018). Difficult peo-

ple: Who is perceived to be demanding in personal networks and why are they there? *American Sociological Review, 83*(1), 111–142.
Pachur, T., Schooler, L. J., & Stevens, J. R. (2014). We'll meet again: Revealing distributional and temporal patterns of social contact. *PLOS ONE, 9*(1), 1–10.
Padgett, J. F., & Ansell, C. K. (1993). Robust action and the rise of the Medici, 1400–1434. *American Journal of Sociology, 98*(6), 1259–1319.
Parigi, P., & Henson, W., II. (2014). Social isolation in America. *Annual Review of Sociology, 40*(1), 153–171.
Park, N., Lee, S., & Kim, J. H. (2012). Individuals' personal network characteristics and patterns of Facebook use: A social network approach. *Computers in Human Behavior, 28*(5), 1700–1707.
Perry, B. L., & Pescosolido, B. A. (2010). Functional specificity in discussion networks: The influence of general and problem-specific networks on health outcomes. *Social Networks, 32*(4), 345–357.
Perry, B. L., & Pescosolido, B. A. (2015). Social network activation: The role of health discussion partners in recovery from mental illness. *Social Science and Medicine, 125*, 116–128.
Pescosolido, B. A. (1991). Illness careers and network ties: A conceptual model of utilization and compliance. In G. L. Albrecht & J. A. Levy (Eds.), *Advances in medical sociology* (pp. 161–184). Greenwich, CT: JAI Press.
Pescosolido, B. A. (1992). Beyond rational choice: The social dynamics of how people seek help. *American Journal of Sociology, 97*, 1096–1134.
Pinfold, V., Sweet, D., Porter, I., Quinn, C., Byng, R., Griffiths, C., et al. (2015). The role of practitioners in personal networks of people with severe mental illness. In V. Pinfold, D. Sweet, I. Porter, et al. (Eds.), *Improving community health networks for people with severe mental illness: A case study investigation*. Southampton, UK: NIHR Journals Library.
Plessard, C. (2014). Les non-relations: Analyse typologique et portee heuristique d'un biais. *Bulletin of Sociological Methodology/Bulletin de Méthodologie Sociologique, 121*, 30–43.
Portes, A. (1998). Social capital: Its origins and applications in modern sociology. *Annual Review of Sociology, 24*(1), 1–24.
Pustejovsky, J. E., & Spillane, J. P. (2009). Question-order effects in social network name generators. *Social Networks, 31*(4), 221–229.
Putnam, R. D. (1993). *Civil traditions in modern Italy*. Princeton, NJ: Princeton University Press.
Putnam, R. D. (2000). *Bowling alone: The collapse and revival of American community*. New York: Simon & Schuster.
Quan-Haase, A., & Wellman, B. (2005). Local virtuality in an organization: Implications for community of practice. In P. Van Den Besselaar, G. De Michelis, J. Preece, & C. Simone (Eds.), *Proceedings of the Second Communities and Technologies Conference, Milano 2005* (pp. 215–238). Dordrecht, the Netherlands: Springer.
Rainie, L., & Wellman, B. (2012). *Networked: The new social operating system*. Cambridge, MA: MIT Press.
Rasbash, J., & Browne, W. J. (2008). Non-hierarchical multilevel models. In J. De Leeuw & E. Meijer (Eds.), *Handbook of multilevel analysis* (pp. 301–334). New York: Springer.
Reyes, C. (2016). Eliciting data on social relationships: The use of hand-drawn network maps in tracing the perception of digitally mediated social ties. *International Review of Social Research, 6*(4), 256–268.
Roberts, S. G. B., Dunbar, R. I. M., Pollet, T. V., & Kuppens, T. (2009). Exploring variation in active network size: Constraints and ego characteristics. *Social Networks, 31*(2), 138–146.
Robins, G. (2016). *Doing social network research: Network based research design for social scientists*. London: SAGE.
Robins, G., Pattison, P., Kalish, Y., & Lusher, D. (2007). An introduction to exponential random graph (p*) models for social networks. *Social Networks, 29*(2), 173–191.
Rodríguez-García, D., Lubbers, M. J., Solana, M., & de Miguel-Luken, V. (2015). Contesting the nexus between intermarriage and integration: Findings from a multi-dimensional study in Spain. *Annals of the American Academy of Political and Social Science, 662*, 223–245.
Rogers, E. M. (2003). *Diffusion of innovations*. New York: Simon & Schuster.
Roman, C. G., Cahill, M., Lachman, P., Lowry, S., Orosco, C., & McCarty, C. (2012). *Social networks, delinquency, and gang membership: Using a neighborhood framework to examine the influence of network composition and struc-*

*ture in a Latino community*. Washington, DC: Urban Institute.

Romano, P. S., Bloom, J., & Syme, S. L. (1991). Smoking, social support, and hassles in an urban African-American community. *American Journal of Public Health, 81*(11), 1415–1422.

Ruan, D. (1998). The content of the general social survey discussion networks: An exploration of general social survey discussion name generator in a Chinese context. *Social Networks, 20*(3), 247–264.

Ryan, L. (2016). Looking for weak ties: Using a mixed methods approach to capture elusive connections. *Sociological Review, 64*(4), 951–969.

Ryan, L., Mulholland, J., & Agoston, A. (2014). Talking ties: Reflecting on network visualisation and qualitative interviewing. *Sociological Research Online, 19*(2), 1–12.

Salganik, M. J. (2017). *Bit by bit: Social research in the digital age*. Princeton, NJ: Princeton University Press.

Salganik, M. J., & Heckathorn, D. C. (2004). Sampling and estimation in hidden populations using respondent-driven sampling. *Sociological Methodology, 34*, 193–239.

Saramäki, J., & Moro, E. (2015). From seconds to months: Multi-scale dynamics of mobile telephone calls. *arXiv:1504.01479v1 [Physics. soc-Ph]*, 1–11.

Schiffer, E., & Hauck, J. (2010). Net-map: Collecting social network data and facilitating network learning through participatory influence network mapping. *Field Methods, 22*(3), 231–249.

Schnettler, S. (Ed.). (2013). *Small world research: Vol. II. Network research*. London: SAGE.

Schweizer, T., Schnegg, M., & Berzborn, S. (1998). Personal networks and social support in a multiethnic community of southern California. *Social Networks, 20*, 1–21.

Scott, G. (2008). "They got their program, and I got mine": A cautionary tale concerning the ethical implications of using respondent-driven sampling to study injection drug users. *International Journal on Drug Policy, 19*(1), 42–51.

Seeman, T. E., Lusignolo, T. M., Albert, M., & Berkman, L. (2001). Social relationships, social support, and patterns of cognitive aging in healthy, high-functioning older adults: MacArthur studies of successful aging. *Health Psychology, 20*(4), 243–255.

Seyfang, G. (2006). Ecological citizenship and sustainable consumption: Examining local organic food networks. *Journal of Rural Studies, 22*(4), 383–395.

Shulman, N. (1976). Network analysis: A new addition to an old bag of tricks. *Acta Sociologica, 19*(4), 307–323.

Singer, J. D., & Willett, J. B. (2003). *Applied longitudinal data analysis: Modeling change and event occurrence*. Oxford, UK: Oxford University Press.

Sloan, L., & Quan-Haase, A. (2017). *The SAGE handbook of social media research methods*. London: SAGE.

Small, M. L. (2009a). "How many cases do I need?": On science and the logic of case selection in field-based research. *Ethnography, 10*(1), 5–38.

Small, M. L. (2009b). *Unanticipated gains: Origins of network inequality in everyday life*. Oxford, UK: Oxford University Press.

Small, M. L. (2013). Weak ties and the core discussion network: Why people regularly discuss important matters with unimportant alters. *Social Networks, 35*(3), 470–483.

Small, M. L. (2017). *Someone to talk to*. New York: Oxford University Press.

Smith, E. J., Marcum, C. S., Boessen, A., Almquist, Z. W., Hipp, J. R., Nagle, N. N., et. al. (2015). The relationship of age to personal network size, relational multiplexity, and proximity to alters in the western United States. *Journals of Gerontology Series B, Psychological Sciences and Social Sciences, 70*(1), 91–99.

Smith, J. A. (2012). Macrostructure from microstructure: Generating whole systems from ego networks. *Sociological Methodology, 42*(1), 155–205.

Smith, J. A., McPherson, M., & Smith-Lovin, L. (2014). Social distance in the United States. *American Sociological Review, 79*(3), 432–456.

Smith, L. E., Greenberg, J. S., & Mailick Seltzer, M. (2012). Social support and well-being at mid-life among mothers of adolescents and adults with autism spectrum disorders. *Journal of Autism and Developmental Disorders, 42*(9), 1818–1826.

Snijders, T. A. B., Spreen, M., & Zwaagstra, R. (1995). The use of multilevel modeling for analysing personal networks: networks of cocaine users in an urban area. *Journal of Quantitative Anthropology, 5*, 85–105.

Snijders, T. A. B., van de Bunt, G. G., & Steglich, C. E. G. (2010). Introduction to stochastic actor-based models for network dynamics. *Social Networks, 32*(1), 44–60.

Sokhey, A. E., & Djupe, P. A. (2014). Name generation in interpersonal political network data: Results from a series of experiments. *Social Networks, 36*, 147–161.

Sommer, E., & Gamper, M. (2018). Transnational entrepreneurial activities: A qualitative network study of self-employed migrants from the former Soviet Union in Germany. *Social Networks, 53*, 136–147.

Song, L., Son, J., & Lin, N. (2011). Social support. In J. S. Carrington & P. J. Carrington (Eds.), *The SAGE handbook of social network analysis* (pp. 116–128). Thousand Oaks, CA: SAGE.

Spencer, L., & Pahl, R. E. (2006). *Rethinking friendship: Hidden solidarities today*. Princeton, NJ: Princeton University Press.

Stark, T. H., & Krosnick, J. A. (2017). GENSI: A new graphical tool to collect ego-centered network data. *Social Networks, 48*, 36–45.

Steglich, C., Snijders, T. A. B., & Pearson, M. (2010). Dynamic networks and behavior: Separating selection from influence. *Sociological Methodology, 40*(1), 329–393.

Takhteyev, Y., Gruzd, A., & Wellman, B. (2012). Geography of Twitter networks. *Social Networks, 34*(1), 73–81.

Taylor, R. J., Mouzon, D. M., Nguyen, A. W., & Chatters, L. M. (2016). Reciprocal family, friendship and church support networks of African Americans: Findings from the National Survey of American Life. *Race and Social Problems, 8*(4), 326–339.

Taylor, S. E. (2011). Social support: A review. In M. S. Friedman (Ed.), *The Handbook of health psychology* (pp. 189–214). New York: Oxford University Press.

Terhell, E. L., Broese van Groenou, M. I., & van Tilburg, T. (2007). Network contact changes in early and later postseparation years. *Social Networks, 29*(1), 11–24.

Tolich, M. (2004). Internal confidentiality: When confidentiality assurances fail relational informants. *Qualitative Sociology, 27*(1), 101–107.

Tranmer, M., Steel, D., & Browne, W. J. (2014). Multiple-membership multiple-classification models for social network and group dependences. *Journal of the Royal Statistical Society: Series A, 177*(2), 439–455.

Tubaro, P., Casilli, A. A., & Mounier, L. (2013). Eliciting personal network data in web surveys through participant-generated sociograms. *Field Methods, 26*(2), 107–125.

Tubaro, P., Casilli, A. A., Mounier, L., Maigron, P., Chardel, P. A., Masson, E., et al. (2013). *ANAMIA Egocenter*. Ecole des Hautes Etudes en Sciences Sociales (EHESS), Centre Edgar-Morin (CEM-IIAC), Paris.

Tucker, J. S., Kennedy, D., Ryan, G., Wenzel, S. L., Golinelli, D., & Zazzali, J. (2009). Homeless women's personal networks: Implications for understanding risk behavior. *Human Organization, 68*(2), 129–140.

Tufte, E. R. (1990). *Envisioning information*. Cheshire, CT: Graphic Press.

UAB. (2013). *Code of good practices in research*. Barcelona, Spain: Universitat Autònoma de Barcelona. Retrieved from *www.uab.cat/doc/Bones-Practiques-Recerca-en*.

Udry, R., & Billy, J. O. G. (1987). Initiation of coitus in early adolescence. *American Sociological Review, 52*, 841–855.

Ugander, J., Karrer, B., Backstrom, L., & Marlow, C. (2011). *The anatomy of the facebook social graph. ArXiv* 1111.4503.

Unsworth, N. (2017). Examining the dynamics of strategic search from long-term memory. *Journal of Memory and Language, 93*, 135–153.

Vacca, R. (2013). *Bridging across nations. The social capital of diversity, brokerage and closure in transnational migrant networks: A study on assimilation patterns in Milan and Barcelona*. Milan, Italy: Università degli Studi di Milano-Bicocca.

Vacca, R. (2018). Multilevel Models for Personal Networks: Methods and Applications. *Statistica Applicata: Italian Journal of Applied Statistics, 30*(1), 59–97.

Vacca, R., Solano, G., Lubbers, M. J., Molina, J. L., & McCarty, C. (2018). A personal network approach to the study of immigrant structural assimilation and transnationalism. *Social Networks, 53*, 72–89.

Vacca, R., Stacciarini, J.-M. R., & Tranmer, M. (n.d.). *Using cross-classified multilevel models to analyze tie variation in overlapping personal networks*. Manuscript under review.

Valente, T. W. (1996). Social network thresholds in the diffusion of innovations. *Social Networks, 18*(1), 69–89.

Valente, T. W. (2010). *Social networks and health: models, methods, and applications*. New York: Oxford University Press.

Valente, T. W., & Saba, W. P. (1998). Mass media and interpersonal influence in a reproductive health communication campaign in Bolivia. *Communication Research, 25*(1), 96–124.

Valente, T. W., Watkins, S. C., Jato, M. N., van der Straten, A., & Tsitsol, L. P. M. (1997). Social network associations with contraceptive use among Cameroonian Women in voluntary associations. *Social Science and Medicine, 45*(5), 677–687.

van de Bunt, G. G., & Groenewegen, P. (2007). An actor-oriented dynamic network approach: The case of interorganizational network evolution. *Organizational Research Methods, 10*(3), 463–482.

van den Berg, P., Arentze, T., & Timmermans, H. (2010). A multilevel path analysis of contact frequency between social network members. *Journal of Geographical Systems, 14*(2), 125–141.

van der Gaag, M. P. J., Appelhof, G. J., & Webber, M. (2012). Ambiguità nelle Risposte al Position Generator. *Sociologia E Politiche Sociali, 2*(15), 113–141.

van der Gaag, M., & Snijders, T. A. B. (2005). The resource generator: Social capital quantification with concrete items. *Social Networks, 27*(1), 1–29.

van der Poel, M. G. M. (1993). Delineating personal support networks. *Social Networks, 15*(1), 49–70.

van Duijn, M. A. J., van Busschbach, J. T., & Snijders, T. A. B. (1999). Multilevel analysis of personal networks as dependent variables. *Social Networks, 21*, 187–210.

van Tilburg, T. (1992). Support networks before and after retirement. *Journal of Social and Personal Relationships, 9*(3), 433–445.

van Tubergen, F. (2015). Ethnic boundaries in core discussion networks: A multilevel social network study of Turks and Moroccans in the Netherlands. *Journal of Ethnic and Migration Studies, 41*(1), 101–116.

Vehovar, V., Lozar Manfreda, K., Koren, G., & Hlebec, V. (2008). Measuring ego-centered social networks on the web: Questionnaire design issues. *Social Networks, 30*(3), 213–222.

Verma, I. M. (2014). Editorial expression of concern: Experimental evidence of massive scale emotional contagion through social networks. *Proceedings of the National Academy of Sciences, 111*(29), 10779.

Viry, G. (2012). Residential mobility and the spatial dispersion of personal networks: Effects on social support. *Social Networks, 34*(1), 59–72.

Volker, B., De Cuyper, R., Mollenhorst, G., Dirkzwager, A., Van der Laan, P., & Nieuwbeerta, P. (2016). Changes in the social networks of prisoners: A comparison of their networks before and after imprisonment. *Social Networks, 47*, 47–58.

Volker, B., & Flap, H. (2001). Weak ties as a liability: The case of East Germany: *Rationality & Society, 13*(4), 397–428.

von der Lippe, H., & Gamper, M. (2016). Drawing or tabulating ego-centered networks?: A mixed-methods comparison of questionnaire vs. visualization-based data collection. *International Journal of Social Research Methodology, 20*(5), 425–441.

Wellman, B. (1979). The community question: The intimate networks of East Yorkers. *American Journal of Sociology, 84*(5), 1201–1231.

Wellman, B. (2002). The rise (and possible fall) of networked individualism. *American Journal of Sociology*, 30–32.

Wellman, B. (2012). Is Dunbar's number up? *British Journal of Psychology, 103*(2), 174–176.

Wellman, B., & Berkowitz, S. D. (1988). *Social structures: A network approach*. Cambridge, UK: Cambridge University Press.

Wellman, B., Carrington, P. J., & Hall, A. (1988). Networks as personal communities. In S. D. Wellman & B. Berkowitz (Eds.), *Social structures: A network analysis*. Cambridge, UK: Cambridge University Press.

Wellman, B., & Frank, K. A. (2001). Network capital in a multi-level world: Getting support from personal communities. In N. Lin, K. S. Cook, & R. Burt (Eds.), *Social capital: Theory and research* (pp. 233–273). Piscataway, NJ: Transaction.

Wellman, B., & Haythornthwaite, C. A. (Eds.). (2002). *The Internet in everyday life*. New York: Wiley-Blackwell.

Wenzel, S. L., Tucker, J., Golinelli, D., Green, H. D., & Zhou, A. J. (2010). Personal network correlates of alcohol, cigarette, and marijuana use among homeless youth. *Drug and Alcohol Dependence, 112*(1–2), 140–149.

White, K., & Watkins, S. C. (2000). Accuracy, stability and reciprocity in informal conversational networks in rural Kenya. *Social Networks, 22*(4), 337–355.

Wills, T. A. (1985). Supportive functions of interpersonal relationships. In S. Cohen & S. L. Syme (Eds.), *Social support and health* (pp. 61–82). Orlando, FL: Academic Press.

Wissink, M., & Mazzucato, V. (2018). In transit: Changing social networks of sub-Saharan African migrants in Turkey and Greece. *Social Networks, 53*, 30–41.

World Medical Association. (2001). World Medical Association Declaration of Helsinki. *Bulletin of the World Health Organization, 79*(4), 373–374.

Yen, T. J., Fu, Y. C., & Hwang, J. S. (2016). Alters as species: Predicting personal network size from contact diaries. *Social Networks, 45*, 78–88.

Zachary, W. W. (1977). An information flow model for conflict and fission in small groups. *Journal of Anthropological Research, 33*(4), 452–473.

Zimmer, M. (2010). "But the data is already public": On the ethics of research in Facebook. *Ethics and Information Technology, 12*(4), 313–325.

# Author Index



## B

## C



## D



## E



## F

## G



## H



## I



## J



## K

## L



## M

## N



## O



## P



## Q



## R



## S

## T



## U



## V



## W

## Y



## Z

# Subject Index

Note. *f* or *t* following a page number indicates a figure or table.

## B



## C

## D

## H



## I



## K



## L

## S

## T

# About the Authors

**Christopher McCarty, PhD,** is Professor and Chair of Anthropology at the University of Florida, where he is also Director of the Bureau of Economic and Business Research. He has done research on personal networks since the 1980s and is the developer of EgoNet, the first program for the collection and analysis of personal network data. Dr. McCarty has conducted studies of migration, disasters, substance abuse, homelessness, and racism. Along with his coauthors, he conducted the largest personal network study of migrants to date, using data from Spain and the United States.

**Miranda J. Lubbers, PhD,** is Associate Professor in the Department of Social and Cultural Anthropology at the Universitat Autònoma de Barcelona, Spain, and Director of the Research Group on Fundamental and Oriented Anthropology. Dr. Lubbers has investigated personal networks in the areas of migration and transnationalism, poverty and livelihood strategies, and social cohesion in Spain. Currently she directs two research projects using personal networks. She also co-organizes a biennial international summer school in Personal Network Analysis.

**Raffaele Vacca, PhD,** is Research Assistant Professor of Sociology at the University of Florida. Dr. Vacca designed and conducted one of the first personal network surveys among international migrants in Italy. In the past few years he has taught courses and workshops on quantitative methods and statistical software for social network analysis at several international conferences and universities in Europe, the United States, and Latin America. His current interests focus on international migration, health disparities, social networks, and science and scientific collaboration.

**José Luis Molina, PhD,** is Associate Professor in the Department of Social and Cultural Anthropology at the Universitat Autònoma de Barcelona, Spain. He is also president of the University's Research Ethics Committee. Dr. Molina is an economic anthropologist who studies the emergence of socioeconomic structures such as migrant enclaves and transnational fields. He is interested in mixed-methods approaches combining ethnography and personal network analysis, with a focus on Southeast Europe, and Romania in particular.